The Journal
of William Charles Macready
1832–1851

Abridged and edited by
J. C. Trewin

Southern Illinois University Press
Carbondale and Edwardsville

Feffer & Simons, Inc.
London and Amsterdam

Copyright © 1967 by J. C. Trewin
All rights reserved
Arcturus Books Edition April 1970

This edition printed by offset lithography
in the United States of America
SBN 8093-0423-6
Library of Congress Catalog Card Number 67-111097

For Wendy

'Words—such at least as I can command—are ineffectual to convey my thanks.'

Macready at Drury Lane, 26 February 1851

Contents

Illustrations

Acknowledgements

My first debt is, naturally, to Macready's previous and devoted editors: Sir Frederick Pollock, Bart. (*Macready's Reminiscences and Selections from his Diaries and Letters*, 2 vols., 1875), and William Toynbee (*The Diaries of William Charles Macready*, 1833–1851, 2 vols., 1912). I have added, after the epilogue, a short list of other works relevant to Macready and his circle.

During the often complex preparation of the present book, I have valued highly the kindness of Raymond Mander and Joe Mitchenson, who have allowed me to examine and quote from the remaining, and hitherto unprinted, leaves of the journal in their Theatre Collection; Herbert van Thal, John Guest, and that confirmed Macreadyan, my wife. It is a pleasure to recall some exhilarating talks with Martin Holmes.

I am very grateful indeed to Miss Nicolette Shawyer for her skill, literary and technical, and her expert solution of a difficult problem of arrangement.

J.C.T.

Introduction: I

William Charles Macready, son of an actor and an actress, was born in London on 3 March 1793, at 3 Mary Street, off Euston Road.[1] He died in Cheltenham eighty years later, on 27 April 1873, and was buried in London on 4 May, at Kensal Green. For more than half of his life (1810–1851) he was an actor, and through the last two decades, a period when he led the English stage, he sustained the copious journal—bred of the moment's mood—that, in its unguarded immediacy, reveals him to us more sharply than we know any other First Player.

He was indeed a First Player—in the line of Burbage, Betterton, Garrick, John Philip Kemble, and Edmund Kean. No other man did so much to lift his profession. During his stage life the theatre, a place of intrigue and rancorous discord, was a breeding-ground for such an adventurer as the showman Alfred Bunn, and for players of a hollow flamboyance. (There were upper-crust Crummleses.) Actors had no social status; technically, they still remained rogues and vagabonds. As Hilton Brown wrote once in another context, 'We are a great people for labels, and we furnish them with well-nigh imperishable gum'. Nobody was less of a rogue and vagabond, or further removed from the grandiloquent 'pomping folk', than William Charles Macready: doubtless if he had been nearer to them, it might have helped his reputation with posterity.

It would have helped because the romantic profligate has always been more cherished than the noble monument, the kind of man Tennyson, in his ode to Macready, called 'moral, grave, sublime', a phrase that later was excessively mocked. Macready wanted a theatre 'in decorum and taste worthy of our country' ('I suppose he asks five pounds a week more for his morality', Byron had said at Drury Lane as early as 1816). In performance he had not the 'cross blue lightning' of a Kean, an actor who, though clearly great when the fit was on him ('indisputable genius' admitted Macready many years afterwards) could often be, I suspect, a glorified stroller when the storm had blown itself out. But we must read his record by the flashes; and probably, in a small group of parts and on his night, Kean could overwhelm any actor that ever lived. (Acting then was a contest: we are told, as if it were a match report, how in the last winter of his life, Kean's Othello blotted out Macready's Iago.) This

[1] Mary Street became Stanhope Street; there is a plaque to Macready at No. 45.

said, Macready had a much wider range. He was never far from the top; Kean's career was a fever chart with impenetrable depths. According to William Archer, summarising the evidence in 1890, Macready, if not so great an actor as Kean, was 'perhaps the greater artist'. Archer need not have been tentative.

Still, I doubt whether these distinctions have much excited a later world for whom Kean is a blazing cometary legend, and Macready a figure hampered by high purpose and classic zeal, by Tennyson's three epithets, and (baffling personage that he was) by his scorn for the profession he led. At this distance he is a figure more complex and contradictory than Kean. His swelling pride would be the tragedy of his life. He would both pity himself for belonging to an inferior calling and rage at any assumed insult to it.[1] Vain and humble; choleric and gentle; impatient and numbingly shy; harsh and yet sensitive to others' feelings; bitter and loving; a despot and a republican: the paradoxes multiply. If he brooded too much on degree, priority, and place, we have to remember that he was brought up, a sensitive, educated youth, in a society, elaborately graded, where an actor—a word to be spoken in italics—was usually odd man out. Macready recognised his contradictions: we have his self-portrait, tortured and desperately honest, in the pages of his journal, a book often spoken about but read too little. The present abridgement seeks to give the pith of nearly half a million words, the absorbing self-revelation of a man who said: 'The universe is but an atom before the vastness of one's self.' In writing of himself Macready managed also to flash up (with a natural sense of the theatre) the people with whom he lived and worked in London, the provinces, and America.

He was a compulsive diarist, unable to sleep[2] without hurrying down in a handwriting that was very like the man, impatient and peremptory, a record of the day's affairs: often it was the second instalment of an entry begun during the day itself. He hid nothing from his diary; it was a relief from much perilous stuff that weighed upon the heart, and he used it as a confessional, noting in it exactly what he had felt about a

---

[1] 'Remember the actors' calling
   Is the finest in the world.
   Is it something a little galling
   When, with a lip politely curled
   And a supercilious smirk,
   You are told to your face
   That the theatre has no place
   Among important things? . . .'
     From Sacha Guitry's Deburau, translated by Granville-Barker.

[2] In New Orleans, 27 March 1844, he wrote: 'I dropped asleep, my pen in hand and cravat off, alas!'

given person at a given time: then his mood would veer, and an entry within a day or so would be a blunt contradiction. The narrative of his relations with that aggressively managing figure, John Forster (of all his friends the closest), shows as sharply as anything the gusty adventure that was a life's friendship with Macready: its progress, while Macready was in the theatre and Forster seemed to be handling the literary and dramatic affairs of half London, can be traced in the pages of this book.

Here are the day-by-day excitements and agonies and angers (Macready inherited his father's temper), the suspicions, the rash-embraced despair. Macready was always several people. In the theatre he was the autocrat, the choleric 'Eminent' affronted by the incompetence and insensitivity of the players he had to act with; by the ignorance of his managers (when they employed him) and his staff (when he was the employer). Nobody must cross him; nobody must divert the public gaze. He was Macready—and to many of the baffled actors round him a tyrant, crying 'Beast! Beast of hell!', and a snob, rigid with dignity, icily withdrawn. He wrote in 1856: 'It has always been in direct contrariety to my disposition and my taste, *even in London*,[1] to adopt the hail-fellow-well-met familiarity of green-rooms into which (when I entered them, which was not often) I carried the manner and address habitual with me in general society.'

Difficult; but the theatre also knew Macready the artist, the compulsive actor. Though he might tell himself that he loathed his task, he was aware at heart (in a phrase mercifully unknown to him) that it was a love-hate relationship; that he could not cease, on the worst of nights,[2] from probing every speech—a search that could impede the free flow of the verse—and from exploring a character to its crevices. He rarely satisfied himself, for he could be as humble as he was vain. When he did, as likely as not he would abuse the audience (in the privacy of his journal) for not responding. Besides the anxious artist, ever at work, and the tyrant—an impression magnified because he was so desperately shy with his fellow-actors—there could be in the theatre a third and surprising Macready, the susceptible romantic. He could fall in love, even if he would never dream of expressing it so baldly; and when actresses were infatuated with him—as they could be; observe the behaviour of

---

[1] My italics.

[2] In his autobiographical fragment he wrote: 'A full attendance is too generally required as a spur to a performer's exertions. . . . It was a rule with me to make what profit I could out of a bad house, and before the most meagre audiences ever assembled, it has been my invariable practice to strive my best. . . . I used to call it "acting to myself"; as indeed it was transferring the study of a character from my own apartment to the stage.'

Helen Faucit—he debated the matter with himself in anxious page upon page when the household was asleep.

There were other Macreadies. One was the affectionate husband and father, a scrupulous head of the household, if a little alarming, more than a little schoolmasterish; he had to be preceptor as well as husband. His wife, an actress, never acted again after marriage, and his children were not allowed to see him on the stage until the last weeks of his career. A further Macready was the loyal and welcoming friend—of Dickens, who understood instinctively how to deal with him; of Forster, who muddled through; and of the others in a circle that remained constant. True, he could not forgive (as with the too eager Talfourd) what appeared to be disloyalty to him. No one must fraternise with his enemies, and he was a merciless hater—of such men as Forrest, in boorish rivalry, and of Bunn of Drury Lane, whom he despised for cupidity and vulgarity. Bunn kept brief occasional diaries. We can observe from this contrast (in the summer of 1833) why there was never any chance of the bouncing manager and his grave tragedian getting on terms. Bunn was in Paris.

BUNN

August 12. . . . Can't 'take it coolly' for the life of me, for with this sun even baths and ices are at a discount. Dined at Anatole's country-seat, a decent little place enough, considering that it is FRENCH and he calls it ENGLISH. . . .

August 15 . . . Navigated the Boulevards with Charles Gore. *Mem.* to do becoming homage to '*miladi*' at two to-morrow. . . . Dined at Meurice's hotel, and thence proceeded to the *Cirque Olympique*: exceedingly amused with the Clown; procured models of two of his tricks—a lark between a *horse* and a goose produced many a *horse* laugh. . . . Saw in an opposite box Dimond, the dramatic author—thought he had been hanged long ago.

August 20. Off for Babylon:

MACREADY

August 12. I finished the chapter of Thucydides' account of the ancient Greeks, and read in Homer the battle array of the Myrmidons, and Achilles' exhortation, which is abrupt and stirring. Practised Lear which I feel to be a benefit. . . .

August 15. This day I wrote a short statement of my wish as to the disposal of my property after my death, which will serve for my will until I can have a better made out. . . . At the Victoria Theatre I saw Miss Keeley and Miss Garrick: why did I not speak to them? It was not pride, but a false shame which is always taken for it and does the exhibitor equal injury.

August 20. Went to the drawing-room, resolute to give the whole morning—or what remained of it—to Lear. Practised the first act,

BUNN

heartily sick of *les braves*, as these fellows call themselves and the very venials who wait upon them. Shall occupy myself *en route* in putting together a farce for the first night of one of the houses.[1]

MACREADY

and, desponding and dissatisfied, was told Mr Best had arrived with bed for the West room. This settled my study. . . .

Yet another Macready was the public man who, in clubs and at dinner-parties, when he was free from those long, turbulent rehearsals, could be a figure self-consciously statuesque, a classic portico given life. Always he was on watch for the apparent insult, society's view of the player, the cut direct, the offering of 'one finger' as a mode of shaking hands, the allusion to himself—away from a playbill—as 'Mr Macready'. At a dinner of the Literary Fund in 1835 he was so described 'among the esquires of the Royal Academy, the King's Printing Office, the Quarterly Review, etc.'

All of these Macreadies, and there were others, an entire cast list, joined in writing the journal. As we read it now we are never sure, from night to night, who will be holding the pen. Macready's rages are frightening, his remorse is even more so; in grief, as at the deathbeds of Joan and Nina, he is entirely unrestrained. In considering him we have to seek the concord of the discord. Micheál MacLiammóir has called him 'an unwavering slow thunderbolt of a man, never asking for our sympathy, never demanding our love, always, in some Sphinx-like fashion of his own, deeply and inexplicably moving'.[2]

This was the man who passed his life at odds with the profession he led. Morosely, he was the high master of his art; glumly, he saved the theatre. He had hoped, when a Rugby schoolboy, to go to the Bar; but his father, a rash actor-manager whose money melted and who was in constant danger of bankruptcy, could not keep him at school; he had to choose the stage. Nearly five decades later, in retirement at Sherborne, he wrote of the morning when he had to make his decision:

> I was not then aware of the distance between the two starting-points of life. My father was impressive in his conviction that the stage was a gentlemanly profession. My experience has taught me that whilst the law, the church, the army and navy give a man the rank of a gentleman, on the stage that designation must be obtained

[1] In *The Stage: Both Before and Behind the Curtain*, 1840.
[2] *Truth*, 7 October 1955.

in society (though the law and the Court decline to recognise it) by the individual bearing. In other callings the profession confers dignity on the initiated, on the stage the player must contribute respect to the exercise of his art. This truth, experienced too late, has given occasion to many moments of depression, many angry swellings of the heart, many painful convictions of the uncertainty of my position.

I was not aware, in taking it, that this step in life was a descent from the equality in which I had felt myself to stand with those of family and fortune whom our education had made my companion. I had to live to learn that an ignorant officer could refuse the satisfaction of a gentleman on the ground that his appellant was a player, and that, whilst any of those above-named vocations, whatever the private character, might be received at Court, the privilege of appearing in the sacred precincts was too exclusive for any, however distinguished, on the stage.

At the age of fifty-seven he left the theatre, never to appear in it again, and the last of the Macreadies arrived: a retiring country gentleman, a scholar (for he was a classic and a linguist), given now only to good works, to the patronage of a Scientific and Literary Institution, and to the writing of some chapters of autobiography gravely urbane and quite out of key with the fury and the fret of the daily entries. He would have a long and in many ways a sorrowful retirement; but he had made his choice; if at any time he was wistful for the stage, he never proclaimed the emotion and we cannot imagine he would have dwelt upon it.

II

In 1875, soon after Macready's death, his friend, Sir Frederick Pollock, edited the chapters of autobiography and the stage diaries. These had to be emasculated. Pollock left in nothing that could offend a living personage. Thus none would have guessed at the Helen Faucit story or the quarrel with Browning. During 1912 the journal was re-edited, this time by William Toynbee who, after forty years, could be far more inclusive: in fact, he printed nearly half a million words (while omitting several important passages from the Pollock text). Obviously a great deal remained unprinted, for Macready was persistent and copious. Though the two volume edition of 1912 is invaluable, it does need to be clarified. In the new abridgement, based on both the previous editions, I have tried to establish the places and circumstances in which Macready wrote.

The original manuscript of the diaries has perished. Before leaving for France as Adjutant-General at the outbreak of the first world war in 1914, [General Sir] Nevil Macready,[1] Macready's only child by his second wife, destroyed the volumes lest they might be used injudiciously. His daughter and Macready's grandchild, the late Mrs Lisa Puckle, wrote during 1960:[2] 'I can speak definitely on this, as . . . my father destroyed the diaries, and I helped him in case they should fall into the wrong hands. My grandfather wrote very freely at times.' Some sixty-four manuscript pages remain, mostly descriptive passages from the journal of the second American tour. Written hastily, and often in the loosest style, on any paper that came to Macready's hand, they were discovered by Mrs Puckle during 1960 in a packing-case long stored at Sir Nevil's bank. These pages are now in the Raymond Mander and Joe Mitchenson Theatre Collection at Sydenham, South London, and a few extracts from them—printed for the first time—appear in their proper chronological order between March and September 1844.

III

Macready began to act (twenty years before he became a voluminous diarist) in a world that in London was ruled by the Patent Theatres, the Theatres Royal—Covent Garden and Drury Lane—and in the provinces depended upon the circuit system. London players would go regularly to act, at a price, for a circuit manager in a specific region, taking their chance with the supporting casts, frequently dire. In youth Macready regarded as a composite home these stock theatres where the pillars might have mouthed blank verse through the night. But he realised that a player with London ambition had to reach either Drury Lane or Covent Garden; no matter how struggling and debt-ridden, they held in theory the sole privilege of presenting the legitimate drama. 'Minor houses', jealously watched, had to employ accepted subterfuges —such as a tactful use of music that would make any drama suitably 'irregular' and therefore playable on a minor stage.[3]

Within his first decade as an actor, Macready learned how to control

---

[1] Later General the Rt. Hon. Sir Nevil Macready, Bart., GCMG, KCB (1862–1946).
[2] To Messrs Raymond Mander and Joe Mitchenson.
[3] The Theatres Act of 1843 ultimately disposed of all this, more than ten years after Bulwer's first efforts.

both a small provincial theatre, such as the elegant Royal at Bristol, a green and gold casket with reeded Doric pillars and a dim blue star-spangled ceiling, and the vast, many-tiered cavern of Covent Garden which held 2,800 people: it seemed a day's march from the stage to the back of the pit. Players had to boom out into the candle-lit immensities, always lighted before the coming of gas made it possible to dim the auditorium. It was in these conditions that Macready rose to lead the theatre. John Philip Kemble, 'Black Jack', retired in 1817 ('Pride of the British stage! A long, a last adieu!'); Kean died in 1833; thenceforward Macready was never seriously challenged. The 'Eminent Tragedian' was five feet ten in height and held himself stiffly erect. He had a flat face with high cheekbones, a mouth small and frowning, a square chin, and a nose that a colleague would call 'a mixture of Grecian, Milesian, and snub'. His eyes were a burning blue. Off-stage he wore his abundant hair clubbed over the ears. His voice was deep and melodious. In private life, says Westland Marston, he spoke 'in a kind of half-smothered bass, which, like his frequent pauses and self-corrections in talk, was too full of individuality to be displeasing'.

As soon as he inherited 'the war-cry and the profit', Macready, though secure enough, would understand the fears that had beset Kean. A major tragedian who had fought for his place, must be wary when it had been won. Like the Priest of Nemi, he had to prowl, sword drawn, about the sacred grove, expecting his murderer. It is impossible to overlook Macready's almost pathological envy and suspicion, the imagination that would see a mortal wound in a mild chafe, a fierce rival in a player transiently acclaimed. But practically everyone at that time would have behaved in the same way: the profession was desperately unsure of itself.

Macready considered his work so deeply that it was never finished. He has been blamed for not making the 'decisive statement' of the great player. To the end he was reconsidering, altering,[1] and even if he seldom failed to enforce attention, he was a variable first-night actor: it was a beginning, not a peak. With constant toil his haughtiness and irritability increased; but no man so impressed himself upon the early Victorian theatre. He was a tragedian; in spite of his Irish descent and a certain gently amusing strain, he jested with difficulty, on the stage or off. (Opinions of his Benedick moved between the actor Anderson's 'mourning-coach in a snowstorm' and Lady Pollock's unqualified

---

[1] Two years before his death, when he could barely speak, he whispered to Lady Pollock: 'I have had some new ideas about Iago. Original, I am sure—true, I think.'

pleasure.) As a tragedian he fought himself clear from the excesses of melodrama, the hollow pomp, the tall spouting gentlemen in tinsel (Leigh Hunt's phrase for Pizarro), and grew closer and closer to the Shakespearean protagonists. It was like Macready to take to himself the notoriously unplayable Macbeth, especially when the dagger of the mind marshalled him the way that he was going, and when in Dunsinane he defied the fates. *Macbeth* governed his stage life. He acted in it at Covent Garden after he left Drury Lane and the stricken Bunn; he acted in it on the night of the Astor Place riot; he acted in it at his farewell. This Macbeth was a great general devil-ridden by his imagination. The performance was haunted from the moment Macbeth saw the air-drawn dagger, not starting in theatrical fear as most actors did, but allowing it to rise slowly as a dagger of the mind, a false creation, that yet turned its handle inexorably to his hand. After the murder the entire agony of that night of storm, storm of the mind and of the elements, was in the cry, 'Wake Duncan with thy knocking; I would thou couldst!' His gaze always averted from the knife, he allowed himself to be dragged from the stage.

His Lear developed an extraordinary pathos, especially in the awakening; and he was, said Lady Pollock, 'a master of the gradations of passion'. Next to these parts his admirers would put the gloating Iago (he was better in Iago's tauromachy than as Othello, which wanted grandeur though its friends were staunch); Cassius, which could have been written for him; the smouldering sunset of Henry IV; and King John. His Hamlet became over-inflected and lachrymose, too shadowed by the pale cast of thought. Several Shakespearean parts, long lost to the repertory, belonged in his day to Macready: again and again recorders return to the tenderness and resolution of Virginius, to the romantic glow of Lytton's Melnotte, the authority of Richelieu ('Beneath the rule of men entirely great/The pen is mightier than the sword'), and the dark sorrow of Byron's Werner. 'He could be the ideal of wretchedness' said Westland Marston.[1] Macready found in this part a famous effect when his son, a murderer, turned upon him with the words: 'Who proclaimed to me/That there were crimes made venial by the occasion?' There, according to Marston, 'with a shrill cry of agony, as if pierced mortally by a dart, [Macready] bounded from his seat, and then, as if all strength had failed him, wavered and fluttered forward . . . until he sank on one knee in front of the stage.'

In aspect he could be strange. A Bath critic wrote elegantly of 'the unaccommodating disposition of Nature in the formation of Mr

[1] *Our Recent Actors*, 1888.

Macready's face'. John Coleman has described the appearance of his Hamlet on the night when Edwin Forrest hissed the so-called *pas de mouchoir* at Edinburgh. Macready—it was the night before his fifty-third birthday—bowed to the audience, an awkward, gaunt figure, hair grizzled, features irregular—'unlike anything else I have seen in the shape of a nose'—and his dark beard close-shaven to his square jaws and unsoftened by a touch of pigment. When he spoke he changed to a 'poetic, subtle, truly human Prince' who 'brightened, irradiated the atmosphere'. Other writers more trustworthy than the emotional Coleman have reported how Macready could overcome his visual strangeness. His voice had the notes of a violoncello. He tried to see a character as a complete whole, not to yield to 'the prescriptive criticism of this country that looks for particular points'. He could humanise an artificial scene, and on occasion give a gleam of domestic truth to a theatre that dreamt it dwelt in marble halls.

On the other side, he had uncomfortable mannerisms. The 'Macready pause' hinted at eternity. Speech upon speech he thickened with redundant syllables, an intercalated 'er' or 'a-a-a'. If a house were unresponsive, he would be 'raw and efforty', or try to extort attention by a declamatory scream. Though he possessed 'the finest and most heroical voice on the stage' (Leigh Hunt), he would endanger a scene by an exaggerated vocal transition, a swoop to some deep crevasse. Often he would stand in the same posture, said Westland Marston, 'one knee, a little bent, before the other'. And he could terrify his fellow-actors. A sword-fight with Macready's Macbeth was usually dangerous. Fanny Kemble wrote: 'My only feeling about acting it [Desdemona] with Mr Macready is dread of his personal violence. I quail at the idea of his laying hold of me in those terrible passionate scenes. . . . As for that smothering in bed, "Heaven have mercy upon me", as poor Desdemona says.' The bitter George Vandenhoff, an actor whom he had borne down in America, catalogued Macready's hardness and angularity of style, his ungainly attitudes and his rolling gait, with an alternate thrusting forward of each shoulder.[1] But even Vandenhoff—who was a hostile witness—agreed that Macready excelled in executive power and certainty of effect, and that he had a voice of astonishing range.

He made many gifts to the stage. For eighteen years he was its most exciting, most debated actor. He sought to restore the texts of Shakespeare (whom he idolised), purging them of the theatrical accretions, the maulings, of Cibber and Tate, bringing back the Fool in *Lear* and Chorus in *Henry V*. In a period singularly devoid of lasting new drama, he

[1] *An Actor's Note-book*, 1860.

strove to foster what seemed potentially good, not only the work of Browning and Lytton and Knowles and Talfourd, but also such plays as Henry Taylor's *Philip van Artevelde* and Marston's *The Patrician's Daughter* ('Blank verse and parasols?' said the actress Mrs Warner to the dramatist; 'Is not that quite a new combination?') Macready had to face the public's incorrigible love of romantic bombast, resonant, platitudinous iambics. It was an audience with a consuming interest in the pseudo-Elizabethan, a refusal to accept modern themes, a masochistic pleasure in the reiteration of certain plays, apart from tinkered Shakespeare, and a relish for the second-rate expressed in Byron's guilty line, 'Otway, *Radcliffe*, Schiller, Shakespeare's art'. In 1825 Thomas Lovell Beddoes, a youth in his early twenties, wrote to a friend about Sheridan Knowles's version of Massinger's *The Fatal Dowry*: 'I am convinced the man who is to awake the drama must be a bold, trampling fellow—no creeper into worm-holes—no reviser even—however good. These reanimations are vampire-cold.' Macready did what he could; and he was always searching. During his four seasons of management he refused to keep his successes running without interruption; had he done so, it might have made all the difference to his balance-sheets and altered the fate of Covent Garden and Drury Lane.

One reason why his colleagues disliked him was his insistence on rehearsal—a discipline that would have a lasting effect upon the stage. His rehearsals were protracted and earnest, never a casual run-through. He was appalled when the players of a provincial stock company, the Lenvilles and Folairs of their time, failed to arrive one morning because it was only *Hamlet* at night, and they thought they knew it. 'Sergeant' Macready would have everything as exact, as finished, as possible. The theatre was all the better for his influence, though during the seasons at Lane and Garden it was tactless to permit the members of his coterie (especially Forster) to attend rehearsals and to join in the debate, amateurs seeking to instruct professionals. Another contradiction, for Macready's view of the amateur could be blistering.

A stage journal during the Covent Garden years printed a brief monologue, a morning with Macready:

'Where is the tailor-man, that Head, fool, brute, beast, ass? How dare you annoy me, sir, in this manner? Have you got a soul or sense? . . . Look, who wrote these calls? Gentlemen, look about you; read for yourselves: here is "Macbeth" spelt "Mackbeth" and Mr Serle's "Afrancesado" spelt "Haffrancishardo". . . . Who is that talking at the wings? Henry! Henry! go down and tell the stage door keeper I expect him to go away—to leave the theatre immediately . . . Mr Forster—oh, show Mr Forster to my room; no, stop! My dear Dickens, how d'ye do? Talfourd! your hand; another and another! Browning! Bulwer! a-a-walk into the green-room. Mr Bender, go on; why do you wait? Where is Mr Willmott? I—I—this is exceedingly bad! Will you make a beginning? Where are the-the-officers? Where is that-a-Paulo—man? Mr Beckett? Mr Smith? What cat is that? Do--do--do-a-a-a-a-damn it!—are you all asleep? . . . Why do we wait, gentlemen? The band? I-I-really will enforce fines without any respect of persons. . . Where's the supernumerary-master? Sir, I desired you not to employ that person without stockings. Do—do find me decent, intelligent men. Gentlemen of the band, be kind enough to discuss your-a-a-*on-dits* —outside the theatre. It is—it-is-a-a-preposterous . . . What is that horrible hubbub in the green-room? I-I really I—Where is the gas-man? Are we rehearsing the-the-a-Black-Hole of Calcutta? Do-do-do-pray lighten our darkness. Man, I have spoken several times about these pewter pots. I—I will not have the theatre turned into a-a-cookshop. . . . You—you—you cannot possibly dine at ten o'clock in the morning. . . . Send in your beds, gentlemen; let us have a-a-caravansery at once.'

This was what the profession would call 'a rap from Mac's sceptre'. Yet at the end of his first season, the Covent Garden actors presented him with a piece of plate, and he said in his reply: 'One of my motives has been the wish to elevate my art, and to establish an asylum for it, and for my brothers and sisters who profess it, where they might be secure of equitable treatment, friendly consideration, and, most of all, that respect which man should show to man, or, most important, which man should show to woman.' Off-stage, his profession, whatever he thought of it, could have had no more impressive symbol. He was only once at fault; and his journal shows how he regretted the clamour after his rash assault on Bunn—an assault no man had deserved so thoroughly. Macready could have remembered some lines of Wordsworth which the poet had recited to him in 1823 (and which Talfourd would echo in *Ion*):

> Action is transitory—a step, a blow,
> The motion of a muscle—this way or that—
> 'Tis done; and in the after vacancy
> We wonder at ourselves like men betrayed.

At his farewell dinner in 1851 the arts and professions gathered to honour Macready. Until Irving there would be no one to fill his place except that conscientious archaeologist, Charles Kean, and Samuel Phelps, an actor Macready esteemed, who was content to stay in his North London kingdom of Sadler's Wells.

'The last of the Mohicans!' cried a voice from the upper gallery of Drury Lane as Macready, to a thunder-burst of cheering, left the stage for ever—bequeathing to it the memories of his angers, his generosity, his shyness, his formality, his egotism, and his greatness. As a man he was 'deeply and inexplicably moving'; as an actor, indubitably great. In his journals man and actor still speak to the years ahead.

J.C.T.

Prologue 1793–1831

'Macready, thou hast pleased me much: till now
(And yet I would not thy fine powers arraign)
I did not think thou hadst that livelier vein,
Nor that clear open spirit upon thy brow. . . .

There is a buoyant air, a passionate tone
That breathes about thee, and lights up thine eye
With fire and freedom; it becomes thee well.
It is the bursting of a good seed, sown
Beneath a cold and artificial sky—
'Tis genius overmastering its spell.'

Barry Cornwall, 1818
Written After Seeing Mr Macready In Rob Roy.

I

His father, William Macready—sometimes McCready or M'Cready—
was an actor, born in 1755, son of a Dublin upholsterer. His mother,
Christina Ann (Birch), ten years younger, was a Derbyshire woman
and a serviceable actress. Three children died in infancy; William
Charles (1793) was the fifth of eight. Macready senior loved his world of
candle-grease and rouge and tinsel as much as his son would hate it.
He had ten years at Covent Garden, usually in the lower ranks—'second-
rate walking gentlemen': Antonio the merchant, Paris, Guildenstern—
and he managed a stock theatre at Birmingham, with others at Leicester
and Stafford. In drama it was a day of adapted Shakespeare and of plays
written largely in exclamation-marks, or in such lines as:

> My flesh creeps still, and my uncurdling blood
> Slowly and fearfully resumes its function. . . .

English poetry now approached a high summer; the drama was facing
the blasts of January.

Christina Macready died in Sheffield at Christmas 1803 when William
was ten. Four years afterwards, at his father's financial crisis—Macready
senior was then managing a theatre in Manchester—he left Rugby and
did what he could to help. During the winter of 1809 his father was
arrested for debt and taken to Lancaster gaol; the sixteen-year-old boy
had both to settle affairs with a hostile company at Chester and to take
charge of another season in Newcastle-on-Tyne. Macready senior,
released from Lancaster, joined him at Newcastle before the spring
season ended; soon it was obvious that William would have to be an
actor. On 7 June 1810, he made his début in Birmingham: 'the part of
Romeo by A YOUNG GENTLEMAN, being his first appearance on any
Stage.' It went well, and William said: 'I feel as if I should like to act it
all over again.' This was an actor speaking: William Charles Macready,
however he might regret it, was born for the theatre.

He became a savagely hard worker, bound to the wheel of the stock
companies. At Newcastle in 1812 he played Beverley in *The Gamester*
and Norval in *Douglas* to Sarah Siddons's Mrs Beverley and Lady
Randolph. The tragedienne, on her farewell tour, offered all encouragement to the young player: 'You are in the right way,' she said, 'but
remember . . . study, study, study, and do not marry until you are
thirty. Keep your mind on your art, and you are certain to succeed.'
Macready took her hardly romantic advice, even if to be what he called
'a most assiduous disciple of patient labour' was to be written off as

priggish. To the ebb of his career he continued to study. In those early years he practised working himself into a passion while remaining stone-still: standing upright against a wall, pinioned by a bandage, he would repeat the most violent speeches of Lear, Othello, or Macbeth.

As the grinding provincial years passed, he found himself spoken of as a London possibility. Edmund Kean, writing to the Drury Lane stage manager during March 1816, referred—ironically perhaps, but nervously—to 'the great W. C. M.' At length, from Bath and Bristol and Dublin, he secured in 1816 a contract to appear at Covent Garden for five years (£16 a week for the first two, £17 for the next two, £18 for the last). His opening part, on the night of 16 September, was Orestes in Ambrose Philips's very poor version[1] of Racine's *Andromaque*; the management's careful choice: no question here of comparisons for it was some time since the previous revival. William Abbott was Pylades; Julia Glover, Andromache; and Mrs Egerton, in the absence of Eliza O'Neill, Hermione. Macready seemed to be an awkward figure when he went on in the Covent Garden idea of a chlamys, and with a curling auburn wig to his shoulders. He pressed too hard at first, but the mad scene closed to cheering, swelled by Edmund Kean himself from a box: Macready had begun, and soon he proceeded to get what he did not want, a name for technical resource in the hollowest of melodramas. Thus they cast him for the Negro in Thomas Morton's tiresome, arid invention, *The Slave*: it meant that he had to appear with black body, legs, and arms, wearing short white cotton trunks, and with coloured beads round arms, neck, and ankles. There were easier things; and, after all, he was now in the presence of the endeared actress Eliza O'Neill ('You tremble before Mrs Siddons,' said an onlooker; 'you weep with Miss O'Neill'); and of Charles Mayne Young, courteous and polished. Pitted against a young rival, Junius Brutus Booth, in a melodrama called *The Conquest of Taranto*, Macready won with ease the kind of pitched battle that at this hour could replace team work.

During 1817, tired of being 'the exponent and apologist of trash', Macready contemplated some other profession. A friend offered to lend him enough to maintain him at Oxford while studying for orders. But when, early in 1818, his brother Edward Nevil Macready had to buy promotion in the Army and leave for India, William borrowed for Edward's sake the sum he might have used himself: he would remain in the theatre to repay it, and by the time he did the actor's son could be nothing but an actor for life.

It was in October 1819 that he had a tumultuous success as Richard

[1] *The Distrest Mother.*

the Third, a character in which Kean had governed London. Here there could be no middle path between disgrace and glory: also it was vital to the theatre (Covent Garden had lost many of its principals) as well as to the actor. Doubtfully, Macready consented; and he won. Twice, after the scene with Tyrrel and at the end of the night, the pit rose, waving its hats and crying 'Macready! Macready!' Leigh Hunt's comment in *The Examiner* was unexpected: 'We certainly never saw the gayer part of Richard to such advantage. His very step, in the more sanguine scenes, had a princely gaiety of self-possession, and seemed to walk off to the music of his approaching triumph.' Hastily, Kean returned to Richard at Drury Lane: the Patent Theatres, as well as individual actors, were in ceaseless conflict, with the same basic repertory. Macready, at Covent Garden, also played Coriolanus, carrying his audience if not all of the critics. Mrs Faucit (Helen's mother) was a Volumnia of whom Leigh Hunt said: 'A Roman matron did not think it essential to her dignity to step about with her head thrown half a yard back, as if she had a contempt for her own chin.'

Soon afterwards, in May 1820, Macready received a new part that would linger with him. In *Virginius; or, The Liberation of Rome*, Sheridan Knowles, the Irish schoolmaster-actor, dramatised the Roman tale of Virginia's slaying by her father in open Forum to save her from dishonour. Macready was asked to 'read the play to the company, and to take on the "getting it up", the arrangement of the action and the grouping of the scenes', the task, that is, of a modern director. He used the methods that companies in future years would find so ferociously intensive, and that exasperated some of the Covent Garden cast, angry at the presumption of a youth who dared 'to order and direct his elders'. At the opening of *Virginius* his pathos was stronger than it had ever been. The *Morning Herald* would allude to 'great and still-growing, genius'.

When he left for the provinces on his next vacation tour, he went with the fame of Kean's rival. On this journey he met in Aberdeen a young actress, still not quite fifteen, called Catherine Frances Atkins. She played the Prince of Wales and Virginia for him, and moved him deeply by more than her acting. In later years he said with some gravity: 'My opportunities of conversation with this interesting creature were very frequent, which, as they occurred, I grew less and less desirous of avoiding.' Macready and Catherine would meet again. Meanwhile, he returned to Covent Garden, to various lean and flashy plays, and to his experiment (which failed to work) of restoring as much of Shakespeare as he dared to the Cibber-choked text of *Richard III*. About this time Hazlitt said contentiously: 'He has talent and a magnificent voice, but he is, I fear, too improving an actor to be a man of genius. That little ill-looking vagabond Kean never improved in anything. On some plays, he could not, and in others he would not.'

II

There followed some seasons with Charles Kemble at Covent Garden. Macready played Hamlet, a self-pitying portrait, though applauded; and as the King in *Henry IV; Part Two*, he startled an audience unprepared for splendour in a part rarely considered:

> O Westmoreland, thou art a summer bird,
> Which ever in the haunch of winter sings
> The lifting-up of day.

At the end of the season of 1822–1823 ('one of perplexity, disquiet, and irritation, much . . . attributable to the excitability of my own undisciplined temperament'), he proposed to Catherine Atkins, who had acted with him on his visits to Bristol, and who was now living in Dublin. She accepted him—and learned, poor girl, that because of the insistence of Letitia, the sister with whom William lived in Conduit Street, she would have to continue her studies as a guest in the house until she was fit to marry: William, it was plain, must not waste himself on a child intellectually his inferior. Sweetly Catherine agreed (and feebly, William also); for everyone's sake, this 'lovely and docile Griselda' gallantly had her mind improved and 'made herself conversant with the works of Milton, Locke, Bacon, and our leading authors in poetry and prose.' It was a blessing that Catherine grew fond of Letitia. They lived together through the Macreadys' married life, and Letitia survived her sister-in-law by six years. The marriage at St Pancras Church was not until 24 June 1824,[1] after Macready's first season at Drury Lane, whither he had gone from Covent Garden. Dubiously, he had accepted Robert William Elliston's offer of an engagement in Kean's lair; Kean himself kept cautiously out of sight. 'I don't mind Young,' he said, 'but I will not act with Macready.' And again: 'Fabius Maximus conquered not by fighting a powerful enemy, but by avoiding him. He weakened his resources, and saved the city of Rome.' At the Lane Macready appeared, among other parts, as Hamlet, Macbeth (Mrs Bunn as Lady Macbeth) and Leontes, as Caius Gracchus in a Roman tragedy by

[1] For a time she had also 'prosecuted her studies in the family of a respectable widow lady at Kensington, most highly recommended'.

Sheridan Knowles that was a kind of popularised *Coriolanus*, and as the Duke in *Measure for Measure* where—unusually at fault—he believed that dignity and lofty declamation were the sole needs. Towards the end of a second Lane season, interrupted by a grave illness, he created (in May 1825) another Knowles part: William Tell in a drama that he helped to construct, and which would be a useful show-piece. All the time Kean stayed at a safe distance, and indeed spent most of 1826 in America.

Macready was westward-bound as well. Accompanied by Catherine and Letitia, he sailed in September 1826 for an eight months' tour in the United States, a country he then admired without reserve. While in New York he saw at the Bowery Theatre a *Julius Caesar* in which a vigorous young man of twenty, Edwin Forrest, played Mark Antony. Nearly thirty years later Macready wrote:

> The 'Bowery lads', as they were termed, made great account of him, and he certainly was possessed of remarkable qualifications. His figure was good, though perhaps a little too heavy; his face might be considered handsome, his voice excellent; he was gifted with extra-ordinary strength of limb, to which he omitted no opportunity of giving prominence. He had received only the commonest education, but in his reading of the text he showed the discernment and good sense of an intellect much upon a level with that of Conway;[1] but he had more energy, and was altogether distinguished by powers that under proper direction might be productive of great effect. I saw him again in *William Tell*. His performance was marked by vehemence and rude force that told upon his hearers; but of pathos in the affecting interview with his son there was not the slightest touch, and it was evident he had not rightly understood some passages in his text. My observation upon him was not hastily pronounced. My impression was that, possessed of natural requi-sites in no ordinary degree, he might, under careful discipline, confi-dently look forward to eminence in his profession. If he would give himself up to a severe study of his art, and improve himself by the practice he could obtain before the audiences of the principal theatres in Great Britain, those of Edinburgh, Liverpool, Glasgow, Birmingham, Manchester, &c. (then good dramatic schools), he might make himself a first-rate actor. But to such a course of self-denying training I was certain he would never submit, as its

---

[1] William Augustus Conway (1789–1828), who played Brutus. A talented but unhappy actor, he threw himself overboard in 1828 while on a voyage to Charleston.

necessity would not be made apparent to him. The injudicious and ignorant flattery, and the factious applause of his supporters in low-priced theatres, would fill his purse, would blind him to his deficiency in taste and judgment, and satisfy his vanity, confirming his self-opinion of attained perfection.

I spoke of him constantly as a young man of unquestionable promise, but I doubted his submission to the inexorable conditions for reaching excellence. The event has been as I anticipated. His robustious style gains applause in the coarse melodramas of *Spartacus* and *Metamora*; but the traits of character in Shakespeare, and the poetry of the legitimate drama are beyond his grasp. My forebodings were prophetic.

On his return to England Macready had in November 1827 his first Drury Lane part for eighteen months. Under the management of Stephen Price, the American, he gave his haunted performance of Macbeth. During the spring of 1828, as Macbeth, Othello, and Virginius, he visited Paris. 'Who would believe', said the critic of *La Réunion* after *Virginius*, 'that a man to whom Nature has refused everything—voice, carriage, and face—would rival Talma for whom she has left nothing undone?' (Kean, who followed Macready in Paris, would get nothing like the same ovation.) That summer, when touring the provinces, William sandwiched Paris between Bridgwater and Exeter, again getting £100 a week—for four weeks instead of three—and acting Tell, Hamlet, and Othello to protracted excitement. For more than two years after this he devoted himself entirely to the provincial theatres, tedious journeys by coach or chaise, long nights in the squalid dressing-rooms and upon the stages he had known as a young actor. Catherine, without effect, was urging him to leave the profession; he was determined to provide for his family.

The 74-year-old Macready senior, who had been a happy man for the past decade as a respected public figure in Bristol, where he managed the Theatre Royal, died in the spring of 1829; his widow, William's step-mother, eventually succeeded him at the theatre. For William himself it was high time to get back to the London stage. He and Catherine, who had been living at Pinner Wood, took a plain, substantial country house at Elm Place, Elstree, three miles beyond Edgware and thirteen miles from Drury Lane. In the autumn of 1830, with *Virginius*, he opened at the Lane, managed now by Captain Polhill and Alexander Lee, with the showman Alfred Bunn in exuberant attendance. Macready entered in his journal on 15 December two words, 'Werner. Succeeded': the briefest of notes on his triumph as the Schiller-worshipping Byron's gloomy figure from a decayed Silesian palace: a personage whose moroseness and pride appealed at once to the actor. On Boxing Day 1830 Catherine gave birth to their first child, a daughter, Christina Letitia (Nina). In 1831 Macready had his only major comedy success, Oakly, the timid husband of George Colman's *The Jealous Wife*.

So, at length, to 1832, the year before he began to make full journal entries. It would be the year in which he and Kean met (a bad night for Macready) as Iago and Othello. There would soon be widening criticism of Patent Theatre monopolists who had broken faith with the drama and made play with 'wild beasts, fire-eaters, sword-swallowers', as Edward Bulwer said in the House of Commons. (He was thinking of 'a grand Oriental spectacle' called *Hyder Ali; or, The Lions of Mysore* at Drury Lane in the autumn of 1831.)

The narrative now, through twenty years, must be in Macready's own voice. He speaks first on an April night in Dublin, and the play is *Macbeth*.

I
Macready and Bunn
(1832–1836)

'It seems . . . that my temper has become worse since this harassing and fretting business has weighed upon and galled it; but of late I have been so irritable that I am shocked as I look back upon my imperious and impatient bearing.'

Journal, 29 June 1836

1832

During this year Macready, who was thirty-nine on 3 March 1832, made only brief daily entries in his journal. In London, where he had lodgings, he was engaged at Drury Lane. His estate, Elm Place, Elstree, was on the borders of Middlesex and Hertfordshire, about thirteen miles from the great 'Patent Theatres' of Drury Lane and Covent Garden. In the spring of 1832, when these extracts begin, he was playing in Dublin.

Dublin, April 12. *Macbeth.* Very unwell indeed. Much disinclined to act, but acted well—really well. Thought of an improvement in third act. Tenderness to Lady Macbeth. Physician came on too late, half undressed, holding his clothes!

London, April 21. Saw Bunn. Business. Took Lodgings, 19, Argyll Street, at £2 12s 6d per week.

[Alfred Bunn, 1798–1860, was now acting manager, soon to be lessee, of Drury Lane. He was a glib vulgarian and a versifier; one day he would write the libretto of 'The Bohemian Girl' (1843), and he would also become the model for Thackeray's theatre manager, Mr Dolphin (Pendennis), 'a portly gentleman with a hooked nose and a profusion of curling brown hair and whiskers; his coat was covered with the richest frogs, braiding, and velvet.']

May 12. Dine at Garrick Club. Dinner to Lord Mulgrave. Very kindly noticed in his speech. Came away as they were about to drink my health. Not nerve for it.

[The Garrick Club was founded in February 1832 at 35 King Street, Covent Garden; it moved in 1864 to its present building in Garrick Street.]

May 23. *Werner.* Dined with H[enry] Smith *[actuary of the Eagle Insurance Company].* Acted very well. Preserved an erect deportment in the midst of passion, and let the mind act.

[Macready first appeared in Byron's tragedy 'Werner' at Drury Lane in December 1830. T. N. Talfourd wrote a sonnet to him that ended: 'When love's disdain round its cold idol twines/How mighty are its weakness and its woe!']

June 25. Saw Kean in *Richard.* Pleased with his energy. Felt his want of abstraction in his soliloquies, and his occasional tricks. *[Edmund Kean, 1787–1833, in 'Richard III' at Drury Lane.]*

August 7. Birth of a son. *[William Charles, second child and eldest son; died in Ceylon, 26 November 1871. Browning wrote 'The Pied Piper' for him in 1842, when Willie was ten, to amuse him during a slight illness.]*

August 8. An idle day, which in duty to myself and my dear children must not be.

September 22. Drury Lane again.

September 25. Read of Walter Scott's death on Friday last. Whatever his defects, a very great man whose loss brings sorrow with it. . . . Walked with Mr Cooper to my chambers, 61, Lincoln's Inn Fields. Signed agreement, £2 5s per week. Came home by Reeves' coach outside. . . . *[This was John Cooper, 1790–1870, actor; later Bunn's stage manager.]*

September 28. Rehearsed *Pizarro*. News of robbery of geese at Elstree. Dined on sausage, brown bread, and soda-water. Lay down on bed. Acted middlingly. Very much cut in the arms.

[Macready played Rolla in Richard Brinsley Sheridan's tragedy, 'Pizarro'; or 'The Spaniards in Peru', from the German of Kotzebue.]

October 2. Newspapers, middling, middling. They persecute me. Why should I regard them? Acted indifferently. . . .

October 17. Came by *Crown Prince* to Elstree. Meditated on the nature and end of life. On the beauty and vivifying qualities of the physical world. Who dares say it is not undesigned or unsustained; looked over the fences, &c., of the fields, and gave directions about farm, &c. Read some of Wycherley's plays—coarse and obscene.

November 10. Lost much time and thought in useless, vain and bad imaginations referring to people indifferent to me, not turning my eyes to the good I possess, but lashing myself into a state of irritation which, if it were wise or just to despise anything in humanity should awaken my contempt. Let me be wiser, O God!

November 12. Saw two acts of Kean's 'Hamlet'. Imperfect, spiritless, uncharacteristic recitation.

November 26. Read Iago in bed. Rehearsed Iago. Met Kean. Lay down on bed. Acted, not satisfactorily, nervous. Called by the audience.

[Kean, tired and ill, had at length to act with the rival he had always avoided. He still ruled the stage, though to do so he had to put out his last strength. If, for two acts of 'Othello', he seemed to be overborne by Macready he managed by constantly 'upstaging' him (standing a few paces back), to force the younger man to appear in profile to the audience. Then, in the third act, after speaking his Farewell resplendently, at the line 'Villain! be sure

thou prove my love a whore!' he seized Iago by the throat, and before the startled gaze of the Drury Lane house, seemed to rise to a stature that blotted out Macready. From this moment the night was Kean's.]

November 27. Looked at Iago. Played well. Chaise to Elstree.

December 10. Iago. Acted well when Kean did not interfere with me. Called for by the audience.

December 27. New cow bought. (Cost £13.)

December 28. Read over Iago. Acted very well. Kean quite strong on his legs and in his voice. Called for by the audience and much applauded. Returned to Elstree in carriage.

1833

More extended entries begin.

January 2. My performance this evening of Macbeth afforded me a striking evidence of the necessity there is for thinking over my characters previous to playing, and establishing, by practice if necessary, the particular modes of each scene and important passage. I acted with much energy, but could not (as I sometimes can, when holding the audience in wrapt attention) listen to my own voice, and feel the truth of its tones. It was crude, and uncertain, though spirited and earnest; but much thought is yet required to give an even energy and finished style to all the great scenes of the play, except perhaps the last, which is among the best things I am capable of. . . .

January 4. . . . My acting to-night was coarse and crude—no identification of myself with the scene; and what increased my chagrin on the subject, some persons in the pit gave frequent vent to indulgent and misplaced admiration. The consciousness of unmerited applause makes it quite painful and even humiliating to me.

January 8. Paid some visits of ceremony—unmeaning, hollow practices, irksome and embarrassing in act and productive of no good results. I allude entirely to the G—s, who are incomprehensible to me; if they like me, why do they not cultivate my society? if they are indifferent, why not relinquish my acquaintance? . . .

January 22. I acted to-night with spirit and in a manly tone, better perhaps than ordinarily in the part Rob Roy. *[In 'Rob Roy McGregor; or, Auld Lang Syne', by Isaac Pocock, a part he had created at Covent Garden in 1818. It moved 'Barry Cornwall' to a lumbering sonnet, with a collector's piece of a first phrase, 'Macready, thou hast pleased me much. . . .']* A curious evidence of egotism and importunate demand of attention to business of no concern to me was afforded me to-night in Mr Heraud's letter. The universe is but an atom before the vastness of one's self!

[John Abraham Heraud, 1799–1887, journalist and critic, had no doubt been asking about a tragedy he had offered to Drury Lane.]

January 24. . . . I was much struck with the scene of the canal and the skaters in the Regent's Park: the kind of indian-ink landscape that the colourless view presented, and the gaiety extorted from the vigour of winter, amused my thoughts. . . .

January 25. Quite made up my mind to leave the managers to their own course in the particular of their pledge to me on the alternation of Othello and Iago. Why did I feel excited and stung into a kind of nervous alacrity by Kean's inability to act? Our interests in this profession come too frequently into collision to ensure, without steady vigilance, that magnanimity which makes the peace of conscience.

He goes on a provincial tour.

To Exeter, February 16. . . . I gave too much to the porter at the coach; this is a very *silly* fault, and a wrong to any poor creature that may need one's charity. There was nothing remarkable in the three passengers with whom I started; the woman was very vulgar, which was not her fault—her husband, an outside, was equally so and rather drunk, but redeemingly civil. . . .

Exeter, February 18. . . . I acted pretty well this evening *[Macbeth]*, but in the dagger scene wanted that fresh natural manner, so real and impressive on an audience. Thank God, was not angry or harsh.

Bristol, February 23. Forgot, in stepping into the coach for Bristol, my many expostulations with myself on the subject of temper, and was guilty of a display of ill humour because a gentleman, a Quaker, claimed, on the right of pre-occupation, the back seats! I notice it to shame and condemn my absurdity! Last night I heard of Kean's illness; a subject which has little interest for me, since his ability to play or not will make no difference in the style of language—qy. cant?—used on him and me.

Dublin, March 3. I AM FORTY YEARS OF AGE! Need I add one word to the solemn reproof conveyed in these, when I reflect on what I am, and what I have done? What has my life been? a betrayal of a great trust, an abuse of great abilities! This morning, as I began to dress, I almost started when it occurred to me that it was my birthday.

To Manchester, March 10. . . . I set off in a carriage with Mr Calcraft and Miss Huddart to Kingstown. We dined at the Royal Hotel. How disenchanting in the female character is a manifestation of relish for the pleasures of the table!

[John William Calcraft, whose real name was Cole, managed the Theatre Royal, Dublin, from 1830 to 1851. Later after financial failure, he wrote the life of Charles Kean, whose secretary he became. He died in 1870.
[Mary Amelia Huddart, later Mrs Warner, 1804-1854, an admired tragedienne, was one of the actresses closest to Macready. In 1836 she married the improvident landlord of a Bow Street tavern. She acted with

Macready at Covent Garden and Drury Lane, aided Phelps at Sadler's Wells, and managed the Marylebone Theatre. After her enforced retirement and her early death (from cancer) Macready helped to provide for her children.]

Manchester, March 13. Have given up the entire day to the rehearsal, consideration, and preparation of *Othello*. The Iago of Cooper was a very bad performance, neither distinctness of outline nor truth of colour. Of my own Othello I am inclined to speak in qualified terms. There was not exactly a lack of spirit in the early scenes, but a want of freshness and freedom in its flow must have been manifest. I was nervous, and under that oppression effort will show itself. The audience, as cold as the snow that was falling at the beginning, waxed warmer and warmer, and actually kindled into enthusiasm at the burst in the third act, which was good, but the part still requires much study. . . .

March 16. . . . I have dispatched a large sum to my bankers today, for which I thank God. In the play I acted Iago pretty well, but was certainly disconcerted, if not annoyed, by the share of applause bestowed on Mr Cooper. What little beings does selfishness make us! . . .

March 24. Read in the newspapers the announcement of Kean and son in *Othello*; it is mere quackery. . . .

[This performance was at Covent Garden on 25 March 1833, with Edmund Kean as Othello and his son Charles, then twenty-two, as Iago. Kean, sustained by brandy-and-water, got through until the third act, but as he attempted his great effect on 'Villain! be sure . . .', his voice went falsetto on the first words, and his head sank upon Charles's shoulder. 'I am dying,' he whispered; 'Speak to them for me.' He was carried from the stage and laid, unconscious, on his dressing-room sofa. 'It must have been a quacking exhibition', Macready said unkindly when he heard the news in Manchester.]

Edinburgh, March 30. . . . I walked upon the Calton Hill after posting my letters. Disliking this city as much as I can suffer myself to dislike any place, I cannot be blind to its extraordinarily grand and beautiful appearance; it is more like a metropolis in the *coup d'œil* it offers than any British city. But I have been ill, and always disregarded here, and I am not patient of the unauthorised pretention of its inhabitants.

April 1. . . . I think I acted Macbeth in a manner that would have gained me fame before any but an Edinburgh audience, which I look upon as one so like the vile pretender to superior wisdom described by Gratiano that I should as soon expect the standing pool to rise in waves, or become clear enough to reflect the images near it, as to observe one genuine display of sympathy from them. They seem to me grave coxcombs. . . . I almost *quite* satisfied myself.

April 5. . . . Struck with the surpassing beauty of this city, which I delight in getting free from. . . .

He left Edinburgh on 7 April and reached home on 9 April.

Elstree, April 25. Saw by newspapers that Mr Bunn is made lessee of Drury Lane Theatre a more dishonest choice could not have been made, but I must 'abide the change of time'.

[Alfred Bunn, bland adventurer, would soon become lessee of both the great Patent Houses, Drury Lane and Covent Garden, which were in difficulties.]

London, April 27. . . . Saw Mr Bunn, who is certainly the lessee of Drury Lane, under Polhill's security, and had some conversation with him; he seems inclined to be very civil; but it is only to try to make me useful to him. I know him to be destitute of honesty and honour. . . .

[Francis Polhill, 1798–1848, Captain, King's Dragoon Guards, and a 'gentleman possessing more money than brains' (J. R. Planché in 'Recollections and Reflections'), had lost £50,000 in four seasons at the Lane. Later, he would be M.P. for Bedford.]

May 4. . . . Called on Mr Cooper and engaged him to go to Birmingham at Whitsuntide. Was surprised to hear him speak in what seemed to me a silly manner on the junction of the two theatres, but he is to be manager of one, and is therefore salaried to approve.

[Bunn tried, during 1833–1835, to run the two theatres together under what a doggerel prologue at the reopening of Drury Lane in October 1833 would call 'the great Grand Junction'. Totally ruthless, he would expect players, if needed, to act in an opening piece at Covent Garden (where opera, spectacle, and ballet predominated), and then to scurry through winter darkness across Bow Street to act in an after-piece at the Lane.]

May 17. *[On the news of Edmund Kean's death]* . . . Kean's death *[at Richmond on 15 May 1833, aged forty-six.]* scarcely awoke a passing thought; he has lived his own choice of life; even his very indecencies have found eulogists, as the worst parts of (often admirable) acting have had loud-throated admirers.

May 18. . . . Made arrangements providing against the necessity of attending Kean's funeral, which I have no wish to do, as I entertain no feeling of respect for his character. . . .

[Macready was a pall-bearer at Kean's funeral. Among names in the entry for May 25 are:

Actors: John Pritt Harley, 1786–1858, noted for his Shakespearean clowns, and Richard 'Gentleman' Jones, 1778–1851, another favourite comedian (Perez is a character in a version of Beaumont and Fletcher's 'Rule a Wife and Have a Wife'); Andrew Ducrow, 1793–1842, equestrian actor ('Cut the cackle, and come to the 'osses') and pantomimist.

Actress: There were two Faucit daughters. The elder was Harriet (Mrs Bland), 1809–1847. The younger, Helen Faucit, 1817–1898, made her debut in January 1836 at Covent Garden as Julia in Knowles's 'The Hunchback'. Frequently Macready's leading lady; she used the name Helena in her later stage years. Married [Sir] Theodore Martin in 1851. Her mother, formerly Harriet Diddear, 1789–1857, left her husband John Saville Faucit to live with the celebrated comedian William Farren, 1786–1861, to whom late in life she was married. Macready, in 1834, found 'the effrontery of the connection extraordinarily disgusting'. In Kean's last years Helen, as a schoolgirl, had met and spoken to him at Richmond: 'A small pale man with a fur cap, and wrapped in a fur cloak. He looks to me as if come from the grave. A stray lock of very dark hair crossed his forehead under which shone eyes which looked dark, and yet as bright as lamps.' (Helena Faucit: 'On Some of Shakespeare's Female Characters', 1888.)

Dramatist: Sheridan Knowles, 1784–1862, in whose 'Virginius' (1820) and 'William Tell' (1824) Macready had had two of his early successes; Knowles was also an actor.

John Braham, 1774–1856, was the popular tenor; Alexander Lee, the musician (composer of 'I'd be a butterfly') who for a time had been Polhill's partner at Drury Lane.

John Forster, 1812–1876, then only twenty-one, stocky, fresh-complexioned, aggressive, and a theatre critic on a journal called 'The True Sun' (he moved later to 'The Examiner'), would become Macready's most intimate friend and adviser, though the friendship was often explosive.

Clarkson Stanfield ('Stanny'), 1793–1867, who became a celebrated marine and landscape artist, was a scene-painter at Drury Lane and one of Macready's inner circle of friends. George Clint, 1770–1854, portrait painter.

May 25. Came early to town . . . On my way to Richmond with Harley, Birch, and Spence, met Jones who promised to do M. Perez for my night. Passed several pedestrian mourners on the road, and some carriages. Among them M. Ducrow's. On alighting among a vulgar crowd saw Mrs and Miss Faucit. Ushered into the room where Kean's remains lay, poor creature! Lee hoped that Mr Harley approved what he had done. In the drawing-room shook hands with young Kean, Stanfield, Knowles. Clint introduced me to Mr Forster. After some delay furnishing mourners, etc., we were summoned, Braham and self first, as supporters; we crossed the Green and paced the crowding streets amid the loud remarks and repetitions of names of the multitude. Kean's coffin, placed before our pew, led me into very sad ruminations—contrasting his moments of burning energy with the mass of cold corruption fronting me. The church was crowded by curious and gay visitors, and was distressingly hot—his son and Mr Lee were much affected; the anthem was beautiful but long. The procession returned to the house in its original order. I could make little observation on anything around me, being under such a surveillance. Braham invited me to dine with him at the 'Star and Garter', but I was obliged to decline. I shook hands very warmly with young Kean, who thanked me; and, with Harley, went in search of the carriage, which met us on the Green and very rapidly took us to town.

He went to Birmingham on 26 May.

Birmingham, May 28. I acted Hamlet, although with much to censure, yet with a spirit, and feeling of words and situations, that I think I have never done before. The first act was the best—still at the exit of the Ghost in both scenes, and afterwards, polish and self-possession are requisite. In the second act, almost general revision. Third act, the soliloquy wants a more entire abandonment to thought, more abstraction. Ophelia's scene wants finish, as does the advice to the players. The play scene was very good, and most of the closet scene, but in parts my voice is apt to rise, and I become rather too vehement. Latter part wants smoothness. End of the play was good. Energy! Energy! Energy!

May 31. . . . Went to rehearsal; made a trifling present to the little boy who, in Albert *[William Tell]* last night, so disconcerted and enraged me. *I deserved a severer penalty.* . . .

London, June 4. At five o'clock left Birmingham in the 'Red Rover', with a guard dressed for the part, in a red coat and red hat . . . I saw Malibran to-night in a state of ridiculous confusion, owing to a tumble she had had in a dance. She would have done better to have laughed.

June 10. Benefit. Amount of House with all the foreign aid—

£408 3s 6d. Profit £116. Our hay began to be cut under the hottest sun of the season; and I left it, with Catherine and Letitia, to attend my *Benefit* in town. . . . Acted as well as I could. Farren was very flat and coarse. Vestris pointless and vulgar. Miss Phillips looked all that the author would have imagined of the beauty and modesty of Maria . . . [Malibran] sang the 'Deep Sea' in quite a poetical manner. She is a creature of genius. And what is Taglioni? A realization of some young poet's dream whose amorous fancy offered to his slumbers beside some stream or fountain the nymph whose divine being consecrated the natural beauty of the scene. She presents to me an idea of the soul of the Peri tenanting a woman's form. . . .

[The Benefit programme included 'The School for Scandal', with Macready as Joseph—'not such a bill' he said glumly, 'as the Tragedian of the Theatre should put out',—and 'The Maid of Cashmere', English version of the opera-ballet, 'Le Dieu et la Bayadère'. The names in the entry are those of Macready's wife Catherine and sister Letitia (who lived with them); William Farren, Helen Faucit's guardian; Maria Felicitá Malibran (1808-1836), the singer; Lucia Elizabeth Vestris, née Bartolozzi (1797-1856), actress and singer, who married Armand Vestris, dancer, when she was sixteen, and would marry the actor Charles James Mathews in 1838; Louisa Anne Phillips, actress, who was the original Ida Stralenheim in 'Werner', and Marie Taglioni (1804-1888), greatest figure in the Romantic era of ballet.]

July 8. Called at Covent Garden theatre on Bunn. . . . He told me much of Farren's and Knowles's absurdity. I promised to send him *Antony and Cleopatra* and *Maid's Tragedy* [*Macready adapted this play, by Beaumont and Fletcher, under the title of 'The Bridal'; Sheridan Knowles added three scenes.*]

Elstree, July 24. . . . Finished the perusal of [Byron's] *Sardanapalus*, which, for the fourth time, I think, I have examined on its capabilities for undergoing adaptation. It *might have been* an acting play, but it is too monotonous, passionless, and devoid of action, I fear, to satisfy an English audience. My whole evening has been spent in revolving the possibility of turning it to a representable form, and of considering the effect of his other plays. I reluctantly conclude upon abandoning the hope of them. We purchased a new cow today, a very interesting event in our farmyard.

July 28. I have begun more seriously this month to apply to the study of my profession, impelled by the necessity which the present state of the drama creates. I do not feel that I have the talent to recall attention to an art from which amusement cannot be drawn but by an exertion of the intellect. The age is too indolent in part, and in part too highly cultivated. But while I see the desperate condition to which, at this late period of my life, my profession is reduced, I am not thereby inclined to let my spirits sink under the disheartening prospect. To do my best is still my duty to myself and to my children, and I *will do it.*

August 6. Received a notification this day from Reynolds[1] of Bunn's intention to act my version of *Antony and Cleopatra*; heard also of Bunn's hostile correspondence with Bulwer, and reflected on Bulwer's recommendation of kicking as a cure for calumny. I look calmly and dispassionately on the irrationality of such reprisals. The character for manly spirit is not wanted where the virtue exists; it is like the loaded gun, if touched in the right place you will soon be made sensible of the danger you incur. Where you can disprove a falsehood, do it as placidly as if in the cause of abstract truth—your end is obtained. Where an insult is offered you by an unworthy person, your best triumph is in an exhibition of utter indifference; the sting is harmless, if the flesh it wounds is not in an inflammatory state. . . .

[Edward George Earle Lytton Bulwer (1803–1873), novelist, dramatist (Macready would act in several of his plays), and politician. In 1838 he became a baronet; he added his mother's maiden name of Lytton to his own surname (as Bulwer-Lytton) when he succeeded in 1843 to her property at Knebworth, Hertfordshire. In 1866 he was created Lord Lytton. Bulwer had enraged Bunn by his campaign against the monopoly of the Patent Theatres.]

August 20. . . . Read the last act of *Antony and Cleopatra*, and Hazlitt's observations on that play and *Lear*. What conceited trash that man has thought to pass upon the public, and how willingly many of them received the counterfeit as sterling.

Between 24 August and 4 September he was in the provinces.

Swansea, August 26. Could not help wishing for the quiet of a country life, as I passed a very neat villa here, that I might dedicate my remaining years to the culture of my own mind and the careful education of my children's.

August 27. I went to my first rehearsal of *Lear*, with which I was much dissatisfied: I am not yet at ease in the character. I have much labour yet

---

[1] Frederick Reynolds (1764–1841), dramatist who was reading for Bunn at Drury Lane.

to bestow upon it before I can hope to make it such a representation as I am ambitious of. Spent five hours in rehearsing, and left the theatre jaded and worn out. Lay down after dinner, and with pain in my limbs, and 'between sleep and wake', made myself perfect in the last scene of *Lear*. A poor player called Dunn, whom I remember in a dirty old coat as D. Dashall at Wexford calling *rouleaux* 'roorloors', sent in a petition to me to buy some fishing-flies from him. Acted particularly well William Tell, with collectedness, energy, and truth; the audience felt it. I spoke in my own manly voice, and took time to discriminate. I was much pleased.

August 29. Endeavoured to make the most of the day by beginning to pack up my clothes before rehearsals. At the rehearsal of *Lear* I found myself very deficient, undecided, uncollected; in short, unprepared for the attempt. After rehearsal took a walk of two miles and more to return the port-reeve's call—the way along the hills about Swansea afforded beautiful views of the bay. Reposed, and tried to think of Lear during the afternoon, but vainly; my thoughts gain an evil mastery over me—a great misfortune, or a great crime; *the latter*. Acted Lear; how? I scarcely know. Certainly not well—not so well as I rehearsed it; crude, fictitious voice, no point; in short, a failure. To succeed in it, I must strain every nerve of thought, or triumph is hopeless. Woulds called and paid me; not a very profitable engagement, but I am seldom discontented.

On 7 September Macready reached Brighton for a short engagement.

Brighton, September 8. . . . Passed the evening in conversation, not very amusing, but affording one further insight into the vanity of human nature, in showing how we colour to ourselves the motives of our conduct. Am already wearied with Brighton, a place to which my aversion increases with my experience of its monotony.

September 11. At rehearsal bore in mind Sir H. B. D.'s[1] criticism, and endeavoured to act from the mind direct, and not lash myself into excitement by physical exertion. Wished to act well, and to bear in mind the principle inculcated in Sir H.B.'s objection. Proceeded with tolerable success to the third act, but, owing to the inattention of the Lucius, my scene at the camp was utterly destroyed, and I incapable of recovering my self-possession through the night. I must not omit to notice the temper I displayed on the occasion, which calls up my bitter regret, as it

---

[1] Toynbee suggests that this might have been Sir Henry Bate Dudley, Bart. (1745-1824), a picaresque figure who was the first editor of the *Morning Post*, an unsuccessful dramatist, and a clergyman, among other things.

merits the heaviest censure. What would I do, or give, to cure myself of this unjustifiable, dangerous, and unhappy disposition? . . .

September 12. . . . In comparing my performances with my rehearsals, when I frequently speak and act with an abandonment and a reality that surprises me, I feel the great advantage which Kean, Miss O'Neill, and Mrs Siddons enjoyed in passing their earliest years upon the stage, and thereby obtaining a power of identification only to be so acquired.

[Eliza O'Neill (1791-1872), actress (later Lady Becher) whom Macready thought the only Juliet: 'It is not altogether the matchless beauty of form and face, but the spirit of perfect innocence and purity that seemed to glisten in her speaking eyes.' *She left the theatre in 1819. Her husband, William Becher, received a baronetcy in 1831.]*

Worthing, September 15. I saw in the *Globe* an announcement of my name for Prospero in the *Tempest* on the opening night of D.L. theatre. I felt very indignant at such an opening part, which Mr Bunn knows very well I except to. . . .

Elstree, September 16. . . . Considered Mr Bunn's letter, which I thought rude and imperious; returned the part of Prospero, as not being yet engaged in the theatre. . . .

Macready and Bunn came, uneasily to an agreement.

Elstree, September 19. Began the morning with reading the dull, ungrammatical version of Prospero by Dryden and Reynolds—oh, the genius! *[Frederick Reynolds was notorious for hack semi-operatic versions of Shakespeare. Macready had met this one before. In later life he wrote:* 'In a *mélange* that was called Shakespeare's *Tempest*, with songs interpolated by Reynolds among the mutilations and barbarous ingraftings of Dryden and Davenant, I had to act, 15 May, 1821 [Covent Garden] the remnant that was left of the character of Prospero, but not for many nights.'*]*

Walked in the garden and yard, and spent the whole of the day in altering and writing out copies of my engagement . . . with a letter to Mr Bunn, intended only to put on record, *litera scripta*, the position in which we stand toward each other. Mr Tomlins called, and offered me £35 for my largest rick, and left me requesting I would not part with it for a pound more. . . . Before I went to bed I read Prospero, and as long as my eyes could keep open to it, in bed too. I am indolent, and my mind is in an unsettled state. I have no good augury, in my feelings, of the engagement I have made. Mr B— is destitute alike of honour and common honesty, and my trust is in Providence only.

London, October 5. To-day being the opening of Drury Lane theatre, I went to town by Billings, and, executing some domestic commissions previously, attended the rehearsal of the *Tempest* at half-past eleven. There was nothing to notice but its tedium, and the offer made me of a night's performance at Richmond, which I declined on the double reason of interference with my attention to business and anticipation of a longer and more lucrative engagement. Received two letters about new plays. Dined on a chop at the Garrick Club (really a blackguard place) . . . Was obliged to force the locks of my trunks for my dress of Prospero acted the part unequally, but maintained myself in the only great passage retained in the characterless, stupid old proser of commonplace which the acted piece calls Prospero. The house was good, and the play went off well.

October 14. Went to the rehearsal of *Venice Preserved*, curious to see the bepuffed Mrs Sloman, who was standing on the stage as I entered. I listened with interest to her opening speech, but the first five lines spoke disappointment to me. I soon, as the play proceeded, became convinced that no permanent success could follow so artificial and vulgar a manner. . . . My acting of Pierre did not satisfy me, though I felt it to be better than my former efforts in the part. Mrs Sloman more than realised my anticipations; it was the worst kind of rant that pervaded her performance. . . .

[Macready had acted Pierre in Thomas Otway's 'Venice Preserved' at Covent Garden in 1819, to the Belvidera of Eliza O'Neill, and at Drury Lane in 1830 to Miss Huddart. Mrs Sloman (1799–1858), was the Belvidera on this occasion, she was daughter of William Dowton (1764–1851), comedian, an applauded Falstaff.]

October 16. Seeing immense placards of Mrs Sloman's success, I called at the Garrick to see yesterday's papers, all of which, except the *Post*, let her down gently. What an injudicious ass Mr Bunn is! Saw Knowles at Garrick. Nothing could be *cooler* than his greeting, as mine, I daresay, to him. If ever a man was at heart ungrateful, it is this man—I would not have his genius for his heart. . . .

October 17. . . . The more I see of the management of Mr Bunn, the more I find cause to blame the proprietors who gave the theatre to him!

October 22. Rehearsed well, but still all was uncertain and unsettled in my mind. Dowton recommended me to try Benedict [*Benedick in 'Much Ado About Nothing'*]. I must pause before I decide on it; I stated positively my inability to act Osmond (!) *[in M.G. ('Monk'* *Lewis's 'The Castle Spectre', a Gothick melodrama]* on Monday. Notes from Captain Medwin *[Thomas Medwin (1788–1869) a cousin of Shelley]* whom I do not like, and a Mr Carroll, wanting an engagement; answered both. Lay down to recruit my spirits and read Hotspur. Acted Hotspur— I scarcely know how. I could and should have done it well if I had had rehearsal to prove myself, and a few days to think upon it. Received a severe blow on the eye and cheek in falling, which I apprehend will be a large black eye. Cooper thinks I am so furious and so strong! Felt tired and dissatisfied with myself.

October 24. . . . Received a book of *Castle Spectre*—a fit play for Mr Bunn's management. In my chambers found a parcel containing notes and a play from Mr Hiscox, a very dull bore, who wanted me to read and champion his rejected play. Answered Mr Hiscox. Lay down and tried to read Werner, but was too tired for anything but sleep. Took especial pains in acting Werner, made due pause, so as to discriminate clearly, and subdued all tendency to exaggeration. Satisfied myself. Read Osmond—ugh! trash!

October 28. Arrived in town, found myself late for the rehearsal, which was called at ten. Went to the theatre, and, under the sensation of wearied body and mind proceeded with the play. In the wardrobe found no dress for me, and lost my temper at the *blackguard* (I have no other word descriptive of the man) Bunn for his behaviour. Reflection, how-ever, convinced and convinces me, that if I want to yield him occasion of success, I shall do so by *passion*. Read some very warm panegyrics on Wolsey and Werner by Forster—dined at the Garrick. . . . Read a little of Leontes, oppressed with weariness. Acted very ill, being literally imperfect—this disgusting management! Notes from Mr Atherstone, an ass! Mr Crooke, a knave! Mr Hiscox, a bore; Mr Young, I know not who; worried and kept up to a late hour in answering them. Sent a note to Cooper stating my inability to play Ford on Tuesday.

October 31. . . . Mr Bunn has announced the *Merry Wives*—if for me, *I will be quiet* . . . [He] appears to me in a Malay humour, ready to run amok—pitiful wretch! . . .

November 1. . . . In a conference with Bunn it was decided that Ford should be laid aside, and that *Antony and Cleopatra* should be done (sacrificed) on Monday sennight. Mr Bunn is such a blackguard, and so out of the pale of respectability, that I have resolved to have no more dealings with him, but transact all my business with Mr Cooper. Acted Macbeth passably, held in check by Mrs Sloman, who I think derived her fire from what would have quenched many others.

November 4. Came to town. Ran directly to rehearsal and very attentively went through *Henry V*. My dress was *beggarly* as usual from the theatre, and inappropriate from my own wardrobe. Dined at the Garrick, where I saw Yates *[Frederick Henry Yates (1797–1842), actor and manager; father of Edmund Yates, journalist and novelist.]* . . . Went home; lay down in bed and read Henry very attentively. Acted it with more self-possession than I have felt before a London audience for years. Three accidents, however, occurred (on such trifles does an actor's success depend!) that damped the general effect of the play which, I incline to think, I acted well: my truncheon broke in my hand during the great speech to Westmoreland, which for a moment disconcerted me— Mr Russell was not called to his time and cut out his part—and Miss Phillips bewildered me in the last scene by forgetting her speech to me. I never, in my own mind, acted the part so well. After the play I marked two acts of *Antony and Cleopatra*, and at a very late hour went to bed and thought upon Othello.

November 11. . . . I acted Hamlet—how? Not so well as I rehearsed it, but still I think *well*. I can infuse more effect, and spread more finish over it, if the newspapers will only give me the confidence in the audience necessary to effect so much. A Mr Hiscox followed me out of the theatre and very ludicrously badgered me about his play.

November 12. Have not yet seen the papers, but can scarcely expect them to gainsay their former opinions on my Hamlet. I must endeavour to 'unassuming win my way.' . . . Set off after the play *[The Tempest]* for Elstree through a fog so dense that I thought at Kilburn we must turn back; we ran on the bank, against a gig, a post, and at last to my great comfort arrived safely.

November 18. . . . Settled dresses for Antony, of which nothing was allowed to be new but a cloak.

November 19. On walking through the streets from the Hummum's *[hotel in Covent Garden, with warm and cold baths]* to my chambers, the inhalation of the air was like breathing prickles. . . . I felt very unwell, cold, hoarse, and with a catch in my breath. Went to rehearsal of *Antony*, which was in a very backward state, and mounted with very inappropriate scenery, though beautifully painted by Stanfield. Earle called to see me, said I ought to lay by for several days, and forbade me to play the morrow. I reported his words to Cooper, and left the rehearsal at a quarter before five. Wallace called, and Cooper sent a note from Bunn requiring 'for the satisfaction of the public', Earle's certificate. On Healey's *[Macready's manservant]* return from Savory and Moore's I sent him to H. Earle; he kept me in a state of some anxiety, not returning till nearly ten—with a certificate, ordering me not to play for 'several days', which I instantly sent—'to Mr Bunn's satisfaction.'

[William Wallace (1786–1839), barrister and writer, was one of Macready's oldest friends.]

November 20. . . . Read Antony through the whole evening and discovering many things to improve and bring out the effect of the part, though unable from a pain at my heart, impeding my respiration, to practise it. I found that I had just got an insight into the general effect, but had no power of furnishing a correct picture or of making any strong hits.

November 21. Went to rehearsal, certainly with amended health, but still rather hoarse, not quite free from the pain at the heart, and generally depressed and weak. I remained there until four o'clock, and protested to Messrs Willmott and Cooper against the hurried manner in which I was thrust before the public. . . . I acted—what shall I say? As well as I could under the circumstances; was raw, efforty, and uncertain in the scenes of passion, but had just taken precaution enough to make my pauses, although not to make use of them—it was not a performance to class with what I have lately done. Wallace and Dow came into my room. Wallace congratulated me! *Beaten.*

[John Willmott, one of the Drury Lane stage management (the prompter) later became Macready's stage director. In this performance of 'Antony and Cleopatra' Louisa Phillips was Cleopatra. Stanfield's settings included the Garden of Cleopatra's Palace; Portico attached to the house of Octavius Caesar, with the Capitol in the distance; Antony's camp near the Promontory of Actium, with a view of the fleets of Antony and Caesar. The newspapers, even 'The Times' ('praiseworthy splendour'), were restrained.

[Macready met Dow, a special pleader of the Temple in 1833, and for some years saw him frequently; he died in 1848.]

November 24. Began a letter to Cooper, which I found too long. Read prayers to my family. Wrote a letter to Cooper, tendering through him the resignation of my engagement, and offering a premium for it.

November 27. I was awoke in the morning by letters from Messrs Bunn and Cooper. Mr Cooper's informing me that Mr B—would reply to my proposal, and Mr Bunn taking up a very friendly tone, saying nothing in extenuation of his annoyance to me, but promising that in future my wishes should be consulted, at the same time refusing to relinquish my engagement. All this is mere froth, and the froth of a venomed dog, too; he has been mighty in his promises before, and they have only become means of alluring me to cajolement. Henceforth *I put no trust in him whatever.* On getting up I applied myself to answer him, which I did—not very satisfactorily to myself, but mildly and in a temper rather inclining to smooth asperities.

December 9. . . . I went to the theatre, thinking first of my dress and secondly of King John! I am ashamed, grieved and distressed to acknowledge the truth: I *acted* disgracefully, worse than I have done for years; I shall shrink from looking into a newspaper tomorrow, for I deserve all that can be said in censure of me. I did what I feared I should do, sacrificed my character to my dress!! Wallace and Talfourd came into my room, and I felt what they thought of my performance; it has made me very unhappy.

[Thomas Noon Talfourd (1795–1854), Serjeant-at-Law; later M.P. for Reading, Judge (1849; knighted); literary executor and editor of Lamb's works; dedicatee of Pickwick*; dramatist; he was the amiably vain author of 'Ion', 'The Athenian Captive', 'Glencoe', all of which would be acted by Macready.]*

December 10. . . . I feared to look into the papers, but found them, on going to meet Fladgate[1] by appointment at the Garrick Club, very indulgent indeed. The *Herald* remarked, in objection, upon my dress; so that I suffered as I ought, but not in the degree I merited. . . .

Elstree, December 12. How strange it is that our experience of the pain as well as unprofitableness of passion should not teach us the lesson of subduing it! How many times this morning had I to accuse myself, and reason myself out of my wrath and impatience, as I drove along, because Healey had brought me a *slow coach* instead of a fast cab? If there be one folly more injurious to man than another, it is the senseless fury of anger. Read the heavy part of [Byron's] *Sardanapalus*. Turned the leaves of Byron's *Don Juan*, a wanton display of thought, wit, and brilliancy. Thought of going by a late coach tomorrow, but the recollection of poor Billings's empty vehicle this morning determined me to rise and go by him.

London, December 31. The last day of the year! . . . I sent a note to a Miss Cope, who I fancy must be crazy, poor creature! as she informed me that the fate of Lucretia bore so close a resemblance to her own! Serle called, and I had a very long conference with him. . . . *[Thomas James Serle (1798–1889), dramatist and actor, was one of Macready's counsellors.]* I could not, on reconsideration, be a party to throwing open the drama indiscriminately, so ruinous did it appear to me to the general

---

[1] ' "Papa" [Frank] Fladgate, epitome of social polish and mine of mundane wisdom, was Father of the Club.' (Guy Boas in *The Garrick Club: 1831–1947*.)

interests of the profession. We at last concurred in the expediency of confining the right of acting the classic drama to the four large theatres of Westminster, restricting its performance elsewhere to a great distance, not including therein the Garrick and the Pavilion. *[The Garrick and Pavilion Theatres were in Whitechapel.]*

1834

London, January 1. Forster related to me an anecdote of much interest—that Hazlitt in his emergency had applied to Kean for the loan of £50, which Kean, on the pretence of inability, refused!

January 9. Went to Talfourd's (from whom I had received a note of invitation to supper in the morning) to meet Charles Lamb; met there Price, Forster, Mr and Mrs Field (I fancy a Gibraltar judge), Charles Lamb, Moxon the publisher, and *not* Mrs Moxon, whose absence was noted by those present as a most ungrateful omission of respect and duty, as he (Lamb) had literally brought her up, and wanted her attention and assistance. I noted one odd saying of Lamb's that 'the last breath he drew in he wished might be through a pipe and exhaled in a pun.' Spent a pleasant evening and walked home under a 'pitiless storm' with Price.

[Among those in this entry are Charles Lamb (1775–1834), essayist; and Edward Moxon (1801–1858), publisher, who in 1833 married Lamb's adopted daughter, Emma Isola.]

January 29. Dined at the Garrick Club with Forster, and made an appointment with Fladgate; had much theatrical conversation, and went out with my friend, who indeed reeled after me, to Covent Garden theatre, where the box-keeper, rudely as I think, knowing who I was, refused me admission. We then went to the Olympic *[the Olympic Theatre, Wych Street, managed then by Madame Vestris.]*, but finding no room returned to my chambers, and took tea. Forster . . . told me in confidence of the *affair de cœur* between Ellen Tree and Mr C. Kean, with the proceedings of the family. [He] kept me up until half-past two—sobered himself and bade me good-night at an advanced hour of the morning. *[Ellen Tree (1805–1880), actress, married Edmund Kean's son, Charles (1811–1868), actor, in Dublin during January 1842.]*

February 12. . . . Wrote to Mr Condy, Manchester, and Rev Mr Butler, Nottingham (who sends his hero into a dog-kennel with the exception of one leg, by which the heroine discovers him, imagining that it is all that is left of him, the dog having eaten the rest!), and returned them their plays from the theatre. . . .

February 18. . . . I have reflected much of late on my condition; my mind, that emanation from and best gift of the Divinity, has elevated me to the mere rank of a player, whose merit, as such, is admitted by few, or when admitted in a degree, grudgingly and with indifference by the many. And it is this for which I have lived! to be classed in common repute with things like Mr H..l.y *[John Pritt ('Quicksilver') Harley]* and Mr Farren, or sunk beneath the ungenerous, vulgar nature of Kean! And in the future no prospect, no hope of redemption; my energies must be, ought to be, and I trust will be, bent to improve myself in my profession, in the dear hope of my heart—its dearest—to leave my children at least independent of a world that, with much of individual good, is a mere material for a higher mind to use in compassing the object of its ambition. Perhaps I might have been far happier had my education been level with my situation; let it be a lesson to me in the formation of my dear children's mind.

February 19. . . . Went out, as soon as I could despatch my business within, and called at the theatre for Mr Bunn, then at his house *[in Prince's Place]*; was denied, afterwards admitted into a richly, not tastefully furnished dining-room. Turkey carpet, damask curtains, liqueurs and cake on the sideboard, easy chairs—which my unpaid £200 and gift of £100 would have more than paid for. He acknowledged Dunn's mistake, and said it was rectified. Talked much ridiculous slang about the theatres—'Knowles's Blind B....r of Bethnal Green', and such like ribaldry; pretended that he merely wished to get afloat, and then give the drama its chance. *Yes!!!*

[Macready watched any contract closely. 'Billy' Dunn was Treasurer of Drury Lane. Planché ('Recollections and Reflections') writes of him: 'During the many years he was treasurer I don't suppose he once witnessed a performance; but regularly after the curtain had fallen on a new piece, it mattered not of what description, he would let himself through with his passkey to the front of the house, as if he had sat it out, and on being asked his opinion, invariably answer, after a long pause and a proportionate pinch of snuff, "Wants cutting".']

During March Macready acted in Dublin and Manchester.

Manchester, March 22. When dressed I scarcely knew how I should get through the work before me, and thought of the peculiarity of this profession, which obliges the sickly frame to dilate itself with heroic energy, and the man of sorrows to affect an immoderate buoyancy of spirits, whilst perhaps his heart is breaking. I was most attentive to the necessity of subduing my voice, and letting the passion rather than the lungs awaken the audience. In consequence I acted well. I fail, when I allow my tongue and action to anticipate my thought. I cannot bear this too strongly in mind—Puff [*In Sheridan's* The Critic] I managed with tolerable vivacity and earnestness, and the audience were evidently disposed to be pleased with me. Clarke paid me £91 odd for the week, which made me think most gratefully of the good I receive.

He returned home on 27 March.

Elstree, April 3. Did not rise so early as yesterday, and received in bed letter from Mr Cooper, announcing *Sardanapalus* for Thursday next with Mrs Mardyn for Myrrha, 'who received the part *vivà voce* from the lips of Lord Byron'. The nasty motives which actuate Mr Bunn in thus presenting to the public a woman, who with youth and beauty to arrest attention was never able to retain it, merely because some suspicion may be circulated of her connexion with Lord Byron, only confirm the disgusting character of the man. His ignorance of the drama, his utter disregard of its interests and respectability, his wish to attract a house by any empirical advertisement, however disgraceful, are so undeniable, that one passes by him and his actions, as we would the most offensive nuisance which the negligence of the police has over-looked. . . . After tea read the last three acts of *Sardanapalus*, which would have been safe with Miss Tree, but cannot, I think, pass with this quadragenarian Myrrha.

[Charlotte Mardyn would have then been in her middle forties; she had once been a Drury Lane actress, a woman beautiful and uneducated. Byron was a director of Drury Lane. Foolishly, their names became coupled, probably because he had sent her home in his carriage after she had called to ask him about a part. In rumour and caricature she was held to be the cause of his severance from his wife and his departure from England in 1816. She had vanished completely from the public mind when Bunn resolved to present the Assyrian tragedy of 'Sardanapalus' which Macready had arranged for the stage, though the manager insisted that the version was by his Drury Lane reader, the dramatist Frederick Reynolds.

It was to Reynolds that a letter came from Paris on 25 March 1834, over the signature of Charlotte Mardyn. It said in the floweriest manner that Byron had wished its writer, as the original of 'Ionian Myrrha', to act the part if the play were ever performed. Bunn promptly offered the Baronne de St Dizier (as she called herself) £100 for an eight weeks' season. Gushing letters duly arrived, some from the Baronne's companion, assumed to be the soi-disant Countess of Annesley. They assured Bunn, in effect, that, at a weekly salary of £20 during eight weeks, a gazelle from Paris would be wafted over by the blue Neptune. He agreed, but he began to doubt. William Dimond, notorious as a man, prolific as a hack dramatist, was in Paris, and Bunn wondered whether it might not be some of his 'humbug'.

Very likely it was, for on 9 April a letter informed Bunn that Charlotte Mardyn was too ill to travel—or, roughly, that she lay, overwhelmed by a medley of mortifications, on the bank of the Rubicon under the evil beam of a cross-grained planet. She was Mr Bunn's 'deepest afflicted but most grateful servant'. Inquiries in Paris showed later that no such person as the Baronne de St Dizier was known at the address from which the letters derived.]

April 7. . . . Went to rehearse *Sardanapalus*; was detained a long while by the prompter; went over three acts of it. Bunn told me of Mrs Mardyn's letters, and said that he began to suspect that it was a humbug of Dimond's. I asked him what he would do, if on rehearsal he found her unpresentable. His answer was: 'kick her—and send her back again!' So much for the caterer to English taste. . . .

London, April 9. Went to rehearsal, where I learned that Mrs Mardyn had not arrived, and had sent a letter declaring herself to be 'too ill to undertake the journey, and begging Mr Bunn not to delay the performance of the play any longer on her account'. I was only confirmed in my former belief, that the whole business was a hoax. We began the rehearsal of the play without any Myrrha, Miss E. Tree having declared, in answer to Mr Cooper's message, that she would not act it. Mr Bunn assumed a dictatorial tone, and after outraging her feelings by taking the character from her, now offered a reparation worthy of himself by endeavouring to compel her to act it at this sudden notice: his observation to Mr Cooper was that 'Punch has no feelings'. Shakespeare alludes to the quotation of Scripture by that imaginary being whose fabled blackness would well typify this unprincipled scoundrel, but who is deficient in the filthy and dastardly vices of his substantial likeness. Why may not Mr Bunn then gabble the trash of Johnson? Miss E. Tree at last *came*, induced or seduced by the cant of the high-souled and upright Bartley. She spoke to me, and I recommended her to stay and rehearse the remainder of the play, which she concurred in thinking most advisable. . . .

[Ellen Tree had been playing at the other 'Grand Junction' theatre, Covent Garden, where George Bartley (1782?–1858), comedian, was stage-manager.]

April 10. . . . Read *Sardanapalus* through. Went to the theatre, and rehearsed it. Came to my chambers very much fatigued, and ordered a

Theatre Royal, Drury L[ane]

This Evening MONDAY, April 7, 18[ ]

Their Majesties' Servants will perform Shakspeare's Tragedy of

MACBETH

Duncan, King of Scotland, Mr. YOUNGE,

Malcolin, Mr. WOOD,   Donalbain, Miss LEE,   Lenox, Mr. [ ]

Macbeth, ...   Mr. MACREADY,

Banquo. Mr. G. BENNETT,   Rosse, Mr. DIDDEA[ ]

Macduff,   Mr. COOPER,

Fleance. Miss MARSHALL,   Siward, Mr. THOMP[ ]

Hecate,   Mr. RANSFORD,

1st Witch, Mr. DOWTON, 2nd Witch, Mr. BLANCHARD, 3rd Witch, Mr. B[ ]

Lady Macbeth, ...   Mrs. SLOMAN[ ]

Gentlewoman, Miss SOMERVILLE.

To conclude with **Auber's Grand Opera** of

Masaniello

Masaniello,   *(a Neapolitan Fisherman)*   Mr. BRAHAM

Don Alphonso, Mr. TEMPLETON,   Lorenzo, Mr. [ ]

Pietro, Mr. BEDFORD,   Ruffino, Mr. THOMPSON,

Moreno, Mr. F. COOKE,   Commissioner, Mr. FENTON,   Selva, Mr. HO[ ]

Elvira, (*Bride of Alphonso*) Miss BETTS.   Inis, Mrs. EAST[ ]

Fenella, (*Masaniello's Sister*) Miss KENNETH.

Mr. BRAHAM

Will appear in the Character of **Masaniello** To-Night, and on Friday next, fo[ ]
Time at Covent Garden Theatre, in his celebrated part of **Don Juan.**

To-morrow, **THE MINISTER AND THE MERCER.** And ANSTE[ ]

On Wednesday, **THE MINISTER AND THE MERCER.** And ANSTE[ ]

On Thursday, will be produced with New Scenery, Machinery, Dresses and Decorations,

Lord Byron's Celebrated Tragedy of

SARDANAPALU[S]

Which has been postponed under the following circumstances:—The Noble [ ]
this Play having, in the event of its being acted, intended the part of *Myrr*[ ]

Mrs. MARDYN,

the Lessee has the gratification to inform the Public, that he has entered into a[ ]
ment with this Lady for the performance of that Character, and she will accordi[ ]
the honor of appearing in it on Thursday next, April 10,

ON WHICH EVENING IT WILL BE POSITIVELY PROD[UCED]

mutton-chop there. After dining I lay down on bed for an hour. Very reluctantly I rose to go to the theatre feeling my spirits and strength much exhausted. The play began—and I acted much better than from my over-laboured spirits and strength I could have expected. I was self-possessed, and often very *real*; the audience were quite prepared to applaud whatever could be interpreted as deserving notice, and my spirits rose to meet their indulgence. In the fifth act I cut a small artery in my thumb against Mr Cooper's dress, which bedabbled my whole dress as well as Mr Cooper's and E. Tree's, flowing profusely at times, and then spurting out like a spring of water. Was called for by the audience, but was ignorant that no one had been sent on, or I would not have gone forward; in the erroneous belief that Mr King had been on, whom I heard desired to give out, I led Ellen Tree forward amid much applause. *['To give out': to announce the next representation.]*

Elstree, April 11. Took a chaise to town, for I felt quite unequal to walk to Edgware; on the road went over Sardanapalus. Arriving at my chambers, which I did in very good time, I found a letter without signature, the seal was the head of Byron, and in the envelope was a folded sheet with merely the words: 'Werner, November 1830; Byron, Ravenna, 1821; and Sardanapalus, April 10 1834.' Encircling the name of Byron, etc., was a lock of grey hair fastened by a gold thread, which I am sure was Byron's, and which I have no doubt was sent to me by his sister, Mrs Leigh.[1] It surprised and pleased me. . . .

London, April 16. . . . Lay down for about half an hour, and read part of *Sardanapalus*. I acted—I know not how; I went prepared and anxious to play well, but I cannot work myself into reality in this part—I have not freedom enough to satisfy myself. Miss Tree and self nearly singed in the last scene *[in the final holocaust when the pyre was kindled for the fate of Sardanapalus and Myrrha]* . . .

April 25. Read with much delight, and not without emotion, several poems by Mrs Hemans *[Felicia Dorothea Hemans (1793–1835). Macready wondered at 'the depth of thought and feeling' in her poems.]* . . .

May 3. . . . A puppy came into the green-room, who sat down, and with perfect familiarity entered into conversation with others in the room and myself, though I believe known to none there. The vulgar coxcomb! . . .

May 5. I awoke very early this morning with the heat of the atmosphere, and my own excited system; was kept awake by a sort of horror that possessed me on thinking that 'tapis' was a Latin word, and that I had used it as a French one. It is ludicrous to remember how much I

[1] The Hon. Augusta Leigh, Byron's half-sister.

suffered from this fancy, and how my silly pride attempted to set me at ease. . . .

May 10. . . . Acted Sardanapalus pretty well to a miserable house—two persons in the second gallery at the opening! From the frequent and almost uninterrupted repetition of this play, I feel myself relapsing into my old habitual sin of striving for effect by dint of muscular exertion, and not restraining my body, while my face and voice alone are allowed to act. It is of the utmost importance to be on my guard against this vicious habit. Came home under a beautiful starlight night, which reminded me of the sweet nights I have travelled in Italy—came home in an hour and a half, and found Letitia sitting up for me.

He prepared to play King Lear which had occupied his mind for some time.

May 20. Before rising, thought over the madness of Lear, which now begins to obtain something resembling that possession of my mind which is necessary to success in whatever we desire to reach excellence.

May 21. Mr Brewster came to cut my hair, and to arrange my Lear's coiffure; he also asked me for tickets. . . . Rehearsed *Lear* very unsatisfactorily—several important persons not being there, and I at intervals tormented with a toothache. Went to the theatre, and acted Henry IV very indifferently indeed: the truth is I can give my mind to nothing until the fate of this Lear, which indeed is my fate, be decided.

May 23. Benefit. *King Lear*—first time—and *Lord of the Manor*. Rose in good time, with the impression that the day was one of serious results to me. Sent tickets to the *Literary Gazette*, *Athenæum*, and *Sunday Times*. I justified myself in my experiment in the reflection that otherwise I should leave unbroken ground to an adventurer who might work it to my disadvantage. Rehearsed—I should say—exceedingly well, giving great promise for the night. Miss Kenneth's wish to see the play, and Cooper's confidence in its going well were all the indications of approval I could pick out from the company. Arranged my dresses, and kept a strong check on myself, not permitting anything like an ebullition of discontent or violence. Returned to my chambers, settled all that was necessary for the night, dined, and went to bed at ten minutes past two, giving orders not to be disturbed—I could not sleep for the state of my mind and the heat—I thought over some of the play. Went to the theatre —dressed—became excessively nervous—took wine—went on the stage —as nervous as the first night I acted in London, without the overbearing ardour that could free me from the thraldom of my fears. My performance in the first two acts was so unlike my rehearsal that, although I goaded myself to resistance by suggestions of my own reputation, of my wife and children's claims upon me—still I sunk under the idea that it was a *failure*. In the third act, the audience struck me as being interested and attentive, and in the fourth and fifth they broke out into loud applause; the last scene went tamely, but I was called for by my friends, and went on—was much applauded, and said that 'gratified as I was by their approbation, I hoped when relieved from the nervousness of a first appearance to offer them a representation more worthy their applause'. Dow, Talfourd and his little boy, Bourne and Forster came into my room—they were all much pleased. Cooper came afterwards and told me that the play was to be repeated on Monday at Covent Garden. . . .

[It was a fairly reasonable version of 'King Lear' on this most testing occasion, for though the Fool was still absent, Macready managed to cut most of Tate's alterations, and Shakespeare's last act was played, as in the Kean-and-Elliston revival a decade earlier. When he repeated the part, at Covent Garden a few nights later, he felt that 'I acted really well . . . my audience were under my sway'. He gave another performance at Covent Garden on 2 June; but was much irritated because Bunn withdrew Bartley (Kent) at short notice to take an insignificant part in an opera at Drury Lane. 'Mr Mathews (Mr Mathews!), without time to learn the words and with one rehearsal, was to be the Kent of Covent Garden. And thus are directed the rational amusements of the English public!']

May 24. The worst is known, and varies little from my expectations. The *Times* does 'damn with faint praise', but the *Herald* writes in a tone of gentlemanly liberality, and the *Post* is not less courteous. I could not sleep; at half-past three I was wide awake, and at a quarter-past four I read *Lear* through and then got up to bring the Foreign *Quarterly* into bed. I looked through an article on home colonisation, and then slept till nearly eight. Sent for the newspapers, and read them with extreme anxiety. . . .

June 3. Called to pay bill at Colnaghi's *[The printseller's in Pall Mall.]* saw the engraving of the cast of Napoleon's face—very striking but, scarcely retaining a resemblance to the portraits of him in life; if the nose were more curved, it might pass for a head of Julius Caesar. Colnaghi related a curious fact of the Countess de Grey, who when stone-blind used to take him to a picture which she had bought at a great price as an *original*, and would feel different parts with her hands, pointing out to him its beauties. She would make him put her hand on the different parts of prints which he would bring her, telling her the subject and the parts of it she touched; and on observing once there was a little cat in the corner of one, she immediately exclaimed, 'Oh, I'll have that.' With only the power of imagining what was before her, which on blank paper she would have done as satisfactorily to herself, it is curious that she should be content to pay money for enjoyment beyond her reach.

Elstree, June 24. On this day ten years ago I was married to my beloved Catherine, whose affection, mildness, and sweet disposition have made the greater part of my life since that dear event most truly happy. . . .

June 26. Began my work of preparation for Dublin by marking the first act of the *Bridal*, which I almost fear rushes too abruptly *in medias res*. *['The Bridal' was adapted by Macready and Sheridan Knowles from Beaumont and Fletcher's 'The Maid's Tragedy'.]*

Elstree, July 18. In the afternoon I received a parcel, containing a note from Mr Bunn, wishing me to open the theatre and perform *Manfred*,[1] postponing for that purpose my Dublin engagement. I do not like the thought of this, as I see no chance for the success of *Manfred*—it is, as I observed, not a monodrama, but a monologue; splendid as the poetry is, it is not at all dramatic.

July 19. Received a letter from Knowles, asking me to act Alfred for his benefit on Monday 28th at the Victoria Theatre *[Formerly the Royal Coburg; it has passed into history as the 'Old Vic'.]*. Came downstairs, and answered Mr Bunn's letter, exposing the impracticability of my studying Manfred before my visit to Dublin. After breakfast sat down to answer Knowles; I confess, though it is a great inconvenience and I feel it rather a descent to play at the Victoria, yet I am gratified in receiving this application from him; it is the best rebuke I can give to his avoidance of me, his coldness to me. . . . I answered him in the kindest tone, assenting to his wish, Finished completely the arrangement of the *Maid's Tragedy*, which I think is improved. . . .

July 21. My dear daughter Catherine Frances Birch born.

[Macready's third child and second daughter; she died at sea on a voyage home from Madeira, 24 March 1869.]

July 22. Took an early vegetable dinner, and afterwards read to the end of [Fielding's] *Amelia*; it cannot, of course, be mentioned with *Tom Jones*, and there are passages of prosiness, puerility of expression, and occasional coarseness, but there is humour, wit, pathos, character, and the justest, most philosophic views of our internal polity. . . .

July 28. Knowles's benefit at the Victoria. On my way to the Victoria

[1] Byron's tragedy. It was produced at Drury Lane on 29 October 1834, with an unlucky actor, Henry Gaskell Denvil, as Manfred.

Theatre called at Drury Lane and sent for Palmer about my clothes. . . . Returned (in company with Forster over the bridge) to chambers to dine, and lay out my clothes, which I gave to Palmer, who called just in time to take them. My dressing-room was more inconvenient and ill-appointed than many provincial ones, and when I went on the stage I found the wings literally choked up with people. I was rather inclined to be out of temper with this, but soon recollected myself, and acted as well as I could—much of the character, Virginius, very well—really and with heart. My reception was *most enthusiastic*—certainly the most of any that appeared. At the end I was called for, but declined going on and went to undress. In consequence of the continued clamour, Abbott[1] promised that I should appear at the end of the farce. . . . Went on the stage, or was rather pulled on by Knowles—the applause was tumultuous —I bowed and retired. Knowles made his speech, in some instances ludicrously familiar, but from its earnestness and from the occasion deeply interesting the audience. He pronounced an enthusiastic eulogium on me, and denied the assertion that I had instigated him to write or heighten characters for myself. This was but an act of justice— tardy, perhaps, but still justice, and therefore obliterates offence.

August 10. . . . Self is such an immense object in every man's eye, and such a little dim shadow to his neighbour's, that it is surprising there are not more instances of human vanity on record than there are—but there are enough and we all swell the list.

Between 1 and 15 September he acted at Bristol.

Bristol, September 2. Went to the theatre. Was disposed to do my best, but acted indifferently. I will not say that it was not my own fault, but Mr Mude, a miserable bawler, who exactly answers Hamlet's description of a 'robustious, periwig-pated fellow', distressed me in the outset of the play, sticking out his arm to me like a ramrod, and I could not recover my temper again, which was often tried during the night, particularly by Lucius and Virginia. And here one of those curious things occurred that show how much we are the victims of our own fears. I thought that Mrs D. Lee did not appear well pleased with my indifference to her, and the distance at which I kept her, and in the fourth act her writhings and gaspings made me think she was going to make a display by a *faint* to excite interest; when I came to stab her, I

---

[1] William Abbott (1789–1843), actor. Played Pylades at Macready's Covent Garden début in 1816. He was managing the Victoria (with Daniel Egerton). Sheridan Knowles, the dramatist, was in the company.

took most especial precaution not to let the knife touch her; she fell, and, as I thought, in a mock faint—nay, I even fancied I heard her hysterics from my room and from the stage, and expected she should impute it all to my violence. I expected her husband every moment to come into my room. I went through the remaining scenes with the ideas of paragraphs —pictures of ruin before my mind that were absolute agonies. I dressed, spoke for some time to Mr Mude on business—nothing was said or hinted, but I went home in a state of mental torture, which was only partially subdued by my reason before bed.

September 3. Awoke more tranquil from sleep, and having considered how utterly groundless were my sickly apprehensions; still, I could not quite reassure myself until I had seen the lady, which I resolved to take occasion to do. The vision, for such it almost may be called, that had haunted me had a manifest effect upon my state of body. I was really unwell from it alone. A woman called with a letter, describing herself as the daughter of Edmund Kean's mother, unpaid by her manager, etc. I felt no compassion even if her tale were true, there is something to me so unredeemably disgusting in the life and character of that man that I feel a sort of sickening to all that belonged to or allied itself to him— Messrs Lee, R. Phillips, J. Hughes, and the whole train of parasitical bl—g—ds. Went to rehearsal in a very low state of mind; rehearsed only the scenes where others were concerned particularly with me. Seized the occasion of sending for Mrs D. Lee on the plea of speaking to her about her dress for Myrrha. When I saw her all smiles and curtseys—oh, what a relief! It is difficult to describe the lightened feeling of my heart, the pleasure which the return of complacency afforded me. I spoke very kindly to her on her dress, and also some points of her acting, by which she seemed much obliged. At my lodgings I looked over what I could of Hamlet, and, going to the theatre, acted it really well—the advice to the players particularly so; and, indeed, the whole performance was good. Came home with a body very much fatigued, but with my mind greatly relieved.

After acting at Swansea (16–18 September) he went up to Chesterfield.

Chesterfield, September 22. Laid out my clothes, sent for a play-bill and a history of Chesterfield—not very interesting. Wish to see Hardwick and Chatsworth, if practicable. Read a little of *Hamlet*, which I acted to the dullest, most insensible audience, and among the most brutish I ever yet had to endure. I did my best, but occasionally felt the lethargy of the audience steal over me. My friend Horatio did everything at night contrary to what I had requested in the morning, but I think I never either looked or offered an ill-natured thing. Was tired, and beginning to grow *home-sick*.

The tour proceeded in October, after a few days at home.

Liverpool, October 7. Dr Lardner[1] came into my room and chatted with me for some time; among other things, in speaking of the tour he had made through Scotland and by the lakes, he mentioned his visit to Southey[2] at Keswick, On passing the drawing-room he noticed several ladies apparently in a very cheerful mood; on giving his name, after waiting about five minutes, Southey came to him, the very image of distraction, took his hand, and led him into his study. For a long time he remained silent—at length told him he believed he must dismiss him; in fine, he disclosed to him that within the last five minutes, since he rang the bell at the lawn gate, Mrs Southey had, without previous indication or symptom, gone raving mad, and to that hopeless degree that within an hour he must take her to an asylum. These are the cruel liabilities of our nature, which no human power can cure, but which only resignation and the hope that religion offers can alleviate and soothe.

Liverpool, October 14. . . . Made some small presents to the servants of the theatre, and after an effort (oh, *mauvaise honte!*) bade the gentlemen of the green-room good-night.

From 20 October until 17 November he acted in Dublin, where he had arrived on 16 October. [His first performance, on 20 October, was Macbeth in which he failed to satisfy himself. In the morning he had had an unfortunate rehearsal: 'There was great confusion and much delay . . . Mr Collins, the prompter, an unfortunate victim of dissipation, was unable to attend, being in a state of raging madness in a straight waistcoat.'] *On 25 October he appeared as Melantius in 'The Bridal', his arrangement of 'The Maid's Tragedy'.*

Dublin, October 25. . . . Laid out my clothes and went to the theatre. Low and distressed; forgot the beginning of my first speech to Amintor; acted as I used to act three or four years ago, not like myself now. Could not do what I proposed at rehearsal. The scene with Amintor and Evadne

---

[1] Dr Dionysius Lardner (1793–1859), notable scientific writer; Professor of Natural Philosophy and Astronomy at London University. Eloped with the wife of a Brighton magistrate. Went to America, and finally settled and died in Paris.
[2] Robert Southey (1774–1843), Poet Laureate.

went very well, that between Amintor and myself very well, also that with Evadne; the scene with the King and the last with Evadne fairly; Evadne's murder scene very fairly, but no enthusiasm throughout; the poor little girl, Miss Allison,[1] was quite a *dépaysagement*. The audience called for me and I was obliged to go on. What I had 'I said better have kept to myself.' I talked of the pleasure I had in announcing, with their permission, the work of those bright names which illuminated the brilliant atmosphere of our poetical region (qn.: what does this mean?) 'those twin stars', etc., touched by the hand of our highly-gifted countryman, Knowles, etc. I hesitated so much as to be quite unhappy.

October 29. . . . Walked out to the Military Hospital; the day was beautiful, and the view up the river of the gate at the bridge, the obelisk and park very striking. Met Colonel and Miss D'Aguilar at the gate of the Hospital, Bulwer came up, to whom he introduced me; he invited me to dine on Friday. . . . *[Colonel George D'Aguilar, 1784–1855, was deputy adjutant-general at Dublin, 1830–1841; he was knighted in 1852.]*

October 31. . . . Met, at Colonel D'Aguilar's, Bulwer, whom I liked very much . . . I urged him to write a play; he told me he had written one, great part of which was lost, on the death of Cromwell.

November 4. Again! and again! I shall really sink into indolence and sensuality altogether if I do not make some permanent reform in my habits. I rose at a shamefully late hour this morning. . . .

November 10. Went to the theatre, where, on dressing, I was seized with a violent bowel complaint; obliged to send for brandy, which affected my head. I played, as might be expected, very unequally, a want to finish from a want of collectedness; but in the last scene of *Macbeth* I was very good, grand in my death—I felt it. My soul would have lived on from very force of will; death could not have been felt by a man so resolute to resist it.

His last Dublin night was on the 17th. Macready had been particularly irascible during this engagement and noted on 15 November that he felt ashamed of 'my morose and petulant behaviour to everybody'. Even so, on 6 November, Miss Allison had amused him by 'her innocent and playful conversation, ending with a request for a lock of my hair'.

On 20 November he began an engagement at Lincoln, from which he proceeded to Boston and Louth.

[1] Laura Allison (1820–1879); actress; later Mrs Seymour and manageress of the St James's, London. Macready saw her Juliet on 21 October, 'a very deplorable exhibition.'

November 27. Arrived at Louth, which seems a miserable little place. After dinner (too good a one!) lounged away some time over old magazines—accounts of young Betty's first appearance—much violent abuse of Napoleon as the 'Corsican assassin', and of Josephine as the most notorious strumpet. Things have mended, judging both from the prose and poetry, which is horrid stuff.

[William Henry West Betty (1791–1874), known as 'the Young Roscius', was transiently astonishing as a boy actor (in Hamlet and other major parts). Finally retired from the stage in 1824.]

Louth, November 29. Walked with Mr Robertson[1] to the post office and to the theatre, which answers also the double purpose of a Sessions House; it is not the worst I have seen. Went to the theatre—dressed in magistrates' room—'quite convenient'. When ready to go on the stage, Mr Robertson appeared with a face full of dismay; he began to apologise, and I guessed the remainder. 'Bad house?' 'Bad? Sir, there's no one!' 'What? nobody at all?' 'Not a soul, sir—except the Warden's party in the boxes.' 'What the d—l! not one person in the pit or gallery?' 'Oh yes, there are one or two.' 'Are there five?' 'Oh, yes, five.' 'Then go on; we have no right to give ourselves airs, if the public do not choose to come and see us; go on at once!' Mr Robertson was astonished at what he thought my philosophy, being accustomed, as he said, to be 'blown up' by his *Stars*, when the houses were bad. I never acted Virginius better in all my life—good taste and earnestness. Smyth, who was contemporary with me at Rugby and has a living in this neighbourhood, came in and sat with me, and saw the play, with which he was greatly pleased.

[In an article in 'The Theatre' (February 1884) Godfrey Turner spoke of Macready's famous death scene in 'Virginius' when he 'died almost standing, with his arms round the neck of Icilius and his back to the audience. But you saw, somehow, it was death. Old actors were touched to tears.']

November 30. Read the newspaper, in which my abhorrence of that wretch Cobbett[2] and his beastly faction was kindled anew. Note came from Mrs Robertson, inviting me to tea, which I accepted. Went there, and was much amused by Mr W. Robertson's account of the extremities of ludicrous distress—though sometimes it was no laughing matter—to

---

[1] William Robertson, manager of the Lincoln circuit; father of a large family, of whom T. W. Robertson, the dramatist, was the eldest, and Margaret Shafto Robertson (Madge Kendal), the youngest.
[2] William Cobbett (1762–1835), essayist and political writer.

which he was reduced in his vagabondizing tours of Scotland and Cumberland.

December 1. Walked out with Mr Robertson; posted my letters, and then walked two miles on the Horncastle road. He related to me two anecdotes of Kean, to which he was witness: once of his having, on coming off the stage in Othello, thrashed a man of the name of Williams, whom I remember well, for distressing him by being imperfect in Iago! and another—a pure specimen of his charlatanry. A vagabond who lived upon petitioning companies and drank their charity, applied for the third or fourth time while Kean was with Mr Robertson. Mr Robertson represented to Kean that he was a worthless, drunken man, and lived upon this practice. Mr K—(there were several present) said: 'You dined very well, yesterday, sir, and you will have a good dinner today; why should you wish to prevent this poor man from doing the same?' And this Kean left his wife without one shilling for herself and son: the woman that lived with him having taken the comparatively small residue left of his disgusting and reckless dissoluteness!! Enjoyed my walk very much; wrote directions for my luggage. Dozed from fatigue after dinner; wrote a letter to Kenneth, made my toilet, and went to theatre. Felt that the house was not very good; but determined to make a study of the night, which I did, and certainly acted great part of Hamlet in a very true and impressive manner. I hit upon the exact feeling in the passage which I have often thought on: 'He was a man', etc.; my intercourse with Horatio, Rosencrantz, Guildenstern, etc., was earnest and real—*ad homines*. Indeed, it was a good performance. Smyth came into my room after the play, and talked of my speaking the closet scene at Rugby. He also told me of endeavouring to commit a poacher. He is a clergyman! . .

Sheffield, December 10. Went to the theatre, where I acted William Tell only tolerably; was a good deal distressed by the actors, imperfect and inattentive, and once or twice rather angry with them, but very kind to the poor child who acted with me, though several times disconcerted by her, but this is from having children of my own, the dear ones. My dresser is a Benedictine monk on leave from the convent in Ireland on account of derangement; his trade is a tailor.

December 11. Went to theatre, where I acted very ill, but should not have been so bad but for the shamefully neglectful and imperfect state of the play. Idenstein, Josephine, and Guba were all more or less imperfect; Ulric did not know two consecutive lines of the last three acts. I sat down at last attempting nothing. I never was so completely *terrassé* in my life. But I was rude and uncivil to no one.

Nottingham, December 12. Went to theatre, and found a horrid fellow

in the part of Gessler, whom I had met at Richmond—it was enough!
Rehearsed, dressed, and acted William Tell to a very good house in a
creditable manner; but was very cross with the little dull boy whom they
had placed in Albert, and fined myself half-a-crown, which I paid him
for my ill-behaviour.

*He was at Elstree for Christmas, and on 31 December left for Bath. His
companions in the coach were* 'very great asses, talking much nonsense
about politics, and vehement Tories'.

1835

Bath, January 8. Acted Othello with a feeling of having no sympathy from my audience; thought myself deficient in earnestness and spirit, but do not regret having done it, as it was a useful rehearsal for me. I never saw the Senate put so well upon the stage. I think I may play Othello well, but the prescriptive criticism of this country, in looking for particular points instead of contemplating one entire character, abates my confidence in myself. Mr Woulds told me that he had heard from Mr Field of general discontent at the prices being restored. The house tonight was wretched, but what could be expected at such a time?

[James Woulds ('Old Jemmy Woulds' or 'miserable Jemmy'), an endeared provincial comedian who was a disappointed tragic lead. Macready was in partnership with him at the theatres of Bath and Bristol, with a company that included (besides Macready himself) Mrs Lovell and Dowton. Bath responded less well than Bristol, and there was a bad loss on the venture.]

January 9. My lady brought me up her bill, and began some inquiries about my stay—the number of my family and some etcs. which showed a disposition to impose; she added that Mr Woulds had not mentioned my *profession*. My blood rose at this impertinence, and I was foolish enough to be so angry as to observe that there was no person in Bath, whether titled or not, that could claim a higher character and that I would relieve her of the inconvenience of such an inmate. She attempted to excuse herself, but I cut the matter short. Heard from Mr Woulds the account of the first week's balance, which was very satisfactory. Read the newspaper, and to my astonishment and satisfaction saw Talfourd member for Reading.

January 10. Expedited the rehearsal as much as possible, but it proceeded slowly owing to the inattention of the actors. What a calling is this! How deeply I feel the degradation of belonging to it, which yet for my dear children's sake I will endeavour cheerfully to pursue. . . .

January 17. In going through the box-office heard a woman inquiring for something entertaining for children. Brownell mentioned that Mr Macready and Dowton would play on Monday. 'Oh, no' she replied, 'they are very good actors, but I want something entertaining for children; when will *Aladdin* be done?' So much for Bath taste! Acted King Lear unequally—wanted the sustaining stimulant of an enthusiastic audience—wanted in them the sensibility to feel quickly what I did, and the ready manifestation of their sympathy; some parts I did tolerably well; acted with some degree of vivacity and nature in Puff.

In mid-February he was in the North, at Manchester, with one night at Halifax.

Halifax, February 18. Went to Rehearsal. Poor Guildenstern had only one eye. From rehearsal one of the actors, Mr Nantz,[1] went with me to show me the Gibbet Hill, where the stone on which the criminals laid their heads is still visible though deeply embedded in earth; from thence he accompanied me to a public-house, formerly the gaol, and now called the Jail Inn, where the blade of the axe, called the Maiden, was shown to me; it is very like the blade of a spade with two holes in it. Not so weighty as I should suppose its office would require. Some of the actors, the principal with his family, lived in the public-house, seemingly domesticated, and mixing in all the business of the place! Such a residence would have suited in every way Mr Kean, and no doubt he often took up his abode contentedly in worse—and I am abused, libelled, and an object of persecution because I do not make companions of actors! Oh, world, what a scene of quackery thou art!

From Manchester he returned to Bath and Bristol.

Bristol, March 3. My birthday . . . I do not recollect a more unhappy anniversary of my birth than this—my forty-second. Went to rehearsal —or rather to my morning's annoyance—striving and wishing to master my fretful, impatient temper, but in vain. Letter from dear Catherine, giving me the news of the house and acquainting me with my being *blackballed* at the Athenaeum. I do not wish to disguise truth; it was a bitter annoyance to me. I had objected to undergoing the trial of the ballot, knowing the dirty tricks practised at this and other clubs, and only consented to the insertion of my name upon the assurance that it was decided on I should be admitted this year. The advantages of the club are not equivalent to the subjection to any blackguard's caprice. I use a strong term, but Mr Croker *[John Wilson Croker (1780–1857), writer and politician]* having been my excluder, justifies it. It shall not occur again. . . . *[Macready was ultimately elected to the Athenaeum in June 1838.]*

[1] Frederic Coleman Nantz wrote a domestic drama called *Dennis; or, The Gibbet Law of Halifax.*

March 6. . . . Went to theatre and should have acted Oakly well, but that in the only scene in which the performers were not *very imperfect* with me, the prompter in every pause I made in a scene where the pauses are *effects*, kept shouting 'the word' to me till I was ready to go and knock him down. I was cut up right and left, root and branch, and—as usual —I grieve and shame to say it—was very angry.

He returned home for a short time before leaving again for Salisbury.

London, March 15. Forster told me of Talfourd having completed a tragedy called *Ion*. What an extraordinary, what an indefatigable man!

Salisbury, March 16. Reached Salisbury at five o'clock, where I went to bed at the Black Horse and was called at ten; rose, breakfasted and went to my lodgings; after some search found the theatre, and went through the rehearsal. My Lady Macbeth was a relic of a style gone by, the veritable 'ti-tum-to' 'jerk and duck and twist' in a most engaging manner. Tried to act Macbeth, but, 'confusion to my Lady!' it was too farcical; she would have been good as Dollalolla [*in Fielding's 'Tom Thumb'*], but quite a travesty in the part she played. Nearly betrayed on one occasion my anger at one of the performers, but was very thankful that I subdued it before an opportunity for explosion was given; most happily I did not expose myself. The end of the play found me very much exhausted. . . .

He acted at Bath, Exeter, and Norwich, with intervals at home.

Elstree, May 7. Read Talfourd's tragedy of *Ion*; pleased with the opening scenes and, as I proceeded, arrested and held by the interest of the story and the characters, as well as by the very beautiful thoughts, and the very noble ones, with which the play is interspersed. . . . After dinner I watered some of the plants in the garden and enjoyed the freshness of the air, the verdure and the flowers, and the lightly clouded sky that was soon naked and bare, one placid depth for the moon's brightness to sail through. It was enjoyment.

He went to Bath, and on to Worcester.

Worcester, May 13. Arrived about five; and, after looking at my rooms, proceeded to the theatre; could not gain admission, and had to wait about a quarter of an hour in a public-house for the arrival of the housekeeper. Unpacked and dressed; though the rain poured down the house was very good, and I acted Virginius very well, and without any anger at all. It was very decently done; only Dentatus had put a surplice over his street clothes and put part of a sheep's fleece on his chin for a beard. Mr Bennett paid me, and I came to the Star, where I read the paper. *[J. Bennett was manager of the Worcester theatre.]*

London, May 21. Called at Forster's chambers to arrange with him a visit to Mr Maclise. Accompanied Forster to Mr Maclise's lodgings— found him a young, prepossessing, intelligent man, anxious to paint my picture. . . . Agreed to sit to him. *[Daniel Maclise (?1806–1870), painter; R.A., 1840.]*

Elstree, June 5. Continued my perusal of *The Provost of Bruges*, and deliberated much upon it when I finished it. The language is not up to that high pitch of imagination, sentiment, or passion which ever seems to approach the sublime, but it is seldom low, generally natural, often-times forcible, and not unfrequently tender and pathetic. I am inclined to attribute its chief merit to its situation, which still is a great merit.

['The Provost of Bruges' by George William Lovell, 1804–1878, dramatist, secretary of the Phoenix Life Assurance Company and husband of the actress Mrs Lovell, is a tragedy about a twelfth-century merchant prince, Bertulphe who discovers that he was born a serf. Macready refers later to its first rehearsal on 2 November 1835 and to its production on 10 February 1836.]

London, June 19. Saw Malibran in *Fidelio*; the dullness of the opera was really wearisome; it was, with the exception of this gifted creature's performance, miserably done; and even she was not in her own element —the part seemed a weight upon her that she energetically but vainly struggled with. The scena at the end of the second act was superior to Schröder-Devrient's, but in all besides she was inferior—straining at effect, melodramatic, elaborate, but not abandoned; her resolution was strong, but her identity never seemed for a moment lost. Her costume was admirable—will our actors never learn?—*Never*. I went into her room after the opera—there were several persons, Mr Cooper among them. She saluted me most affectionately, and, perhaps, to her I was what she was to me—a memorial of years of careless, joyous hope and excitement; she said I was not altered; I could not say what I did not think of her. I could have loved—once almost did love her, and I believe she was not indifferent to me. It often occurs to me on such recollections: how would my destiny have been altered! I should have possibly been an *ambitieux*—should I have been happier?—should I have had my Nina, my Willie, and little Catherine? Left Malibran with a very great depression of spirits.

July 15. . . . I drove to the Garrick Club. On entering, Talfourd and Price uttered joyous exclamations, and I shook them both cordially by the hand; a person with his back to the room at their table, turning round displayed the face of Mr C. Kemble,[1] and to my great surprise, said, *'Come!'* and took hold of my hand, which I instantly withdrew; he said, 'What, you won't shake hands with me?'—which I believe he repeated. He was drunk, or nearly so. I am not quite clear how I should have behaved. I do not mean as to whether I should have accepted his offer of reconciliation—for really to do that would be tantamount to making alliance with fraud, treachery, falsehood, the meanest and most malignant species of intrigue: in fact, with vileness and profligacy of the most barefaced character—but whether I should have resented the liberty he took. I felt no anger; but really it was a gross impertinence. Talked with Talfourd, who was tipsy. . . .

Elstree, July 18. I wish I were anything rather than an actor—except a critic; let me be unhappy rather than vile! If I meant by this that men who *usually criticise* are vile I should convict myself of equal folly and injustice. It is the assumption of the high duties of criticism (demanding genius and enthusiasm tempered by the most exact judgment and refined taste) by mere dealers in words, with no pretensions to integrity of purpose or the advancement of literature, that disgusts and depresses me. The sight of the *Quarterly Review*—the arena of Croker, Lockhart, Harness, Hall, etc.—which H. Smith has sent me, induced a train of thought upon the (so-called) criticism of the country. Generally speaking, it takes its tone from faction. The most profound ignorance is no obstruction to the most dogmatic assertions—these are made, of course, on points that few persons are interested in contradicting, or in seeing contradicted, therefore they remain as texts for the declaimers from the particular *Review* to preach from. It is really my opinion that in the classification of minds such a one as Lockhart's—hireling, defamer, corrupt (not by direct means of pecuniary bribe, but by party and power), malignant trader in sentences pointed to stab, and draw by slow droppings the life-blood of a man's heart—is of the base the basest.

[Among names in this entry are: John Gibson Lockhart (1794–1854), editor of the 'Quarterly Review', 1824–1853, and son-in-law of Sir Walter Scott, whose 'Life' he wrote; the Rev. William Harness (1790–1869), friend of Byron, and Shakespearean editor; Samuel Carter Hall (1800–1869),

[1] Charles Kemble (1775–1854), John Philip Kemble's youngest brother; actor and sometime manager of Covent Garden; Fanny Kemble's father.

writer chiefly on art, husband of the novelist Anna Maria Hall (1800–1881), and identified with Dickens's Pecksniff.]

Between 8 and 19 August Macready was in Dublin.

Dublin, August 8. Went to theatre and acted Werner with considerable care, and I think with much earnestness and sometimes with reality; occasionally I sank into my old muscular efforts, and was cut out of the most striking opportunities for effect in the play by that very imperfect actor, Mr Pritchard. I was very angry, but did not allow my displeasure to interfere with the performance.

Elstree, September 8. Had just sat down to dinner when a loud knock came, and, in vain denying ourselves, we heard Talfourd and Forster give their names. We asked them to dine as we were dining; and adding a little to our table, we soon replaced ourselves, though with the loss of dear Nina and Willie, and dined. In the evening we discussed the whole, and read the greater part, of *Ion*. Talfourd was amusing in resisting several of the proposed cuttings as the best in the play, and that it would be better not to act the play, but he took it all in good part. His account of Wordsworth's silence about his play *disgusted* me. They left me a little after ten.

September 9. Practised part of Othello, to which I do not find I yet give that real pathos and terrible fury which belongs to the character. Read over attentively the whole of Melantius *[in The Bridal]*. I do not much fancy it.

He prepared for the new Drury Lane season. His agreement with Bunn gave him a salary of thirty pounds a week of four nights over a period of thirty weeks and a half, with no fines and a veto on any part Macready might consider melodramatic. Bunn agreed to stage immediately after Christmas the tragedy of 'The Bridal' on the usual terms of £33–6s–8d per night to the ninth night and £100 for the twentieth'. And there was this clause: 'That W. C. Macready shall not be required or asked to act the characters of Sir Giles Overreach, Joseph Surface, or Rob Roy, and that he is to have a dressing-room to himself, secure from removal or intrusion.' Though Bunn loathed Macready, he was eager to have him back. The 'Grand Junction' had been uncoupled; Bunn, left on his own (Covent Garden having refused his suggestion of a lower rent), had only the Lane to play with.

Elstree, September 9. I returned to Macbeth. It is strange that I do not feel myself at all *satisfied* with myself; *I cannot reach in execution the standard of my own conception.* I cannot do it; and I am about to enter on the season which will decide my fortune, with the drawback of the consciousness of not being able to realise my own imaginations.

London, October 1. Went to the theatre, played ill *[Macbeth]*, I must presume, because ineffectively; and yet I never tried so much to play well, and never, never was it of so much importance to me to play well. The audience called for me—a kindness on their part—and I went on, but when Talfourd, Forster, and Wallace came to my room, not one had a word of comfort or congratulation. What have I omitted to make this evening successful? I do not know, but the bitterness of my feelings is such, with the anticipation of the newspapers tomorrow, that if I had not ties which bind me to this profession (and I could curse the hour that it was suggested to me) I would eat a crust, or eat nothing, rather than belong to it. I scarcely recollect when my feelings have been so wrought up to a state of agonising bitterness as tonight; I feel almost desperate.

October 2. . . . Arose very little better; my bath composed my spirits a little, and the *Times* newspaper, which, though not highly laudatory, was not written in an unkind spirit, gave me back some portion of my wonted tranquillity. The other papers were very cold; I sent them with a letter to my dear Catherine.

October 5. . . . In acting Macbeth felt that I carried my audience along with me. I was earnest, majestic, and impassioned. The applause was enthusiastic, and I was obliged to go on at the close of the play. I redeemed myself, and most grateful do I feel in saying 'Thank God'. Talfourd came into my room and said he had 'never seen me finer, if indeed I had ever played it so well'. Wallace asked 'Why the d—l didn't I play it so on Thursday?'

October 12. . . . Went to the theatre, and acted Macbeth before Her Majesty [Queen Adelaide] and a full house. The audience did not come solely and purposely to see *Macbeth*, and the labour to keep their attention fixed was extreme. Wallace came round and said I acted very well; I tried to do so, but am not confident of my success. Talfourd and Forster came to my room. Bunn told me he must do *Othello* on Thursday. I said '*I* could not'. He 'must'. I 'would not'. He sent me up a note to know which I would do, Othello or Iago, on Thursday. I returned for answer, Iago, and would not do Othello at all. He then sent Cooper to me, to whom I said the same, and in answer to his inquiry said, 'I would not do Othello under a week's notice'. He left me without fixing anything. I was very much fatigued. Talfourd suggested the propriety of ascertaining the intentions of the management, and I waited for Cooper;

while speaking to him Bunn came up, and wished me to go into the room and talk it over. He was as civil as a dog, the dragooning attempt had failed; and after some conversation *Othello* was fixed for Wednesday week, and *The Provoked Husband [a comedy by Vanbrugh, completed by Cibber]* for Thursday next.

October 13. Opened newspapers; the *Post* was the only one that had a lengthened criticism, and stated that my performance of Macbeth had 'created quite a sensation'.

October 14. Went to the Garrick Club; met Forster there and Meadows; saw Mr C. Kean who made a very formal bow to me. This young man appears very conceited, and surely not amiable in any part of his conduct that has come under my cognizance. He owes me civility. . . . *[Drinkwater Meadows (1799–1869), comedian, was later Secretary to the Covent Garden Theatrical Fund.]*

October 15. . . . Acted Lord Townley *[i.e. Lord Townly in 'The Provoked Husband']* in a very mediocre manner, occasionally with spirit, but with an utter absence of finish and high deportment.

October 16. Note from Forster, enclosing the *Morning Herald's* criticism on my Lord Townley, which *very justly* objected to my want of ease and formality. I cannot contradict or question the fairness of the remark. . . . Went to theatre and acted Hamlet, not as I did the last time—I felt then the inspiration of the part; tonight I felt as if I had a load upon my shoulders. The actors said I played well. The audience called for me and made me go forward. Wallace, Forster, and H. Smith who came into my room, all thought I played well—but I did not. I was not satisfied with myself—there was effort, and very little free flow of passion. I *fear* the papers may notice me tomorrow. Mr Bunn came into my room, and spoke to me about *Othello* for Wednesday. I refused; he wished to see me in his room, and there I was witness to a great deal of gross and blackguard conversation; was very quiet, and left without any settlement.

October 17. . . . In the club saw Planché,[1] who related to me the circumstance of a very beautiful girl being enwrapt and violently agitated with the play last night, so as to attract observation. It is pleasing to hear this. Saw Knowles, wild as the wind.

October 21. Went to the theatre, and felt very nervous and unsettled; reasoned with myself, and partially recovered my self-possession; but, in truth, was hurried out in the part of Othello, and was not perfectly

---

[1] James Robinson Planché (1796–1880), dramatist; student of heraldry (he became Somerset Herald). In the theatre he was known particularly for his extravaganzas which clearly influenced W. S. Gilbert.

possessed of it. The criticism I passed on Malibran's Fidelio will exactly suit my own Othello—it was 'elaborate, but not abandoned.' In the early scenes I was abroad, making effort, but not feeling my audience; in the jealous scenes I had attention, and certainly had no reason to be discontented by the degree of intelligence, skill, or effort shown by Iago; but the audience seemed to wait for Kean's points, and this rather threw me off my balance. In the soliloquy after Iago's exit I in some degree asserted myself, and though not up to my own expectations in the 'Farewell', etc., yet in the grand burst I carried the house with me. From that point I should say the performance averaged good, but was not in any, except that one outbreak, great. *The newspapers will, of course, annoy me. They will!* Dow and Forster came into my room— rather satisfied; Wallace, on whom I can better depend, not so much so. *He is my barometer.* I was obliged to go on before the audience, which, as Mr Vandenhoff was also called for, I had rather not have done.

[Forster, certainly was satisfied. In the 'Examiner' he would talk about the 'most astonishing elevation of anguished passion into a fixed and sublime despair that [playgoers] have ever been permitted to see.' On the first night a woman in the pit fainted hysterically at Macready's 'ghastly and tremendous appearance' [Forster] after Desdemona's murder, when he started with extended arms through the curtain drawn in front of the bed.

John M. Vandenhoff (1790–1861), was much approved as a provincial tragedian; father of the actor, George Vandenhoff.]

October 22. After a restless night (which indisposition of body as well as an uncomfortable state of mind tended to make long and unrefreshing) I rose with very uneasy anticipations of the newspapers' report of my Othello. I came at last to the resolution not to see them . . . Forster sent me the notice of the *Times* which, for the *Times*, was highly favourable. It set my mind at peace instantly—as much from the value it set on Mr Vandenhoff's performance, as for the praise it gave to mine. This man has intrigued and caballed much with country newspapers, and through his instrumentality I have been systematically abused at Liverpool, Edinburgh, etc. He has puffed himself and stuffed some few of his listeners with the notion that I had usurped his place. He had the opportunity of showing his talent last night; he did show it—a poorer, more unmeaning, slouching, ungainly, mindless, unimaginative performance I have never witnessed in any person making pretensions to high rank. He is a man of a very poor, very little, and very vulgar mind. Called on Forster, saw the *Post*, badly written, but highly encomiastic.

Truly grateful am I for the impression which my performance seems to have made. . . .

October 23. Felt so unwell *[he had a very bad cold]* that I could not come to any resolution as to acting or being excused; tried to nurse myself, and hoped each hour would find me better, but no; at twelve I sent for Forster, who thought I ought not to risk Othello if I did not feel equal to it. This decided me, and I wished to write a note, but he seemed anxious to bear the communication, and I did not refuse him. He returned at two, to say that Bunn was a most atrocious beast, and that he had behaved most cavalierly to him. This he might have expected on such a message, if he had known the man; but Cooper was to call presently. Cooper did call, and after much conversation they both agreed that it would be better I should make the effort at all risks, as Bunn might seek to do me some mischief. Cooper offered to make an apology for me, which I declined—I did not fully coincide with their reasonings but felt myself so much better that I yielded. . . . Went to theatre and had a short conversation on very good terms with Bunn. Acted Othello. I am puzzled to say how, for both Dow and Forster, who came into my room afterwards, seemed to think me not so good as on Wednesday night, and in many particulars I thought myself better. The reception which the audience gave me was very marked tonight, and in the presence of Mr Vandenhoff must and did show him that they considered we stood at a wide distance. He was visibly agitated with—must I not say from this man's previous low and illiberal behaviour?—envy. . . .

October 28. . . . I think succeeded in performing the whole character better—more grandly, deeply, and nobly—than I have yet done.

[In 'Theatre' (February 1884) Godfrey Turner recalled Macready's death scene in 'Othello': 'After the speech which ends with the self-inflicted stab, corresponding with the words "And smote him—thus," Othello, as if to save himself from falling, clutched Montano's shoulder, and then, turning towards the bed, which was in the middle of the scene at the back of the stage, endeavoured to reach it, staggering from one piece of furniture to another. Just as it seemed that Macready had approached near enough to fling himself on the body of Desdemona, "to die upon a kiss," he sank rather than fell backwards with his head towards the audience. The failing support of the limbs and the uncontrolled sway of the body were wonderfully death-like.']

Elstree, October 29. Lay very late, thinking over the play of last night (*Othello*) and revolving in my mind the slow and comparatively unprofitable advance of my reputation; the danger it runs from the appearance of every new aspirant, and the reluctant admissions that are made to it. Walked in the garden, and inhaled, with grateful and tranquil pleasure, the pure air of the country.

London, October 31. Went to Garrick Club, where I saw the papers, and the new magazines, in which there was nothing to interest me; several of the performers were there and I learned that the success of the new Opera had been very great, and that *Othello* was removed from the play-bills. It is as impolitic to take it down from that night, being put up, as it was to announce it: but this fellow Bunn was, is, and will be a beast to the last days of his disgusting existence.

November 2. Went to town, was just in time for the rehearsal of the *Provost of Bruges*, to which I went. My hopes were not raised by the nearer glimpse of it which this first rehearsal gave me. . . .

Owing to the Drury Lane triumph of Balfe's opera, 'The Siege of Rochelle', and of Planché's version of Scribe's three-act melodramatic spectacle, 'The Jewess (La Juive)'—Bunn packed them into a double bill—there was now no chance for Macready to act. He had refused the part of Eleazar in 'The Jewess', which Vandenhoff played, and from 28 October until 3 February, though his salary was paid, he remained idle, chafing.

November 21. Rising, I felt the peculiarity of my situation as regards my profession—quite interdicted from its exercise during the greater part, if not the entire, of the season, and all the hopes of profit from new characters, upon the strength of which I made this engagement, utterly falsified. . . .

November 26. Read a review, and some beautiful and touching extracts from a dramatic poem called 'Paracelsus', by Robert Browning.[1]

November 27. Went from chambers to dine with Rev. William Fox,[2] Bayswater. . . . I like Mr Fox very much; he is an original and profound thinker, and most eloquent and ingenious in supporting the penetrating views he takes. Mr Robert Browning, the author of *Paracelsus*, came in after dinner; I was very much pleased to meet him. His face is full of intelligence. My time passed most agreeably. Mr Fox's defence of the suggestion that Lady Macbeth should be a woman of delicate and fragile frame pleased me very much, though he opposed me, and of course triumphantly. I took Mr Browning on, and requested to be allowed to improve my acquaintance with him. He expressed himself warmly, as gratified by the proposal; wished to send me his book; we exchanged cards, and parted.

[1] Robert Browning (1812–1889), poet and dramatist, was then twenty-three.
[2] The Rev. William Johnson Fox (1786–1864), preacher, drama critic of the *Morning Chronicle*, and politician.

December 16. Went to Mr Buller's[1]—passed an unpleasant day—did not feel myself at home; my spirits were sunk still more by the accident of the coach-window falling out, and my expectation of a summons every moment from the coachman to dispute with me the payment of it. . . .

Elstree, December 31. Frederick Reynolds arrived a little after four o'clock. . . . Our other guests were Miss Kenney, Forster, Cattermole,[2] Browning, and Mr Munro. Mr Browning was very popular with the whole party; his simple and enthusiastic manner engaged attention and won opinions from all present; he looks and speaks more like a youthful poet than any man I ever saw. . . .

[1] Father of Charles Buller (1806–1848), M.P. for the Cornish borough of Liskeard, who would be a valued friend of Macready.
[2] George Cattermole (1800–1868), painter. Co-illustrator of *The Old Curiosity Shop* and *Barnaby Rudge.*

1836

Elstree, January 1. Our visitors, except Frederick Reynolds, left us. I wished to detain Mr Browning, but had no opportunity. . . .

London, January 11. . . . Went with Dow to Covent Garden, saw Miss H. Faucit in the *Hunchback*, thought she had force and some intelligence, but no elegance, little real abandonment, and little true pathos—occasionally violent, flurried, *larmoyante*, and almost always stagey. Kemble looked like an old and faithful footman—his shoulders bending under long service, nor did his gestures, attitudes, or intonations betray the slightest variance with his air and aspect.

[Covent Garden was then under the management of D. W. Osbaldiston. Helen Faucit, aged eighteen, had made her début on 5 January as Julia in a revival of Sheridan Knowles's 'The Hunchback', with Charles Kemble as Sir Thomas Clifford. She had expected to play Juliet, but no Romeo young enough could be found. Though intensely nervous at first, she came through in triumph, helped by the warm-hearted encouragement of Harriet Taylor, the Helen; and next morning she entered into an agreement as leading actress at Covent Garden for three years.]

Macready goes to a short engagement at Bristol.

Bristol, January 18. Went to rehearsal at eleven o'clock; was kept waiting for some time; found things in a decent state, but the Lady Macbeth bad beyond all former out-doings—detestable! . . . Mr Denvil, who was my Macduff with a pair of well-grown moustaches, told me of his having pitched Mr Eliot, a pantomimist, from a height of eighteen feet, in which the pitched Elliot gloried to that degree that he even suffered pain from the surmise that some of the audience might suppose it was a *dummy* that was thrown! Now, what is ambition in the pleasure its success conveys? Was the Duke of Wellington more inwardly gratified after a victory than this man would be if three or four rounds of applause were to follow him into the black hole into which Mr Denvil or any other person might pitch him? *Gloria mundi!* Proceeded to the theatre. The house was very fair, and I tried to act with the millstone of Lady Macbeth round my neck. Oh!—Muses! I acted Macbeth very unequally

—some parts I thought I did very well; the scene before the banquet and the melancholy of the fifth act particularly. I should, however, say that it was not sustained.

January 21. Rehearsed *Othello*. Mrs D. Lee, who played Virginia last night, told me 'how much I had hurt her'; on asking *where*, she said 'her arms.' 'Why, I do not touch your arms with any degree of force through the play—scarcely touch them at all; do you remember the scene?' 'I think in the scene where you rush on.' Now, here is another example of the vileness of these people! I never touch her arms through the play with the remotest possibility of hurting her, but I had occasion twice in the course of the play to remind her of the business she forgot— *hinc illae lacrimae!* Hence this trumped-up story!

January 22. Heard before I went on the stage that Mr Denvil had been bled by Dr Riley in the green-room! And yet for £5 he was able to play Iago! I could not have done this—I could not have played Iago so badly as he did under any circumstances, but, under his peculiar ones, could not have done it at all. I acted a little of Othello very fairly, but this Mr Denvil was trying to *get behind* me (for what Heaven only knows!) and very much inconvenienced and embarrassed me.

London, January 27. . . . I learnt that the Covent Garden manager had renewed an engagement with Mr Kemble, that he had put the hypothetical question to him of performing with me, and that his answer was, he would play nothing but *first!* Here is an old coxcomb, who never yet was permitted, but as a substitute, to appear in first characters, who dared not act them even when manager, and now before his four-shilling audiences is obliged to descend to such things as Charles II and Sir Thomas Clifford, talking about playing *first* business with a first artist! What a wretched old coxcomb! *[Charles II in 'Charles the Second; or, The Merry Monarch' by J. Howard Payne (Covent Garden, 1824); Sir Thomas Clifford in Knowles's 'The Hunchback' (Covent Garden, 1832; Fanny Kemble was the original Julia in this play). 'The Hunchback' became a familiar 'stock' drama. In Pinero's 'Trelawny of the "Wells" ' the Bagnigge Wells actor, Ferdinand Gadd, says: 'I'm hitting them hard this season. To-night, Sir Thomas Clifford. They're simply waiting for my Clifford.']*

Bunn was now ready to stage 'The Bridal'; Macready held that the contract which stipulated immediately after Christmas, had been violated; he refused to let the play be acted and claimed compensation. Bunn said that Macready, for his part, had violated his agreement by acting out of London.

January 28. Mr Cooper came to say that they had rehearsed the *Bridal* that day, and that Mr Bunn was ready, in compliance with my agreement to act it on Tuesday next; that he himself thought it a shocking play; that Mr Warde,[1] the pure-minded, highly cultivated critic, thought it monstrous: this I endured, and waived, by observing it was nothing to the purpose, the agreement was violated. I then asked who had been cast as Aspatia?—Miss Tree. Who, then, is to do Evadne? I declare I pause as I write the name: Mrs Sloman! To her, whom they would not permit to play the easy part of Emilia at my suggestion, as being so bad, they give a character that only Mrs Siddons could realise! I said 'That is enough; if you were to pay me one or two thousand pounds for it, I would not suffer it to be so acted; but I confine myself to the legal objection, and on the violated contract I demand compensation.' Mr Cooper said: 'I am instructed to offer £33 6s 8d and to withdraw the play.' I observed that the same offer had been made by Mr Yates, which I had treated with the same indignant contempt. 'Well, then,' said Mr Cooper, 'I am now declared to ask you upon whose authority you went to Bristol.' I now lost all temper. I answered: 'Upon my own!' and that the question was a gross impertinence. Mr Cooper proceeded to state that he thought it was not justifiable on former usage, and I replied it was. Dow entered, and he observed that I was ready to perform, if required, in London, and that my Bristol engagement was made dependent on and subject to that of Drury Lane. In the course of our conversation [Cooper] had said that Miss Ellen Tree would have flung the part of Evadne in his face if it had been offered to her. I observed: 'She would not have flung it in mine.' 'Oh, yes' he said, 'she would.' This question I shall ask of Miss Tree. This disgusting and servile booby at length left us—if ever a man answered to the description of the moral being of an individual, as sketched by a poet's pencil, go, Mr Cooper, into the hide of Austria in the play of *King John*, and find your own fitting in the dullness, conceit, falsehood, treachery and cowardice of the Viscount Limoges. After dinner I wrote notes—statements—to Mr Bunn, and one to Mr Cooper, desiring him to confine himself to the duties of his office. . . . Looked over my engagement, by which I think Mr Bunn had no pretence for touching my salary—none. . . . How bitterly do I quarrel with and reproach myself for my want of self-control and master over my passions.

Elstree, January 29. The midday post brought a letter from Cooper, wishing to know when I could be ready in [G. W. Lovell's] the *Provost of Bruges*. I answered that I had long since applied for subjects of study

[1] Possibly James Prescott Warde (1792–1840), actor.

and had received no answer, that I had laid aside the *Provost of Bruges* and could not immediately state when I should be ready, in two or three days I might be able to do so. I added that, having found that my last week's salary had not been paid, I desired it might be immediately. . . .

January 30. Received a call for the rehearsal of the *Provost of Bruges* on Monday next. Resolved not to attend the rehearsal unless my salary was duly paid. Read over the part of Bertulphe, of which I do not entertain very sanguine hopes, it is too sketchy and skeleton like; there is a want of strength and substance in the thoughts, which are thin and poor; its situation is all its actual power. If it be successful, it will owe much to the acting.

London, February 1. On my arrival at chambers I found a note from Cooper informing me that 'I had violated my engagement in going to Bristol, and in consequence Mr Bunn had stopped a week and a half of my salary, but that if I chose to give my best services to the theatre in a more harmonious way than of late, Mr Bunn would be very happy to remit the stoppage.' To which I immediately answered—receiving a note from good old Dow, with a play-bill containing an announcement of myself for Othello and Werner, that instantly decided me—that 'my engagement, in the opinion of an eminent special pleader and a leading barrister, did not allow of Mr Bunn's deduction; that if he did not intimate to me that my demands were paid, I should at once close the correspondence; that I should wait in town until three o'clock.' . . . Mr Cooper called. He said it seemed the dispute was only about terms of speech; that he had signified Mr Bunn's willingness to pay the money due; and that he supposed, of course, I should give him my best services. I distinctly stated that it was merely a question of whether my salary, according to my engagement, was or was not paid, without any other consideration; if paid I should go to the theatre, if not, I should end my engagement. He complained of being obliged to do 'Mr Bunn's dirty work'—which I thought to myself he might very well avoid. The beginning, as the end, of our conversation was this, that I would not answer his note, but *stood upon my legal claim*, which he promised should be answered, and I told him I should go to rehearsal tomorrow.

Macready now reappeared as Othello in the first legitimate drama at Drury Lane for three months.

February 3. Rehearsed the women's scenes of *Othello*; in suggesting two or three things to Miss E. Tree, she begged me not to demur at giving her any information; but my disgust at witnessing the impertinent forwardness of Mr Vandenhoff tutoring persons capable of teaching him made me tender of hazarding my own opinions. I did not feel *at home*, but felt resolved to do my best. . . . I began Othello with resolution, which was confirmed by the kind reception of the audience; but I found myself a little disconcerted by the strangeness of the theatre during the apology to the Senate, in which my back is turned to the audience. I recovered myself, and threw myself more into the character than I think I had previously done. I was called for by the audience, but this, if a compliment, was certainly much reduced in value by Mr Vandenhoff receiving the same for playing Iago like a great, creeping, cunning cat. Grimalkin would be a better name for his part than the 'honest fellow', the 'bold Iago'. Mr Westmacott[1] was in the green-room, and I was indiscreet enough (having drunk some wine) to show my contempt for him in a manner not to be mistaken; he half bowed to me, and I turned my back upon him with the word 'beast' quite loud enough for him to hear. This, *though provoked*, had been better omitted. What can I do against a repetition of his insults? . . .

February 6. At my chambers I found Palmer to whom I gave orders for my dress [Bertulphe's in *The Provost of Bruges*] which is to be of cotton velvet and not to exceed in cost £5.

February 7. Dow called and informed me of the wretch Westmacott's abuse of me in the *Age:* 'that an automaton might be made to play Othello as well; that it was very cold, that the new play would probably fail, and that Virginius was melodrama, etc., also that Mr Vandenhoff's Iago was the best since Cooke!'[2] I had at least the sense to feel no anger at all this nonsense.

February 9. Went to rehearsal of *Provost of Bruges*, which was long and heavy. . . . I am quite uncertain of the play, and am certain of my own very crude and unpractised conception of my own character.

February 10. Went to rehearsal (*Provost of Bruges*), sparing myself as much as I could. In the wardrobe was told that Mr Bunn would not find me pantaloons, and I was resolved to purchase none; was very angry, and therefore very blameable. . . . Went to the theatre very tranquil in spirits, but was slightly disconcerted by the very culpable negligence of my dresser. Resolved to take no wine before I came on and to trust to my spirits to bear me up until fatigue came on. Misjudged in doing so; my nervousness, from want of due preparation, was so great as to mar my

---

[1] Charles Molloy Westmacott (1787–1868), editor from 1827 to 1843 of a scurrilous journal, *The Age*. Charles Kemble had once thrashed him in Covent Garden Theatre for libelling Fanny Kemble.

[2] G. F. Cooke (1756–1812), actor.

efforts in the first scene, which, in spite of my best attempts at self-possession, was hurried and characterless. Gulped down a draught of wine, and, growing more steady from scene to scene, increased in power and effect; but it was a hasty, unprepared performance, the power of which was mainly derived from the moment's inspiration. The applause was enthusiastic, and I was obliged, after long delay, to go before the audience. Dow, Cattermole, Forster, Browning, and Talfourd came into my room and expressed themselves greatly pleased with my performance but did not highly estimate the play. . . .

[It had eight nights at a loss; Macready at this period was not a draw. But Helen Faucit, who saw the play on 16 February, wrote in her journal: 'How splendidly did Mr Macready act in it! . . . There is such an earnestness and meaning about everything he does, even the most trifling word or action, that carries such 'truth' with it. I hear a great many talk of his faults of declamation, pauses, and so on, but I don't know it is, he never gives me time to see them. He may not be, and certainly is not, so graceful in his manner and bearing as Mr Kemble (but then how very, very few are!); his overpowering earnestness makes amends for all, and leaves no fault that I can see.']

February 11. . . . Forster brought me the notices of the newspapers, which were all highly commendatory; the writer of the *Times* is, I think, acquainted with Mr Bunn. . . .

February 16. Forster and Browning called, and talked over the plot of a tragedy which Browning had begun to think of; the subject, Narses. He said that I had bit him by my performance of Othello, and I told him I hoped I should make the blood come. . . .

February 17. Dear Edward born *[Edward Nevil Bourne Macready, second son and fourth child.]* . . . Read Joanna Baillie's[1] play of *Basil*, which I think can scarcely be made pathetic enough for representation; there is a stiffness in her style, a want of appropriateness and peculiarity distinguishing each person, that I cannot overcome in reading her plays: it is a sort of brocaded style, a thick kind of silk, that has no fall or play— it is not flexibility of nature.

February 23. Called on Bulwer, whom I found in very handsome chambers in the Albany, dressed, or rather *déshabillé*, in the most lamentable style of foppery—a hookah in his mouth, his hair, whiskers, tuft, etc., all grievously cared for. I felt deep regret to see a man of such worthy and profound thought yield for a moment to pettiness so

---

[1] Joanna Baillie (1762–1851), dramatist and poet.

unworthy of him. His manner was frank, manly, and cordial in the extreme—so contradictory of his appearance. He told me, after talking about the *Provost of Bruges* and recalling our conversation in Dublin, that he had written a play; that he did not know whether I might think the part intended for me worthy of my powers, for that inevitably the weight of the action fell upon the woman; that the subject was La Vallière. He handed me a paper in which I read that it was dedicated to myself. It almost affected me to tears. I could not read it. He wished me to read the play, give my opinion, and that he would make any alterations I might suggest. . . . Acted Bertulphe pretty well, though much disconcerted by the din of carpenters. . . . Found at my chambers Bulwer's play. Read it. What talent he possesses! I must read it again.

[Edward George Lytton Bulwer, later Lord Lytton (1803–1873): his luckless marriage (1827) with Rosina [Wheeler] was breaking up, and a deed of judicial separation was signed in April 1836. An extraordinarily versatile writer (novelist, poet, editor), and a politician, he was now to become a popular dramatist, and he proposed to Macready his tragedy of 'The Duchess de la Vallière.' Louise de la Vallière was mistress of Louis XIV.]

February 24. Received a letter from Mr Lovell, offering to have his play acted for nothing rather than let it be stopped, which from the appearance of the playbills seems intended. . . . Spoke to Bunn, without mentioning the author's name, of Bulwer's play, and asked him what remuneration he would offer. Would he give £100—3rd, 6th, 9th, 16th, and 25th nights? He said 'Yes.' Read very attentively over the play of La Vallière, and made my notes upon what I thought it needed.

February 25. . . . Received a parcel—another play—from Mr Wightwick of Plymouth. I could have dispensed with it, but he cherishes kindly feelings towards me, and is entitled to my best offices. *[George Wightwick, a Plymouth architect, was an admirer of Macready for whom, in later years, he adapted Sherborne House.]* Called on Bulwer (shopping on the way) and found him less carefully set up than on my former visit. We talked over the play, and I mentioned my objections, at the same time suggesting some remedies. He yielded all readily except the fifth act; upon that he seemed inclined to do battle, but at length I understood him to yield. We talked over terms. He was not satisfied with Bunn's proposal, but added to that £200 down, and to be paid through the two following seasons £5 a night, after which the copyright to revert to him. This is rather a hard bargain; I do not think Bunn will concede so much. . . .

February 27. Read the two last acts of [Talfourd's] *Ion*, which if I had personal advantages, I am confident I could make effective in performance. . . . Forster and Browning called in. My nerves and spirits were quite quelled, and I was rejoiced in seeing them leave me—excepting Browning, whose gentle manners always make his presence acceptable. I acted Othello—I scarcely know in what way—not to please myself; the truth is, I have lost the tone, the pitch of voice, the directness of the part, and I strive in vain to recall it; perhaps and as I believe, because I do not *strive enough*. . . .

March 1. Mr Lovell called. . . . I told him the cause of the withdrawal of the *Provost of Bruges*—the dresses having been cut up for *Chevy Chase!* [*'Chevy Chase', a melodramatic spectacle or grand chivalric entertainment, by the versatile James Robinson Planché.*] . . . Acted Macbeth very unequally; latter part of first act—second act—part of third act—part of fourth—first and last scenes of fifth act—well; the rest badly. I cannot act Macbeth without *being Macbeth*, which I must have time to prepare my mind for. I cannot work myself into such a tempest of ever-waking thought. . . . Mr Willmott told me that the reason of Mr Ward[e]'s nervousness—oh! how nervous he is!—was that he drank nearly a bottle of gin every night!! Spoke to Bunn about *La Vallière;* he would say nothing *until he knew the author.* A man came into the room with a 'Hurrah'! I took him for a vulgar auctioneer, or one of the blackguard hangers-on of Bunn. Bunn, however, introduced him to me as *Lord Allen!* . . .

March 2. . . . Called on Bulwer, and evidently came on him by surprise; he could not well avoid seeing me; indeed he did not demur, though evidently a little discomposed. He was in complete *déshabillé*—a white nightcap on his head, looking like a head of Gay or some poet of that time—it was a picture; his busts, papers, etc., around him, and the unornamented man of genius undandified. I told him of Bunn's desire to know the author's name before he committed himself, and that I could not counsel it, as I know Mr B——to be *utterly faithless and treacherous.* He at last commissioned me to give his name to Mr Bunn, but would not consent to his seeing the play to judge of it; the price down was for *his name*. We talked over the objections to his play, and I think he inclined at last to my view.

March 5. Went to the theatre; saw Bunn, delivered Bulwer's proposal of his play without being looked at. Bunn refused*[he refused to 'buy what the profane call a pig in a poke']*, but said he would write to Bulwer. . . . A woman called for relief, 'because she was of the same name'. I paid a shilling for the unlucky accident. . . .

He was in the provinces until late in March.

To Bath, March 6. . . . *[In the stage-coach]* Captain Bourchier *[a passenger]*, as I soon learned his name to be, talked much; among other subjects mentioned young Kean's success at Bath, told me that he knew him, and that his dresses cost him £300 per annum, that he was very pleasant, and related many amusing stories about the theatre. One of Macready, who is a good actor, but he can never play without applause. He went on one night to play and no notice was taken of him, on which he said to the manager, 'I cannot get on, if they do not applaud me'. Upon which the manager went round and told the audience that Mr Macready could not act if they did not applaud him. When Macready reappeared, the applause was so incessant as to disconcert him, and he observed, 'Why, now I cannot act, there is so much applause'. I told him I rather discredited the story, 'In short,' I observed, 'perhaps I ought to apologise to you for allowing you to tell it without first giving you my name—my name is Macready.' He was very much confused, and I as courteous in apologising as I could be.

Bath, March 8. . . . *[Virginius]* The Icilius (a Mr Savile) was either half-stupidly drunk, or, as is very probable, a born ass. Virginia would have made an excellent representation of Appius' cook, as far as appearance went, added to which she seemed to think that she was playing Virginius, not Virginia, and fortified herself for some extraordinary efforts by a stimulant which was too easily detected on a near approach to her. The whole business was most slovenly—and last year this play was actually a *pattern* of correctness. Therefore last year there was a loss on the theatre, and now there is a considerable profit. So much for the judgement and taste of a Bath public. Pshaw! It is all quackery.

March 10. . . . Received a letter from Bulwer, apprising me of the expected termination of negotiations with Mr Bunn on the subject of his play, and wishing me to impress on Mr Bunn that the communication was confidential. . . . *[Macready replied that he would write to Bunn, 'not that an oath upon the best Bible or the most holy relic in Christendom would have any retentive power for him'.]*

Exeter, March 18. . . . Between the third and fourth acts *[of Virginius]* the manager came into my room to apologise for a delay of some minutes, while Mr Hughes stripped the togas and decemviral insignia from Appius Claudius, a Mr H. Bartlett, and invested himself with them to finish the character, Mr Bartlett having been so excessively drunk as to tumble from the *sella curulis* in the Forum. Oh Rome! If the man had been acting Cato, it might have been taken for a point of character.

This is the profession which the vulgar envy, and the proud seem justified in despising! . . .

Plymouth, March 23. My endeavour to act Werner well was completely frustrated. The whole play was acted very indifferently; Josephine was dressed like a flower-girl for a fancy ball; Idenstein, Fritz, Stralenheim all bad—Gabor not good—but Ulric was beyond all power of description—winking with his eyes, then starting, and looking very fine, mysterious, and assassin-like—then as flippant as a man-milliner. He quite *paralysed* me. I contended with this oppressive incubus, and made some effect, but the heart was absent.

Exeter, March 24. . . . Saw an Edinburgh newspaper, containing an account of the extraordinary success of young Kean—'the houses literally crammed every night'. *Can this be bad?* . . . Letter from Mr Cooper, giving me notice of *Richard III* for Easter Monday. Oh, Mr Bunn—I was distressed at first, and, as usual, angry, but soon reasoned myself into complacency, or at least resolution not to let it be any advantage to the man who thinks to annoy me and perhaps to make me relinquish my engagement—but it is a night's uncomfortable feeling and then an end! It cannot kill my reputation, for my reputation does not rest upon the past; I will, however, do my best with it.

Elstree, April 4. Letter from Talfourd, proposing to be here on Friday. Read over *Ion [a production of which was contemplated]* in order to get a general idea of its arrangement.

April 8. A letter from Talfourd mentioned the time of his arrival, and enclosed Mr Vandenhoff's refusal to act Adrastus.[1] I did not expect the man to do it from any feeling to me, since he would pay a premium to have my throat cut, and he has no sense of delicacy, but to the character of Talfourd and to the merit of his play, some consideration was due. He excused himself on the plea of his daughter's début, which takes place on Monday next—a *fortnight* before the representation of *Ion!* He is, as I have ever observed him, *a nasty fellow!* On Talfourd's arrival about three o'clock we went over the play, he not offering an objection to all my omissions. . . . Talfourd's easiness of disposition, his general indulgence for others' faults, and good-natured aversion to dispute, has proved, in the happiness that has resulted from such amiability, the best wisdom.

London, April 9. Called on Miss Tree. To my distress and consternation, she was not at home, nor expected to return until May. Reflected on my situation and thought the matter hopeless without Miss Tree.

[1] Adrastus, King of Argos, in Talfourd's *Ion*. He is a tyrant who holds bacchanalian revels in the plague-stricken city.

Called on Talfourd; proved to him the impossibility of acting the play of *Ion* without Miss Tree, but luckily thought of writing to her, to ask her to assist me on a more distant day—if Bunn, as I doubted not, would consent to its postponement. We walked together to Drury Lane theatre, and I went in to see Mr Bunn. I proposed the delay, to which he assented, and I left him to carry the news to Talfourd at the Garrick Club.

April 14. . . . Talfourd came in to the theatre from the House where he had been speaking on flogging in the Army. He said that he was nervous and rapid, but listened to with great indulgence. Showed him a letter from Ellen Tree which I had just received, in which she mentioned her intention of being in town 22nd May, and her willingness to study Clemanthe *[heroine of Talfourd's Ion]* for me. Neither Cooper nor Bunn was in the theatre, so that nothing could be settled.

On 15 April Macready saw that he had been announced, degradingly, to play William Tell in the Drury Lane after-piece on 16 April. This, for a First Tragedian, was humiliating, but Macready agreed, on the understanding that Bunn would pledge his word that nothing of the sort should recur. He would not give the undertaking, and Macready had to play.

April 16. . . . There seemed to be a very general feeling of disgust at Mr Bunn's behaviour among the people connected with the theatres. Had not been able to read *William Tell*, but took all the pains in my power with its performance, and rendered it very effective, particularly when the lateness of the hour is taken into account. The audience did not move until the very last, and after going to my room, I was obliged to return at the call of the remaining audience, who would not depart, and who cheered me most enthusiastically. . . . Thus was passed over a threatening danger, which might have had an evil influence, with a different issue, on my whole future life. . . .

Macready spoke too soon. On 25 April he learned that if he refused to act in after-pieces, Bunn proposed to 'play me on Malibran's off-nights through my range of characters at half-price.'

April 26. At Garrick Club, where I dined and saw the papers. Met Thackeray,[1] who has spent all his fortune and is now about to settle at Paris,

April 27. Going out met Dow, and we set out, he attending to

[1] William Makepeace Thackeray (1811–1863), novelist.

accompany me to the theatre; as we passed along, he stopped to read the play-bill, and exclaimed, 'What's that?—'The first three acts of *Richard III.*' So it was announced in the play-bill. He observed, 'You will not do it?' and recommended me to go and declare before a witness to Mr Cooper that I would go on and ask the audience whether they would have the play in its mutilated state or complete. I parted with him at the stage door, and taking the prompter into Mr Cooper's room, I said as much, not at all angrily, but rather amused. Mr Cooper said he would communicate the message to Mr Bunn. . . . Dined at the Garrick Club where I saw newspapers and looked over *Sketches by Boz.* . . . Acted Macbeth very fairly; I had to goad my mind into the character, for my thoughts wandered to the feverish state of things about me. Mrs Bartley[1] was the Lady Macbeth; she should take some of the blame for my occasional inefficiency; she was so bad, so monotonous, so devoid of all thought or feeling of character, so artificial, and yet, as it were, elaborating nothing. There was no misconception, because there was no conception, no attempt at assumption; it was Mrs Bartley. I gave Mr Warde a hard knock on the head inadvertently, or rather through his own awkwardness, for which I was sorry, but had I laid it open he could not have displayed more agony. . . .

April 28. Went to the theatre and rehearsed in the saloon *'the first three acts of "King Richard III".'* Every actor expressing his indignation at the proceeding. *[Bunn who realised very well that the last act of 'Richard III' was known to be Macready's best, maliciously broke off the play in the middle and announced the truncated version in the same bill as 'The Jewess' and the first act of 'Chevy Chase'.]* . . . Tried in chambers to read—in vain; tried to compose myself by sleep, till I was depressed and unable to think on my character for tomorrow night; I tried and could not. Took tea, did what I could to compose and soothe my spirits—it would not be; my inability to prepare myself in the part of Richard—which I have not acted for more than four years—by tomorrow night, quite weighed me down; I tried the part; the consciousness of not having time to duly consider and practice it quite rendered unavailing all attempts. Passion and angry thoughts, angry to a degree of savageness and desperation, agitated me long and painfully. What can recompense me for being subject to the spite of such a reptile as this Bunn? If I were prepared in the character, I should laugh; I am tormented by painful doubts and misgivings. Sometimes I think of resigning my engagement, which is at least £250. I cannot do it; let what may happen, I must trust in God, for God knows I have very few friends here. I am very unhappy.

[1] Mrs George Bartley (1782–1850), tragic actress.

April 29. Rose with uneasy thoughts and in a very disturbed state of mind, which I reasoned into more placidity as I proceeded with my toilet, but I had difficulty in controlling my mind, labouring under the alternate sensations of exasperation and depression. Wrote to Dow that I had settled on doing the three acts tonight, although it was against my engagement. Called on Forster on my way to rehearsal, who told me of Kemble's expression of his indignation at Mr Bunn's behaviour. At rehearsal I spoke to Cooper on the stage to the effect that it was not worth my while to record any protest, but that I would not do such a thing again as act in a mutilated play, my engagement not warranting the fact. . . . *[He went to the Garrick Club, then to chambers]* . . . My spirits were so very much depressed, so overweighed by the situation in which I was placed, that I lay down to compose myself, and thought over the part of Richard as well as I could. Went to the theatre; was tetchy and unhappy, but pushed through the part in a sort of desperate way as well as I could. It is not easy to describe the state of pent-up feeling of anger, shame, and desperate passion that I endured. As I came off the stage, ending the third act of *Richard*, in passing by Bunn's door I opened it, and unfortunately he was there. I could not contain myself; I exclaimed: 'You damned scoundrel! How dare you use me in this manner?' And going up to him as he sat on the other side of the table, I struck him as he rose a back-handed slap across the face. I did not hear what he said, but I dug my fist into him as effectively as I could; he caught hold of me, and got at one time the little finger of my left hand in his mouth, and bit it. I exclaimed: 'You rascal! Would you bite?' He shouted out: 'Murder! Murder!' and, after some little time, several persons came into the room. I was then upon the sofa, the struggle having brought us right round the table. Willmott, the prompter, said to me: 'Sir, you had better go to your room, you had better go to your room.' I got up accordingly, and walked away, whilst he, I believe—for I did not distinctly hear him —was speaking in abuse of me. Dow came into my room, then Forster and young Longman. Wallace soon after, evidently deeply grieved at the occurrence. They talked and I dressed, and we left the theatre together. Wallace and Forster, on Dow leaving us, went home with me, and taking tea, discussed the probable consequences of this most indiscreet, most imprudent, most blameable action. Forster was strongly for attempting to throw Mr Bunn overboard on the score of character; but Wallace manifestly felt, as I felt, that I had descended to his level by raising my hand against him, and that I was personally responsible for so doing. I feel that I am; and, serious and painful as it is, I will do my duty. As I read the above lines, I am still more struck with my own intemperate and unfortunate rashness. I would have gone through my engagement in forbearance and peace, still enduring wrong on wrong, as for six years I have been doing, but my passions mastered me, and I sought to wreak them. No one can more severely condemn my precipitation than myself. No enemy can censure me more harshly, no friend lament more deeply my forgetfulness of all I ought to have thought upon. My character will suffer for descending so low, and the newspapers will make themselves profit of my folly. Words cannot express the contrition I feel, the shame I endure. . . .

[In the second volume of 'The Stage: Both Before and Behind the Curtain' (1840) Bunn gave his own version of the incident: 'On Friday the 29th April I was sitting at my desk, a few minutes before nine o'clock, and by the light of a lamp, so shaded as to reflect on the table but obscure the room generally, I was examining bills and documents, previous to their payment on the following morning; when without the slightest note of preparation, my door was opened, and after an ejaculation of "There, you villain, take that—and that!" I was knocked down, one of my eyes completely closed up, the ankle of my left leg, which I am in the habit of passing round the leg of the chair when writing, violently sprained, my person plentifully soiled with blood, lamp oil, and ink, the table upset, and Richard the Third *holding me down. On my naturally inquiring if he meant to murder me, and on his replying in the affirmative, I made a struggle for it, threw him off, and got up on my one leg, holding him fast by the collar, and finally succeeded in getting him down on the sofa, where, mutilated as I was, I would have made him "remember me", but for the interposition of the people who had soon filled the room.']*

April 30. Read for about an hour in bed last night, and though at first restless and dreaming of being in the custody of an officer, my sleep was sweet and refreshing. In opening Johnson's *Lives* in bed I began upon the narration of Savage's unfortunate rencontre with Sinclair; the idea of murder presented itself so painfully and strongly to my mind that I turned directly for relief to another subject. My thoughts have been scorpions to me; the estimation I have lost in society, the uncertainty and shame with which, if I am again invited by those who respected me, I shall meet their looks, is a punishment which has anguish in it. All I can do, as I have reduced myself to a level with this reptile, is to allow him the whole advantage of it, and accept any message for a meeting that he may choose to send me. . . . Who will say this alternative is not a most painful one? I acknowledge it, but I will go through with it. . . .

Henry Smith called; it was evident the disastrous report of last night had brought him. I asked him if there was anything in the paper. He said: 'Yes'; that he was surprised at the paragraph in the *Morning Chronicle*, and had come to ask if anything could be done. Wallace, Forster, and afterwards Dow, came and consulted on what was best to be done; looked at the *Morning Chronicle*, and Wallace declining to be a party to any draught of a counter-statement, the others adjourned to Forster's chambers and soon afterwards returned, having come to the conclusion that it was better to let the thing pass. Wallace thought differently, and so did I, agreeing that it would be better a proper statement should appear in preference to an improper one. . . . Sent a note to C. Jones for my salary. The words 'no answer' was returned. Sent to Dunn saying, if not paid I should proceed against Mr Bunn for this amount. Mathews[1] called to see me. . . . Felt ashamed to walk through the streets, and took a coach; ashamed even to meet the look of the people in the street. Dined with Power.[2] Letters from Dunn, saying that Mr Bunn was ill at Brompton; and from Mr Fox, kindly offering to do anything to set the matter right with the public. Drove home in Dow's cab. Told dearest Catherine and Letty of the unfortunate rashness I had been guilty of. They were deeply distressed.

May 1. . . . Forster informed me that Stephen Price had been stating at the Garrick Club that he had cautioned this reptile 'that if he persisted in goading me with the annoyances he was practising against me, that I should lose my self-restraint and inflict severe retribution upon him.' He knew me, it appears, far better than I knew myself. . . . Went to dine with Talfourd. Saw on the placard of the *Age:* 'Great Fight. B–nn and M——y.' It made me sick to think of it. Felt occasionally uncomfortable at Talfourd's, but on the whole was more comfortable than I had anticipated. . . .

May 2. . . . On my way to the Garrick Club saw a face in a carriage I thought I knew, and immediately, as I passed, Malibran put her head out of the window and waved her hand to me. She seemed bridally attired. How different her lot from mine! She with fame, affluence, idolatry, on every side; I, poor, struggling to maintain a doubtful reputation, which my own rashness endangers, and looking, as my greatest good, to an independence which may be just large enough to

---

[1] Charles James Mathews (1803–1878), comedian; son of the great Charles Mathews (1775–1835); second husband of Madame Vestris whom he married in 1838.

[2] Tyrone Power (1795–1841), Irish actor popular in London and New York; he was drowned in 1841 when the steamship *President* sank on her return voyage from America. Sir Tyrone Guthrie, the director, is his great-grandson.

educate my children liberally and raise them above want; even this is now very doubtful. . . .

May 3. . . . Mr Bartley informed me that they had found a boy, a nephew of Algar's to come forward to say that he was at Bunn's door when I approached it, that I pushed him aside, entered, and that he saw me strike him, then ran to the prompter Willmott, and said: 'Mr Macready and Mr Bunn are fighting.' Mr Willmott then declares that he came into the room, and saw me upon the sofa, holding Mr Bunn's hair in my two hands, Mr Bunn over me and striking me; that he swung Mr Bunn round to the other side and desired me to go to my room. As gross a perjury as ever the mouth of a villain uttered—so help me God! So may my soul know peace here and hereafter! Talfourd called. I thought he seemed as much disconcerted at *Ion* being withdrawn as at my suffering. He recommended a note to Cooper to extort, if possible, a notice of dismissal. I wrote it and he approved it. . . .

May 5. Dear Catherine brought a letter from Kenneth with an offer of £200 for twelve nights from Mr Osbaldiston *[David Webster Osbaldiston, manager of the Theatre Royal, Covent Garden.]*, and an invitation from Calcraft *[of Dublin]*. I wrote to Kenneth wishing to see him. Kenneth called; we talked on the matter, and he took down my modification of Mr Osbaldiston's offer. I observed that I did not wish to trade upon, or raise my terms on, this unfortunate occurrence; but that I could not, under the circumstances of the season, take less than had been offered to other actors; that I did not wish him to say £240 for twelve nights, but would he say £200 for ten nights, or £120 for six? For *Ion* I also stipulated. At my chambers I found Dow, who went upstairs with me. A letter was lying on the table for me, the hand strange to me. On opening the envelope I found a letter from the wretched villain who has caused me all this suffering—to the effect that he considered my engagement, etc., '*cancelled and determined*' by my '*attempt to assassinate*' him on Friday evening and that he had given orders to the doorkeepers, etc., not to admit me 'on any pretence whatever.' It was a great relief to me to receive this letter—and I was as much, if not more, gratified by his accusation of my '*attempt to assassinate*' than by the release I have obtained from the perplexing dilemma in which his silence left me. I trust it is for good. . . . *[Kenneth was a London agent.]*

May 6. In reflecting on the letter received from Mr Bunn last night, it occurred to me that the occasion should not be lost of fixing the question as to the honourable feeling which has actuated me. I wrote to Wallace, wishing his presence and advice, and wrote out the substance of what I thought ought to be returned to Mr Bunn. A note from

Mr Conquest[1] of the Garrick theatre, Whitechapel (!), offering me an engagement for six nights—to divide the house, ensuring me £100. A very kind letter, and one that would comfort me, if anything could, from Colonel Birch; an offer from Clarke *[Manager of the Liverpool and Manchester theatre]* of £165 for ten nights at Liverpool, etc. Answered Mr Conquest, civilly declining his offer. . . .

He accepted Osbaldiston's terms for Covent Garden, '£200 for ten nights, and a Benefit divided, after £20, beginning Wednesday 17 May and ending Saturday, 11 June'. Also to act two nights gratuitously.

May 7. Walked out to call on Henry Smith; in the Covent Garden playbills my name was blazing in large red letters at the head of the announcement. May it be prosperous! . . . *[Later, at the Garrick Club.]* Kemble came in as I was going out. I told the waiter to ask him to step into the strangers' room, which he did. I said that it had gratified me much to hear of the liberal way in which he had spoken of me before and subsequently to this unfortunate affair; that I had commissioned my friend Talfourd to say as much to him, but, seeing him there, I chose to anticipate his intention and to express myself the sense I entertained of his liberal manner of mentioning my name, having so long been in a state of hostility with him. He replied that he had never cherished any hostile feeling towards me, and that his language had always been in the same tone; that everyone must feel indignant at the infamous conduct of this Bunn towards me, and that he had ever entertained the best feelings for me. I drew off my glove, and said that I had much pleasure in acknowledging the liberality of his conduct. He shook hands very cordially, saying that it had always been a matter of regret to him that our acquaintance had been interrupted, and I replied that I regretted this reconcilement had been forced from me by the generous and liberal behaviour which he had shown, and had not proceeded spontaneously from me. . . . We parted in the hall; my feelings were excited and won over on this occasion; but I cannot help pausing to remark how very much I yield to impulse instead of guiding my course through life on a stern, undeviating principle of justice. I call charity only justice. I fear I am often weak on this account, and seem vacillating where I ought to be unmoving. I certainly feel no ill-will to Kemble . . . but [he] has not redeemed those errors in his character which leave him open to overwhelming censure. Should I then have obeyed a kindly sort of grateful

[1] Benjamin Conquest (Oliver) (1804–1872), of the Garrick, Leman Street, Whitechapel.

feeling, or have weighed in my judgment the value, motive, and sincerity of his conduct? *I am not quite clear. . . .*

Macready was quite clear by 8 August, when he added a note: 'I now *am*—that I was, as I too frequently am, precipitate, and acted on impulse in a matter that should have been duly deliberated on.'

May 9. . . . Called at Covent Garden theatre. Saw Mr Osbaldiston. Settled the night of *Ion:* 26th instant. Spoke about orders, dressing-room, etc., in all of which Mr O—— seemed desirous of accommodating me. Was introduced to Mr Fitzball(!), the Victor Hugo, as he terms himself, of England—the 'Victor No-go' in Mr Keeley's[1] nomenclature. Dined at the Garrick Club, where I am regarded with an 'eye askance' by the *roué* set . . . this will not kill me.

[Edward Fitzball (1792–1873), prolific dramatist, was originally apprenticed to a Norwich printer. In a rash moment became lessee of Covent Garden in 1835. According to Saxe Wyndham in 'The Annals of Covent Garden Theatre', 'Mr Fitzball came down to breakfast one morning, and, seeing that the day was a fine one, and that, moreover, Covent Garden Theatre was advertised in "The Times" to let, went and took it.' Fortunately his friend Osbaldiston relieved him, Fitzball 'securing to myself the position of emergency author, at a good salary, for two years'.]

May 11. . . . Went to the theatre, and, in dressing, still felt my nerves were untrue to me; looked over the early part of the play, and just before I went on I screwed up myself to care for nothing, and went boldly and resolutely forward. On my entrance in *Macbeth* the pit—indeed the house—rose, and waved hats and handkerchiefs, cheering in the most fervent and enthusiastic manner. It lasted so long that it rather overcame me; but I entered on my own task, determined to do my best, and, I think, I never acted Macbeth more really, or altogether better. The applause was tumultuous at the fall of the curtain, and the person who went on was driven back with cries of 'No,' and I went before them. When silence was gained, I spoke an address as follows: 'Ladies and Gentlemen,—Under ordinary circumstances I should receive the manifestation of your kindness with silent acknowledgement; but I cannot disguise from myself the fact that the circumstances which have led to my engagement at this theatre, after an absence of many years, are uppermost in your minds. Into those circumstances I will not

[1] Robert Keeley (1793–1869), comedian. His wife was the equally celebrated comedienne, Mary Ann Keeley (1805–1899).

enter further than by two general observations: first, that I was subjected in cold blood, from motives which I will not characterise, to a series of studied and annoying and mortifying provocations, personal and professional. The second, that, suffering under these accumulated provocations, I was betrayed, in a moment of unguarded passion, into an intemperate and imprudent act, for which I feel, and shall never cease to feel, the deepest and most poignant self-reproach and regret. It is to you ladies and gentlemen, and to myself, that I owe this declaration, and I make it with unaffected sincerity. To liberal and generous minds, I think I need say no more. I cannot resist thanking you.' This seemed to affect many and engage the sympathies of all. Talfourd, Dow, Smith, Forster, Wallace, Maclise, and the editors of the *Post* and *Herald*, who wished a report of the speech, came into my room, but I was too nervous to have pleasure from their presence. . . .

May 13. Passed on to the Garrick Club, where I saw the evening papers of yesterday, which were all kind, and the *Times* of this day. It is difficult to speak or think with temper of such a nasty fellow as the conductor of this paper; it is a waste of honest indignation to lose words or thought on anything so profligate and flagitious. It copied my address, and added the falsest and most offensive comments it could apply. I could eat little dinner after reading it. . . .

May 14. I allowed my candle to burn till some time after one, and again woke in twilight at about three—lying in a very restless state both as to mind and body. *I am not what I have been! Ichabod! Ichabod!* It was a night of misery. The shoemaker Davies called about some sandals. I do not like the man; he is *inaccurate*. . . . A poor man called to ask for a subscription. I am in no state of mind to shut my heart or purse to the necessitous. Called at the office of Messrs White and Whitmore *[his solicitors]*. Found there that the process had been served by Evans, Bunn's attorney, and that they, W— and W—, had entered an appearance for me, so the battle is begun. . . . I returned to chambers. Forster called, and in referring to the blackguard behaviour of the *Times*, I could not speak. I covered my face with my grasping hands, and was obliged to go into the next room, where some cold water, etc., restored me to a composed appearance, and I returned with an appearance of cheerfulness. . . . Sent the advertisement of *Ion* to the newspapers. Came home by Bryant *[Coach to Elstree]*, whom I very nearly lost by being late. Read the kind, the very kind, notices in the *Court Journal* and the *Literary Gazette*. Had gone several miles before I could sufficiently withdraw my mind from this *hateful subject* to attend to anything; at length began to *try* to read *Ion*. Oh what a state am I in to read! . . .

May 15. Rehearsed *Stranger*. Talfourd and White came. Talfourd read *Ion* in the green-room, and was evidently happy in his employment. Who would not be? Should have acted the *Stranger* well, but was quite *bouleversé* by the *drunken* or *insane fustian* efforts of Mr Barnett in Steinfax*[sic]*. He was really disgusting. I was called for by the audience, but would not go on without Miss H. Faucit, whom I led forward. . . .

['The Stranger' was translated and adapted by Benjamin Thompson from the German of A. v. Kotzebue. (Drury Lane, 1798. The play in which Miss Fotheringay appeared as Mrs Haller at 'Chatteris' in the fourth chapter of Thackeray's 'Pendennis'.) Helen Faucit and Macready rehearsed together once only, on the morning of the performance. She wrote later: 'He came up to me and congratulated me very kindly upon my success, but with all this I feel very much afraid of him, there is something so cold and distant, and almost repulsive in his manner. I don't think I shall ever like him. Mr Macready took me on after the play, but how different his manner of doing it was to Mr Kemble's! I felt that he thought it a great bore. I may be wrong, but his manner gave me that impression.' The part of Steinfort was taken by Morris Barnett (1800–1856).]

May 19. Rehearsed *Ion*, which seems to me to *come out* in the acting— we shall see. Spoke about my name being put in the bills by Mr Osbaldiston after Mr Kemble's. This is to me of no importance, but I have no right to be placed out of my own rank before the public. They, as a body, know nothing of the art and only take their opinions from what they are told, therefore I have no right to let them be told what is not true and against my interest. A note from Heraud for tickets, which I answered, addressing him, 'My dear sir.' When my note had gone I perceived his style to me was 'My dear Macready.' I therefore wrote another note to despatch in the morning, that he may not think me repulsive or proud.

May 20. Acted Hamlet as well as I could under a most excruciating attack of rheumatism and much fatigue. I think I did much of the part well, though not so well as when last I played at Drury Lane: I was called for and made my obeisances. Knowles, Forster, and Talfourd afterwards came into my room. Talfourd talked much of his play; my cause seems quite an unimportant matter; he is right to revel in his happiness: he *deserves* it, he has earned it, and it is fit he should enjoy it. But the contrast of our several conditions now, and sixteen years ago, is most humiliating to me. I seemed then to have fortune and honour before me, and he was a clever, industrious young lawyer. *I am now a wretch!* . . .

May 21. A note from Bulwer told me that his play was rejected at Covent Garden.

May 26. Rehearsed *Ion* with much care. Went to the theatre and acted the character as well as I have ever played any previous one, with more of inspiration, more of complete abandonment, more infusion of myself into another being, than I have been able to attain in my performances for some time, particularly in the devotion of Ion to the destruction of Adrastus, the parting with Clemanthe, and the last scene. But . . . I lost my temper again tonight; a particular scene for a particular picturesque effect had been decided on in the morning and when I came to look at its disposition, I found another, to which I had objected in the morning, substituted for it. I was foolish enough to be *very angry*, very much agitated, and yet all passed off, and I might have been so much better by the government of my temper, which *effected nothing but my own exposure*. Oh! how bitter— how very bitter is the reflection that follows these unwise, unworthy transports of passion! Was called for very enthusiastically. . . . *[later, at Talfourd's]* I met Wordsworth,[1] who pinned me; Walter Savage Landor[2], to whom I was introduced, and, whom I very much liked; Stanfield, Browning, Price, Miss Mitford[3] —I cannot remember all. Forster came to me after supper, which was served in a very elegant style, and insisted that it was expected in the room that I should propose Talfourd's health, whose birthday it was. . . . *[He did so; Talfourd then proposed Macready's]* . . . It became a succession of personal toasts, Miss E. Tree, Miss Mitford, Mr Stanfield, Mr Price, Mr Poole,[4] who made a most egregious ass of himself; Browning, and who else I do not know. I was very happily placed between Wordsworth and Landor, with Browning opposite, and Mrs Talfourd next but one—Talfourd within two. I talked much with my two illustrious neighbours. Wordsworth seemed pleased when I pointed out the passage in *Ion*, of a 'devious fancy', etc., as having been suggested by the lines *he* had once quoted to me from a MS tragedy of his; he smiled and said. 'Yes, I noticed them,' and then he went on:

> 'Action is transitory—a step—a blow,
> The motion of a muscle—this way or that—
> 'Tis done; and in the after vacancy
> We wonder at ourselves like men betrayed.'[5]

[1] William Wordsworth (1770–1850), poet.
[2] Walter Savage Landor (1775–1864), poet and writer.
[3] Mary Russell Mitford (1787–1855), author of *Our Village*.
[4] John Poole (1786–1872), writer of comedies and farces.
[5] The passage from *Ion* occurs at the end of IV. iii, Ion's
>   What have I to forgive?
> A devious fancy, and a muscle raised
> Obedient to its impulse!

Landor, in speaking of dramatic composition, said he had not the constructive faculty, that he could only set persons talking, all the rest was chance. He promised to send me his play of *Count Julian*, and expressed himself desirous of improving his acquaintance with me. . . . We reached home about two, and went to bed with the birds singing their morning song in our tired ears.

Elstree, May 27. Rose, quite worn out—with a feeling of weariness and incapacity to employ myself that was almost distressing. . . .

London, May 30. . . . Received in bed a note from Forster requesting me to call or to receive him, as *Landor* was with him and desirous of seeing me. I could not get up and dress myself, and thus lost the pleasure of again seeing Landor. Went to the theatre *[Julius Caesar]*; the audience were rather noisy through the early scenes, but I was not disposed to yield to them. I do not think that my reception was quite as long as Kemble's, or I did not use sufficient generalship with it; but I acted Cassius in my very best style, and made the audience feel it. I was good; I was the character; I felt it. The audience were rapid and vehement in their applause. . . .

June 1. Rehearsed *Ion*, and have all the feeling of *second* night about me, and the uncomfortable addition of a strange actress, Miss H. Faucit, whom I do not like; she wants heart. . . . This lawsuit hangs heavy and wearingly upon my mind—my thoughts are prevented and dogged by the alternate conjectures and misgivings about this odious business. Went to the theatre. . . . I acted Ion but indifferently. . . .

[Ellen Tree acted Clemanthe on the first night. Against her will, for she thought it a bad part, Helen Faucit had consented to play at later performances. At the première on 26 May she had much admired Macready ('You hear with distinctness his lowest whisper . . . Mr P. Farren tells me it is not only the voice that causes this, but the clear and open articulation'). Rehearsals were difficult: 'There is something about Mr Macready that is quite awful. I wonder if I shall ever get over this silly feeling? I fear not; for I think, if I may judge from the freezing and proud coldness of his manner, he 'dislikes' me, and if so, he is not likely to be more agreeable in 'my' eyes. . . . I don't yet like him, nor do I think I ever can. Still there is something about him that commands one's respect.']

June 2. . . . Forster called. Went with me to the Temple, where I met Talfourd, Whitmore, and Gray. Talfourd said that Lord Denman had said the damages ought to be a farthing; but my nature is not sanguine. It was all but concluded on to let judgment go by default. I cannot, of course, be a judge in such a case. . . .

Elstree, June 7. . . . There was a fracas in the kitchen—the footman and housemaid fighting.

London, June 8. Before setting out to come to town by Billings, I had the disagreeable and painful task to perform of discharging Connor for his behaviour last night. This is the world! I am obliged to punish a fellow creature for the same vice—intemperance of conduct—in which I stand condemned. There is the aggravation of my servant's case, that he tried to raise his hand against a woman—an unpardonable offence. . . .

June 11. Mr Gray called, and talked over the matter of my lawsuits with the scoundrel Bunn—about which I am altogether in the dark. I have not even the power of a guess at the result, but my apprehensions picture something bad. A moment's indiscretion must be paid for by perhaps the labour of a year, whilst this fellow's villainy actually makes a premium for itself by the extent of his knavery—*it is too bad!* . . . I went to the theatre, where I saw Mr Osbaldiston, who would most gladly engage me for a succession of nights to continue the run of *Ion*. I acted Ion fairly—pretty well. . . .

This was the last performance of the season; but Macready signed with Osbaldiston to return in the autumn for twenty-two weeks at a salary of £40 a week, with 'half a clear benefit'. On 12 June he travelled into the provinces, first for an engagement on the Lincolnshire Circuit.

June 12. The principal, indeed the entire, occupation of my day was packing for my journey and my next Birmingham engagement. Forster called and remained for some time. . . . He seemed to think that Talfourd is quite in earnest about getting up *Ion* as 'private theatricals' and acting Ion himself. He alluded to it at supper last night, but I humoured what I supposed the joke. It begins to look serious, for private actors are very awful personages. . . .

Wisbech, June 13. . . . Acted Hamlet with a load on every limb, sore feet, and my mind in a doze. I was dissatisfied with myself and everyone about me. . . .

June 14. I looked into some papers, and saw that Mr Morris *[D. E. Morris, manager of the Haymarket]* was said to have obtained Talfourd's permission to perform *Ion* with Ellen Tree as Ion. Here was another instance of my exacting temper. I felt *displeased*. My interest was menaced and I only looked at my own supposed degree of damage. In strict justice, I do think that having arranged the play (which Talfourd would not have done successfully—see *his* version) and put it upon the stage, it is scarcely fair, before the attraction is decided as past, to turn over my labours to any other persons. But it is not *worth* caring for. . . .

June 15. Went to rehearsal, where I found Mrs Robertson, my Lady Macbeth—very old, poor woman, not very perfect, and cutting out the passage 'I have given suck,' etc., as too *horrible*! . . . *[at night]* Met the several checks to the abandonment of myself to Macbeth with tolerable evenness. Lady Macbeth acted, and hauled and patted me, and I endured most heroically—most philosophically. It was a trial. . . . *[Mrs Robertson was William Robertson's aunt.]*

He was at Birmingham from 19 June to 30 June.

June 27. Went to the theatre, and laboured under the great disadvantage of a *wretchedly* cast play: the Virginia, Icilius, Lucius, Numitorius were too bad for the smallest theatre. I really contended with the depressing effect of such disenchanting persons, and in the latter part of the play acted with some correctness and reality. . . .

Elstree, June 30. Was called earlier than I had ordered. . . . Paid my bill, which was a very exorbitant one, satisfied the servants, and passing through the market-place, which is very fine, went to the Nelson Hotel, from whence I set out at seven o'clock. At Brickhill Major Smith left us; an outside passenger had come in, and the guard lent him a *Morning Chronicle* of this day—which, as I caught a glimpse of the words Bunn *v.* Macready, I begged him to let me see for one instant. I looked for the damages, which I saw were £150. I felt relieved and satisfied as far as the pecuniary consideration went; but when he had read through the paper he handed it to me. I found the statement of Mr Thesiger—the plaintiff's counsel—to be a gross and scandalous misrepresentation from beginning to end: direct falsehood, most groundless inferences, and the basest imputations on my character. My agitation was so far suppressed as not to be visible to my fellow-passenger, but the wolf was tearing at my heart. My mind was away while he was speaking to me. I was suffering an inward torture, which only persons of acute sensibility can conceive or sympathise with. I could not confront the passengers who stayed at Redbourn to dinner but walked on with my *compagnon de voyage*. Reached home by a little after six, and found my dear family quite well.

[What Macready read on this return journey from Birmingham was that the assessment in damages in Bunn v. Macready (action for assault) had taken place on the previous day before Mr Under-Sheriff Burchell and a

jury, at the Sheriff's Court, Red Lion Square. Mr Frederick Thesiger and Mr Ogle were the plaintiff's counsel; Serjeant Talfourd and Mr Whitmore the defendant's. No evidence was given for the defendant, and damages were assessed at £150.

Frederick Thesiger (1794–1878) was later Lord Chelmsford and twice Lord Chancellor. Macready, violently enraged to know that Thesiger had called the assault 'unmanly, dastardly, and cowardly', wrote in his journal on 2 July about 'the mendacious assertions of a fee'd scoundrel', and never really forgave Talfourd for a poorly-judged speech of defence in what could be nothing but a lost cause.]

July 8. A note from Talfourd, with the information that he had concluded with Morris an agreement allowing him to perform *Ion* at the Haymarket theatre, and wishing the loan of my book, as marked for representation. This naturally caused me to think much upon the effects and motives of the proceeding. I had much rather it had not taken place, and something like dissatisfaction arose in my mind on perceiving the credit I had gained partially endangered by the possible success of a performer inferior in rank. A little consideration, however, made me see that selfishness was the mainspring of my reasonings, and that I thought chiefly of my interests and fame, as Talfourd, very justifiably, did of his. I cannot hope the experiment to succeed, and I trust it will not, as it cannot harm Talfourd by failure, and in its triumph may take much from me. Such is an actor's reputation! Walked in the garden, enjoying the freshness of the air and perfume of the flowers. Answered Talfourd, and sent him by Drinkwater the book requested, giving him the use of it till Tuesday or Wednesday. . . .

July 9. Heard with much satisfaction of the failure of Malibran's renowned engagement *[at Drury Lane]*. It is most unjust that a foreigner should be brought into a national theatre to receive enormous terms at the expense of the actors of the establishment.

On 2 August he played Virginius with a company of amateurs at Cambridge, and noted: 'The president of the club is a solicitor, which seems the aristocratic order of the club. I heard of no grade above it; an artist, an apothecary, stage-coachman, innkeeper, &c., make up the society for which I took a journey, gave up my time and labour, and very much inconvenienced myself.'

August 8. Went to the Haymarket to *Ion*; it was tiresome and sleepy to a degree; over at ten o'clock. Miss Tree's performance of Ion is a very pretty effort, and a very creditable woman's effort, but it is no more like a young man than a coat and waistcoat are. Vandenhoff was frequently very false and very tiresome; some things he did very well. The play was very drowsy, very unreal.

August 9. . . . Coming up—I think—Hanover Street I saw that dirty wretch Bunn arm-in-arm with Calcraft! I looked forth at them both, with a smile of contempt at that reptile, but the one *dared not* and the other *would not* look across the narrow street in which they *must have seen me*. It would be exacting, indeed, in me, if I could expect men should relinquish intimacies or friendships on my account—but here is quite a different case. Mr Calcraft told me yesterday that Mr Bunn was a coward; he has before told me that he would be hanged, and then changed his opinion on the conviction that he was too great a coward to peril his life in any way; he was privy to his rascality in cheating me in Dublin; he was privy to his cheating his friend, young Kean; Mr Bunn charged him with a dishonourable mode of getting the Dublin theatre into his own hands—and I see this person, whom I have essentially served, who holds a commission in the King's service, walking arm-in-arm and manifestly on terms of intimacy with a man whom he proclaims one of the greatest rascals living and an irreclaimable coward! Can I entertain respect for the character of Mr Calcraft? My suspicions—my strong suspicions of his mind and heart are confirmed.

Between 22 August and the beginning of October, Macready (with intervals at home) acted at such towns as Swansea, Cheltenham, Bristol, Shrewsbury, and Worcester.

Swansea, August 27. Went to the theatre and rehearsed *Ion*, which I no longer feel pleasure in performing. I feel, I fancy, rather *dégoûté* with Talfourd's 'delight' at seeing Miss Tree's performance in the part; if it is the author's feeling that it is the nasty sort of epicene animal which a woman so dressed up renders it, I am very loth to appear in it, and to this notion the author seems to lend his opinion.

Elstree, September 22. Wrote a letter, which I copied, to Miss Ellen Tree, expressing my desire to offer her a mark of regard, and suggesting a farewell Benefit as the most serviceable mode of doing so, mentioning Mr Osbaldiston's assent to the proposal of having it at Covent Garden theatre, and offering to do anything myself upon the occasion—to study Adrastus for her, if she would wish to have *Ion* for her play. I was glad when I had done it, as a kind thing to her, and an evidence to Talfourd and his friends that I had no unworthy feeling in respect to this play's subsequent performance.

Shrewsbury, September 27. . . . In thinking over Miss E. Tree's letter, I do not feel that it is quite responsive to the act of kindness shown to her. I may be mistaken, but the tone of the epistle is rather cold and, I think, *lofty*. I hope I misconceive it. Returning *[from rehearsal]* to my inn . . . I asked for the newspaper. I had read three pages of it, and one or two columns of the fourth—it was the *Standard*—when my eyes struck upon the words: '*Malibran is no more!*' The loudest clap of thunder in the calmest sunshine could not have given me a greater start. I felt as if my mind was stunned; it was a shock that left me no power to think for some little time. I read on, when recovered from the horror and surprise of the news, and was quite restored by the stuff—the *newspaper sentiment* and string of falsehoods that went to disfigure the melancholy and affecting truth of one—in youth, so rich in talent, once so lovely, with so much to enchant and fascinate, and so much to blame and regret —suddenly taken from a world so full of delight to her, and to which she was so frequently a minister of delight. I once could have loved her, and she has since said that she loved—'was in love with'—me. Had I known it for certain, I might have been more miserable than I am. Latterly, she had decreased in my regard, and in my esteem she had no place. This world is a sad loss to her, and she to it. Poor Malibran!

[Malibran (Madame Malibran de Beriot) had arrived in Manchester from Brussels on 10 September to sing at the coming music festival. On 14 September, after repeating, with Madame Caradori, a duet from Merca-dante's 'Andronico', she was taken ill, and on 23 September, at the age of twenty-eight, she died. For some time she had been overtaxing her strength.]

Worcester, October 1. A Mr Brough saluted me from the coach that met us, and came down to speak to me—for the *sake of speaking* to me. One of his fellow-passengers, who had learned from him who I was, accosted me (!)—told me I was anxiously looked for at Worcester. I bowed. He went up to his coach, and I suppose told someone inside that I was on this coach. I heard the vulgar fellow say: "Ask him how Mr Bunn is?" On which this person again approached the box where I sat, and said: 'Pray, how is Mr Bunn?' I suppose I looked rather surprised, but said nothing. The man laughed very loudly, and seemed to think it a very witty thing. I do not know whether he was intoxicated or no. . . .

Macready opened a twenty-two weeks' Covent Garden engagement, at forty pounds a week, with 'that very ignorant and incapable man', Osbaldi-ston. He began on 3 October with 'Macbeth'.

October 4. At the theatre, whither I went to rehearse *King John* and *Werner*, was much amused by [Charles] Kemble, when I met him, not offering to shake hands with me, and it occurred to me that the reception of the play last night *[Macbeth]* might have cooled his cordiality. *I believe it to be so.* Spoke to Mr Osbaldiston about Miss Tree's Benefit. Called on her after rehearsal and sat some time with her; she seemed very grateful for my disposition to serve her. . . . Forster told me of a tragedy which Browning had completed in ten days (!) on the subject of Strafford. I cannot put faith in its dramatic qualities—the thing seems, not to say incredible, but almost impossible. *I cannot place reliance on the world.*

October 10. Called on Forster, at whose chambers I saw Browning, who had not yet finished his play, which I think a circumstance to rejoice at. An application for relief from Mr Y——, an indifferent actor and not a good man. He strove to run his sword into my father on the stage at Manchester, and when my father asked him why he was so violent, he said: 'Because you struck me, sir!' which, in the character of Cassio, my father had to do. I gave him what I ought not to have given him. Went to theatre. Acted Macbeth as badly as I acted well on Monday last. The gallery was noisy, but that is no excuse for me; I could not feel myself in the part. I was labouring to play Macbeth; on Monday last I *was* Macbeth. Mr Pritchard came into my room to try over the fight and asked me not to 'strike so hard'. I observed to him that he struck much harder than I did, to which he replied: 'Yes, but I am obliged to do it' . . . I said I could not act gently on purpose, and that it was a mere accident that he was struck; he was disposed to be very absurd, and said that I had 'damned him' on the previous night. This I declare to be a shameful *falsehood*. I never uttered a word to him. He made me extremely angry and threw me into great agitation, just as I was going on the stage. I was *very much to blame—very much indeed*—for losing my presence of mind, and especially to such a fool, for he is really no better. Oh, God! Oh, God! *Shall I never learn to act with wisdom?*

[Edwin Forrest (1806–1872), an American actor who would be Macready's bitter rival. William Winter called him 'a vast animal, bewildered by a grain of genius.' His first Drury Lane performance, preceded by vigorous publicity, was as Spartacus in 'The Gladiator', by the American dramatist Robert M. Bird, a tragedy that 'offered abundant opportunities for muscular exertion, ferocious passion, and reiteration of the freedom-loving sentiments he held so dear' (Richard Moody: 'Edwin Forrest', 1960).]

October 14. Went to Adam Street, to the Garrick Club, to Covent

Garden theatre, inquiring for the address of Mr Forrest; called at Mr Hughes's for it, and found him there. Like him much—a noble appearance, and a manly, mild, and interesting demeanour. I welcomed him—wished him success, and invited him to my house. He mentioned to me his purpose of leaving the stage, and devoting himself to politics—if he should become President! In going to the Club, I met Mr Bartley, who told me that Mr Forrest would do, that his play was good, and he himself likely to hit. This I could *sincerely wish*, while it did no injury to myself; but my home is so dear to me that charity must satisfy itself there before it can range abroad.

Elstree, October 15. Rose late, and canvassed with my counsel of the Home Department the best mode of arrangement in inviting Mr Forrest to our home. Wrote a note of invitation to him.

London, October 17. Dow called, and brought me the news of the Drury Lane representation, viz. that Mr Forrest had quite succeeded, and that the play had been as completely damned. His opinion was that he was a very good actor, but he did not think him a great one. I cannot of course have, as yet, any opinion; but this I know, that when I saw him nine years ago, he had everything within himself to make a very great actor.

October 18. Woke late and much fatigued. . . . Looked at *The Times* for the account of Mr Forrest, whom they pronounced to be 'more spirited than any tragic actor now on the stage'. It is not surprising; the only wonder is how I have retained any spirit at all. . . . Acted Ion, judging from the little applause, *very feebly*, and yet I strove to be in earnest and energetic. Miss [Faucit] would make me think, if I were a young man, that she had designs upon me—but I suppose it is all the truth of acting.

October 19. Called on Forster, and learned there that my misgivings about Talfourd's coldness were not ill-founded; he has taken some caprice into his head, and is weak enough to indulge it. I am sorry, very sorry, for this; but it is most unjust, for I have ever acted honestly, zealously, and with pure disinterestedness in my whole course of friendship with him. He has twice sought my intimacy, and I suppose will twice relinquish. This is not well—but here is the *rise* of pride. Very very unworthy.

October 20. Wrote to Forster urging him to deal liberally and kindly by Forrest in his notice. Began to read *Othello*, which occupied me the whole evening. Debated upon the propriety of writing a note to Talfourd, but am so entirely at a loss to guess at the cause of his conduct that I really know not how.

William Charles Macready, 1843. From an engraving of a miniature by Robert Thorburn, A.R.A.

Edwin Forrest, aged 45.

Alfred Bunn.

October 21. *[Othello]* . . . Suffered very much from want of self-possession—in truth from want of time to have prepared myself. Very fortunately there was a riot from the exceeding crowd in the theatre, which made, I fancy, other persons as nervous as myself, and I was pleased and encouraged on hearing the other actors in the play receive as little applause as myself—if indeed they did not meet with less. But in the third act of *Othello* I rose into energy, though wanting finish, and produced a great deal of applause; in fact, I felt myself lauded, but I was very much distressed. I held the audience through the play, and was called for at the end; when I went on, I was very enthusiastically received.

Elstree, October 22. It was a great relief—a great gratification to me to read in *The Times* a very laudatory notice of my Othello.

[Forrest played Othello at Drury Lane just after Macready had appeared in the same part at Covent Garden. Though Forrest had generally good notices, Forster attacked him in the 'Examiner', asserting that the public taste must be guarded against a vicious style in art of which Forrest was one of the professors.]

London, October 24. My spirits were very low, and I had begun the page on which I am now writing, when old Dow—staunch old Dow—came in; shortly after him, Forster. They gave me an account of Mr Forrest's performance of Othello. It would be stupid and shallow hypocrisy to say that I was indifferent to the result—careless whether he is likely to be esteemed less or more than myself; it is of great importance to me to retain my superiority, and my wishes for his success follow the desire I have to be considered above him! Is this illiberal? I hope not. Their accounts of his performance have certainly reduced very much my opinion of his mind, which from the particulars they related cannot be of the highest order. Forster says that he will be greatly praised in the papers, but both agree that he will not attract.

October 25. Looked at the newspapers with great anxiety for the account of Mr Forrest's Othello. *The Times*[1] had a most insidious article—a *Times* article!—upon which, if charged, it would disclaim all intention of comparison, but intended to convey the idea of superiority in Mr Forrest, still unable to use strong terms of praise—to apologise for and offer excuses and reasons for *much* which it admitted to be feeble and ineffective. The *Herald* and *Post* were both qualified; felt the performance not to have been a thoroughly successful one. . . . Lay down, my spirits depressed by the unfair tone of the newspapers, and read over

[1] Macready's syntax suffers from his emotion.

Othello. At the theatre there was a violent disturbance from the over-crowded state of the pit; the audience demanded that the money should be returned, the play could not be heard. Charles Kemble went forward, addressed the audience, spoke to Mr Wallack [Henry Wallack (1790–1870), stage manager at Covent Garden]—but by merely temporising he effected nothing. The first scene ended in dumb show. Mr H. Wallack went forward in the next scene, but his speech was shuffling, evasive—anything but an answer to the downright demand of 'Return the money!' The audience would not allow the play to proceed, and at last, after speaking to Mr Vandenhoff, I went forward. I said that 'under the circumstances of peculiar inconvenience from which so many seemed to be suffering, I scarcely knew what to say, and that if I should say anything that might appear to give offence either to them or the management, I hoped I should stand excused; but as the only means of remedy-ing the present inconvenience and relieving both those who were desirous of going and those who wished to remain, if the ladies or gentle-men who could not obtain room would require their money from the doorkeeper, and tell him to charge it to my account, I should be most happy to be responsible for it.' The whole house cheered very enthusi-astically, and like the sea under the word of Neptune, the waves were instantly stilled. Kemble said afterwards, 'If he had thought of it, he should have said the same, but it never entered his head.' Voilà Kemble!

October 27. I sent in to Forster, and heard further from him of the set that is making against me to elevate Mr Forrest. This is ungenerous, but as I did not wish to be an ungenerous rival to him, I again requested Forster not to write in harshness or hostility upon his performance. He was very peremptory and distinct in his expressed resolution to keep his own course. At Garrick Club I saw the papers—the Morning Herald also of yesterday, of which the Editor ought to be ashamed. It was an effort to abuse and depreciate me, but in the most positive manifestation of his own ignorance the writer seemed as if he could not or dared not—I do not know what he means. The playbills of Drury Lane pronounce Mr Forrest the 'most extraordinary actor of the day'. He has never been cheated by, nor punished the writer—it is therefore true! Saw Kemble, Fladgate, and Price, who came to me with a list of names for a compli-mentary dinner to Mr Forrest, asking me to put my name to it. I had no alternative, but it is very indelicate, to say the very least, that an Ameri-can should thus make himself a party in such a business. [Stephen Price (1783–1840), American speculative showman, who managed the Park Theatre in New York for thirty years, had been lessee of Drury Lane in 1826–1828.]

October 28. Mr G. Dance told me that C. Kemble had been appointed without solicitation to the office of Licenser *vice* George Colman,[1] who died the day before yesterday. How poorly he has shrunk out of existence—a man of some talent, much humour, and little principle. Fortune seems to shower her benefits on those who certainly from their talents and virtues can make little claim to them. For character, look at C. Kemble—what he really *is* and what he *passes for!* I feel discontented (am I envious?) at seeing place and wealth conferred so unmeritedly; but thus it almost always has been, and I suppose ever will be. They called me to go on the stage, but I heard one or two voices roaring out 'Vandenhoff'. and I declined the honour. I do not know if they had him on. Talfourd came into my room and seemed very glad to see me. Dow walked home with me and sat very late. I expressed to him strongly how very much annoyed and distressed I felt at Forster's expressed resolution to write a severe article on Mr Forrest; he being known to be a friend of mine, my situation was particularly painful.

October 29. Read Forster's criticism on Mr Forrest, which gave me very great pain. I thought it ill-natured and not just—omitting all mention of his merit, with the enumeration of his faults. I would have done much to have prevented it. Forster came, and I expressed candidly my dissatisfaction to him.

October 30. Browning arrived, told me of a most exaggerated notice of Mr Forrest's Othello in the *Athenæum*—'Decius (Mr C. Dance) was once my friend'; he is now the close ally of Mr Price, and thus we obtain just and correct criticism. Whilst I was dressing, Messrs Forrest, S. Price and Jones arrived. We talked in the drawing-room with Browning and Dow, till the arrival of Talfourd and Mr T. R. Price and White. Introduced all to Forrest. Asked him to take Mrs Macready down. Spent an agreeable and cheerful afternoon. My American friends did not return to the drawing-room. I was very much relieved from any feeling of regret I may have felt in learning from Talfourd that he thought Forster's article in the *Examiner* borne out in its fidelity by the evidence it gave; he thought it well done.

London, *October* 31. Forster and Browning called. Browning who, said his play of *Strafford* was finished, soon left. . . . Went to Garrick Club, where I dined and saw newspapers—and puffings of Mr Forrest in all directions: 'Macready's opinion of Mr Forrest: "Sir, there has been nothing like him since Kemble"!' Fact! *Globe.* This is rather too bad. My spirits were low. Every one around me seems helped on by fortune;

[1] George Colman, the younger (1762–1836), dramatist; theatrical manager; ultimately Licenser of Plays.

I have the dogged course of labour to pursue, with all its uncertainties. Acted King John tolerably well—the second scene with Hubert better than before by *taking time* between the periods of passion:

November 2. Read Bulwer's play of the *Duchess of La Vallière* in Mr Osbaldiston's room. The actors and actresses were, or seemed to be, very much pleased with the play, but I cannot put much confidence in them. . . .

November 3. Called on Miss Martineau,[1] who told me of many friends she had seen in the United States, and of her intended book upon the country. I was surprised and sorry to hear her say of Webster[2] that his private character was bad. Alas! Alas! She liked Clay[3] the best of the American statesmen. . . .

November 4. Acted Othello—not perhaps quite equally—but, taking one part with another, very fairly. Is Miss [Faucit] disposed to coquette with me? I cannot quite understand her. . . .

November 10. . . . Mr W. Jones[4] was behind the scenes [at Covent Garden] and I was talking to him. I asked him to step into my room after the play; inquired of him when Forrest's engagement was likely to close, as I should like to pay some professional compliment to him. He said it was uncertain, it might end in a week or go on for months. He added that Mr Forrest was very much gratified by the attention I had paid him. I told him I wished to be pleased with his visit, and, while speaking on the subject, in strict confidence, wished to observe that the articles which were so severe in the *Examiner*, having been written by Mr Forster, who was a particular friend of mine, I begged to assure him that, knowing Mr Forster's opinion of Mr Forrest to be less flattering than that of other persons and other newspapers, I had used all my influence with him—by word of mouth, by writing, and by the mediation of friends, to induce him to abandon his intention of expressing an unfavourable opinion; that he had yielded partially in his first review, but had peremptorily and repeatedly refused to suppress or qualify his opinion on the subsequent performances. Jones said that it had been said the articles were *through me,* but that neither he nor Mr Forrest had ever given attention to the insinuations and assertions of the base persons

---

[1] Harriet Martineau (1802–1876), author.
[2] Daniel Webster (1782–1852), American orator and statesman.
[3] Henry Clay (1777–1852), American statesman; defeated by James Polk in the Presidential election of 1844.
[4] Thomas Willis Jones, who was at first Forrest's London adviser; later, and amicably, Forrest entrusted his affairs to Bunn. Jones, as manager of the Richmond Theatre, had persuaded the young Helen Faucit to make her first tentative appearance there.

who are to be found about a theatre. I observed to him, that to contradict any such persons would be quite beneath me; that if my character were vulnerable to the attacks of such persons as Mr Westmacott, etc., it really was not worth the care necessary for its preservation. He told me that Talfourd had sent him, Mr Forrest, his play of *Ion* with a very kind note, which he had pointed to in refutation of *my* interference to his prejudice, and that Forrest was more gratified by my calling on him, etc., than by anything he had met with here.

November 19. Browning came with Dow to bring me his tragedy of *Strafford;* the fourth act was incomplete. I requested him to write in the plot of what was deficient. Dow drove me to the Garrick Club, while Browning wrote out the story of the omitted parts. I found remaining of the party of eighteen who sat down to the dinner given to Mr Forrest—himself, Talfourd (in the chair), Mr Blood opposite, S. Price, C. Kemble, W. Jones, Zachary (!), Dance, Murphy, Raymond, and three others unknown. I greeted Forrest, and told him I was anxious to be among his hosts; Talfourd mentioned that my health had been drunk very cordially, but repeated it in my presence. I was drunk to, and briefly stated that 'the attention was unexpected; that I came to pay, not to receive, a compliment; and could assure my highly-talented friend that no one extended the hand of welcome to him more fervently or sincerely than myself, in doing which I only endeavoured to repay a small part of the debt of gratitude which had been heaped on me by the kindness of his countrymen, etc. C. Kemble wished that we should take wine together, which we did. Browning and Dow soon summoned me, and I received the MS, started in a cab to Kilburn, where I found a chaise, *vice* fly, waiting for me. I bought a couple of cigars and smoked to Edgware. Got comfortably to Elstree and found, thank God, all in tolerable health.

[When Macready and Browning had been fellow-guests of Talfourd on 26 May 1836, after the first night of 'Ion', Macready had said as they left the house: 'Write a tragedy, Browning, and keep me from going to America.' Browning, who had revised the manuscript of Forster's just-published life of Thomas Wentworth, Earl of Strafford, during the author's illness, replied: 'Shall it be historical or English? What do you say to Strafford?'

Blood was a singer, Charles Dance a dramatist and critic, Francis Stack Murphy a Serjeant-at-Law, and George Raymond the author of a life of Elliston, the actor-manager. After this occasion Forrest wrote to an American friend that Macready's 'delicate courtesies and attentions demonstrated his great refinement, good breeding, and the native kindness of his heart.']

Elstree, November 20. Applied myself to the perusal of Browning's MS of *Strafford*. I was greatly pleased with it, read portions of it to Catherine and Letitia. My little remainder of the day was spent with my darling children—playing with and telling them stories.

London, November 21. Browning called in some anxiety to have my opinion of his play. I told it frankly, and he was very much pleased, agreeing in my objections, and promising to do everything needful to the play's amendment. He sat very long. Read some part of Brutus—acted the part—partially well—not altogether. . . .

Elstree, November 23. Began *very attentively* to read over the tragedy of *Strafford* in which I find more grounds for exception than I had anticipated. I had been too much carried away by the truth of character to observe the meanness of plot, and occasional obscurity. Went into the garden to induce my children to exercise; set them at play and returned to my work on *Strafford*.

London, November 24. Browning called, and I told him that I could not look at his play again until Bulwer's was produced, in which he acquiesced. Dow called when I was trying to snatch a few minutes' sleep; he told me that the *Age* abused me in Brutus for having a '*pug nose* and *massive* face', *I laughed sincerely*. Acted Brutus very well, better on the whole than I think I had done before. . . .

November 30. Went to rehearsal. Bulwer came with Forster; went over part of the play. Is the frank—the volunteered expression of admiration and partiality on the part of Miss [Faucit] simplicity, deceit, coquetry, *or* passion? I really do not know, but suspect that neither the first nor last have much to do with it. Mr Farren has, in my mind, seriously injured this play by his intrusion of himself into the part of Lauzun. He does not understand it. He is a very, *very ignorant* man.

[Macready had wanted William Farren, the comedian, to play the small comic part of M. de Montespan; but Farren insisted on the important part of the Duke de Lauzun (the smooth villain) which Charles Kemble had declined. G.H. Lewes, in 'On Actors and the Art of Acting', said of Farren (1786–1861) that, in spite of his fine qualities, he had none of the personal regard usually felt for public favourites: 'He had no geniality; he had no gaiety; there was none of the fervid animation which acts like electricity upon the speaker.']

Sent coat of arms to Johnson and Allen, coachmakers. I already repent the order for the carriage, and wish my money in my pocket and the horse in Yorkshire. Acted King John tolerably well, but was much less applauded than either Miss Faucit or Kemble. I do not think that *low prices* raise the judgment of the audience, for they hail rant and roar with an ardent spirit of reciprocity. *[At the beginning of Osbaldiston's management he had lowered Covent Garden prices considerably.]*

December 1. Saw the papers and was amused to read the *Times'* criticism on Mr Forrest's Macbeth[1]—as 'inferior to his former efforts—in the last act tame and not sufficiently studied—deficient in that robust power, which is the main characteristic and essential quality of his acting'—his 'variations of tone not in accordance with the text'; but 'it is *questionable* if his second act could be surpassed by any actor now on the stage—on the whole, considering the state of the stage, the performance is entitled to considerable praise.' Has Forster said worse than this? He has spoken truth honestly and not like a craven parasite, as the writer of this recanting article is. *It is too bad.* Went to the Garrick Club; took up *Post*, saw that it was a flaming panegyric upon Macbeth, about which even the playbills are cold, and laid it down again. Saw a notice of myself in Brutus in the *Athenæum*—trash!

December 7. Went to rehearsal of *La Vallière*. Mrs Glover observed to me, hoping I should not be offended at the observation, that she had never seen such an improvement in any person as in myself lately. I told her I was extremely gratified to hear her say so, since every art needed study and was progressive in its course towards perfection. Rehearsed Bragelone. I cannot make out Miss [Faucit].

[Mrs (Julia) Glover (1779–1850), famous comedienne, was the actress who fainted on the stage during the final scene of Kean's Sir Giles Overreach in 'A New Way to Pay Old Debts'.]

December 9. Went much fatigued to an early rehearsal of *La Vallière*, of which I begin to entertain strong and painful apprehensions. Mr Farren does not convey to me the least tinge of resemblance in the character of Lauzun. Webster seems very unmeaning and inefficient in Montespan; Vandenhoff not very impassioned in the King, Miss Pelham awfully bad in Madame Montespan, and Miss Faucit frequently feeble and monotonous in La Vallière. I do not feel that I can do anything worthy of myself in the part, but I will do my utmost. Bulwer and Count D'Orsay were at rehearsal. The necessity of deferring the play until after Christmas was suggested, and upon reflection espoused by Bulwer. Dined at that vulgar place, the Garrick Club, where the principal conversation is eating, drinking, or the American Presidency! . . .

[Benjamin Nottingham Webster (1797–1882), actor. Manager of the

---

[1] Forrest's Drury Lane engagement continued until 19 December.

Haymarket Theatre, 1837–1853. Miss Pelham was a minor Covent Garden actress.]

December 13. Called on Forster, and proposed to him to write a courteous valedictory notice of Mr Forrest, disclaiming personal feelings and paying a tribute to his private character. Forster very decidedly refused—upon the belief or suspicion that Mr Forrest had looked, if not with a gratified, at least an indifferent eye upon the attacks that had been made upon me.

December 20. Browning called and left with me the omitted scenes in his play. I called on Forster, who reported to me of Mr Forrest's *Virginius* last night that it was the worst of his performances—he almost seems now in each new character to fit to himself the line, 'but worse remains behind.' *[Macready regarded Virginius as his own part. Forrest chose it for his Drury Lane farewell and benefit night; Sheridan Knowles, the author, appeared in the cast, and afterwards the Drury Lane company presented Forrest with a gold snuff-box.]* . . .

I have performed for the last time with Mr C. Kemble who had been playing Mark Antony—my professional account is closed with him, and I part with him without regret or esteem. As an artist, I think him by comparison *good* in second and third-rate characters; *excellent* in parts of them, as in the drunkenness of Cassio, but complete in scarcely any, great in none, and very bad in those of a *higher class*. There is no *character*, no assumption in anything he does—the only difference between the serious scenes of Cassio and Mark Antony are, with him, a Roman-looking dress in this and in the other doublet and hose.

December 24. After breakfast I lost some time in calculating and reflecting on my means, and my chance of increasing them. Last night Mr C. Kemble left the stage with an income of, at least I should suppose, £1200. Seven years ago—or indeed five years ago, this man, after having enjoyed an excellent income all his married life, was *worse than nothing!* With a moderate degree of talent, without learning, without one amiable or estimable trait of character, he makes us wonder at his good fortune, and would create discontent and doubt in the minds of those who believed the recompenses of Providence to be distributed in this world. It has been his luck—and luck, as the sun shines, smiles indiscriminately.

December 28. Called at Johnson and Allen's, where I saw our new carriage and gave order for horses to it, desiring Mr Johnson to call and be paid. Paid Mr Johnson £100 for the carriage. Placed dearest Catherine and Willie in it, with my secret wishes that they might long enjoy it.

II
The Leader (1837–1840)

'No exertion will be spared in presenting the National Drama, whether as a branch of literature or as a department of art, with every advantage.' *Announcement of Macready's second season at the Theatre Royal, Covent Garden (September 1838).*

1837

January 2. Acted Lord Hastings [*Jane Shore* by Nicholas Rowe] very, very ill indeed, in the worst possible taste and style. I really am ashamed to think of it; the audience applauded, but I deserve some reprobation. I have no right to trifle with any, the least important, character; whatever is good enough to play is good enough to play well, and I could have acted this character very well if I had prepared myself as I should have done. Without study I can do nothing. I am worse than a common nightly drudge.

January 4. [*The Duchess de la Vallière*] . . . Acted Bragelone well, with earnestness and freshness; some passages were deficient in polish. Being called for, I did not choose to go on without Miss Faucit, whom I led forward. The applause was fervent, but there had been considerable impatience manifested through the play, which did not end until eleven o'clock. I fear it will not have any considerable success. Dow, Fitzgerald[1] Browning, Talfourd and his son Frank, C. Buller,[2] came into my room; they all seemed to think much of my performance, but otherwise thought the play much under-acted. It was *shamefully performed*. Bulwer came in when they had gone, and in most energetic and ardent manner thanked me for my performance, and for making him cut out the first scene of the fifth act, which I had done. Mr Standish took Forster and myself to Lady Blessington's;[3] Count D'Orsay and herself received me most warmly. We had too rich a supper; our talk was all on the play. Bulwer did not seem happy—his mind was 'away! away!' . . . [He] drove me home, all his talk was *La Vallière*.

January 5. Sent for the newspapers; they were all in a faint tone, except *The Times* which was maliciously abusive. [*'It is in the worst taste of the worst school, the school of the modern French romance. We have all but an enforcement under the crucifix. . . .'*] . . . Forster called, and accompanied me to the theatre, where the process of cutting was in act. Bulwer was there; Forster proposed his own rearrangement, which was acceded to. Mr Farren came to explain to me that 'merely to oblige the

[1] Edward Marlborough Fitzgerald, journalist.
[2] Charles Buller, M.P.
[3] Marguerite, Countess of Blessington (1789–1849), novelist. Hostess at Gore House, Kensington, in association with her stepson-in-law, the French dandy, Alfred Guillaume, Count D'Orsay (1801–1852), who liked to be known as the 'general *arbiter elegantiarum* of London society'.

theatre, Mr Bulwer, etc., he had undertaken Lauzun, which was not in his line'; this part, and only this the man insisted on doing, and was certainly one of the causes of the play's ill-success. . . .

January 6. Bulwer and Forster called, and after talking on the proposed omission of the third act, on which I did not feel competent to speak decisively, they left me to urge it on Mr Osbaldiston. I agreed that it was a desperate experiment, but perhaps worth making. Acted pretty well. I thought Miss Faucit was inclined to play some tricks to mar my effects, but it did not much disconcert me. I was called for, and went on; as far as I could judge, the play seemed to run on very smoothly, but I heard that there was disapprobation expressed at the short third act—not ten minutes long! Bulwer, full of delight at my performance, came into my room with Forster. They have concocted some plan for a new scene for me—to which I decidedly objected; indeed, as far as I can judge, it would destroy the character.

January 7. A note from Bulwer was couched in the strongest terms, asking as 'a personal favour' that I would act the scene he had written and sent me. I did not stay to read the scene, but wrote back by his servant to say that I could not resist the impulse of striving to show my appreciation of the honour he had done me, and that I would do it. Forster called, and I explained to him wherein I thought it hazardous and impolitic, but he seemed to regard it as another desperate stroke to retrieve the cast-down nature of Bulwer's fame. I felt it so and did not repent having assented.

Elstree, January 8. Read over—both to correct and to study—the introduced scene of Bragelone. *There is nothing in it*, and no play can derive strength from a scene which is not missed when omitted, and which does not contain some new and striking effect with regard to the character. I think this has no power, and is merely to make time!—the worst motive for a scene.

London, January 10. Forster called, and I inquired of him how far I was right in the alterations I had made in the scene. He smiled at me, which decided me in retaining the original of Bulwer—which was very feeble. Went to theatre, anxious to make an effort with Bragelone, but did not act the part to satisfy myself, being disconcerted by the inaudibility of Miss Faucit, who was ill, and the nervousness I endured about the new scene. . . . Bulwer came into my room, and was in very good spirits. I did not myself feel the play to go as well as he, Messrs Osbaldiston and Wallack seemed to think it had done; and I fear the report of it will not be very cordial. Bulwer took Forster and myself in his cab to the Albion, Aldersgate Street, where the Garrick Club gave their complimentary dinner to C. Kemble. . . . I was beckoned soon to the cross-table and taken there by Captain Williams and placed between Sir G. Warrender and Standish. Sir G. Warrender introduced me to the Chairman, Lord Francis Egerton.[1] Mr Knowles returned thanks for the dramatic authors in a very rambling drunken speech—it was nothing, and a little worse. Captain W—— had come to me twice or three times, to ask me to return thanks when 'The stage and its professors' was drunk. I declined, but saw at last that I had no power of retreat. The toast was given by Mr S. Price, in rather a confused manner, and his want of self-possession restored my confidence. I replied . . . as good a complimentary effusion as J could hope to make, where my heart was not interested and my esteem was not conciliated. Supped on oysters, as I came home with Forster. I forgot to notice Mr Yates's speech, which was in the worst style and taste of the worst green-room.

January 11. A note from Bulwer with the altered passage of the introduced scene; informing me also that Mr Farren had written to him to be removed from the part of Lauzun; really the ignorant effrontery of this empty coxcomb is most offensive.

January 17. After dinner read over the part of Bragelone. Bulwer has, I fear, added very little to the general effect of the play by the insertion of the new scene, and in my particular case he has done actual mischief. If he has not diminished the interest by lessening the probability (which I think, he has) in the too sudden change of Bragelone from the warrior to the monk—yet he has so flurried me, so thrown me off my centre by the want of due preparation and proper harmonising of the scene with the rest of the character, and so distresses me nightly by the hurry and fret into which I am thrown by the very brief allowance of time for my metamorphosis, that I am confident he would have acted more judiciously in leaving the play as it stood on the third night—or of restoring some other person's scene. Acted Bragelone as well as I could, but not well. I am *spoiled* in it by Bulwer's injudicious amendments. There was disapprobation at the end of the play. *['La Vallière' was performed for only nine nights.]*

Macready went to Manchester, and later to Dublin.

Manchester, February 6. Clarke talked much of Mr C. Kean, giving his opinion that he would not succeed in London, that he did not

[1] Lord Francis Egerton (1800–1857), author, politician, and afterwards first Earl of Ellesmere.

improve; it is natural to ask how should he. He observed that he was *arrogant* and extravagant—lived at hotels and squandered the money. This young man ought to have started into wisdom from the sight and consequence of his father's follies and vices, but it is not improbable that he has been spoiled. It is very hard (qu. is it possible?) for a person on the stage to preserve a well-regulated mind.

Dublin, March 3. Today I am forty-four years of age. Before I left my bed, I gave my mind to long and earnest reflection on the occurrences of my past life—on the unhappiness which, in my portion of good and ill, had fallen to my lot, and of its cause. Most of it is to be traced to myself, to my own violent passions, to the want of self-direction and command under events, which seemed at war with my interests or feelings. The necessity of renewing and increasing my efforts to subdue my will; to bring my irritable will under the strong curb of reason; to think less of myself in relation to others; to extirpate the envious and vindictive feelings which still lurk within my disposition; the indispensable necessity of this regenerating my mind . . . appeared clearly and palpably to me.

March 11. . . . Acted the tragedy scene of Puff in *The Critic* very well for the last time that I ever will appear in that part—it is *infra dig*.

March 12. *[on leaving Dublin]*—. . . Calcraft *[the manager]* observed that I had not dined with him during my stay. I recalled to him that he had been twice in London for long periods and had never come to our house, and that I kept away from him designedly. He seemed rather relieved in thinking that was the sole cause. I did not choose to tell him —it was not my business—that I had met him arm-in-arm with Mr Bunn shortly after he had been struck by me.

Elstree, March 20. Forster and Browning arrived—cheerful evening —though more of the conversation turned on Dow than I could have wished. Browning related an amusing story of his application to him for an epitaph on his father—to which, when Browning had promised it, he added his mother, her sister, and an infant two years old; and subsequently, on receiving the report of the marble-mason of Barnsley, wished two more lines to be added to the complete epitaph as the stone would hold two more! . . .

March 21. Browning came with me into the study, and with much interruption over the discussion of points and passages, we read through his tragedy of *Strafford;* I must confess my disappointment at the management of the story—I doubt its interest. Walked out with Browning round the reservoir. After dinner Browning and myself resumed our conversation about *Strafford*, and I resolved—seeing no other means—

to read it again to-night—after tea I did so, but I am by no means sanguine, I lament to say, on its success.

March 22. Resumed with Browning the conversation of last night on *Strafford;* showed the necessity—as far as Mr Osbaldiston was concerned—of his direct declarations, yes or no, as to his ability to give the finished play on Saturday. After some deliberation he decided in the negative, and preferred withholding the play till my Benefit. He seemed to think much of the objections and suggestions I had offered. He left us. Looked over the play of the *Death of Socrates* by a person signing himself 'Nemo'. If he is not deranged, he is the most enormous ass I have yet encountered. . . .

March 25. On coming downstairs I gave my attention to the remainder of the heap of MS. that awaited my examination. Looked over *Pandolfo*—trash! *Corsair*—do. *Robert the Bruce*—id. *Recluse*—better. *Lass of Hawthorndene*—ohlie Hieland—trash. *Marriage-à-la-mode*—trash. Read over *verbatim* Mr Solly's play, *Gonzaga di Capponi*—in which there is some talent—and by that cleared off my debt of MSS.

London, March 28. . . . A youth called to know if I taught elocution, and on my information he went off very abruptly. . . .

March 29. Browning called and brought me the play of *Strafford;* he looked very unwell, jaded, and thought-sick. . . .

March 30. I read to Mr Osbaldiston the play of *Strafford;* he caught at it with avidity, agreed to produce it without delay on his part, and to give the author £12 per night for twenty-five nights, and £10 per night for ten nights beyond. He also promised to offer Mr Elton an engagement to strengthen the play. Browning and Forster came in; I had the pleasure of narrating what had passed between Mr Osbaldiston and myself, and of making Browning very happy; I went over the memoranda I had made of corrigenda in his MS; the suggestion of the children's voices being heard in the pause following the announcement of Strafford's death he was quite *enraptured* with; he took the book and promised to work hard. Forster is trying to induce the Longmans to publish it; I doubt his success. Browning asked me if I would allow him to dedicate the play to me. I told him, of course, how much I should value such an honour.

March 31. Called at the theatre and proceeded to the box office, paid in (more reluctantly, I think, than I ever paid money in my life) a cheque for £2 2s. to the subscription for plate to Mr C. Kemble. . . .

April 5. After thinking in bed of the want of connection in the scenes of Browning's play, and also thinking on the necessity of continuing my study of my art—going over the fourth act scene of King John—I rose and sent for Forster; explained to him the dangerous state of the play, and the importance it was of to remedy this defect. We sat down to work—he first mentioning an attack on him in *The Times* through a piece of trash by that very wretched creature, Mr Poole, and also showing me a notice of my Richard in the *True Sun*. We went over the play of *Strafford*, altered, omitted, and made up one new scene; we were occupied from eleven till four o'clock; the day entirely surrendered to it. . . .

April 7. Forster and Browning both came to my room—Browning with some of the passages to be supplied—very feebly written. Forster and he had rather a warm altercation. . . .

April 8. Browning called, whom I accompanied to the theatre. Read over *Strafford* to the persons in the green-room, but did not produce the impression I had hoped—it dragged its slow length along. . . .

April 12. . . . Spoke to Osbaldiston about *Strafford*, and, having been anxious to find some of the actors restive about their parts, to furnish Browning with a decent excuse to withdraw the play, was disappointed at their general acquiescence. Forster called, and went twice over the play of *Strafford* approving of all the omissions and expressing himself much raised in hope by the alterations. He thought my view of the work quite a clear one, and in the most earnest spirit of devotion set off to find and communicate with Browning on the subject—a fearful rencontre. . . There were mutual complaints—much temper—sullenness, I should say, on the part of Forster, who was very much out of humour with Browning who said and did all that man could do to expiate any offence he might have given. Forster (who has behaved most nobly all through the matter of this play—no expression of praise is too high) showed an absence of sense and generosity in his behaviour which I grieved to see. There was a *scene*. Browning afterwards told me how much injury he did himself in society by this temper, corroborating what Talfourd had just before said of my poor friend Forster's *unpopularity*. I was truly sorry to hear from Browning much that rendered his unpopularity scarcely doubtful. Browning assented to all the proposed alterations and expressed his wish, that *coûte que coûte*, the hazard should be made, and the play proceeded with. . . .

April 14. Calling at Forster's, met Browning, who came upstairs and who produced some scraps of paper with hints and unconnected lines—the full amount of his labour upon the alterations agreed on. It was too bad to trifle in this way, but it was useless to complain; he had wasted his time in striving to improve the fourth act scene, which was ejected from the play as impracticable for any good result. We went all over the play *again* (!) very carefully, and he resolved to bring the amendments

Helen Faucit, from a drawing by Sir Frederic Burton.

John Forster in 1840, from a drawing by Daniel Maclise, R.A.

The second Theatre Royal, Covent Garden, opened September 1809.

The Theatre Royal, Drury Lane, October 1842. The Wrestling Scene in Macready's production of *As You Like It*. From a drawing by T. H. Shepherd.

suggested by eleven o'clock this evening. *[Later]* Met Browning at the gate of my chambers; he came upstairs and, after some subjects of general interest, proceeded to that of his tragedy. He had done nothing to it; had been oppressed and incapable of carrying his intentions into action. He *wished to withdraw it.* I cautioned him against any precipitate step—warned him of the consequences, and at last got him to offer to go and bring Forster, whom I wished to be a party to all this business. He came with Browning, and we turned over all the pros and cons—for acting or not acting the play. They both decided on its performance, Browning to have more time than he had asked for the completion of his alterations. It was fixed to be done. Heaven speed us all! I thank God I felt quite satisfied with my conduct throughout this delicate affair of Browning.

April 21. Miss Faucit said to me that her part in Browning's play was very bad, and that she did not know if she should do it. She wanted me to ask her to do it. But I would not, for I wish she would refuse it, that even at this late point of time the play might be withdrawn—*it will do no one good.* Forster and Talfourd came into my room. Mr Fitzball also asked me if I would play Iago to Mr Forrest in *Othello*, to which I gave an unqualified refusal. 'Would I refuse to play with him?'—to which I answered, *'By no means,* but *I must play my own parts'.*

April 22. Browning came to breakfast, very pale, and apparently suffering from over-excitement. I think it unfortunate that without due consideration and time for arranging and digesting his thoughts in a work so difficult as a tragedy, he should have committed himself to the production of one. I should be too glad of any accident that would impede its representation, and give me a *fair* occasion for withdrawing it; but this I cannot now do without incurring the suspicion of selfishness and of injustice to him. . . .

April 28. Thought over some scenes of *Strafford* before I rose, and went out very soon to the rehearsal of it. There is no chance in my opinion for the play but in the acting, which by possibility might carry it to the end without disapprobation; but that the curtain can fall without considerable opposition I cannot venture to anticipate. . . . In all the historical plays of Shakespeare, the great poet has only introduced such events as act on the individuals concerned, and of which they are themselves a part; the persons are all in direct relation to each other, and the facts are present to the audience. But in Browning's play we have a long scene of passion—upon what? A plan destroyed, by whom or for what we know not, and a parliament dissolved, which merely seems to inconvenience Strafford in his arrangements. There is a sad want of judgement and tact in the whole composition. Would it were over! It must fail—and it grieves me to think that *I am so placed*. Browning will efface its memory by the production of *Sordello*; but it will strike me hard, I fear. God grant that it may not be a heavy blow. . . . Forster introduced me to young Mr Longman,[1] who consulted with me upon the publication, and yielded to my reasons for delaying it until Monday afternoon.

April 29. Brewster called with my wig for Strafford. Went to the theatre and rehearsed *Strafford*, which I am disposed to think might *pass muster*—not more—if it were equally and respectably acted, but Mr Dale in the King must ensure its utter failure. Browning was incensed at Mr Dale's unhappy attempts—*it is too bad*. . . .

Elstree, April 30. . . . I repeat my conviction that it *must fail*—if, by some happy chance, not at once tomorrow, yet still at best it will only stagger out a lingering existence of a few nights and then die out—and for ever. It is dedicated to me most kindly by Browning. *['Dedicated, in all affectionate admiration, to William C. Macready.']* . . .

London, May 1. Called at the box-office about the boxes and places for which I had been applied to. Rehearsed *Strafford*. Was gratified with the extreme delight Browning testified at the rehearsal of my part, which he said was to him a full recompense for having written the play, inasmuch as he had seen his utmost hopes of character perfectly embodied. He was quite in raptures, I warning him that I did not anticipate success. . . . Read Strafford in bed, and acted it as well as I could under the nervous sensations that I experienced. Edward and Henry Bulwer, Fitzgerald, Talfourd, Forster, Dow, Browning (who brought his father to shake hands with me) and Jerdan came into my room. Went back to chambers, whence I proceeded with Catherine to Elstree. Arrived there about half-past one.

[Besides Macready—the portrait (said 'The Examiner') of 'the great and ill-fated Earl stepping from the living canvas of Van Dyck'—the cast included Helen Faucit as Lucy Carlisle, John Vandenhoff as Pym, J. Webster as young Vane, Dale as Charles I. 'Macready', said Browning himself, 'acted very finely, as did Miss Faucit. Pym received tolerable treatment. The rest—for the sake of whose incompetence the play had to be reduced by at least one-third of its dialogue—"non ragionam di lor!"' The authorship remained an open secret until the last of five performances when the playbill on May 30 spoke of '— Browning, Esq.'

William Jerdan (1782–1869) was editor of 'The Literary Gazette', 1817–1850).]

[1] Thomas Longman (1804–1879), publisher.

May 2. Looked at newspapers, which I was gratified to find lenient and even kind to Browning. On myself—the 'brutal and ruffianly' journal observed that I 'acquitted myself exceedingly well'. . . . Called on Forster—with whom I found Browning. I told him the play was a grand escape, and that he ought to regard it only as such, a mere step to the fame which his talents must procure him.

May 4. Looked at newspapers; read a criticism on *Strafford* in the *Morning Herald*—it extolled the play as 'the best that had been produced for many years', and abused me for 'pantings—a-a-s, etc.' which the writer supposed 'it was too late to cure'. This attempt to fasten upon my acting a general censure for a vice that was only detectable in one unstudied character is made by Mr Conan, who has quarrelled with Forster.

May 7. Looked at the *Examiner*, and thought that Forster had given a very kind and judicious criticism on *Strafford*. . . .

May 8. Called on Forster, who informed me how much he had been hurt by Browning's expressions of discontent at his criticism which I myself think only too indulgent for such a play as *Strafford*. After all that has been done for Browning with the painful apprehension of failure before us, it is not pleasing to read in his note, 'Let —— write any future tragedies'. Now, really, this is too bad—without *great assistance* his tragedy could never have been put in a condition to be proposed for representation—without great assistance it never could have been put upon the stage—nor without great assistance could it ever have been carried through its 'perilous' experiment. It is very unreasonable and indeed *ungrateful* in him to write thus.

May 18. Acted Posthumus *[Cymbeline]* in a most discreditable manner undigested, unstudied. Oh, it was most culpable to hazard so my reputation! I was ashamed of myself. . . .

[Helen Faucit played Imogen; Elton, Iachimo, and Farren, Cloten. Macready's other principal parts during the spring season were King John to the Bastard of Vandenhoff and Helen Faucit's Constance; Brutus to Vandenhoff's Cassius and Sheridan Knowles's Mark Antony; Leontes to Helen Faucit's Hermione, Mrs Glover's Paulina, and William Farren's Autolycus.]

May 22. Called on Forster, who gave me a letter from Browning, at which I was surprised and annoyed; as if I had done nothing for him—having worn down my spirits and strength as I have done—he now asks me to study a speech at the end of the second act, and an entire scene which I am to restore in the fourth act. Such a selfish, absurd, and use-less imposition to lay on me could scarcely have entered into any one's imagination. I was at first disgusted by the sickly and fretful over-estimate of his work and was angry; but reflected that he did not know what he required me to do, and had forgotten what I have done; 'so let him pass, a blessing on his head!' I shall not do it.

May 23. [Benjamin] Webster came into my room, and after a long conversation upon the bargain, it was concluded. For two months at the Haymarket theatre, £20 per night, at three nights per week, the first fortnight; to return £10 per night the third week if the *Bridal* be pro-duced, for which I am to receive £12 per night additional; during its run to throw in an additional night per week, or, if it fails, to be liable to be called on for a fourth night, extra work at £10 per night.

Elstree, May 31. Miss [Faucit],[1] in her nightly flirtation, told me that she thought of going to the Haymarket, and chiefly because I was to be there. *Nous verrons!*

June 3. A person calling himself Mr Monteagle, of good property, wished to know what I should require for instructing him so completely as to bring him not exactly up to my own degree of talent, but very near it. I told him I would pay very willingly to be taught, if anyone could teach. I civilly dismissed him, after enduring the bore for some time. Acted Othello pretty well—unequally, but some parts, in the third act particularly, forcibly *[with Elton as Iago; Helen Faucit as Desdemona]*. Was called for at the end of the play and well received. Thus ended my Covent Garden engagement which, thank God, has been profitable and agreeable to me. God be praised.

June 15. Went to the Haymarket, and read the *Bridal* in the green-room, which seemed to interest the actors much.

June 16. Sent to the theatre about the rehearsal, and after looking at the newspaper to ascertain the state of the King's[2] health—what an absurdity that the natural ailment of an old and ungifted man should cause so much perplexity and annoyance!—went to the Haymarket and rehearsed, with some care, Othello. Acted Othello in some respects very well, but want much attention to it still. Mr Elton is not good, and is unfair. I was called for, and after long delay went forward. Forster came into my room with a gentleman, whom he introduced as Dickens, alias Boz—I was glad to see him.

---

[1] The omission of Miss Faucit's name will become familiar.

[2] King William IV (1765–1837). When Duke of Clarence he had ten children by his mistress, the comedienne, Mrs Jordan. Married Adelaide of Saxe-Meiningen in 1818.

[Edward William Elton (1794–1843) was in both Macready's Covent Garden and Drury Lane seasons between 1837 and 1843. He was drowned in the wreck of the 'Pegasus', on the Farne Islands on its voyage from Leith to London, leaving a wife and seven children for whom a large sum was raised.

Charles Dickens (1812–1870), novelist, became one of Macready's dearest friends. From the moment he met the tall, smiling young man with lustrous eyes and thick, wavy hair—Dickens was then twenty-five—there was no one through life that he was happier to see.]

June 17. . . . Drove up to No 8 Kent Terrace, where I saw the house and lady of the house, and agreed with her to take it, and take possession on Wednesday. . . .

June 19. Went to rehearsal, having previously looked at the newspaper for the King's health. Went to theatre; when half dressed a person passed my door saying the King 'was off'. Upon inquiry I heard that notices of the event—his death—had been fixed up at the offices of the *Courier* and *Observer*, and it was said that it had been up at the Mansion House more than two hours since. The state of suspense in which I was kept to the very moment of the beginning of the play so agitated me that when I went on the stage I was weaker than I often am when I finish a character. I laboured through Richard, but it was labour, and most ineffectual. I was very bad, very bad.

June 23. Went in a cab to chambers, where I busied myself in the melancholy labour of further dismantling them. My long acquaintance with them—four or five years—has given me a sort of attachment to them. Disposed of the ricketty furniture which I had bought from Mr Brougham, my predecessor, to a broker for £2 10s. I should have taken anything he offered in order to rid myself of the incumbrance of these things.

June 26. Acted Melantius in the *Bridal*, which I had altered with some scenes by Knowles, from Beaumont and Fletcher's *Maid's Tragedy*. The play went with considerable applause. I did not please myself in the acting of Melantius, which was a crude, unfinished, performance. Being called for, I led on Miss Huddart. . . .

June 27. Called at Forster's, where a note had been left, which I got at 61, Lincoln's Inn Fields, and on its direction proceeded to Dickens's in Doughty Street. Another note directed me, under the guidance of his brother, to Cold-Bath Fields *[The House of Correction, Clerkenwell: 'used for criminals generally'.]*, where I found Dickens, Forster, Cattermole and Browne, the Pickwick artist. I went through this sad scene of punishment and shame, and my heart sank in its hope for the elevation of my kind. From this place we proceeded to Newgate, over which we went, and in the second room into which we were shown I saw a man reading; he turned as we entered—it was Wainewright—with large, heavy moustaches—the wretched man overlaid with crime. Several in solitary cells under sentence, and one to be hanged for rape. He seemed the most cheerful of them all; but in all the pride of our nature seemed eradicated or trodden down—it was a most depressing sight. We proceeded to Dickens's to dinner, where Harley, Mr Hogarth, and a Mr Banks (who had married Maclise's sister) joined us. Our evening was very cheerful, and we laughed much at Mr Harley's theatrical efforts to entertain.

[Hablot Knight Browne ('Phiz', 1815–1882), Dickens's illustrator.

Thomas Griffiths Wainewright (1794–1852), art critic ('Janus Weathercock'), forger, suspected poisoner.

George Hogarth (1783–1870), Dickens's father-in-law; musical critic.]

Macready, for some weeks, had been considering a plan for becoming director of Covent Garden.

July 14. . . . Fladgate, T. Hill, and some others spoke to me about 'having taken Covent Garden theatre'. I told them I had not taken it. *[Thomas Hill (1760–1840), book collector and retired drysalter, was a friend of Dickens.]*

July 18. . . . Saw Webster, and learned from him that it was true Mr Phelps was to have a trial there *[at the Haymarket]* whom I thought of engaging if he should prove good. *[Samuel Phelps (1804–1878), actor, especially in Shakespeare. Managed Sadler's Wells, 1844–1862. In the summer of 1837, when he had some celebrity as a provincial tragedian, the actress Mrs Nisbett gave him an introduction to Webster at the Haymarket].*

July 19. Acted Melantius not well. The occupation of my mind in other matters is already beginning to display its effect on my acting. . . .

July 24. Went into the theatre *[Covent Garden]* to take possession of it, invoking the blessing of Almighty God upon my undertaking. . . .

July 25. Mr Buckstone called. *[John Baldwin Buckstone (1802–1879), comedian, playwright and manager, was lessee of the Haymarket, 1853–1876.]* I received him very courteously, but was by no means captivated by his manners, or sentiments. I thought him a coxcomb.

July 27. Called on Wallace to ask his opinion of memorializing the Queen for her special patronage, and the liberty to assume the title of Her Majesty's Company of Performers. He thought, if obtained, it would be of great service, and assented to the proposal to get an introduction to Lord Durham, and ask his interest. Later went on to Lady Blessington's . . . Lord Durham was announced. I was introduced, and in a short time mentioned my desire to see him, and to ask his opinion on the Queen's acquiescence in my wish. He thought she would not and ought not to give a preference to one theatre, but that the title of Her Majesty's Servants he thought she ought to give, and would say a word or two to the official persons to induce her.

July 29. Dickens and Forster called, and I walked out with them, Dickens speaking to me of the comedy he was desirous of attempting. . . Walked to Oxford Street, took cab home. The cabman insisted on two shillings, which I resisted; and, on his persisting, I made him drive me to the police office, where a deposit was made for the measurement of the ground. I walked home. . . .

August 1. Went to the police-office, where I found I was cast in costs of 3s., which I very cheerfully paid, though I can scarcely yet believe myself wrong. . . .

On 11 August Macready ended his first Haymarket engagement; on 12 August he agreed to take, for seven months from 21 September, a furnished house, 8 York Gate; and on 14 August he went by coach to Southampton to see Samuel Phelps acting in 'The Iron Chest'.

Southampton, August 14. Saw the play of *The Iron Chest* [by George Colman the younger]; what a thing it is. I was disgusted with the patches of sentiment and claptraps upon national privileges, humanity, and all the other virtues in which G. Colman was so rich—on paper. Mr Phelps in Sir Edmund Mortimer displayed intelligence, occasionally great energy, some imagination—not much; want of finish, of experience, of logic in the working out of the character—(to lay violent hands on the term)—of *depth* in all the great parts. His best scene decidedly was his death, but even there was a want of method. His level speaking is often very pleasing—always sensible. I expected from his opening more than he achieved. There was no *absorbing* feeling *through* the great scenes, no evidence of the 'slow fire' 'wearing his vitals'; this was particularly manifest in the last act, where he was direct and straightforward even to commonplaceness. I think he will improve. . . . He called at the Dolphin and I offered him either the salary he might take from Mr Webster, or to give him now a salary, if he would name one, that I might meet. He preferred waiting for Mr Webster, and we interchanged agreements to that effect. I liked his tone and manner.

[On the next day, 15 August, Phelps wrote from Southampton to his wife: 'I did not know if any person was in the house from London; but at the end of 'The Iron Chest' a note was sent round to me from Macready, who had been there all the time himself. I was with him last night for upwards of an hour, and the result was I go to Covent Garden on the 16th of October. He wanted me to name my salary, which I declined doing until I have played in London; but at last I agreed to take the same salary that I may agree for at the Haymarket—which, if I succeed, I will take care shall be a good one, or I will not go at all.']

Elstree, August 23. Bartley came; he brought me letters, news, and a message from the Lord Chamberlain. In answer to my memorial the Queen had expressed herself much interested in Covent Garden; stated that she had great respect for Mr Macready and admiration for his talent, that the precise object of his request required consideration, but if it should be found impracticable to concede, that she trusted other means might be found of rendering assistance to his undertaking. . . .

Macready went to Bristol; in the coach he met a Frenchman.

August 27. . . . I fell into conversation with Monsieur, but found my French very rusty; we talked on various subjects, and at last the theatre was mentioned by him, and shortly after my name. I told him I was the person he was speaking of—his surprise and pleasure were extreme. His enthusiasm broke forth . . . and again made me lament that the destiny which made me a player, had not made me a French one. After long silence, on resuming our conversation, he repeated to me some lines, which he wrote down for me when we reached the White Lion, Bristol:

À L'ILLUSTRE MACREDÉ

Toi, dont le désespoir m'a glacé de terreur,
  Quand la main frémissante immolait Virginie;
Fils de Shakespeare, adieu! c'est dans ton noble cœur
  Que le ciel a jeté le feu de ton génie.

August 29. . . . Acted Virginius miserably; it was painful to myself, and could have been satisfactory to no one. Sent for the *Morning Herald*, and read the account of Mr Phelps' appearance *[as Shylock at the Haymarket]* which seems to me a decided success. It depressed my spirits, though perhaps it should not do so. If he is greatly successful, I shall reap the profits; if moderately, he will strengthen my company. But an actor's fame and his dependent income is so precarious, that we start at every shadow of an actor. It is an unhappy life!

From 11 to 22 September he acted in Birmingham.

Birmingham, September 11.—Rather unwell, and a little disconcerted by the conceit and presumption of the actors here.

September 15. . . . After the terrible moral of the play *[The Bridal]* in which she had just been acting for the first time, Miss —— preferred coming to my room rather than receive me in hers, because she knew in hers some one would be present. It seems a weakness in her, an *unconsciousness of wrong*—yet what does she propose to herself? Is it that she does not know, or does not set the due estimation on the worth of character? Does she think? or does she *only feel*—and obey a *feeling?* What a world this is! And how little of it beyond its thin surface do those in it know of it!

September 16. The uncomfortable position in which I am placed with this girl disturbed me, but I came to the resolution of not allowing myself to suffer from my own vanity or weakness. I really like her much as a friend, and I will be a friend to her. Gave Miss — the part of Clothilde in the *Novice.* She told me that she had not been to see her sister, and that she had expected me to call in the afternoon! She had no grounds for doing so.

[Helen Faucit appeared as Clotilda Lilienstein in 'The Novice' by William Dimond. When produced, the play was a failure. On 16 August William Farren had signed, on Helen Faucit's behalf, her agreement to become the principal tragic actress at Covent Garden during the season 1837–1838 at fifteen pounds a week.]

September 18. Went to call on Miss —, who, I hoped, would not have returned from Wavertree, but she was at home. I received the book of *Foscari*[1] from her, and she decided on the character of Mariana [Marina] in preference to that of Isabella, *Measure for Measure.* She told me that she had made up her mind not to be disappointed in travelling to town with me, so that I had no alternative—not that I had even expected she would change her mind. I cannot affect or doubt as to her affection for me. She must either love me, or be one of the most extraordinary and senseless deceivers that ever existed. I would to God it were not so, or that I could believe it not so.

[1] Byron's tragedy of *The Two Foscari.* The part was Marina, wife of young Foscari, not (in spite of Macready's ambiguous phrasing) the Shakespearean Mariana of *Measure for Measure.*

September 19. Miss — did not like to say she would act Hester in *To Marry*[1], and feared she had incurred blame by taking Miss Dorrillon, from which I relieved her at once. I sent in a note afterwards, requiring a *Yes* or *No* answer to the part of the *Novice*. She wrote back very affectionately and promptly 'Yes'. . . .

September 20. . . . Miss — declined Hester in *To Marry or Not*, also refused to act Emma in *William Tell* for me.

London, September 24. Robertson told me that Sir H. Wheatley had, on the part of the Queen, expressed a wish that the price of her box should be reduced from £400 to £350. If this be Royal Patronage, commend me to popular favour! Patronage to a declining art!

At the end of September Macready went into management at Covent Garden. Negotiations had been complex; but it seems that Macready had agreed to pay a rent of £40 a night, over a period of 180 nights, as a first charge on the receipts. He would pay himself a salary of £30 a week. Surplus would go at the rate of two-fifths to himself, three-fifths to the proprietors until the remainder of £8,800 had been paid to them. His company was ready to take salaries lower than usual (but Macready at the end of a losing season paid what the cast would normally have received). Helen Faucit agreed to £15 a week instead of £30; Elton to ten guineas, Phelps to ten (that summer he had appeared as Shylock, Hamlet, Othello, and Richard III at the Haymarket), Mrs Glover and Vining to £9 10s, and so on. The stage director and prompter, John Willmott, had £4 10s. Next to Macready, the highest salary went to Miss Shirreff, a popular singer, £18 a week. Prices ranged from box seats, 5s., to upper gallery, 1s. H. Robertson was the Treasurer.

The opening play was 'The Winter's Tale': Macready as Leontes, Helen Faucit as Hermione, Miss Huddart as Paulina, Bartley as Autolycus, Harriet Taylor as Perdita, James Anderson (his London début) as Florizel. Macready had an extraordinary moment when the statuesque Hermione quivered into life and descended from her dais. As Leontes touched her hand with the cry, 'Oh! she's warm!' his passionate joy seemed beyond control; now he was prone at her feet, then embracing her and caressing the unbound hair that escaped from beneath the veil. Helen Faucit cried out hysterically, and Macready whispered to her: 'Don't be frightened, my child! Don't be frightened! Control yourself.' All the while applause was in tumult. Earlier, Anderson (an actor whose fame would die with him) had been cheered so loudly after his fourth-act scene with Camillo that Macready rushed to the prompter's box to ask what had caused the noise. On the stage Harriet

[1] *To Marry, Or Not to Marry* (1805) by Mrs Elizabeth Inchbald.

Taylor, the Perdita, was whispering to Anderson: 'Isn't this glorious! Haven't you hit 'em hard!'

September 30. When I am actor I must forget that I am manager. Covent Garden theatre opens . . . Rehearsed the play, and attended to the various claims on my notice; received many letters of acknowledgment for the freedom of the theatre. Took every occasion of repeating the address [by Talfourd]. Bartley and Robertson came into my room with a slip from one of the newspapers of an address to the public by that reptile, Mr Bunn; it was meant as an answer or comment upon mine. I thought it inconsiderate in Bartley to pester me with such a thing at such a time, and gave as little attention to it as I could; it simply left the notion with me of being an *ebullition* of temper from *such* a person! I thought little of it. It consumed some time to arrange my dresses, etc., and when this was done I lay down in bed. Repeatedly went over my address, and also read over the first scene of Leontes. . . . Being called to the address, went and found the overture only just begun. Much agitated, the thought of the Rubicon-like plunge I was about to make and my home came upon me and affected me for a moment. When I went on the stage the enthusiasm of the audience was very great; I began my address with tolerable composure, but in the last part of it I stopped—it was a pause of about half a minute—but in agony of feeling, longer than time can measure; I recovered myself, and tripped slightly again before the conclusion of the address. . . . Acted Leontes artist-like but not, until the last act, very effectively. . . . Sat up late, and when I went to bed slept very little.

October 2. Rose in good time and tried to keep my thoughts on *Hamlet*. Went in coach to the theatre, and arriving there spoke about the bad delivery of the bills. Robertson sank my spirits very low by an account of the *Times*' report of our opening, which he represented as altogether blame. I went through the rehearsal of the play—taking pains with it, and attending to other business as it fell out. Among other letters was one—I should say ruffianly, if intended, as I suspected, to convey a personal menace—from that wretched profligate, Mr —. Other letters. I dined, and lay down in bed. Very, very much dejected. Felt myself quite unequal to perform. As the time drew near I rallied, dressed. . . . I acted the greater part of *Hamlet* in my best manner; and the play was put beautifully on the stage. The audience noticed with applause several of the improvements.

October 9. Among notes received one, very kindly written, from Rogers *[Samuel Rogers, poet, 1763-1855]*. Lay down, and glad to do so, in bed. My mind a good deal excited, but I acted Hamlet pretty well.

My self-possession returns to me in a surprising way. . . . The house falling off in the half-price, decided, with my council, on putting up *Othello* for next Monday.

October 10. Rose, after a night of very little sleep, in which I thought of Othello, at an early hour, and reached the theatre by nine o'clock; found no carpenter, in fact no workmen there! . . . Wrote eight notes or letters, and then gave myself entirely to the rehearsal of the play of the *Novice*; took great pains in endeavouring to infuse a spirit into the actors engaged in it. Settled the cast of *Othello* with Mr Bartley for the Duke, as an example to the other actors and to show that here would be no impediments to the best possible disposition of the characters in a play. Looked over the papers and dined at the Garrick Club, saw only disagreeable and most vulgar persons there . . . Miss — has begun to talk to me in a way that inclines me to waver in my opinion of her constancy or sincerity. We shall see! . . .

October 11. Rose much fatigued. Went to the theatre. Letters from a French pantomimist, wishing to represent animals and a fly! . . . The play of the *Novice*, which if acted well in the part of Carolstadt would have been most effective, was marred and almost ruined by the inefficiency of Mr Vining *[Frederick Vining, ?1790–1871]*. It escaped, but will do no good. Forster, Talfourd, Wallace, etc., came into my room. The house was wretched.

October 15. Rose with feelings of heavy weariness, and, coming downstairs, gave my first attention to my domestic accounts. Then looked at the theatrical business of the week. It is, I think, this week which will show me the degree of hope that a reasoning man may entertain of the final issue of my enterprise. The impossibility of revoking the step I have made enforces the propriety of putting a resolute and cheerful face upon the matter; and though I go forward with very little hope, yet still I do not bate much of heart in urging my purpose forward. There is at present a loss upon the concern, and this is beginning early, but the statements laid before me could not be accurate; and though I do not think that Robertson has wilfully deceived me, yet certainly things are not as he represented them to be. . . .

October 16. . . . Mr Anderson came to inform me that he had received from an agent of Drury Lane an offer, which I afterwards heard was 'double his present salary, to act what he pleased, and to play a new part in a play which the author would only consent to his performing'. *[James Anderson (1811–1895), actor. His salary then was six pounds a week.]* Mr Bunn is certainly an honest man, and his friends are honest men. Lay down and tried to think over Othello. Very much dissatisfied with my own performance of the part of Othello, very much indeed. I can scarcely tell why I was so heavy and cold, except that the fatigues of management are beginning to tell upon my acting. The Council of Forty was a scene of beautiful effect, one of the most real things I ever saw. . . .

October 17. . . . Looked at the papers, not one of which noticed the *mise en scène* of *Othello!* So much for the assistance of the Press! Spoke to Miss Faucit about Virginia; she promised to do her best. . . .

October 18. Went to theatre. Miss Huddart, in talking to me, showed *temper*, which I did not like to see. Miss Faucit assented to Virginia, saying that her mother was very much against it, etc.

October 19. Saw Bartley and asked him his opinion of our prospect; he said that he began to be afraid of it.

October 23. Called on [Clarkson] Stanfield, taking Letitia and Catherine with me on their way to Shoolbred's. Asked Stanfield to paint me a diorama for the pantomime. He almost promised, and in the kindest manner. He is a fine creature. Went to theatre, where of course business awaited me. Signed engagement with Mr Howe. Business with Robertson and Bartley, who went down on a message to the Vice-Chamberlain's Office, and brought word that the Queen would come to the theatre in November. Agreed with Mr Phelps. . . .

[Henry Howe [Hutchinson] (1812–1896), was at the end of his life the 'Daddy Howe' of Irving's Lyceum company, one of the most respected of Victorian supporting players.]

October 24. C. Buller called and stayed with me some time. He mentioned his disappointment in my Othello not being more tender, a criticism that I will not forget. Settled with Mr Phelps to do Othello in November.

October 25. Called on Stanfield, whom I found what he is said to be, and must be thought to be, the very spirit of kindly feeling. He assented to my request and promised to make all arrangements with me. I told him I could not thank him, both for the act itself, and its moral influence on the undertaking I have in hand.

October 28. Went to theatre. Acted Werner to a *wretched, wretched* house as well as I could, but not well. I spoke with Miss Faucit after the play, asked her to play the part in the new drama to *oblige me*, to which she kindly assented, but told me that she suffered much at home for it. When Robertson heard of her acquiescence, he observed that 'there was nothing like a little rational conversation', to which I assented. She is a kind, good-hearted girl.

107

November 1. Browning came into my room. Robertson, etc. As this day closes I begin to have doubts of my ability to rally. I fear 'it is a hopeless struggle'.

November 2. Uneasy and unhappy thoughts. I begin to despair, but I hope I shall not despond. The hopelessness of the struggle, unaided by the Press, and thwarted by the knavery of one and the indolence of another, begins to weigh upon me. Still, I bate nothing of resolution. . . .

November 3. Thought over part of Macbeth before I rose; went to the theatre. Superintended the rehearsal of three acts of *Macbeth*, which was not satisfactorily proceeding. Sat down to my letters and wrote ten, dining on my daily chop. *What am I doing all this for? What is to be my recompense?* Indifference, pity, and, from some very few, respect; I should have thought of this before. . . .

November 5. . . . A Monsieur Lasnes sent up his name—he was the person who first gave me instruction in Italian; he had been in the French Army and served under Napoleon. He was then a handsome, interesting young man; he looked now a sort of person that one would expect to see in the farce of *Victorine*, and smelt strong of drams. He asked me for Wallace's address, and for pecuniary relief. I gave him five shillings. Read prayers to the family. . . .

November 6. . . . Tried my best to act Macbeth well, and did much of it very well—particularly the scene before the banquet. The whole play was very beautifully put upon the stage, and the audience seemed to appreciate it . . . I heard of the complete failure of the *mélange* called *Caractacus [Planché's adaptation of Beaumont and Fletcher's 'Bonduca', music by Balfe]* at Drury Lane theatre, and took hope and heart from the issues of both experiments. I had drunk much wine, and was very vehement, swearing rather loudly (unwise, ungentlemanly, and dangerous passion!) at Mr Phelps in the fight. . . .

November 7. Arose wearied and with headache; went to theatre, where much of the morning was talked away; my spirits and body were equally wearied. Had a long conversation with Mr Phelps, to whom I sent in order to excuse myself for my last night's violence. He did not take offence at it. I was *very much to blame*. . . .

[Phelps had no luck this season. After one performance as Othello (to Macready's Iago) his manager made sure that he would not be too prominent again. Cassius (February 1838) would be his best chance: two performances only.]

November 10. Bartley came to tell me that the Queen had sent to command me Friday night. . . .

November 12. Resolved on advertising no change of price on the occasion of the Queen's visit. Rose very late, at four o'clock in the afternoon. Bartley called to inform me of a communication from the Lord Chamberlain's Office, signifying the Queen's command that *Werner* and the *Irish Ambassador* (with Mr Power from the Adelphi theatre) should be acted on Friday night. . . . *[J. Kenney's 'The Irish Ambassador' (1831).]*

November 13. Received a note from Mr Martin, the Vice-Chamberlain which I answered in the strongest terms, putting before him, and whomsoever it might reach, the injury and injustice done to me by foisting Mr Power upon me. He shortly afterwards called, and, in discussing the subject, admitted the prejudicial effect that such a partial proceeding would have upon my arrangements. . . .

November 14. Received a note from Mr Martin that the performances would be, for the command, *Werner* and *Roland for an Oliver*—was much gratified to learn that I was freed from this *embarras*. . . . Heard from Lord Conyngham that he had no hand in recommending Mr Power and that it was not easy to alter the first proposal. . . .

November 15. Sent for Jones—Edward's tailor—to measure me for a Court suit—a livery of servility. Came home to dinner; returned to theatre; answered a very nice note from Dickens. . . .

November 16. Mr Martin, Vice-Chamberlain, called to say that the farce commanded was the first act of *Fra Diavolo*, and that 'all was right' about the matter lately agitated.

November 17. *[Queen's visit]* . . . I could not help thinking, as I sat dressed for Werner, waiting for my call and listening to the acclamations of the audience on the Queen's arrival, of the folly and impiety of this pampering and spoiling the mind of one human being, and in the same act debasing those of millions. There was a great tumult arising from the overcrowded state of the pit, a great number were lifted over the boxes in a fainted and exhausted state. Mr Bartley had leave from the Queen to address the audience, which he did, tendering the price of admission to those who, not having room, might wish to return. When order was restored, the play proceeded. I acted, not to please myself; I could not recover my self-possession. The Queen sent to say she expected to see me as she retired. I dressed myself in full dress and went with Bartley to wait on her. Thanked Lord Conyngham for his kind attention to my request about Mr Power. The ladies-in-waiting and the officers, etc. passed through the room, and at length the Queen—a very pretty little girl—came. Lord Conyngham told her who I was. She smiled and bowed, and said, 'I am very much obliged to you.' Pointed me out to the

Duchess of Kent, and bowed repeatedly to me. I went home with Miss Martineau and Catherine, very, very tired.

November 18. . . . Walked to the Prince of Wales's tavern, where a party were assembled to dine with Dickens, on the completion of his Pickwick volume. We were detained long for dinner, but the day was interesting. Ainsworth,[1] Forster, Lever,[2] Talfourd, etc., were there. Talfourd proposed Dickens's health in a very good speech and Dickens replied—under strong emotion—most admirably. Left them directly that ceremony was over. . . .

November 19. Went to Talfourd's—met Dickens, Forster, Ainsworth, Keating, Hill, etc. Passed rather a heavy day. Gave my opinion injudiciously upon some actors—C. Kemble, etc. Forster informed me that Thackeray had inquired of him today the reason why Mr Price so violently and constantly spoke against me! . . .

November 20. . . . Mr Phelps refused the part of Exeter [Henry V]—is afraid to play the first and averse to take the second characters. I told Bartley to tell him I should shut the theatre if he did not play it.

December 2. Went to theatre, where I sat for some time revolving the hopeless condition of the concern. I strove to calm my spirits, and devise the best means of meeting and winding up the losses that appear hanging over me. I could not rally, my heart had quite sunk within me.

December 8. Rose later than I should have done. Looked over the debate, and was amused with the farcical failure of B. Disraeli. . . .

December 16. Went to the theatre, where I attended to business, looking out for plays, etc., after Christmas. Had the account from Robertson, which I looked over, and found myself about £2200 to make up, to bring in even balance; profit is therefore beyond all hope!

On 18 December the Queen came to Macready's Macbeth. 'Was called for, but her Majesty took precedence, and I hid my diminished head.'

December 19. Awoke at five o'clock much disturbed by the thought which crossed me, that possibly the subject of the pantomime [Harlequin and Peeping Tom of Coventry] might be considered indelicate from the indecent character of the farce acted at Drury Lane and the Haymarket last night; lay thinking upon it, until at a late hour I fell asleep. Rose late, and looked at the papers; The Times gave us [Macbeth] no notice, the Herald a very cold one coupled with a very impertinent one

[1] William Harrison Ainsworth (1805–1882), novelist; author of *Old St Paul's, The Tower of London*, etc.
[2] Charles Lever (1806–1872), novelist.

on the Drury Lane performance. Are not these newspaper reporters wretches? Is it easy to imagine men made up of viler materials? . . . Went to theatre. Expressed my apprehensions about the possible attempt to fix the character of indecency on our story, and recommended a slight alteration in its conduct, to which they agreed, Mr Young asking me to do it for him. Bartley told me that Lord Conyngham [the Lord Chamberlain] had sent to say that the Queen was very much pleased with the last evening's entertainment.

So much depended on the pantomime that he was at the theatre on Christmas Day. On Boxing Day it would follow the tragedy of 'Jane Shore'.

December 26. . . . All was in a state of anxious preparation for 'the great work', the pantomime. Rehearsed Lord Hastings; watched the rehearsal of the pantomime, which I could not leave, for had I gone to my own room I could not have given my attention to my own character, my thoughts would have been with the success of the pantomime. Rehearsing on the stage, which was not over till ten minutes past five. Dickens, Cattermole, and Forster sat it through. . . . The pantomime succeeded completely, for which I feel most gratified.

December 29. Acted Werner very indifferently. I am falling off in my art through my attention to the management. I must reform it altogether.

December 31. . . . Since my entry on this unhappy speculation of management, my mind has, if not retrograded, certainly stood still. . . . Forster called. As I went out to call on Bulwer, I set him (Forster) down in Oxford Street. Talked with Bulwer about his play [The Lady of Lyons]; he has not settled his fifth act, and I cannot help him. A Dr Quin, a homoeopathic, called and inquired into his state. [Frederic Hervey Foster Quin (1799-1878), who founded the London Homoeopathic Hospital in 1850, was the first homoeopathic physician in England.]

1838

January began with Macready's plans for King Lear, *restored as written, with the character of the Fool.*

January 2. Read over part of *King Lear*, and then went to the theatre, where I found a letter from Miss Faucit, returning the part of Cordelia. . . . Spoke with Bartley, and wrote to Miss Faucit, sending back the part of Cordelia with a very kind note of remonstrance. . . .

January 3. Heard at the box-office that Mr C. Kean had called there to ask Notter *[the box-office manager]* how he did!—to complain that he had lost his voice—through nervousness! and asked Notter if *we did not wish him at the Devil!* The conceit and effrontery of this puppy is really disgusting. . . . Note from Miss Faucit, very ungraciously consenting to act Cordelia.

[Charles Kean, who had refused to act for Macready at Covent Garden, was now appearing for Bunn at Drury Lane (twenty nights at fifty pounds a night).]

January 4. Went to the theatre, where I went on a first rehearsal of *King Lear*. My opinion of the introduction of the Fool is that, like many such terrible contrasts in poetry and painting, in acting representation it will fail of effect; it will either weary and annoy or distract the spectator. I have no hope of it, and think that at the last we shall be obliged to dispense with it. Settled the scenery, which will be very striking. Received the last act of Bulwer's play, with a note from him. Read it, and have my apprehensions about it; he writes too hastily, he does not do himself justice. . . .

[Bulwer said in this note: 'The only titles I can think of for the play are as follows: 1st (your own) 'Nobility'; 2, 'How Will It End'; 3, 'Lost and Won'; 4, 'Love and Pride'.]

January 5. Speaking to Willmott and Bartley about the part of the Fool in *Lear*, and mentioning my apprehension that, with *[Drinkwater]* Meadows, we should be obliged to omit the part, I described the sort of fragile, hectic, beautiful-faced, half-idiot-looking boy that it should be, and stated my belief that it never could be acted. Bartley observed that a woman should play it. I caught at the idea, and instantly exclaimed: 'Miss P. Horton is the very person.' I was delighted at the thought.

January 6. Spoke to Miss Faucit, who seems to have taken up a very discontented tone.

January 7. . . . Finished the perusal of Bulwer's play, which I think, considering the time in which it has been planned and written, is really wonderful.

January 8. Waited with some impatience until eleven o'clock for the arrival of Bartley and Robertson from Drury Lane; they came with Forster, and gave an account of the reception and performance of Mr C. Kean [Hamlet]. In going over the different points, each one enumerated confirmed me in the opinion I had long since taken up on very good grounds, that this young man has been trading in the part of Hamlet upon my conception and performance. Willmott exclaimed as they detailed the various passages: 'Every point is Mr Macready's!' They spoke of it as a dull affair. The papers will, of course, laud it beyond all measure. We must trust in the strength of truth, and the God of truth. [Charles Kean, spluttering and adenoidal, was not a major Shakespearean; but playgoers, remembering his father, warmed themselves at a vanished blaze. His triumph on this occasion was largely a sentimental one.]

January 10. . . . Read Talfourd's tragedy of The Athenian Captive. This was a great disappointment to me; no one could believe it to be by the author of Ion; it has nothing of it but its faults of style exaggerated. How am I to tell Talfourd this I scarcely know. . . .

January 11. Talfourd called to know the fate of his tragedy. . . . I told him he should dictate as to its performance; that if he wished it, I would act it, but as a friend I advised him on every account not to do so. It was painful—he was evidently much disappointed. I said I would read it again, and talk with him upon it. I think he will have it done—and if he does, it will be a serious calamity to him. I feel sure of it.

January 18. Received a querulous note from Talfourd, who seems annoyed at my opinion upon his play, which, he says, having been written for the most disinterested purpose of serving the cause I uphold, he cannot consent to let his labour perish, and insists on its performance. How different from Bulwer! . . .

January 24. I gave up the whole morning to the rehearsal and superintendence of King Lear which, to a classic or Shakespearean eye, looks very striking, and, as I think, very harmoniously arranged. . . .

January 25. Lay down and tried to think of Lear. Was very nervous in the morning, but prepared for the play much more collected than I had been. I scarcely know how I acted the part. I did not satisfy myself.

. . . Was occasionally pretty good, but I was not what I wished to have been.

[Macready as Lear, Helen Faucit as Cordelia, Bartley as Kent, Priscilla Horton as the Fool, and the text (in the words of 'John Bull') 'freed from the interpolations which have disgraced it for nearly two centuries'. The play was staged magnificently, its castles heavy, sombre, solid, their halls adorned with weapons and trophies of the chase; on the heath Druid circles rose spectrally; the storm was sustained. Dickens, writing in 'The Examiner' (4 February 1838) on 'The Restoration of Shakespeare's "Lear" to the Stage', said that Macready's performance, 'remarkable before for a masterly completeness of conception, is heightened by this introduction of the Fool to a surprising degree.' The article ended with the words: 'The only perfect picture that we have had of "Lear" since the age of Betterton.']

January 26. . . . The pain of suspense, until I read the papers, was never more severely felt by me. They at length arrived, and being far more favourable than my anticipation, my serenity in some degree returned, but my mind and body were both weighed down by fatigue. Went to the theatre. . . . The impression created by *King Lear* seemed to be wide and strong.

Dramatists and actors were troubling him. 'I wish,' he wrote on 3 February 'they were all tied in a sack together! They worry my heart out.' Bulwer's play, so far untitled, began to occupy his attention. Over at Bunn's Drury Lane 'this Mr C. Kean' was playing to an average of £310 a night.

February 9. . . . Bulwer came into my room at the end of the second act [of *King Lear*]. I sent him round to a private box and he returned to me at the end of the play. Expressed himself in very warm terms upon what he styled my 'gigantic' performance, talked about the play, with the arrangements for which he seemed well satisfied.

The play set in post-Revolution France (1795–1798), was to be called 'The Lady of Lyons; or, Love and Pride'. Various other titles had been suggested, such as 'The Adventurer' and 'The Gardener's Son'. Bulwer hit finally upon the title that was used (letter to Macready, 4 February 1838, in Charles H. Shattuck's Bulwer and Macready, 1958). Helen Faucit had credited the naming to an incident at rehearsal when Bartley, the Damas, bowed to her and said: 'Shall it not be called 'The Lady of Lyons'? At first it was staged without an author's name. 'The Times' attacked the dramatist for 'Republican claptraps'.

February 15. Went to an early rehearsal of the new play. Message from the Vice-Chamberlain to say that the Queen was not coming, which I hailed as excellent news. Acted Claude Melnotte pretty well; the audience felt it very much, and were carried away by it; the play in the acting was completely successful. Was called for, and leading on Miss Faucit was well received.

[The cast included Macready as the romantic impostor, Claude Melnotte, a character half his age; Helen Faucit as Pauline Deschappelles, the Beauty of Lyons ('as pretty as Venus, and as proud as Juno'); Bartley as Colonel Damas, Elton as Beauséant, Meadows as Glavis, Strickland and Mrs W. Clifford as M. and Madame Deschappelles. Helen Faucit, as the duped girl, had probably the ovation of her life.]

February 24. Saw an attack in *The Times* newspaper on Bulwer and the play, arising from the publication of his name; it was vulgar, virulent, and impotent from its display of malice—such an article as I could *wish* my enemy to write against me.

[Bulwer, in a preface, dated 26 February 1838, to the first printed text of 'The Lady of Lyons', wrote: 'I can honestly say that I endeavoured, as much as possible, to avoid every political allusion applicable to our own time and land—our own party prejudices and passions. How difficult a task this was, a reference to any drama in which the characters are supposed to live under Republican institutions will prove.']

February 27. Forster came into my room, and told me of some very paltry meanness on the part of Talfourd about Bulwer's play, which, he said, perfectly *disgusted* him. . . .

March 1. A violent love-letter from some person who had seen me in *Melnotte*. Heard that the Queen had gone again to Drury Lane this evening. . . . Her patronage of the effort I am making to uphold the drama—to preserve decency behind the curtain—is quite intelligible!

March 3. Acted Claude Melnotte very well. The Queen came to see the play—no notice was taken of her. Received books of the play, which is dedicated to Talfourd. This is heaping coals of fire on his head with a vengeance.

March 8. . . . Bulwer came into my room and seemed very much delighted with the success of his play. He told me of a message he had received from the Queen, full of courteous expressions to him about the play, and wishing him to communicate to me how very much she was delighted with my acting the comedy, the third act and the fifth. He added that she did not like Miss Faucit. It was curious to see a man of

Bulwer's great mind evidently so much delighted by the praise and compliments of a little girl—because a Queen!

March 12. *[Coriolanus]*. The house was very indifferent; this was a blow. The reputation of this theatre for producing Shakespearean plays ought to have commanded more attention. I give up all hope! Lay down to rest. Acted parts of Coriolanus well; parts not to satisfy myself. Jerdan, Dickens, Bulwer, Blanchard,[1] Forster, came into my room.

[Macready never fully mastered Coriolanus. On this occasion Mrs Warner (Miss Huddart now used the name) was cast as Volumnia, Bartley as Menenius, Anderson as Aufidius, Warde as Cominius. The staging startled even Alfred Bunn who had to call it 'worthy of any theatre and any manager'.]

March 21. Went to the theatre, reading the *Foscari* [Byron] upon my way. Arrived there, I had to *encounter* Mrs Glover, who came in the highest tone of offended dignity to complain of the treatment she had received in my neither having called on her nor sent the money. The fact was, I informed myself of her health through the messages taken by Partridge, and did not think it right to pay her salary, as she had met with her accident in seeking to deceive and defraud me in asking leave to go to Brighton to see her son, when, as it afterwards appeared, she went to Coventry to play. She wished to have her engagement returned to her. I told her I would give the matter consideration, but could not answer her immediately. . . .

[Mrs Glover had been expected to play Madame Deschappelles in 'The Lady of Lyons', but when she did not appear at the theatre on 3 February the part was given to Mrs Clifford.]

March 23. Looked at the newspapers, in which I read an advertisement for a dinner to Mr C. Kean, to present him with a piece of plate, Lord Morpeth in the chair! This is to take place in the saloon of Drury Lane theatre (a fitting place for such an exhibition) on the 30th inst. How long is the intelligence of this country to be insulted by his quackeries? . . .

March 27. A pretty girl, with a strong lisp, came to present herself as a would-be Thespian. I thought she had mistaken her vocation and seemed much better adapted for a Cyprian. I did not, however, tell her so . . . Faraday sent me a note with his pamphlet on electricity.

April 7. Acted Foscari very well. Was very warmly received on my appearance; was called for at the end of the tragedy and received by the

[1] Samuel Laman Blanchard (1804–1845), editor and writer.

whole house standing up and waving handkerchiefs with great enthusiasm . . . The operetta of *Windsor Castle* was in active process of damnation as I left the theatre.

April 14. Thackeray came to the evening rehearsal and told me that he had written the criticism on Macbeth in *The Times*, but that much of it had been cut out—that in what he wrote of Bulwer every word of praise was omitted. How sick I am of that scoundrel paper!

April 16. Went to the theatre where I was engaged incessantly the whole day with the superintendence of the Easter piece [*Sindbad, the Sailor; or, The Valley of Diamonds*]. The labour was oppressive. Here I am sacrificing myself, and still I must ask for what—for whom? . . . Acted Macbeth in an odious style; was called for and well received.

After all, he was planning to do Talfourd's 'The Athenian Captive'.

April 20. Gave the evening to the study of Thoas, a bitter drug. Account from the theatre most wretched. £55. So that this at least tells the value of *Coriolanus*, and even the *Foscari*.

April 21. Saw the papers, and went to the theatre, where I was startled at learning that there was only just enough cash to meet the day's demands; and this included the remainder of my Benefit. The prospect is fearful. I sent for Willmott, and immediately made arrangements to dismiss *Sindbad* from the bills, and reduce every expense. . . . In the evening learned second act of Thoas. Oh, what a life!

Mrs Warner—who had been Miss Huddart—was in childbirth; Macready asked Helen Faucit to take over her part, Talfourd and Forster going as emissaries.

April 27. Miss Faucit . . . agreed to play Ismene in *The Athenian Captive*, but just before her entrance a note came from Mrs Talfourd,[1] written in a less courteous strain than I would write to any servant, or poor tradespeople—it is an outrage on good breeding and decency which I would never have permitted a wife or sister of mine to have been guilty of—it was *shocking*. I sent it to Forster, from whom I had just received a note of inquiry, and detained Miss Faucit that I might tell her what she was to do. Mrs Talfourd's note was to the effect of declining Miss Faucit's performance of Ismene, which Talfourd had last night requested her to perform! I had sent Bartley in quest of Talfourd to

[1] Rachel Talfourd (they were married in 1822) was the eldest daughter of John Towill Rutt (1760–1841), a leading Unitarian.

Westminster Hall, to learn from him distinctly whether the play was or was not to be acted. Bartley had been calling on Mrs Talfourd, and described her in a state of excitement little short of frenzy. I fear he has done no good, if he has not done actual mischief. Forster and Dickens came, the former loudly indignant at Talfourd's weakness, and at being made, as he termed it, such an ass of by Talfourd. They sat long waiting for Bartley's return, who came unsuccessfully back, and whom I again despatched to Talfourd's chambers. Dickens told me one thing that pained me much—for human nature, as well as for the individual. I had mentioned to him Mrs Talfourd's visit here (after her *very cold* reception at her own house of Catherine and Letitia) and her extravagant tone of cordiality. He said: 'Yes, I saw her after, and she told me she was "quite *fatigued* with *over-acting*".' This is about as bad an instance of duplicity and bad feeling as I ever heard of in friendly social intercourse. Bartley at length arrived with Talfourd—and a more melancholy, pitiable sight I think I never saw than the poor dejected fellow. I truly pitied him. He was depressed almost to tears. I got Willmott out of the room, as I thought he might wish to say something, and I did not desire Willmott to witness the pain he endured. He said very little—endeavoured to get from me an expression of a wish that the play should be done. I said, as I had from the first said, that 'I would not utter one word.' I mentioned having received a note from Mrs Talfourd, which too manifestly was the result of feeling and temper—that as written by a lady I could not comment upon it further than to say: 'It was unmerited, that I had not deserved it—it was an injustice.' I added that had I the same occasion twenty or twenty thousand times, I should in all I had said or done, do and say exactly what I had done—that I had acted by Talfourd as I should have done by my own brother; that it was at an end, etc. We shook hands, and they left me to my labours.

April 28. Rehearsed the play of *Romeo and Juliet*, with my part of Friar Lawrence. . . .

April 29. . . . Forster called, and showed me a note from Talfourd, in which I must say he manifested an *abject spirit*, observing that 'if Bartley were to call at his house whilst he were at home, Mrs Talfourd might perhaps be worked upon to consent to its performance'. The tone of the note was most unmanly and most pitiable. Forster told me much about Mr Bartley that leads me to believe he has been most impertinently communicative, if not treacherous. Much of Mrs Talfourd's silly intemperance of conduct has been evidently fomented by the busy interference of this faithless servant. . . .

April 30. Rehearsed the play of *Romeo and Juliet* with much attention.

Received two books of *The Athenian Captive* from Talfourd with his 'regards, thanks, and regrets'. Read over Friar Lawrence. Acted it. I find the playing a part of this sort, with no direct character to sustain, no effort to make, no power of perceiving an impression made, to be a very disagreeable and unprofitable task. Having required many of the actors to do what they conceived beneath them, perhaps it was only a just sacrifice to their opinions to concede so far—but it is for the first and last time.

[Anderson and Helen Faucit were Romeo and Juliet, and Vining the Mercutio. There were two performances. 'The Athenian Captive' was abandoned]

May 2. Bartley called in, and told me that the Edinburgh papers had turned round upon Mr C. Kean. I lay down on bed to rest and read Lear. Acted the part—not to my own satisfaction, but apparently to the content of the audience. Liston was in the green-room, and rather drunk. I saw him for a few minutes. *[John Liston (1776–1846), the famous comedian; retired from the stage in 1837.]*

May 9. . . . Saw Dickens, Blanchard, and Cruikshank the caricaturist *[George Cruikshank 1792–1878]*, who seemed set in for a *booze* in Forster's study. I am much more comfortable with a cool head and quiet thoughts.

May 19. Rehearsed *Woman's Wit*. Knowles and Forster were present at the early part of the rehearsal. Knowles was very much struck with the beauty of the scene for the opening of the play; he observed to me, 'My dear Mac, for all the plays I have ever written, there has never been done so much as is given in this one scene.'

['Woman's Wit; or, Love's Defiance' by Sheridan Knowles: Macready played Walsingham, Helen Faucit, Hero. The play was about a young woman, Hero, who had shocked her unavowed lover by waltzing with a roué. Resolved to conquer the frigid fellow, she dressed like a Quaker girl and got him to visit her (as Hero's sister) in a house at Greenwich. The play had thirty-one performances for six of which Elton appeared as Walsingham.]

May 21. Gave up the entire morning to the rehearsal of Knowles's play. . . . Knowles was very much struck with the mode of putting the play upon the stage, drilling the actors, and teaching them their business; I was glad he was present that he might know, in any event, his trust had not been misplaced. He told me the proprietors, if they knew their interests, ought to give me £4,000 per annum to conduct their theatre—about the amount I shall give them!

May 23. From six o'clock to eight I was boring at the concluding speech of the play, having closed my eyes with it last night, and could not get it into my head. . . . Rehearsed the play of *Woman's Wit*, and attended to all the various matters connected with it; scenes, dresses, etc. Read over my own part, and laboured at the concluding speech, writing it out repeatedly from memory, but unavailingly, to make a secure lodgment with it. Acted Walsingham in a very crude, nervous, unsatisfactory manner. . . .

May 26. Wrote to Bulwer, saying I should be glad to see him if he were strolling near; I wish to ask him if I can be of any use to him in improving his elocution.

May 29. Had a long conversation with Bartley and Robertson on the conduct of next season; they, but more particularly Bartley, seemed to be very anxious that I should be continued, with safety to myself, in the management. Bartley mentioned that the actors were to meet on Thursday, and that Serle had a plan to propose, but that this plan included an operatic company. I am nearly certain Serle's plan must be of a republican character, with which I said I would have nothing to do; as a director I must be a *despot*, or *serve*. Dined with Forster and Dickens. Forster told me of Talfourd's *little* conduct—eulogising Mr C. Kean's great talents and no word to bestow on Knowles in his play, nor on me except as to my sacrifices and getting up of plays! Dickens and Forster were disgusted with him.

May 30. Finished the number of *Nickleby* in bed; talked with Forster on the subject of next season's management, upon which he is as usual very sanguine. Miss Faucit came, at my invitation, into my room. I wished to speak with her, but our conference was very short, as she was rather sullen and reserved. Bulwer came in. I told him that Forster had mentioned to me how anxious he was to endeavour to improve his elocution, and that if *I* could be of any assistance to him in that respect, I should be most happy. He seemed very much obliged and pleased, and though doubtful of a good result, would be happy to receive my assistance.

May 31. After the interlude was over, Warde, Harley, Meadows, and Stanfield came into my room to ask me to step into the green-room where I found my company assembled. They all stood up as I entered, and I bowed to them, and Bartley addressed me in their names, deputed by them. . . .

The players, said Bartley, appreciated what Macready had done to champion the fallen drama. They recognised his sacrifices, and as a testimonial they had their names engraved on a salver which Bartley handed to him. Macready replied with feeling. 'One of my motives', *he said*, 'has been the wish to elevate my art, and to establish an asylum for it, and for my brothers and sisters who profess it, where they might be secure of equitable treatment. friendly consideration, and, most of all, that respect which man should show to man, or, most important, which man should show to woman.'

June 5. Read the essay on 'Envy' in Bacon—endeavouring to examine myself by it. Heard a strange story (an incredible one, I should say) of a present having been sent from that wretched fellow at Drury Lane to the Queen. Talked away my time, all upon the subject of next year's management. Willmott told me of the extravagant expectations of the actors, who expected to share with me in the chance of their salaries, and also to divide any surplus! I see the impracticability of the attempt to raise them from the condition of serfs; they have not the nobleness to be really free. . . .

June 11. Miss H. Faucit came in, and I had a long conversation with her on the subject of her next year's engagement, she saying that her friends would expect her to receive a higher salary; I observing that I would not conduct the theatre to give it, and warning her to be liberal and just in her engagements.

June 14. Leigh Hunt[1] called on Forster; I saw him and talked with him about his play, assuring him that I would give my whole attention to it, and do all in my power for it. I was quite moved in speaking to him. It is curious to mark the revolutions in human affairs. I remember when Leigh Hunt, as the editor of the *Examiner*, seemed to hold my destinies in his grasp; as the person on whom, in respect to this play, he now depends, I appear to have his in my keeping. Mr Webster sent up his card and came in. He proposed an engagement—asked me if I would take £20 per night. I said, No; that I did not wish to act, and would take nothing under £25 per night for four nights per week for five weeks. He said, 'Well, Mr Macready, I will give it,' and named the time—the middle of July. He then detained me till past five o'clock, disclaiming any malice towards me, making very lame excuses, and saying he did not remember that I had made him a present of £50 when leaving the theatre. I told him I would not act Shakespeare's tragedies at the Haymarket, to which he agreed—Knowles's play was the object. Put

[1] James Henry Leigh Hunt (1784–1859), critic, essayist, and poet; the original of Dickens's Skimpole in *Bleak House*. Presumably the play was *A Legend of Florence*.

him on the free list. Forster called to tell me of Knowles's distress and to ask if I would give him a Benefit, dividing after £105. I said *No*; but I would divide with him after £60.

June 15. Reflected much on the circumstance of —. It is scarcely to be wondered at that she should be keenly alive to the influence of passion— but it is not right. A sterner rule of conduct must be adopted if I wish to be happy and at peace with myself. . . .

Elstree, June 17. Sat down to read Leigh Hunt's play, which I did, not without difficulty; the unhappy construction so deprives it of interest that I cannot entertain a hope for it, which on every account gives me great concern. . . .

London, June 21. Dickens came in. Miss Faucit had written me a note, assenting to the salary, but desiring the right to refuse parts, and wishing for a dressing-room to herself. She came to my room, and after trying if she would give up the point, I told her she might as well have done so, for I should not be manager. She was much concerned.

June 23. . . . Drury Lane, with its advertisements in the papers, has closed—only opening for the Coronation night! Thus ends for the present season the impudence, falsehood, knavery, and swagger of that disgusting scoundrel.

June 26. Blanchard told me that at the theatre on Friday night Mr C. Kean, with two companions, by his indecent behaviour—sneering and observing upon the performance of the *Lady of Lyons*—attracted the attention and frequent notice of those around him; that no language of his could convey at all an adequate idea of the insolent and offensive conduct of this vulgar-minded and conceited young man. There is no genius in such a nature. . . .

Macready arranged to continue at Covent Garden during the next season.

July 2. Webster called, and seemed greatly disappointed at my continuance at Covent Garden theatre. He, however, expressed the most friendly intentions. . . .

July 5. Acted Claude Melnotte very well, was called for, and led on Miss Faucit. . . . The last night of my performance this season at Covent Garden.

July 6. Went into the box to hear Bartley deliver the closing speech; he had said to me a little before that it had occurred to him the audience might call for me; I said if they did I would instantly run out of the theatre, so that he might with perfect safety say I was not in it. The audience did call from the time the curtain fell, but not strongly enough till Bartley appeared, when their vociferation a good deal disconcerted him, and a momentary darkening of the lights, which made the audience laugh, did not tend to restore his self-possession. The cheering was so loud and long on his announcement of my continuance in the lessee-ship that I thought it time to decamp, and went out of the theatre.

From 23 July he acted at the Haymarket.

July 31. Called on Mr Anderson at the Fleet Prison—passing through the galleries and seeing the persons confined there, was struck with the inutility of such a punishment! Saw Anderson, who seemed surprised to see me; gave him a cheque for £20; wished to know if I could do anything further for him or his wife—near her confinement; expected that he would discharge all his *real* debts on his release, and parted very kindly from him. . . .

[Anderson had been sued unexpectedly for managerial debts from his days in Cheltenham. He could do only one thing: he went to the Fleet Prison for three months, a kind of holiday enforced, spent in reading, writing, studying Shakespeare, and playing rackets.]

August 3. My mind was occupied for some time in endeavouring to compute my pecuniary loss by management. I find I managed to lose, as I first thought, judging from actual decrease of capital, and absence of profit by my labour, £2500, or, measuring my receipt by the previous year, £1800. It is a painful subject for rumination. . . .

Talfourd's 'The Athenian Captive' was in production at last.

August 4. Felt at the rehearsal that my part *must fail* of effect, and in consequence became very low-spirited and uncomfortable. . . . Later acted Thoas with vigour and effect; quite bore the play on my own strength. Was called for by the audience; went on leading Mrs Warner [Ismene], and was very cordially received. Talfourd came into my room in a state of high excitement and delight; was lavish in his acknowledgments, and surprised, as he expressed himself, at the effect I had produced. Dickens, Browning, Forster, Horne, came into my room. *[Richard Hengist Horne (1803-1884), poet was author of the so-called 'farthing epic', 'Orion' (1843; sold for a farthing).]*

August 22. Agreed to take 13, Cumberland Terrace, from 15th September to 24th March at £7 10s. per week.

For his second season at Covent Garden Macready had roughly the same company, with the addition of Vandenhoff and his daughter. He began to consider 'The Tempest' and was much exercised about Priscilla Horton's dress and the 'flying' of her Ariel. He also planned to light the theatre with the newly invented 'liquid gas'. The season began on 24 September with 'Coriolanus': Vandenhoff as Caius Marcius, Phelps as Aufidius.

September 25. . . . Read the papers: heard that *The Times* was as disgusting in its insidious treatment of me and my exertions as ever.

September 26. Spoke to Miss Faucit about her boy's dress for Imogen [*Cymbeline*], and suggested to her, on the supposition that her legs were rather thin, the use of a pair of fleeced stockings 'such as Malibran used to wear'. I managed this 'delicate negotiation' as dexterously as I could, and reconciled her easily to the experiment; went out and purchased a pair for her, which were sent home at three o'clock, with a pair of my own, and I gave them to her. Surprised at the return of the house, which far exceeded my expectations.

October 1. . . . Annoyed by finding my orders and intentions completely frustrated through the indolence and ignorance of the persons employed; the closet scene [*Hamlet*] which I had intended to be a beautiful effect, was necessarily left in its original state. Rehearsed the play very feebly and unsatisfactorily; in one or two places I proved to myself that I could act the character well if I could only throw myself heartily and naturally into it. Looked at my letters. Lay down on my bed, which I was obliged to make up with cloaks, etc. Rose almost hopeless, nerved myself as I dressed, and acted Hamlet perhaps altogether as well as I have ever done. . . .

October 13. [*The Tempest*]. Rehearsed the play and made some valuable alterations, Received letters, one informing me that the writer, a creditor of Mr W—, would arrest him, and prevent his performance this evening if I did not 'intercede' and settle the debt. Read Prospero as well as I could; acted it as well as I could—but how could I act it well with the excitement and load of such a production on my mind? Was greatly received. Called for after the play, and received again with enthusiasm. Dickens and Forster went to our box. Spoke to Miss P. Horton on her performance; thanked her and kissed her. Gave largess to the carpenters.

[This was one of the major successes of Macready's management. Previously 'The Tempest' had always been staged in the Dryden-Davenant perversion. Miranda had a sister, Dorinda; she, in turn, had a lover called Hippolito, an island-youth who had never seen a man just as Miranda had never before

*seen a woman. It was very symmetrical, and rather foolish. Macready
abandoned it and brought back Shakespeare's text—or much of it. Priscilla
Horton's skimming flights as Ariel delighted the house, though 'John Bull'
complained testily that she had been whisked about by wires and a cog-wheel
like the 'Cinderella' fairies. Macready was Prospero; Helen Faucit,
Miranda; George Bennett, Caliban. There were fifty-five performances to
an average of £230 a night, and the revival could have lasted much longer
if Macready had wished.]*

October 14. Could not recover myself from the excitement of last
night. The scenes of the storm, the flights of Ariel, and the enthusiasm
of the house were constantly recurring to me.

October 15. Went to the theatre, where I saw the newspapers, renewed
the excitement that I thought had subsided. I tried to tranquillize myself,
but vainly. This is not a life to live for one who wishes to improve himself by living—it is a tempest indeed.

October 16. Acted Prospero very roughly—was called for, and led on
Miss P. Horton. Spoke to Willmott about inaccuracies; to Mr W— about
his probable arrest, of which I had been apprised by Notter. Would not
permit the sheriff's officer to enter the theatre, nor would I consent to
Mr W.'s request to let him through the private boxes.

October 22. Bartley brought the news of the failure of the 'horse and
beast' piece at Drury Lane. *[A spectacle called 'Charlemagne', with
Ducrow's horsemanship and Van Amburgh's lions, tigers, and leopards.]*
I do *feel thankful* for this defeat of a bad man's attempt to debase still
lower the art and artists he has so long and brutally oppressed. . . .

October 24. Letter from Bulwer informing me that he had made out
the rough sketch of a play, an historical comedy, on the subject of
Richelieu. I answered him, delighted at the news.

November 1. Miss Faucit returned me her part in the new tragedy
with a note, which made me very angry. I began a note to her under
much irritation, but had just sense enough to resolve to defer it till
to-morrow. *Never do anything in passion.*

November 2. . . . Wrote to Miss Faucit, sending back the part of
Lady Catherine to her.

November 3. Miss Faucit again wrote to me, again returning the part
in Haynes's tragedy *[Ruthven]*. I sent for her and spoke to her between
the first and third acts. She remained obstinate. Acted Prospero pretty
well. . . . Went into the box to see the new opera; received a note from
Miss Faucit consenting to act the part. Went down and spoke to her. . . .

November 4. . . . Wrote a copy of letter to return the letter of that offensive fool, Mr Pritchard, who now tells me that he was insulted last 13th of November by me! I told him then I wished him to go, but he chose to remain—to take my money—to profit by his engagement—to pass me every day without decent courtesy—and now he lets me know that his feelings were insulted!

November 8. Forster came into my room and proposed on the part of Dickens the dramatization of *Oliver Twist*, with Dickens's name. Nothing can be kinder than this generous intention of Dickens, but I fear it is not acceptable.

November 9. . . . The skimming over *Oliver Twist* occupied me more than the whole day.

November 10. Forster and Dickens called; and I told them of the utter impracticability of *Oliver Twist* for any dramatic purpose.

November 12. Bulwer called, and promised to send his play of *Richelieu* up to Cumberland Terrace. Acted Macbeth but indifferently, not altogether well. . . . Found Bulwer's play at home; sat up till half-past two to read it.

November 15. Read greater part of Bulwer's play of *Richelieu*, which, though excellent in parts, is deficient in the important point of conti-nuity of interest. . . . I fear the play will not do—cannot be made effective.

November 17. Called on Bulwer, and talked over the play of *Richelieu*. He combated my objections, and acceded to them, as his judgment swayed him; but when I developed the object of the whole plan of alterations he was in ecstasies. I never saw him so excited, several times exclaiming he was 'enchanted' with the plan, and observed in high spirits, 'What a fellow you are!' He was indeed delightful. I left him the play, and he promised to let me have it in a week! He is a wonderful man. . . .

November 18. Sir E. Bulwer called, and showed me two scenes, good ones, that he had already written. Settled the plot of the remainder. . . .

November 21. . . . Bulwer called, bringing with him the completed *Richelieu*. . . . Arrived at home, read through the play. I begin to be deadened to the interest of its story; it seems to be occasionally lengthy. I fear it has not the clinging interest of his present successful play, but hope and trust are good supporters.

November 25. Sir Edward Bulwer and Forster came to dinner; after which I read the play of *Richelieu* to them and Catherine and Letitia; its effect was not what I had hoped, and in the fifth act Forster was asleep. This evidently hurt Bulwer, and we talked long after it. Forster, when Bulwer had gone, sat long talking over it, and admitted (what he never would have done but for this accident) that the interest of the play was not sufficient. I deeply feel the disappointment on Bulwer's account, to whom I am *so much indebted*.

November 26. Forster came into my room, and went to our box where Catherine gave me a letter from Bulwer; chagrined and evidently *angry* with Forster. It gave me great pain. Forster was importunate on its purport, which I was obliged to tell him I could not (according to Bulwer's expressed wish) communicate, He has warmth of feeling (Forster) but not much judgment, and wants the tact of good breeding[1] . . . . I acted Iago ill. . . .

November 27. Wrote to Bulwer in answer to his note, expressing to him how foremost in my consideration was his reputation; that his play would have been valuable from any other person, but that it would not serve his interest, whether in reference to his literary fame, his station, or his political position. *[In his letter Macready added: 'Forster, with all his faults, is so warm-hearted, and I think so thoroughly enwrapt in an ardent admiration of you, that I apprehend you misjudge the intent of anything he may have said.']* Acted Prospero rather better than I have done lately. . . . Bulwer came into my room, and in a very warm manner expressed himself most gratified with my note, and much obliged. He sat and talked about *Richelieu*, and left me the note (a very valuable one) that he had written to me.

November 29. Forster called, and showed me a very kind letter from Bulwer to him. . . .

December 5. Dickens brought me his farce *[The Lamplighter]*, which he read to me. The dialogue is very good, full of point, but I am not sure about the meagreness of the plot. He reads as well as an experienced actor would—he is a surprising man.

December 6. . . . Wrote to the editor of the *Weekly Dispatch*, striking that paper off the free list.

December 7. . . . A very grossly insulting letter from the editor of the *Weekly Dispatch*—which, in my first impulse, I re-enclosed in its own *turned cover*; but hesitated, under the supposition that it might seem too haughty, and wrote a gentlemanly letter of retort, quietly repeating that falsehood had been my provocation and that the subsequent reply to me was impertinent. Brydone suggested the return of the letter, as I had at first intended, and I, concurring with him, re-enclosed it in its own cover, and sent it back to the editor.

December 8. . . . Mr Willmott told me that Mr Williams, the editor

[1] Augustine Birrell would describe Forster as 'the best of all disagreeable friends'. (*The London Mercury*, May 1920.)

of the *Dispatch*, had published my letter and the one he sent me (which I returned to him) in the paper—the wretched blackguard! He had not said that I had returned it. Miss Faucit asked me to write my name on a print of Virginius, which I did. Note from Bulwer with his play, which I read; it is greatly improved, but still not quite to the point of success.

December 11. Dickens came with Forster and read his farce. There was manifest disappointment; it went flatly, a few ready laughs, but generally an even smile, broken in upon by the horse-laugh of Forster, the most *indiscreet* friend that ever allied himself to any person. He has goaded Dickens to write this farce, and now (without testing its chances of success) would *drive* it upon the stage. Defend me from my friends! It was agreed that it should be put into rehearsal, and, when nearly ready, should be seen and judged of by Dickens! I cannot sufficiently condemn the officious folly of this marplot, Forster, who embroils his friends in difficulties and distress in this most determined manner. It is quite too bad.

December 12. A long discussion on Dickens's farce; called in for their opinion Messrs Bartley and Harley. The result was that Forster decided on withdrawing the farce.

December 13. Wrote to Bulwer, and to Dickens, about his farce, explaining to him my motives for wishing to withdraw it, and my great obligation to him. He returned me an answer which is an honour to him. How truly delightful it is to meet with high-minded and warm-hearted men. Dickens and Bulwer have been certainly to me noble specimens of human nature, and show out strongly the pitiful contrast that a man like Talfourd offers. . . .

December 16. Attended to my accounts, and then gave the whole morning to the conclusion of the marking of *Richelieu*. Henry Smith and Serle called first, then Browning, Fox, Blanchard, and Lane *[John Bryant Lane (1788–1868), portrait painter]* to hear the reading of the play. I told them that no one must speak during the process, gave pencils and paper to each, with which they were severally to write down their opinions. The play was listened to with the deepest interest, and the opinions, all of which were favourable, were given in. I then spoke to them individually, and endeavoured to gain their precise opinions more in detail. . . .

December 19. Received a letter and MS of a play from Mrs Butler of Philadelphia, brought by Mr Power. *[Mrs Butler was Frances Anne (Fanny) Kemble (1809–1893), actress and writer, daughter of Charles Kemble, who married Pierce Butler, a Southern planter, in 1834.]*

December 20. . . . Finished the reading of Mrs Butler's play, which is one of the most powerful of the modern plays I have seen—most painful, almost shocking, but full of power, poetry, and pathos. She is one of the most remarkable women of the present day.

December 21. A son born *[Henry Frederick Bulwer Macready (1838–1857)]*. . . .Wrote to a person of the name of Rahles, who very kindly sent me a rich velvet cap in testimony of the pleasure he had received from my performance.

December 23. Looked through the unused plays of Shakespeare for *cementing* lines for the *Richard III*. . . .

The year's pantomime, Harlequin and Fair Rosamond; or, Old Dame Nature and the Fairy Art, *was apparently disastrous at first.*

December 26. Went to Covent Garden theatre, and rehearsed Hastings *[Jane Shore]*; then giving my attention to the pantomime until twenty minutes past five o'clock. Acted Lord Hastings indifferently; my mind was on the pantomime. From the utter absence of arrangement on the part of Mr Marshall, his clumsy attempt at contrivance, and the deficiency of his work, the pantomime completely failed. What will be the result I cannot guess—it will go near to ruin me. It is a terrible blow. *[Charles Marshall was the scene-painter.]*

December 27. . . . On my way *[to the theatre]* looked through the often-searched Shakespeare for some play. Thought of *King Henry V*, with the choruses to be spoken by Vandenhoff. Attended to the pantomime, which I cut, and set the performers and the carpenters about. Serle, when I suggested *Henry*, observed that the choruses would admit of illustration, a hint which I instantly caught at, and determined upon doing it. Attended to the performance of the pantomime, which, thank God, went off very smoothly. Afterwards arranged business for rehearsing it. . . .

December 29. I spoke to Miss P. Horton about her insubordinate language. She was much distressed about it.

December 30. Forster sent the papers to Letitia, by which it seems our pantomime stands fair for attraction. L.D. *[Laus Deo]*. . . . After dinner continued the attentive perusal of *Henry V*. . . . Resolved to defer it to Easter, and make it the last Shakespearean revival of my management.

1839

January 5. Read Bulwer's play of *Richelieu* to the actors, and was most agreeably surprised to find it excited them in a very extraordinary manner. *['Richelieu; or, The Conspiracy'. 'Triumph!' wrote Macready to Bulwer. 'The enthusiasm which accompanied the reading and followed the conclusion of the play was beyond any I have ever witnessed in a green-room.']* . . . Read a very strange note from some woman, threatening to destroy herself for love of me. The ugly need never despair after this. Answered it shortly.

January 7. Went to supper at Dickens's, where there was a large party for the christening of his youngest and the birthday of his eldest. At the supper there were speeches, which much annoyed me.

January 8. A note from the woman who had written to me on Saturday with so much *abandon*, enclosing her address, and begging for an answer. Answered the note I had received, saying that I would see the writer in Newman Street this evening, and hear what she had to say. . . . Left my coach at Newman Street, and met there the writer of the letters a fine-looking young woman, of modest deportment. I inquired of her, as we walked, her object in writing to me, and wishing to see me. She begged my pardon, and I learned that she had been living at Sir —'s. She asked if I was married. I told her I was, which seemed a bitter shock to her. I told her I was many years older than herself, and spoke to her with kindness. She made me uneasy from the deep and—as it seemed to me—*desperate* melancholy of her expression. I told her to let me know if I could do anything to serve her, and I would do it. I parted from her by Westminster Hall. I felt quite uneasy and dejected at what seemed to me her unhappiness. She had evidently encouraged the hope of *marrying* the ideal that had filled her mind from the representation of Claude Melnotte. Poor girl! I was quite depressed. How much are we the victims of an inevitable destiny! . . .

January 9. I was in very low spirits, and could not disguise the dejection into which the thought of that poor girl whom I saw last night sunk me. . . .

January 16. . . . Letter from Mary —; poor girl, she must suffer very much. I feel for her. She is evidently possessed with a deep and absorbing passion, and has right notions. I feel (what I have in reality endured) for her when she speaks of her agony as she will see the curtain fall and shut me for ever from her sight. Poor, poor girl! . . .

January 23. Note from the Vice-Chamberlain informing me of the Queen's intention to command next week, and wishing a list of plays. . . . Dickens sent me his *Oliver Twist*.

January 24. Heard that the Queen was going to pay a third visit to Drury Lane theatre to see the lions, and after the performance to go on the stage!

January 25. Read in the *Morning Post* the account of the Queen's third visit to Drury Lane theatre to see the beasts, and of her going upon the stage after the pantomime to see them fed. Mr Martin, the Vice-Chamberlain, called, wishing to know if we could send him word of the *length* of each that I could offer. He did not *exactly* know the night she would come (I believe he was enjoined not to communicate what he *did* know) and thought the *Lady of Lyons* would be the play.

January 26. Mr Martin, the Vice-Chamberlain, arrived to inform me of the night on which the Queen would command (which they knew two days ago!) and of the plays she had selected: *Lady of Lyons* and *Rob Roy*. Received a note from Dickens, wishing me to look in upon the Shakespeare Club in the course of the evening. Went to the Shakespeare Club, where I had to return thanks greatly to my annoyance.

January 31. Found my desk covered with notes and letters; one from Count D'Orsay, most kindly suggesting to me the avoidance of several defects complained of by the Queen at Drury Lane. . . .

February 1. . . . Acted Claude Melnotte very fairly. Her Majesty did not arrive until twenty-five minutes past seven. . . . *[Later]*. I had undressed, and was preparing to put on my court suit, when an equerry came from her Majesty to desire me to go on, as the audience were calling for me. I did not know what to do—told him, and showed him that I was quite undressed, but that I would do whatever her Majesty desired. He left me, and I thought it better to put on my dress again, which I did, and receiving a second message from her Majesty, went on as Melnotte before the audience, and met with a most enthusiastic reception, her Majesty and the Lord Chamberlain joining in the applause . . . Dressed in full court dress. Went into the antechamber when her Majesty came out. Lord Conyngham called me to her, and she condescended to say 'I have been very much pleased.' I bowed, and lighted her down. Glad to conclude a day that has been very wearying to me. . . .

February 2. Saw the newspapers. The *Morning Post* reported the proceedings of the night in a fair spirit. The *Morning Herald* and *The*

Times merely mentioned what related to the Queen—these honest persons. Saw the *Court Journal*, which contains a wretched piece of trash, justifying the Queen's patronage of Mr Van Amburgh. *[An American, Isaac Van Amburgh (1805–1865), the lion-tamer at Drury Lane.]*

February 11. . . . Note from D'Orsay. Found a note informing me that he had a play from B. *Disraeli!!!*

[This was 'The Tragedy of Count Alarcos' by Benjamin Disraeli, later Earl of Beaconsfield (1805–1881), politician and novelist. Set in Spain and founded on a 13th-century ballad, it was published in 1839 but not acted until 1868 at Astley's. It includes the lines on a storm:

> *The lightnings play*
> *Upon our turrets that no human step*
> *Can keep the watch. Each forky flash seems mission'd*
> *To scath our roof, and the whole platform flows*
> *With a blue sea of flame. . . .]*

February 18. Letter from the equerry-in-waiting, apprising me of the Queen's intended visit to Covent Garden this evening. Read over *King Lear*. . . . Acted King Lear well. The Queen was present, and I pointed at her the beautiful lines, 'Poor naked wretches!' . . .

February 20. . . . Gave my attention to the consideration of the character of Richelieu, which Bulwer has made particularly difficult by his inconsistency; he has made him resort to low jest, which outrages one's notions of the ideal of Cardinal Richelieu, with all his vanity and suppleness and craft.

February 21. . . . A MS. tragedy and note from B. Disraeli.

February 22. . . . A letter from Wightwick (who had heard that I was coming to Plymouth) informing me that Mr C. Kean had been playing to houses of £140 and £150 each—more than the theatre will hold!—and entreating me not to come, as I should be mortified by the contrast. It was kind in him, but I had no thought of going, as I told him in my answer. Resumed *Richelieu*, which I must *fabricate*. . . .

February 28. . . . Rehearsed the play of *Richelieu*, which occupied the whole morning till past four o'clock. Forster was present for most of the time. Bulwer called to seek him after he had gone. A letter from Knowles inquiring 'when the play of *Woman's Wit* would be done'! A play that was only sustained by the proprietors foregoing rent and I salary! Miss Faucit wished to speak to me—to ask for leave of absence tomorrow, I could not grant.

March 2. Went to Covent Garden theatre, where I rehearsed *Richelieu;* was much annoyed by Mr —'s absence, who is confined by gout—induced by a system of nightly intoxications. He is too bad—a wretched man on whom there is no dependence. Paid constant attention to the progress of the play, and thought it wore an improved appearance. Miss Faucit dined with me at half-past four. . . .

March 5. [*Richelieu* rehearsal]. By an accident of the printers Mrs Warner's name was inserted in the bills for Catherine in the farce instead of Miss Faucit's; notice was sent to her, and she came in very ill temper to speak about it. I accosted her very kindly, and she attacked me, asserting that the measure had been adopted 'for the mere accommodation of Miss Faucit'. This was too bad from a person under such obligations as Mrs Warner is to me. It is indeed *most ungrateful.* She wished to speak to me again, and I went to hear what she had to say, expecting to find her anxious to express her regret for her previous intemperance, but she only aggravated what had passed before. Bulwer came in, and saw the last three acts rehearsed with which he seemed very well satisfied.

The Queen decided to come to the première, and was sent a book of the play.

March 7. Colonel Cavendish and his two sons called; his business was to tell me that the Queen would come this evening. Lay down after dinner to compose my shaken nerves. Bulwer called, and *disturbed* me—to give me a book for the Queen. At the same time a letter was delivered to me; when Bulwer had left me I opened the letter. It was from Colonel Cavendish to inform me that the Queen would *not* come this evening. Acted Cardinal Richelieu very nervously; lost my self-possession, and was obliged to use too much effort; it did not satisfy me at all, there were no artist-like touches through the play. How can a person get up such a play and do justice at the same time to such a character? It is not possible. . . . What will the papers say?

[Macready as the 'blood-red comet', the Cardinal who mingled Wolsey and Iago, had no idea of the effect he had made. But the great Covent Garden pit had appeared to rock and sway with enthusiasm. At the end, according to Jerdan in the 'Literary Gazette', the entire audience rose and cheered Macready for some moments. London would talk of the scene in which Richelieu, sheltering his ward Julie in her bridal dress, threatened to launch the curse of Rome on Baradas. The cast included Helen Faucit as Julie, Elton as Louis XIII, Warde as the Count de Baradas, Anderson as the Chevalier de Mauprat, Diddear as the Duke of Orleans, Vining as the Sieur de

Beringhen, Phelps as Father Joseph. The production would have thirty-seven performances during the season.]

March 8. Saw the papers. The *Morning Chronicle* was as usual most kind and eulogistic; *The Times*, although trying to damn with faint praise, admitting much more than I expected, and enough to give to its readers, who knew its baseness, the assurance of success. Went to the theatre, where I cut the play with the performers, and expressed myself much obliged by their zeal and industry. When we had separated, Bulwer came and altered that we had arranged—annoying and disconcerting me very much. I struggled for the omission of several passages, but he was triumphant, and therefore no longer so *docile* as I had heretofore found him.

March 9. Met Mrs Warner, who looked very differently at me, poor foolish woman. . . . Colonel Cavendish brought me word that the Queen, prevented by the weather on Thursday night, would come this evening.

March 13. Two long notes from Bulwer—with more last words—and a lengthy criticism on some points of my performance, in which he wishes me to substitute coarse and vulgar attempt at low farcical point in one instance, and melodramatic rant in another for the more delicate shadings of character that I endeavour to give. I have long had surmises about Bulwer's taste from several things in the comedy of *La Vallière*—in the original of *The Lady of Lyons* and in the original copy of this play. I am *sure* that his taste is not to be depended on. Saw *The Times*, in which was a letter from that contemptible wretch, Mr Bunn. His anger and indiscretion look as if he were near the end. God grant it! Amen. Difficulty in answering Bulwer's notes without giving offence—at last dismissed his worrying prosings with brief generalities.

March 14. Received a note from Bulwer proposing another subject for a play this season, if I wished it. What an indefatigable man! Read over *Richelieu*. Acted the part very fairly. . . . The Queen was in the theatre.

March 21. Webster called, and expressed his anxiety to give me £100 per week—£25 per night for four nights a week, for his whole season, to the 15th of January. I promised him that I would sign with him directly the proprietors of Covent Garden theatre declined my offer.

March 23. . . . Robertson came into my room, and I explained to him the nature of the offer which I intended to make to the proprietors. He seemed to think it not unlikely to be entertained by them. . . . Miss Faucit came for my signature to two prints of Virginius.

March 26. . . . Coming home, I finished the perusal of Disraeli's play, which will never come to any good. It is taken from an old Spanish ballad on the Count Alarcos, and the Infanta Solisa, etc. . . .

March 27. Read the newspaper; was disgusted with the tone of the American Press anticipating a war with England. War! war! That men, the creatures of a God of wisdom and of love, should rush forward in savage delight to mangle and slay each other! . . .

March 28. Forster called at the theatre, and told me that Bulwer had nearly finished his play, which is most powerful. . . .

The Shakespeare Club gave a dinner to Macready, Dickens in the chair: some forty present, including Stanfield, Leigh Hunt, Maclise, Jerrold, Thackeray, Lover, Forster.

March 30. . . . The most hearty sympathy I almost ever witnessed was unbroken through the evening. I was obliged to remain until the business of the day was done, and was astonished to learn from the waiter that it was a quarter past twelve. I set Mr Harley down, and on coming home, racked with headache from the heat of the room, reported all to Catherine and Letty, whilst I had the power of remembering. Dickens's speech in proposing my health was most earnest, eloquent, and touching. It took a review of my enterprise at Covent Garden, and summed up with an eulogy on myself that quite overpowered me. . . . *[Macready replied]*. . . . Leigh Hunt was called up, being honorary member and guest of the day, and in a rambling, conversational style talked of what Shakespeare would think if he could walk into the room and ask on what man's account all this festivity and sympathy was raised, and how surprised and pleased he would be to learn that it was himself. . . . I rose to propose Dickens's health, and spoke my sincere opinion of him as the highest eulogy, by alluding to the verisimilitude of his characters. I said that I should not be surprised at receiving the offer of an engagement from Crummles for the next vacation. All went off in the happiest spirit. Procter—*mirabile dictu!*—so yielded to the spirit of enjoyment that he fell at last into a profound sleep of nearly two hours; we parted, in the best of spirits, at past one o'clock. *[This was Bryan Waller Procter ('Barry Cornwall'; 1787–1874), writer and lawyer; biographer of Edmund Kean.]*

March 31. Wrote a very courteous note to J. [B.] Disraeli on his play, and to Mr G. P. James *[G. P. R. James, 1801–1860, historical novelist]* on his; it is not so easy to write a play as a novel.

April 6. . . . Went with Forster to Covent Garden. Robertson had been inquiring for me. When he came in, he had nothing to say—looked very gloomy and seemed to understand that the business of my separation from the theatre was finally settled. Decided on announcing my retirement. Drew up the advertisement.

April 7. Called on Stanfield, and told him the state of affairs at Covent Garden theatre—that I should get out *King Henry V* and wish to have his aid. He most readily—heart and hand—went with my views, blaming extremely the stupidity of the proprietors. . . .

April 8. Willmott came in, spoke of the grief and gloom that had been spread over the theatre. Robertson came; informed me that Mr C. Kean was engaged by Mr Webster. I was not disposed to believe it . . . Webster called. I questioned him about Mr C. Kean; he admitted it; I thought it very disingenuous in him and was not pleased. I recommended —*if* he could with prudence and safety to his financial arrangements and *if* he wished to make his theatre a miniature Covent Garden, that he should strengthen his company by engaging Mr Anderson, Willmott, and Mrs Warner. He said he certainly would, though the recommendation did not seem very palatable to him.

April 9. . . . Willmott came into my room to tell me that a notice had been put up in the Hall, requiring 'the performers to meet the proprietors in the Saloon at three o'clock.—Signed, H. Robertson.' I was shocked at this gross impertinence of my servant, Mr Robertson and the vulgar outrage on my rights by the proprietors. Passing by the green-room, I saw the same notice on the glass, I pulled it down and threw it into the fire. As the play proceeded I saw more clearly the very low conduct of these men, and my equanimity returned—particularly on reading and repeating some of the beautiful maxims of Prospero. There is some *virtue* in poetry; it has often helped my mind in its struggles. Acted fairly Prospero. (Miss P. Horton and Miss Faucit came to speak to me. I desired them both to go to the Actors' Meeting.) Talfourd thought that they might just as well have called the 'meeting' in my private room, or even in my 'drawing-room at Cumberland Terrace'. Talfourd thought it a most happy thing that I was released from the management, which was actually consuming life, health, and all delight.

A week of anger followed, with a quarrel between Macready and the proprietors over the sums due to him. He discovered that he was 'manacled in every way as, literally, the servant—*instead of the tenant—of the proprietors'. Robertson, in particular, had been perfidious. On 15 April Macready addressed the players in the green-room for an hour and a quarter, stigmatising the proprietors' 'shameful falsehood and dishonourable con-*

duct', explaining that he had been 'for two years juggled into the belief that I was the lessee', only to find himself the theatre's 'salaried foreman'. His speech and his promise—under all the indignities he endured—to carry on the theatre to the end, for the company's sake, produced a message of unqualified admiration and gratitude. But when his back was turned, some players repented. The text of their first strong attack on the proprietors was so 'altered and emasculated' when it reached Macready, that he forbade its publication. He would not submit to paltering.

April 16. Went to Covent Garden theatre. I sent for Mr Elton and told him that I supposed it was unnecessary to see the whole deputation of performers, but that I might communicate to him for the body that I had read the *resolution* and wished it not to be printed. He was very much confused, and evidently distressed. He said he feared that it was not altogether satisfactory to me. I told him that it was useless to enter upon any question upon the subject, that I had said all that was necessary last night, and that I had only today to return an answer to the question of publication. He left me very uncomfortably. . . . Acted King Lear *very well*—as well, if not better than I had ever done.

April 28. Woke early, and fell into reflections, painful at first from the indignation and disgust which must arise in thinking upon baseness and evil; but I have thought myself into a happier state of mind by considering the *actual* amount of injury which these base and bad men the proprietors have the power of doing me. If I do not injure myself, if I only preserve my temper, and let the facts between us speak, I must remain with a great increase of reputation, and they, when their conduct is known, must be condemned; they may rob me of my claims for surplus, but what is £350 to the peaceful possession of the honour that must attach to me for what I have done, and striven to do! I feel myself *above them*.

April 30. Went to Elstree in the carriage with Catherine and Willie; enjoyed to a degree I cannot describe the air, the freedom, the sight of the country, and the old familiar objects of my passage to and from Elstree. . . .

May 6. . . . Rehearsed *Coriolanus*, which gave me much uneasiness, for it ought to have been prepared on Saturday. I was much fatigued by the rehearsal. Was in a state of extreme nervousness—dispirited and unwell. . . . Acted Coriolanus. Was quite struck, as by a shock, on seeing the pit *not full* at my entrance. I instantly, whilst I bowed to the audience, rallied and resolved to do my best. It is a useful lesson to teach me how I ought to estimate my own exertion. The public is, *of course*, the most selfish of human bodies, and a sensible man ought to act upon it accordingly. Acted the part moderately, not very satisfactorily...

May 25. Letter from White and Whitmore with the version of the proprietors' agreement—a string of falsehoods. It made me very angry, and I went *very imprudently* to speak to Bartley about his friend Robertson. I could see that the wretched fellow *enjoyed* my anger. I soon cooled, but was ill through it. Acted ill—called for. Forster came—*ill—ill*.

May 26. What a dreadful calamity to me—what a source of continued suffering is this excitability of temper to me. . . . I have scarcely slept the whole night, the pressure on my head made me at one time alarmed for my clearness of reason. I got up and took medicine, and tried to think (though vainly for a long time) on other subjects than the detested theatre. . . . Browning called, told me *Sordello* was finished.

May 27. Phelps came in and asked for leave to quit the theatre; he had become security for a relation who had embezzled money, and was in dread of the consequences. I asked him of the particulars, and, on his acquainting me with them, recommended him not to think of going, but that I would endeavour to advance him the money, and he should repay me on his salary. *[Macready handed Phelps a cheque for £450.]* Miss Faucit came in to speak to me about stuffed stockings. . . .

June 1. Saw in the *Gazette* the name of that bad man, Bunn, as having sold the commission of Gentleman Pensioner, purchased out of the pillage of the actors' salaries. I could not see without some satisfaction that retribution has been at last awarded to him. . . .

June 3. . . . The last night, the fifty-fifth, of *The Tempest* was crowded. I felt quite melancholy as we approached the end of the play; it had become endeared to me from success and the benefit it had occurred upon my undertaking. . . . I look back on its production with satisfaction, for it has given to the public a play of Shakespeare which had never been seen before, and it has proved the charm of simplicity and poetry.

June 5. Had a long rehearsal of four acts of *King Henry V*. Tried on the armour of Henry and dined in it. . . .

June 8. Tried on my armour, which I wore through the afternoon, and was obliged at last to put off for its weight. . . .

June 9. Put on my armour for *King Henry V*, and moved and sat in it until half-past three o'clock. . . .

June 10. . . . Began the play of *King Henry V* in a very nervous state, but endeavouring to keep my mind clear. Acted sensibly at first, and very spiritedly at last; was very greatly received, and when called on at last, the whole house stood up and cheered me in a most fervent manner. I gave out the repetition of the play for four nights a week till the close of the season. . . . Catherine and Letitia were there, and I accompanied them back to Elstree in a state of the greatest excitement. It is the last of my attempts to present to the audience Shakespeare's own meaning.

[This performance of 'King Henry V', the most elaborate production Covent Garden had known, restored to the stage the Chorus (John Vandenhoff) in the character of Time, with glass and scythe. Macready used various tableaux and a diorama: 'To impress more strongly on the auditor, and render more palpable those portions of the story which have not the advantage of action, and still are requisite to the Drama's completeness, the narrative and descriptive poetry spoken by the Chorus is accompanied with Pictorial Illustrations from the pencil of Mr Stanfield.' Macready represented the battle by a transformation before the audience. Troops painted on the backcloth turned suddenly to troops that peopled a true field of battle. Smoke that had whirled across the scene was puffed away, and there in depth, on the vast Covent Garden stage, were the contending armies, 'the very casques that did affright the air at Agincourt'. The company included Elton (Exeter), Meadows (Fluellen), Anderson (Gower), Harley (Pistol), Priscilla Horton (Boy), Bennett (Charles VI), Vining (Dauphin), Phelps (Constable of France), Miss Vandenhoff (Katharine). Mrs C. Jones acted Quickly instead of Anne Humby who threw up the part at the last rehearsal, angered by constant interruptions from John Forster whom mischievous colleagues told her had written the play.]

June 11. . . . At three o'clock returned in the carriage to town, Catherine and Letitia accompanying me. Stopped Billings's coach, and got from it a parcel containing the newspapers which Forster had sent. They were all favourable. . . . Thank God that it is over, and so well over.

June 16. Came to town with Catherine and Letitia, reading Bulwer's play of *Norman*[1] by the way. *I do not like it.* Dressed in great haste, and went with Catherine to Horace Twiss's to dinner. *[Horace Twiss (1787–1849), lawyer and M.P., was nephew of Mrs Siddons.]* . . . Rather an agreeable day, though we arrived after all had sat down. Disraeli made acquaintance with me, and told me a good story of Hume. I found that Daniel Webster had called on my return home.

June 17. Daniel Webster called and sat a short time. He seemed greatly pleased with England. Settled on closing the theatre, July 16th, with Willmott. I am anxious to feel free of it.

June 18. . . . Sent for the *Sunday Times*, with the notice of *King*

---

[1] Became *The Sea-Captain; or, The Birthright.*

Henry in it. I was disgusted—these ignorant coxcombs are our *critics!*

June 20. Read *Norman* again; was much struck with the *effect* of the two last acts, though I do not altogether like the play, it is far too melodramatic. . . . Saw in the Court news that the Websters were at the Queen's ball, which I was glad to know. Bulwer, C. Buller, and Talfourd were also there. It is not a pleasing reflection, without caring for the thing itself, that my pariah profession should entitle me to the lavish expression of public praise, and exclude me from distinctions which all my compeers enjoy. . . . Brydone *[Macready's business manager at the time]* came in and spoke about accounts. It appears that we have acted *The Tempest* fifty-five nights to an average exceeding £230. This is not a common event. Forster came, and hearing that I had hashed venison, consented to have a dish sent for.

June 21. . . . Came to town in a chaise that seemed to have hatched all the poultry in the village for half a century back. I was ashamed to be seen in such a thing, and slept my journey to town away in it. The driver took me all down Regent Street to Carlton Place, Pall Mall, then round the National Gallery, up St Martin's Lane, through Long Acre, down Bow Street to the stage-door, Covent Garden theatre. My patience was quite exhausted. . . .

June 24. Called on Mr D. Webster, whom I found at home, some gentlemen calling on him. I did not think he seemed quite easy at my call. Is it that he has been much caressed, and not met me in the *high regions*, where he has been spending his days in England, or to what am I to attribute what, without anything like jealousy or even uncomfortableness of feeling. I cannot help perceiving to be a changed and, I should say, an awkward demeanour? . . .

June 30. Came to the conclusion that if it were ever proposed to me to undertake the management of a theatre again, I should give no answer *until I had read carefully over the diaries of the two years now past*.

July 8. . . . Sent to Head about my clothes, which he brought; but he informed me that he had received an order from Mr Robertson, that by order of the proprietors he was not to allow me to take away any of the clothes which I had had made for myself! I really did not well know what to say to him; he was very civil; I told him he was quite right, but to bring the clothes—he was my servant, and if he did not obey my orders I should discharge him. He brought them immediately, and I locked them in my imperials. . . .

July 15. Addressed the performers assembled in the green-room. Told them that. . . . I wished merely to say that at our last meeting I had pledged myself to keep the theatre open to the latest possible period, without requiring any condition from them. I had done so under every species of outrage and petty insult that these persons, the proprietors, could put on me through my own servants; that I had laid a moral obligation on myself; as to what I had said to them on the subject of my undertaking not being a mercenary one, I was here today to discharge it. At the same time, in the kindest spirit, as my connection with them must end here, I felt that they had not done me justice in evading the direct statement of the proprietor's conduct, which they *admitted* to be false and treacherous. . . . Vining and Bennett said something in exculpation, but it went to nothing. . . .

[Helen Faucit wrote to him that day from 30 Brompton Square: 'Your manner and expressions at the meeting called by you this morning evidently evinced an impression on your part that the performers of Covent Garden Theatre in your dispute with the Proprietors had not acted towards you with the fair dealing which was your expectation and due . . . I know and recognise but 'yourself', and feeling as I do the warmest gratitude for the honourable and kind manner with which I have been treated, I cannot but express my earnest hope that you do not even in thought extend to me a censure on my part so truly undeserved.' (Letter in Raymond Mander and Joe Mitchenson Theatre Collection).]

July 16. Prepared to play in a very depressed condition. My reception was so great, from a house crowded in every part, that I was shaken by it. I acted King Henry V better than I had yet done, and the house responded to the spirit in which I played. The curtain fell amidst the loudest applause, and when I had changed my dress I went before the curtain, and amidst shoutings and wavings of hats and handkerchiefs by the whole audience standing up, the stage was literally covered with wreaths, bouquets, and branches of laurel. When at last the dense mass resumed their seats, and the tumult subsided to the stillest silence, I began my address. The cheering was renewed as I bowed and left the stage, and as I passed through the lane which the actors and people, crowding behind, made for me, they cheered me also. Forster came in my room and was much affected; Fox was quite shaken; Dickens, Maclise, Stanfield, T. Cooke *[Thomas Simpson Cooke (1782-1848), musical director of Drury Lane]*, Blanchard, Lord Nugent (who had not been in the theatre), Bulwer, Hockley of Guildford, Browning, Serle, Brydone, Willmott, came into my room; most of them asked for memorials from the baskets and heaps of flowers, chaplets, and laurels that were strewn upon the floor. Went home with Catherine and Letitia, carrying the wreaths, etc.

Elstree, July 17. . . . Received the newspapers. . . . *The Times* was consistent in its open knavery—not one word in report or comment upon the speech or the evening. . . .

On 20 July he was entertained to a dinner at the Freemasons' Tavern, with the Duke of Sussex[1] in the chair, and most of his staunch friends present. 'The Duke talked much to me, more than I wished; but a full glass of sherry seemed to steady my nerves a little, though I looked very grave and pale, as I was afterwards told, and Bulwer said I looked like "a baffled tyrant".' *When Macready rose, after the Duke had proposed his health, the whole room, with the ladies in the gallery, stood up, cheering and waving handkerchiefs as if it had been a Covent Garden first night. He spoke briefly, saying that he had tried to present the works of the dramatic poets, chiefly Shakespeare's, with the truth of illustration they merited, a truth that a public with such a dramatic literature had a right to demand. He had hoped, if he had stayed in management, to produce the complete Shakespearean series in a text purified from interpolation and distortion. His poverty, not his will, compelled him to desist.*

Elstree, July 21. . . . Rose very late; could only talk—only think over the exciting circumstances of yesterday and last night. My head ached much. . . . Went to afternoon church; overcome by fatigue and drowsiness. In the garden afterwards. Read prayers to the family.

Elstree, August 7. Went to church with Dickens, Forster, Maclise—to meet Catherine and her party with darling little Henry who was christened by Dr Morris. Dickens gave him a silver cup—as his godfather. He is one to be proud of. After the children's dinner went to the reservoir, where Dickens, Maclise and Forster joined us; pulled on the water with Dickens. Welsh came to the bank to tell me I was wanted; saw Bulwer and Willie as I went up the field. They returned with me, and Forster landed and joined us. I talked much with Bulwer about a play. Forster, Bulwer, and myself went into the field and shot with the bow for some time. A pleasant day. . . .

On 19 August Macready began a Haymarket Theatre engagement that lasted until 15 January 1840. Though he began by alternating Othello and Iago with Phelps (Helen Faucit as Desdemona), the arrangement ceased immediately when Phelps was too successful as Othello.

London August 19. . . . Acted Othello, in part well, in part languidly.

[1] Augustus Frederick, Duke of Sussex (1773–1843), sixth son of George III.

The audience did not seem to be of the same quality of intellect as I had been used to at Covent Garden. But let us hope.

August 21. Went to theatre for rehearsal. I sensibly feel the descent from Covent Garden into this dog-hole of a theatre—dirt, slovenliness, and puffery make up the sum of its character. Found Browning at my lodgings on my return, and was kept by him long, but he left me where he found me. His object, if he exactly knew it, was to learn from me whether, if he wrote a really good play, it would have a secure chance of acceptance. I told him certainly, and after much vague conversation, he left me to read and rest as I could.

Elstree, August 27. Continued Leigh Hunt's play, of which I read four acts; they are hopeless; he *cannot* write a dramatic work.

[This was presumably 'The Secret Marriage,' later 'The Prince's Marriage'. In his 'Autobiography' Hunt wrote that 'A Legend of Florence' was 'declined by the principal manager then reigning. I wrote another blank-verse play in five acts, thinking to please better by adapting it to his taste, but I succeeded as little by this innocent artifice.']

London September, 2. . . . Acted Iago very unsatisfactorily, and *quite lost my temper—an inexcusable fault.* The audience applauded Othello, Mr Phelps, who got through the part very respectably, but seemed not to understand me. . . .

September 5. Read Browning's play on Victor, King of Sardinia—it turned out to be a *great mistake.* I called Browning into my room and most explicitly told him so, and gave him my reasons for coming to such a conclusion.

September 17. Letitia mentioned to-night that Forster had told them that Dickens intended to dedicate *Nickleby* to me. I was sorry he had mentioned it, for such an honour—as great a one as a man can receive— should not be divulged, for fear of accident.

September 18. Rehearsed Shylock with very few persons, and did not feel at all at home in it. I have not got the key to the character, and must sternly and resolutely take the part in hand.

[He had always argued—maybe fearing, subconsciously, a challenge to Kean —that success as Shylock would not aid his reputation, and failure must do some harm. The Haymarket cast included Helen Faucit as Portia, Phelps as Antonio, and Buckstone as Launcelot Gobbo.]

September 22. Received a most kind letter from Dickens with the proof sheet of the dedication of *Nickleby* to me. Surely this is something to gratify me. . . .

September 25. Read Bulwer's play *[The Sea-Captain]*, which I did not like so well as the original *Norman*. . . . Miss Faucit wished to speak to me after the play *[The Lady of Lyons]*; she was very open in her disclosures. Webster came to speak to me about Mrs Warner, who is not so.

September 30. Rose in a very nervous and wandering state of mind; very much magnifying to myself the possibilities attendant on my experiment of Shylock this evening, and suffering under imaginations and apprehensions that appear absurd upon the occasion. The unpleasant position of this character is that its success would not be any great accession to my reputation, and failure must do some harm in any undertaking. . . . Acted Shylock, and tried to do my best; but how unavailing is all reasoning against painful facts—the performance was an utter failure. I felt it, and suffered very much for it. Browning came into my room and said all that sympathy and friendly feeling could suggest.

October 4. . . . I acted Shylock in many instances very fairly.

On 5 October he proposed Dickens's health at a 'too splendid dinner', at the Albion, Aldersgate Street, to celebrate the publication of Nickleby. '*I did not get through well.*'

October 9. Arriving, waited for Miss H. Faucit, to whom I gave some very excellent advice upon the part of Portia, and other things, for which she was very much obliged. I dismissed her very kindly and properly. Webster and Willmott called, and I read to them the three acts of Bulwer's play. Bulwer came in while we were thus engaged, and was gratified in hearing that the acts had made so favourable an impression. He left with me the other two acts, which I read to them. They approved, and I observed that my hands were now washed of the business; if Webster chose to accept it he had only to signify as much to Sir Edward Bulwer and arrange all the rest with him. *[Macready and Webster much needed a new play; Webster paid £600 to Bulwer for the London rights for three years.]* They left me. A letter from Mr —, pestering me with his disgusting play of *Catiline*, wishing me to give it with a note from him to Mr Webster—which I did. . . .

October 12. Spoke to Mrs Warner about her very ill-judged and unseemly conduct. Miss H. Faucit is ill, and makes me quite uncomfortable in playing. . . . Webster spoke to me about Mrs Warner. I advised him to promise her to give her in every respect fair play with *every other* actress, as to announcements, etc., but to do no more. Came home to our newly-taken house, York Gate, Regent's Park.

October 15. Webster called. . . . We settled the terms of an engagement for next season at £100 per week, play or no play, with the choice of a month's vacation on my part. Devoted the whole day, without inter-mission, to Bulwer's play. . . .

October 28. Rehearsed the new play. Bulwer was very doubtful about its success, Forster and Willmott equally confident. There was a long debate upon the question of withdrawing it, to which Bulwer seemed inclined. I could not give any opinion, for I have not had time to form one. It was at last decided to trust to Caesar and his fortune. Webster came into my room and told me that the proprietors of Covent Garden had let it to Vestris for £5000! They have made a good bargain.

October 30. . . . Bulwer became more confident as the rehearsal proceeded, and seemed at ease in his mind when it had concluded. I am not. I want time for myself and much more for other persons and things. . . .

October 31. Went in great anxiety, and uncomfortably, to the theatre. . . . Acted Norman in Bulwer's new play with some energy and occa-sional enthusiasm. Was received very warmly. . . . I am most thankful to God for what I feel a great escape.

[The play, a melodrama with an English Elizabethan setting (which mattered little), was very poor work. Thackeray chopped it to bits in a 'Yellowplush' paper in 'Fraser's Magazine', and Richard Barham rhymed its plot in one of the 'Ingoldsby Legends'. Eventually it would have forty performances between production and the following March. (Sheridan Knowles's 'Love', put on early in November by the rival Vestris manage-ment at Covent Garden, had nearly fifty nights). Macready, Phelps, Helen Faucit, and Mrs Warner headed the cast of 'The Sea-Captain'. Nearly thirty years later, Hermann Vezin acted in Lytton's revised version, 'The Rightful Heir' at the Lyceum (1868), but it was still a failure.]

November 21. Went to theatre; acted fairly. Spoke to Miss Faucit on the stage. She seemed low-spirited and unwell. On coming off, I asked her what was the matter. She said she had been very much shaken by some ill-natured thing—that she did not like to speak of it then, as it would upset her. She was passing my room, and I said, 'You had better come in and sit down.' She did, and to my request explained to me that she had been greatly distressed by information that Mesdames Warner, Ellen Tree, and Lacy[1] had been talking in a very malignant manner about her coming into my room to speak with me after the play, as they said, 'every night', Mrs Warner observing it was a great pity, it being the

[1] Mrs Lacy (1807–1874), actress, was formerly Harriet Taylor. She married the light comedian Walter Lacy (1809–1898).

talk of the Haymarket and Covent Garden theatres; Miss E. Tree adding her charitable compassion to the stock, and thinking it a pity that some one did not speak to Miss Faucit; Mrs Lacy, in a similar strain, saying also that there had been a paragraph in *The Satirist* to a like effect. I told her not to disturb herself about the matter; that my door had always been opened to every one who came; that my brother had come in without knocking; that Messrs Webster and Willmott were informed of the subject of every conversation we had had, and that on no one occasion of her speaking to me in my room had I omitted to mention it, and the matter spoken of on going home at night. I told her not to distress herself, painful as it was, for that I was quite sure Mrs Macready would show her sense of it by making a party on purpose to invite her. She was very thankful. This occurred in two conversations, during and after the play. Webster and Willmott came in and spoke, but to little purpose. On going home I mentioned all that had occurred, and my wish that Catherine should invite Miss Faucit, to which she instantly assented.

November 22. Catherine sent a note with a card of invitation to Miss Faucit. At Mr Webster's request, spoke with Miss Faucit about playing Lydia Languish, which she said she would give an answer to to-morrow.

November 23. . . . Miss Faucit wished to speak to me in my room, but I told her on her account I thought it better not; the few things I had to say I said to her behind the scenes.

December 6. Dickens gave me a play to read, called *Glencoe*,

December 7. Finished the play of *Glencoe*, which has so much to praise in it. . . .

December 8. Arranged my accounts, and found myself possessed of £10,000, a small realisation out of such a receipt as mine has been the last twenty years. But I have lost much, given away much, and, I fear, spent much; but what I have lost, and what given, would leave me with all my spendings a rich man. . . .

December 12. Thought much about Miss Faucit. Let me hope that I may yet be able to advance her in her profession, and to see her happy and respected. Went to dine with Talfourd, calling on Dickens, who said he was too ill to accompany me. Dined. Talfourd, Forster, and self. After dinner the conversation turned on plays. I mentioned one I had of a striking character upon a popular subject; Talfourd asked me the title. I told him *Glencoe*. He questioned me about its possible melodramatic tendency. I told him that the treatment avoided the melodrama of the stage; that the style was an imitation of his writing, but without the point that terminated his speeches; that the story was well managed and dramatic; and that I intended to act it. At last, to my utter astonishment, he pulled out two books from his pocket and said, 'Well, I will no longer conceal it—it is my play'; and he gave each of us a copy! I never in my life experienced a greater surprise. This play had been represented to me as Mr Collinson's. Forster affected great indignation, and really stormed; I laughed, loud and long, and put down his *affected* feeling; it was really a romance to me. Talfourd told us that he had written this to preserve his recollections of Glencoe. I strongly advised him to take one of two courses, either to flood the town with the edition, published anonymously, and to engage the suffrages of the Press, and leave it to be acted with his name, as it might escape; or to preserve it a profound secret, giving him at the same time a right to call upon me if he heard it anywhere through me. *Forster showed a character of sycophancy—* affected friendship where he felt it not—*bad acting*—super-enthusiastic. We went in a coach to Dickens, whom we found at home, and Talfourd dismissed the coach, expecting to 'be kept late'. Forster and self went with Dickens into another room, and we there discussed the business, Forster again *affecting the right to dance on the high ropes! Foolish man!* I put him down again, and spoke coolly to Dickens, urging him strongly to go with Talfourd to Moxon, and impress upon him the necessity of enforcing him to silence. I invited him to dinner on Sunday, and Talfourd, who could not answer for the power to 'get away'. Came home.

December 13. Read through the play of *Glencoe*, which I trust is destined to be a great success, but my opinion of its poetical merits is still unchanged: it is superior to, in dramatic construction, and very much below in poetry, the play of *Ion*.

December 18. Read an account of that wretched fellow Bunn's examination in the bankruptcy court. No one appeared to make any complaint, and though there is no doubt the swindler has secreted at least £700, to say nothing of goods, yet the Commission actually dismissed him with praise!!! My God! What is the value of character or fair dealing in this world? . . .

December 26. Gave the entire morning to Miss Faucit, entering into the subject, generally and in detail, of the study of the art of acting, cautioning her not to entertain the subject unless resolved to give herself up to it. Told her of all the faults I could recollect in her style, and showed her how to remove them. She was most grateful, and seemed sensible that what I said was true. I was very glad indeed to have her here. Catherine received her very kindly, and saw her two or three times.

December 28. Spoke to Miss Faucit for two or three minutes about the effect of her subdued acting, and explained to her how much might be done. . . .

December 30. Went to the theatre. Miss Faucit sent me a note enclosing a certificate from Dr Babington, stating her inability to continue her professional exertions; it threw me quite into low spirits. I rallied, and played Othello very fairly. . . . Spoke after the play to poor dear Miss Faucit who was in very low spirits. I urged her strongly not to go to Hastings, but, if not abroad, at least to go to Devonshire.

1840

London, January 1. Willmott informed me as we went to Drury Lane that the women in the dressing-rooms had been saying that [Miss Faucit] left the theatre from 'being in the family way'. It is monstrous and terrible to live and carry on one's daily occupations among such a set of —s and bl—g—ds as this profession (!) is composed of! Scarcely one among them that would not think it a *gain* to obtain a profitable paramour, and all ready to fabricate the grossest and most unfounded calumnies to justify their own profligacy.

January 5. . . . The T. Twisses *[Members of a family Macready had met first in Bath during 1815]*, Browning, and Miss Faucit came to dinner. We passed a cheerful day. I gave Miss Faucit de Staël's *Germany*, and Schlegel's *Dramatic Literature*. I asked her, as I took her to her carriage, if I should not see her again. She said no—she thought not. I felt very low at parting with her, and did not know how deep and tender an interest I felt for her. I do entertain a most sincere and affectionate regard for her. God bless her! dear girl! I go to bed in very low spirits—I feel great apprehension for her. God bless and assist her!

January 9. Wrote out after tea the memoranda of rules and hints on acting for Miss Faucit, read them to Catherine, and enclosed them with a note to Miss Faucit, but before the servant had taken it a note arrived from her, not wishing to receive it until she reached Hastings where she is going. . . .

January 12. Read, Mr—'s trash—which I still believe to be more malignant than silly—he mentions my name with Miss Faucit in a way that I think is intended to convey gross insinuations. I care more for her sake, if such innuendoes should reach her, than for anything else— these are your *gentlemen of the Press!*

Macready was now rehearsing at Drury Lane for a season under the direction of W. J. Hammond, the comedian, who was managing the theatre unsuccessfully, and who failed at the end of February for £8000.

January 18. . . . Went to Drury Lane theatre; began to rehearse *Macbeth:* thought Mr Archer drunk from his rude and insolent manner; in the banquet scene he became so wantonly rude that at length I took up my umbrella and left the stage. . . . Came home; dined. Lunn called to tell me that Mr Archer was discharged. . . . I wrote to Hammond and Willmott, to say that it was not my wish Mr Archer should be discharged, that I should discharge my obligations with *whatever performers*, claiming the right of absenting myself from disagreeable rehearsals. Went with Catherine to look at a house—Clarence Terrace—which I liked. . . .

January 20. . . . Acted Macbeth tolerably fairly. . . . Was very grateful to see so excellent a house.

January 22. . . . Rehearsed the play of *Mary Stuart* [by James Haynes]. Returned home and assisted Willie in his exercise—*instead of attending to my own business, and reading my part*. I did it most reluctantly but could not bear to leave him to his own apprehensions. Rested for about half-an-hour. Went to Drury Lane theatre, and acted Ruthven; was nervous, and, to my own surprise—in fact I cannot now understand the cause—I lost the words in the great effect of the fourth act. I came off the stage in a state of desperate fury, rushed to my book, and, when I looked at the words in which I had been perfect six weeks ago, I saw that if my life depended on it I could not have spoken them—they had gone out of my head. . . .

[There were twenty performances of 'Mary Stuart', in which Macready played Ruthven; Elton, Rizzio; Phelps, Darnley; Mrs Warner, Queen Mary.]

January 28. . . . Found Forster at home, who dined with us. The conversation, in turning on the twaddle of the *Observer*, led us to speak of the reflection upon Miss Faucit—of which Forster had also heard, and our conversation turned very much upon it. As I told him, the ill-treatment which this poor girl has received only binds me more strongly to her. I will not desert her.

February 16. Forster told me of Leigh Hunt's ingratitude to him, who has done everything for him for years; he is not a good man, nor a good-*natured* man.

February 19. Went to Drury Lane theatre. Acted Ruthven fairly. . . . Very disgusted and irritated by Mr Elton *walking out* in the last scene, and converting what was arranged as a most terrible and picturesque murder into a miserable hustle! I was excessively annoyed, but on reflection thought it wiser to leave him to a beggar's consolation—of having had his own way, and paying for it; he is a most wretched specimen of imbecile vanity.

February 21. A Mr Esdaile called, wishing for instruction to aid him in going on the stage; I with kindness and earnestness dissuaded him from following so unprofitable and demoralising a calling, and told him

I had rather see one of my children dead than on the stage. He left me, very grateful for my advice.

February 24. Spoke to Mrs Warner, requesting her to be more careful as she struck the dagger in my face. She said, 'I beg your pardon, sir, etc.' It was most painful to me to think that a woman, for whom I had entertained an affection, and who had once loved me, could be so estranged from me. Such is the world!

Hammond, of Drury Lane, went bankrupt for £8000. Automatically, the players' agreements ended, but through the week Macready acted gratuitously on behalf of his poorer colleagues. He had arranged to open a new engagement at the Haymarket on 16 March. Meanwhile he continued to be distressed by the 'calumnies' about Miss Faucit. On 7 March at an interview with her friends, he 'strongly urged, against all lawyers, the necessity of commencing an action against Miss Faucit's defamers and of putting up the notice in the green-room.' From 8 to 13 March he was at Bristol.

March 8. Went with Edward to the railway station. Took my seat, and reached Twyford in an hour and five minutes. Continued my journey by coach. . . . There is no doubt — had felt an admiration for me, which amounted to love. Her manner in parting with me was manifest proof of it. Her subsequent meeting with me strengthened this feeling in her and made her an object of interest to me. I could not—at least I did not feel that I could—show coldness to her, though I really wished her good angel had removed her from me. Time has made her partiality a passion and her injuries and sufferings have deepened my interest for her into a sincere affection, but one which I can avow without any self-reproach for the feeling. My anxiety for her is quite a painful sensation.

Bristol, March 9. . . . Went to the theatre and tried to act Macbeth but, the witches first—ducking or burning could only have properly rewarded them; then Banquo, shutting his eyes, and making himself amiable and heroic in turns; then Duncan, an out-and-out wretch; but it was all so bad—Banquo coming on as the ghost with his face painted exactly like the clown in a pantomime! It was so bad that I felt and said, 'Money could not pay for the sense of degradation endured in such a set of persons'. . . .

March 10. . . . I am the victim of an ill-regulated, and morbid imagination, and to what its agency may lead me I cannot see. . . .

March 12. . . . Received letters from dearest Catherine; very comfortable and comforting, except in the account of her mother's health; and one from —; the latter is very nicely written, but she signs it —.

Is this in her fond gratitude, or that she does not see, that she has not learned the necessity of wrestling with a passion, and moderating it to a deep and tender friendship? Such is the feeling, before God, that I desire to preserve and prove to her. . . . Went to the theatre to play; but all the day, and all the night, through the whole play, I was *haunted* by one word—it was in my brain as I walked behind the scenes, and seemed written down before me as I sat at my toilet, each time that I returned to my room. This word was —. Does it mean anything? *Does it not?* Does she examine her own heart? I fear not. She really is amiable, but I believe she is *blind* to her own position. She would seem to intimate to me that she loves me with a love beyond what friends indulge in, or why —? Here is evidence of the ill-effect of the absence of a *principle*. She may very naturally love me more than she has ever done. She may think or feel she has more reason. But she has noble and solacing motives to sustain her in at least the *struggle* with her emotions. It is a subject on which I cannot write to her, lest her letters be seen, but I pray to God that I may act rightly towards her. . . . *[Later]* This *word* still pursues me. . . . But I will do what is right. I will believe all that is good of her, and think, as is probable, it is the mere want of the strong terms, 'affectionate, etc.,' which her feelings *need* to express themselves, that she has recourse to this most familiar method. God bless her, and make her, and keep her a good girl.

He opened at the Haymarket, an engagement that continued until 13 March 1841.

March 16. Was nervous and uncertain about the performance of Hamlet to-night—regretting that I had not made myself secure of my feeling through the part. Went to the theatre and rehearsed Hamlet; took pains with Miss Horton [Ophelia] also. . . . Acted very carefully and very well. The new effect of the pictures on the wall of the apartment was a very great improvement on the old stupid custom. . . . *[At 'Look here, upon this picture, and on this' in the Closet Scene, instead of comparing two miniatures, Macready gestured towards a wall hung with full-length paintings; the Ghost appeared through his own portrait and later vanished through it.]*

March 19. Went with dear little Edward to Elstree, reading *Wilhelm Meister* by the way. . . . All [at Elm Place] was in the confusion of packing and removal. The once cheerful little rooms looked desolate, sad, and dreary, and poor Mrs East looked the picture of melancholy. I looked at all around me perhaps for the last time.

March 29. Browning called, and presented me with his book of

Sordello; he sat some time, and the Procters called. When they had gone I asked Browning to stay to dinner, which he did. He gave his account of his quarrel with Forster, in which certainly Forster appears the blameable party.

April 1. A letter from Miss Helen Faucit, informing me that she had fallen back in health, and was now going for change to Brighton. I do not think she will recover; she has been cared for too late. How very, very much we miss her now, with these Mrs Warners and Yarnolds! *[In a letter to Miss Faucit on 26 March Macready had said: 'You grieve me very much in throwing a doubt about the resumption of your art, for independently of the strong personal interest which I must always take in you, I have looked on you as one in whom I could hope to see left a surviving specimen of the purer style of the theatrical art, which seems now rushing to decay. I look around and perceive no intelligence or sensibility among those engaged in our theatres to lend the least encouragement to hope beyond yourself. . . .']*

Copy of *Lear* from C. Knight, who gives a long disquisition upon the bad taste of N. Tate and those who acted his version of *King Lear*, but cannot spare one word for the successful attempt to place Shakespeare in his own form again upon the stage.

April 9. Letter from Miss Faucit, informing me of the improvement in her health, which I was truly grateful to learn. . . . Walked to Regent Street with Dickens, and took a cab home. Rested after dinner. The servant brought me in a card, Mr Thomas Moore,[1] and told me the gentleman would take no denial. I could not imagine it to be Tom Moore, and went out in a very ill humour; to my surprise, it was the bright little man himself. We went upstairs, and he wanted to visit the Haymarket with Mrs Moore and his son, who is going out to India. I told him to ask for his own private box, which I procured for him when I went to the theatre.

April 11. Webster called after dinner, and asked me about Miss Faucit's first appearance, having received a letter from her. She wished to open in *The Lady of Lyons*. I think it would have been as well *not*.

April 25. Rehearsed *The Lady of Lyons;* saw Miss Helen Faucit. I was quite pleased to see her so well and apparently so strong; she was very glad to see me. Acted Claude Melnotte partially well; was called for, but hearing Miss Faucit's name, thought it right she should have her undivided applause, and desired that some one else should lead her on, which was done. Went on afterwards, to the continued call, and was well received. . . .

[1] Thomas Moore (1779-1852), poet.

May 8. Attended Carlyle's[1] lecture, 'The Hero as a Prophet: Mahomet'; on which he descanted with a fervour and eloquence that only a conviction of truth could give. I was charmed, carried away by him. Met Browning there. . . .

May 11. . . . Rehearsed *Glencoe*, which wears an appearance of much promise. Acted Claude Melnotte fairly. Miss [Faucit] said something about striving to overcome her fondness for me, and that she thought I wished it. I do wish it. For I have a sincere and strong regard—an affectionate one for her, and do not wish it be endangered or interrupted.

May 12. Went to Carlyle's lecture on Dante and Shakespeare. Saw Browning and Mrs Jameson there; was disappointed in his treatment of the subject; his comments were not up to the height of his great argument. He said little that was impressive; he quoted a passage about 'histriones et nebulones', and spoke of managers of playhouses being the most insignificant of human beings, which made me smile, but sent the blood into my face, as I fancied the thoughts of many present would revert to myself—but possibly they never descended from the subject to me.

May 18. Went to the theatre, reading *Glencoe*. Began the rehearsal, but only proceeded in it for two scenes, Messrs Warde, Phelps, and J. Webster being absent. . . . Miss P. Horton told me that I was the subject of general abuse in the green-room, which I can easily believe. I have had experience enough of players to know that their ignorance and their vanity combine to make them a most ungrateful set of persons.

May 19. Went to the theatre, where I found confusion and uncertainty. After some time rehearsed the fifth and first acts. . . . The play is not cast to its demand, and is *hurried* forward. . . . Went with Maclise and Forster to Carlyle's lecture on the man of letters as the great man; was very interested and edified.

May 23. . . . Went to the theatre, and, in the character of Halbert Macdonald in Talfourd's play of *Glencoe*, I did all I could do—all that the very short period allowed for preparation allowed me to do. The audience became very fervent, although I felt, in the second act, that the persons in the front were disposed to be ill-natured. Was called for by the house, and, when silence was obtained, I informed them that I had a little history to relate concerning the play; that it had been placed in my hands by a friend, as the work of a gentleman named Collinson. . . . Mr Webster accepted it unhesitatingly, and it was some time after that I was made acquainted with the real author, a name which I had pleasure in communicating . . . it was Mr Serjeant Talfourd's. This

[1] Thomas Carlyle (1799–1881), author and historian.

was greatly applauded, and I gave out the play for three nights' representation per week till further notice. Talfourd rushed into my room to thank me, and Dickens, Maclise, etc., also came. Went to sup with Talfourd—a heavy supper—taking David Colden *[New York friend of Dickens and Macready]* with me. Speech-making was the order of a dull evening.

['Glencoe; or The Fate of the Macdonalds' has rightly been called an unsatisfactory 'compromise between the methods of Greek tragedy and romantic drama' (Dr Ernest Reynolds, in 'Early Victorian Drama'). In this production, with Macready as Halbert Macdonald, Helen Faucit appeared as Helen Campbell, Mrs Warner as Lady Macdonald, Phelps as Glenlyon and Webster as MacIan.]

June 2. Acted Halbert Macdonald indifferently. . . . Spoke to dear Helen Faucit about her languor in acting; she did not seem to meet my objections with the strength of mind and good sense that I had anticipated. She was much depressed. I am much concerned about her. Miss Horton had told me, in reference to Mr C. Kean, that she thought there was none like myself. I wish the public would think so; but it is pleasant to see oneself loved, if only by a few individuals.

June 6. Saw dear, dear old Elstree; looked over with the clerk the fixtures, etc. . . . and, under the faint silver of the afternoon's moon, bade my last adieu to the scene of many, many joys. . . .

June 17. After dinner tried—another attempt—utterly desperate—on *Sordello;* it is *not* readable.

June 23. . . . Looked at *Timon of Athens*, but it is (for the stage) only an incident with comments on it. The story is not complete enough—not furnished, I ought to say—with the requisite varieties of passion for a play; it is heavy and monotonous. . . .

June 26. Thought much on the subject of [Helen Faucit]. Concluded that I must explain to her the dangers that beset her in cherishing feelings which cannot be indulged without all the pain of apprehension, of consciousness, of self-reproach. . . . I must prevent her lapsing into danger, but I fear—and I shall grieve if it be so—that I cannot hold possession of her friendship if I discourage her love.

June 27. A son born. *[Walter Francis Sheil Macready (1840–1853), fourth son and seventh child.]*

July 2. Spoke with — on the subject of her attachment to me. She is truly amiable. In explaining to her that my motive in seeking to occupy and engross her mind was to weaken the strength of that affection which had excited so much apprehension in my breast for her health and happiness, and divert her thoughts, I went fully into the description of the course of study and artistical discipline which she should undertake, and particularly urged upon her the distress it occasioned me to think that she was, as it were, widowing her heart, in its youth and freshness and fulness of feeling, by allowing it to dwell upon one object, whose rare opportunities of enjoying her society afforded him no power of recompensing her tenderness; at the same time assuring her how truly and devotedly I was her friend, how firmly I was bound to her interests and care for her happiness by the very persons whose persecutions had sought to make my regard destructive to her. She said she could not, as I wished, and as her friends wished, think of any person as a husband (on which I remonstrated), that she feared I blamed her, and that she would try to do what was right. She told me of her family—so wearing, so sordid, so vulgar, so cruel as they are. I hope she may leave them. . . . *[Later]* Spoke again with —, who could *not* bring herself at present to entertain the thought of any connection, as unjust to someone who might trust her, and distressingly painful to herself. But she would try to do all I wished. She feared I might not respect her, and could not bear the idea of altering my present demeanour or feeling towards her. I assured her, if that would tend to give peace to her heart, that whilst I had life, she might regard my devoted friendship and affectionate care for her as unalterable. She left me in a more cheerful state of mind, and I trust in God will be happy. . . . In my conversation with —, expatiating upon the hopelessness of her affections so bestowed, I observed that I was now advancing into age, to which she answered: 'Ah! your mind must always be young.'

July 4. Looked at the paper, in which was a review of Mr Bunn's book.[1] There is nothing, it appears, so low, so vile, so degraded— regarding it either as respects honour or common morality—that reaches a level which the sympathies of the gentlemen of the Press cannot descend to . . .

[On 9 July Macready had 'a most distressing interview . . . a bitter, a most afflicting scene' with —, who told him that she had not known until her illness how deeply her affections were engaged, when she knew that her love was all she had to live for. 'I took one little remembrance from her, which will always be precious to me. I kissed her forehead—and no more. Our

[1] *The Stage: Both Before and Behind the Curtain*, from 'Observations Taken on the Spot'. By Alfred Bunn. Late lessee of the Theatres Royal Drury Lane and Covent Garden. In three volumes published by Richard Bentley, New Burlington Street. On the title-page was the epigraph, 'I am (not) forbid/To tell the secrets of my prison-house.'

parting was really terrible. . . . All the love that with due regard to her
honour I can bear her she shall have, while I can feel or think.' Next day he
felt 'utterly weighed down in spirit. . . . It is very sad to think of her and her
sweet mode of binding up her resolution to do right.']

July 15. Was detained a very long time in endeavouring to tinker
together a few lines in verse for dear —'s album. My muse is cold—she
never had much vitality.
[Macready's verses in Helen Faucit's album ran:

> *'Tis not the dove-like softness of thine eyes*
> *My pensive gaze that draws, however fair;*
> *A holier charm within their beauty lies,*
> *The unspotted soul, that's mirrored always there.*

> *There every thought of thy young heart is seen,*
> *Radiant and pure, by truth and genius given,*
> *As, on the surface of the lake serene*
> *Reflected, gleam the perfect lights of heaven.]*

Webster had engaged Charles Kean for the Haymarket.

July 17. Went down to the Haymarket to see *Macbeth*. Mr C. Kean
was really so bad—so idealless, made up of long pauses, whimpering,
rant, and the falsest system of intonation, all built up on the most
offensive imitation of his father's worst habits and tricks, that I could
not stay beyond the second act. Mrs Warner seemed noble and Mr
Phelps fresh and vigorous beside such acting.

July 21. Began to act Jacques very fairly, but was thrown off my
balance by a man in the gallery vociferating: 'What do you go on for,
spoiling Shakespeare,' etc. I caught no more, for the audience was
roused until he was turned out. But he was right in judgment, however
barbarous and ungentlemanly his method of giving publicity to it. I
ought not to have resumed those speeches, which I always censured as
so misappropriated, and which I restored to the First Lord when I was
in Covent Garden. It made me low-spirited and ill-humoured for a
time.

July 27. I made the best of my way to Brompton and called on Mrs
Braysher *[A friend with whom Helen Faucit lived]* to meet Miss Helen
Faucit there by appointment. Mrs Braysher sat some little time with us
and left us, observing that she understood my call was one of business.
I entered unreservedly into the examination of H. Faucit's defects in

acting, and pointed out to her the remedies. I gave her a lecture of more than two hours, chiefly on the characters of Rosalind and Lady Townley. She seemed very sensible of the truth of what I urged, and appeared very grateful.

July 31. Browning called and gave me his play *[The Return of the Druses]*, which does *not* look well.

August 3. . . . Read Browning's play, and with the deepest concern I yield to the belief that he will *never write again*—to any purpose. I fear his intellect is not quite clear. I do not know how to write to Browning.

August 12. Browning called, and walked out with me on my way to the theatre. As he accompanied me he talked of his play and of *Sordello*, and I most honestly told him my opinion on both, expressing myself most anxious, as I am, that he should justify the expectations formed of him, but that he could not do so by placing himself in opposition to the world. He wished me to have his play done for nothing. I explained to him that Mr Webster *would not* do it; we walked to the Haymarket, and in parting I promised to read it again. Forster called and read me a letter from Bulwer, who has already written one-third of the comedy *[Money]*. His expedition is wonderful! . . . Acted Jaques fairly. Watched one scene of Miss Faucit's Rosalind, which is not humorous and joyous enough.

August 16. Went to dine with Dickens, and was witness to a most painful scene after dinner Forster, Maclise, and myself were the guests. Forster got on to one of his headlong streams of talk (which he thinks argument) and waxed warm, and at last some sharp observations led to personal retorts between him and Dickens. He displayed his usual want of tact, and Dickens flew into so violent a passion as quite to forget himself and give Forster to understand that he was in his house which he should be glad if he would leave. Forster behaved very foolishly. I stopped him; spoke to both of them and observed that for an angry instant they were about to destroy a friendship valuable to both. I drew from Dickens the admission that he had spoken in passion and would not have said what he said, could he have reflected; but he added he could not answer for his temper under Forster's provocations, and that he would do just the same again. Forster behaved very *weakly;* would not accept the repeated acknowledgment communicated to him that Dickens regretted the passion, etc., but stayed skimbling-skambling a parcel of unmeaning words, and at last finding he could obtain no more, made a sort of speech, accepting what he had before declined. He was silent and not recovered—no wonder!—during the whole evening. Mrs Dickens had gone out in tears. It was a very painful scene.

August 20. . . . Talked much with Dickens, whose views on politics and religion seem very much to square with mine. We talked about Forster, and he said that he assumed a supercilious tone before people to give the idea that he was the patron, or *padrone*. How little and how silly!

August 27. Browning came before I had finished my bath, and really *wearied* me with his obstinate faith in his poem of *Sordello*, and of his eventual celebrity, and also with his self-opinionated persuasions upon his *Return of the Druses*. I fear he is for ever gone.

After a very brief vacation at Broadstairs, Macready was back at the Haymarket.

September 3. . . . Received a very pretty flower and note, affectionately written, from —.

September 7. Walked down to the theatre. On going into a private box I started back and called to the box-keeper on seeing Mrs Glover satined-out and acting Violante. He told me that Miss Faucit was indisposed and that an apology had been made. Sat through part of the second, the third, fourth, and part of the fifth acts—it was very, very badly acted. It does not surprise me that the taste for the drama—as acted—should wax feeble. Who would go to see such a performance? I did not hear one line given with propriety—not to say with an artist's discrimination. The play too *[The Wonder]* was bunglingly arranged. Mr Wallack was quite out of place in Don Felix—quite below the part, but it was throughout a very indifferent provincial representation.

September 11. Maclise, Forster, and Talfourd came to dine, our dinner was very cheerful. Talfourd grew so tipsy that he quite impeded conversation. I was sorry to see him; otherwise it would have been very pleasant. . . .

September 13. Brydone called, and gave me a picture of Covent Garden and its management, that tends to confirm my belief of its rottenness. Luck alone can sustain it, and chance acts two ways. It is not a fitting spectacle—the national drama in the hands of Mrs Vestris and Mr Charles Mathews! . . .

September 14. . . . Acted Hamlet—in bad spirits—*against the grain*— *no flow*. The soliloquy on death I never spoke so well, but altogether I did not satisfy myself. Was depressed by the bad house, and became very much irritated in thinking of that blackguard —; was quite out of temper, and lost the keynote of the character. . . .

September 15. . . . Again read what I could of Browning's mystical, strange, and heavy play of *The Return of the Druses*. It is not good.

159

Wrote to him, and, offering to do all in my power, gave him my recon-sidered opinion. . . .

September 18. . . . Received by post a letter and two acts, fourth and fifth, of a comedy from Bulwer; the others are sent by the Ambassador's bag—it is completed! *[Bulwer wrote from Aix-la-Chapelle. The play was 'Money'.]*

September 19. . . . Received the other three acts of Bulwer's comedy. Began the play as I came home in a cab. . . .

September 23. . . . Went into the Oxford Street theatre *[the Prin-cess's on the north side of Oxford Street; closed finally in 1902]*; was denied, but on giving my name, was conducted over it by a sort of superinten-dent. It is really beautiful: well placed, it would be a fortune; but, where it is, I have no faith in its success.

September 27. . . . My darling boy, Henry, very unwell; he seems wasting and sinking away—my heart fell down within me as I looked at the thin face of the dear, dear child. . . .

September 28. Mr Pope called and saw dear little Henry, who, I fear, is very, very ill. My hopes are wretchedly low about him. . . .

September 30. Gave my whole morning to the consideration, revision and arrangement for the stage of *Money*, the comedy of Sir E. Bulwer. Wrote my remarks and suggestions to Bulwer. Mr and Mrs Carlyle called. . . .

October 3. Mr Pope called, and most grateful to God am I to know that my dear Henry is better. . . .

October 6. Went to Covent Garden theatre *[under the management of Madame Vestris and Charles Mathews]* to see Knowles's play of *John of Procida*. I paid for entrance—a slight reproach, I think, to the manners, taste, and feeling of the present management. The play was not interes-ting; there were good scenes, or rather parts of good scenes, in it. Mr Anderson was by far the best actor in the play; he is much improved. I saw an interlude after it, full of practical jokes, which was very fairly acted by Messrs Keeley and Mathews, but it was poor stuff. I was, or seemed to be, quite unknown in the theatre, where not a year and a half ago I was the observed of all observers. Such is the world! Walked home thinking on my art, and meditating on *Othello*.

October 8. Gave lessons to some of the children, and revolved much the decisive step I was about to take in relinquishing my engagement for next season at the Haymarket, but reflection showed me its necessity . . . *[Later]* Mr Webster, it seems, only received my letter declining any engagement beyond the present season, as he came to dress. Before the play began, he came into my room in great tribulation and humiliation

. . . he almost wept. I listened, and quietly observed upon his conduct; but he was obliged to go on the stage.

October 9. . . . Played at piquet in order to learn the game for the new play, *Money*. . . .

October 13. . . . Called for Dickens, and went to see *The Spanish Curate [by Beaumont and Fletcher, adapted by Planché]* at Covent Garden; with the exception of Messrs Anderson and Keeley the play was very, very badly acted, dressed with no regard to costume, and, upholstered for all times, the characters were not understood. I expected and sat shrinking to hear the hiss, which did not come; the audience applauded, though coldly and flatly. . . .

He was now working steadily on Bulwer's Money

October 25. After dinner continued my work on *Money*, about which I begin to have my usual apprehensions.

October 29. Went to the theatre where I rehearsed three acts of *Money*. Spoke to Mr Webster about the scenery and dresses, observing most emphatically that I did not wish to have anything whatever to do with them—that I would aid the acting as much as I could, but that I had rather he arranged the other matters in his own way. . . .

[Macready and Webster had had a series of disagreements about Lytton's new modern comedy.]

October 31. Acted *The Stranger* feebly. Spoke with Helen Faucit after the play. She told me that Mr Farren had said, on the faith of Mr Robertson, that on one occasion *1000* persons went in free during my Covent Garden management!!!

November 5. Went to the theatre, where I spent two hours in the rehearsal of one page of the club scene of the new comedy. As I write, doubts and misgivings arise in my mind. I have nothing great or striking in situation, character, humour, or passion to develop. . . .

[On 7 November he would write to Bulwer: 'We are creeping:—advancing as miners through a porphyry dyke—but we are advancing.']

November 12. Gave the morning, not very sternly or diligently, to the reading of *Money*. A boy called for an order for Mr Barnes of the *Times* office! I told him he was fortunate that I did not give him in custody to a police officer. . . .

November 13. Received a most kind and candid exposition of the state of the public theatrical feeling at Plymouth from Wightwick, giving it as his opinion that the town would be more likely to make greater houses to Mr C. Kean than to me—a piece of information which I received with the most placid philosophy. . . .

November 14. Received a letter from Bulwer with further alterations, which I thought improvements. Went to the theatre and rehearsed with much care two scenes—only two scenes in three hours—of the play, which really *ought*, well acted, to be a success; it is most painful to see the desperate hazard it incurs in this theatre. Forster came in and saw part of the rehearsal, with which he was greatly pleased. Mr Webster came to express his wish to leave the rehearsal, in order to go to a sale and make a bargain of some card-tables! Came home with Forster, and, after dinner, half asleep, wrote a letter to Bulwer. Rested, overcome with fatigue. Read Sir Oswin Mortland [*in Mrs Inchbald's 'To Marry, Or Not to Marry'*]. Went to the theatre. Acted Sir Oswin very feebly, being completely paralysed by the vulgarity of Mrs Glover. Willmott spoke to me after the play about the manner in which the theatre is carried on. The curtain would not descend at the close—the man had gone away! Coming home, found a letter from Mrs —, whom I think very anxious to dispose of her virtue from the stress she lays upon it. . . .

November 18. Rehearsed with much care and much exertion the fourth and fifth acts of *Money*, which we got into a rough shape. Was painfully struck to see dearest, dearest Henry. He looked so sad and so thin. I fear, I fear I shall lose the darling boy. . . . Went to the theatre and acted Claude Melnotte with considerable *spirit*, which is a virtue in my acting that I fear I am losing at the Haymarket theatre. I hope not.

November 20. Very much fatigued by the wakeful night I had through the dear, dear little Henry, who seems falling back. . . .

November 21. Went to the theatre. Bulwer was there, and Forster during part of the morning. Much of the play went so heavily and unsatisfactorily that Bulwer became very nervous—quite ill-tempered, and spoke harshly to the actors—haughtily, I should say, certainly unphilosophically; but how much has he to excuse the manifestation of his suffering! I quite feel for him. I did and said all I could. Did not reach home till nearly half-past four o'clock. Spoke to Miss Helen Faucit wishing her to *act* at the rehearsal on Monday morning.

Macready had to divide his mind, agonisingly, between Clarence Terrace and the Haymarket. Henry was ill through the night of the 22nd. Next morning he lay exhausted while his father, in distraction, went to a rehearsal of the play, which had begun to sag; that night the boy was better, and on the 24th, everything being tinged by his state of mind, Macready discerned 'a golden promise' in the first three acts of Money. *On the 25th, leaving the theatre where Forster's arrogance had annoyed him, and where he had finally settled with Webster for the new season, he came home to learn the words of an altered passage in the fourth act. He was startled by the news that Henry was no better, and that little Joan, at only three years and four months, was very ill indeed, dangerously so. The journal (25th) proceeds:*

I left my study to go up to bed—as well as I can remember, for my head is not clear upon the exact course of wretched circumstances that seemed in some sort to stupefy me. I went up to the nursery. . . . Catherine waved me back with her hand, and begged me not to come— that I could do no good. I felt—I do not know what I felt—a strange agony, a weight at my heart and head, that made me irresolute and tortured what to do. I had nowhere to go, no one to go to. All were around this blessed precious infant making despairing efforts. I threw myself on my bed and, wrapping the coverlid over my head, lay in a state of misery such as I never felt before, till dearest Letty came down to me in tears, wrung my hand, and spoke a few words to me. I asked her if the blessed creature was dead. My child, my beautiful, my lovely little Joan was gone; I was in a state of desperate wretchedness. . . . *[This was Harriet Joanna (1837–1840)]*

During four days Macready was in despair

November 26. . . . Forster called, and was much affected on seeing me. He had supposed it was Henry who had gone, and when he learned that dear Joan had been taken from us, he lost all self-control. He rushed out of the study, and remained away at least half-an-hour. When he returned he could say nothing; he left me greatly agitated. Received a dear and most affectionate note from Dickens which comforted me as much as I can be comforted. But I have lost my child. There is no comfort for that sorrow; *there is endurance*—that is all. . . . Darling Henry is very restless and in pain. . . .

November 28. . . . Dr Elliotson[1] and Mr Pope called to see Henry. I met them returning, and Elliotson said that 'there was no reason he should not get well', but his tone was not assured and his manner evasive. . . .

November 29. . . . Went in to see dearest Catherine, and found her weak and wearied, but thinking Henry better. . . .

[1] Dr John Elliotson (1791–1868), a distinguished physician. A friend of Dickens; deeply interested in hypnotism.

November 30. *[Joan's funeral]*. . . . Forster remained with me the whole day. Elliotson and Pope called, and having seen darling Henry pronounced him certainly better. Devoutly do I thank God.

Henry continued to improve. The première of Money *should have been on Saturday, 28 November, but on the previous night Webster announced its deferment because of 'the very severe domestic calamity of Mr Macready'.*

December 2. . . . Forster called, and we walked round the Park together. I enjoyed the exercise very much. . . .

December 3. . . . A note from Forster, informing me that Webster would not listen to the suggestion of deferring Bulwer's play, as I confidently expected. Went to the theatre. Rehearsed the play of *Money*. Found at home an anonymous note, cautioning me against a ruffianly person, a low man, called Dr —, who goes behind the scenes of the Haymarket theatre.

Henry's condition—he suffered from an attack of thrush—fluctuated; but by 7 December he was 'much easier', and Macready had recovered enough to act at the Haymarket in Werner *to a very dull audience. Finally on the night of 8 December, the postponed première brought London to the Haymarket. Macready was faced with the long part of Alfred Evelyn who, by feigning to lose a large fortune at cards, tests the loyalty of his entourage.* Money, *at once a success (though Bulwer was unhappy about the performance), continued for what in those days was the extraordinary run of eighty consecutive nights. Besides Macready as Evelyn, a long part that he had called that of 'a damned walking gentleman', the cast included Helen Faucit, Mrs Glover, Priscilla Horton, David Rees, Walter Lacy, Webster (as Graves), Strickland, Benjamin Wrench, Vining. Lacy (who relinquished Sir Frederick Blount when he decided to join the Covent Garden company) said in a reminiscent 'Theatre' article (February 1880): 'Macready's Alfred Evelyn was amazingly bright and telling, the forced gaiety being as natural to the man as appropriate to the character. The man who made the heartiest impression was David Rees [as Benjamin Stout, M.P.] . . . There was a breezy freshness about the man, his great round red face luminous, full of breath and explosive power; he rushed in like an express engine, puffing with electioneering excitement.'*

December 8. . . . Went to the Haymarket and rehearsed the play of *Money*. I was much depressed and low-spirited. Coming home, read over the part and resolved to do my best with it. Laid out and put up my clothes. Acted the part of Evelyn. Not satisfied. I wanted lightness, self-possession, and, in the serious scenes, truth. I was not good—I feel it. In the last scene Miss Faucit, as I had anticipated, had quite the advantage over me; this was natural. Bulwer came into my room; he was, as usual, obliged by my exertions.

By the end of the year Henry was genuinely better. But it had been an anxious time for Macready; and, as usual, he had theatre worries.

December 19. . . . Acted Evelyn pretty fairly, not pleased with some unfair advantages taken by Helen Faucit; it is not wise. She was very prone to this habit once, but I thought had discarded it. Mr Webster was laughing during the concluding speech, which checked me twice and very nearly made me lose the word. I spoke (which there was no need to do) to him about it when the curtain fell, and he flatly denied it. I (*indiscreetly*) said it was of little consequence to me what he asserted or what he denied! I was very hasty, *but nothing can justify anger!* Bulwer came in and spoke about cutting the play, and made with Willmott some short cuts. He is very much dissatisfied with the success, and swears he will never write another play.

December 21. . . . A note was given me, half asleep and only as I was going to the theatre, from the poor actor, Green, in Whitecross Street prison, and brought by his wife. I apologised to her for the delay, and gave her a cheque for £4 to release him from a debt of £3 10s. A human being incarcerated—shut from exercise, industry and his house, his wife and children for £3 10s. *Happy, aristocratical England!!!*

December 28. . . . Was grieved to see Miss H. Faucit ill and low-spirited in her performance. Spoke to her after the play; some wretch had been writing a gross and ribald letter of abuse to her! I requested her not to give any thought to it. She is a very sweet girl. . . .

December 29. . . . Talfourd thought the play 'the merest trash—nothing in it; that it was a great stretch of friendship in me to play Evelyn.' He is very anxious. Evelyn is not a good part, but I have played, too, *The Athenian Captive*. . . . Mrs Warner is discharged! I am truly sorry for her.

III
Drury Lane (1841–1843)

'The whole house rose with such continued shouting and waving of hats and handkerchiefs that I was quite overcome; I was never so affected by the expression of sympathy by an audience.'
Journal, 14 June 1843

1841

January 3. Forster called, and we walked round the Park together, which I very much enjoyed. Confided to him my notion of engrossing a large share of Drury Lane theatre, which he thought very much of, and which I think may be a great thing if I have energy and constancy to carry it through.

January 8. . . . Mrs Warner was in the theatre, and I sent to say I should be glad to speak with her after the play. She came to my room, and I told her I was sorry she was to leave the theatre, and that, as we might not meet again, I did not wish to part with her on terms of estrangement after the affectionate understanding that had subsisted between us. She went into the scandalous affair of last year, endeavouring to make out her case, but making admissions that proved her indiscretion. . . . I told her she might still consider herself as having the right and power of applying to me if ever I could be of service to her. I shook hands with her. She told me she had passed *a most unhappy year*. I was sorry—very sorry to hear it. . . .

January 9. Mrs Warner sent to ask to speak to me again. . . . She talked long, giving me the history of her transactions with Mr Webster. She admitted her indiscretion and injustice to me, and I parted with her—*very late*—reassuring her of all the kindness I had proffered her yesterday.

January 10. Coming down, I saw dearest Henry, who, thank God, is wonderfully better; wonderfully. It is indeed almost a miracle. *[It was only a partial recovery. Epileptic tendencies developed later, and Henry died on 12 August 1857 at the age of eighteen.]*

January 21. . . . Asked Dickens to spare the life of Nell in his story (*Master Humphrey's Clock*) *['The Old Curiosity Shop' was appearing in 'Master Humphrey's Clock'],* and observed that he was cruel. He blushed and, men who blush are said to be either proud or cruel; he is not proud, and therefore—or, as Dickens added—the axiom is false.

January 22. . . . Found at home note from Dickens with an onward number of *Master Humphrey's Clock*. I saw one print in it of the dear dead child that gave a dead chill through my blood. I dread to read it, but must get it over. Later I have read the two numbers; I never have read printed words that gave me so much pain, I could not weep for some time. . . .

January 27. Thought a good deal upon my prospects and claims; calculated for my children's good, and see little to reason me from the necessity of again entering management, if I can do so without hazard of what I possess. The stage seems to want me. There is no theatre, but that to a man with a family is no argument; there is no theatre for me, and that is an overwhelming plea. Then much may be done of good in all ways.

February 5. Was guilty of bad taste in telling an unbecoming (for *me*) story in the green-room. I did not think of it.

February 14. Anderson called. I . . . developed to him [in confidence] my views on Drury Lane in case the proprietors were willing to entrust the theatre to me; observing to him that if he were not satisfied with his condition at Covent Garden theatre (which he represented himself not to be), that I should be willing to regard him as one attached to the undertaking, if it reached anything; that I should place him in an official situation, and should look forward to him as my successor in the course of time. He expressed his readiness and happiness to be made a participator in such an undertaking. . . .

February 28. Called on Mrs Butler; saw C. Kemble, wasted, old, decrepit; he said he had suffered much, but that now he thought he was 'landed'; he looked as if he would be soon, but he had walked down to the Garrick Club and back! and felt that it was a little too much for him. Pierce Butler[1] seemed glad to see me; an American, General Hamilton, came in and we talked. He and Mr Butler went out to dine with Trelawny,[2] after Mrs Butler came in. I liked her frank and genuine manner very much indeed; it is rarely that I have seen a person I have been so taken with. We talked long. . . .

March 3. I am forty-eight years old today.

March 7. Went out to call on Dickens, who read me part of his preface to *Oliver Twist*—which I liked; on Lord Denman, who was not at home; on Mr and Mrs Pierce Butler (with whom I found Mr Bartley!), and with whom I talked some time, and asked them to dine. . . . Going home passed that bad man Bunn, looking rather shabby. Dickens was strong for me to resume the direction of a theatre. Fox, etc., also. I resolved to so do, and saw what looked auguries of good.

March 23. Beazley and Dunn called, and we talked over the feasibility of re-opening Drury Lane theatre *as a theatre. [Samuel Beazley (1786–1851), playwright and architect, was on the Drury Lane Committee.]* I

[1] Pierce Butler had married Fanny Kemble in 1834; they were divorced in 1847.
[2] Edward John Trelawny (1792–1881), traveller and writer; friend of Shelley and Byron.

mentioned what must form the basis of any agreement—liberty to close at a day's notice; no compulsion to pay any rent; no rent to be paid before Christmas; my salary to be included among the working expenses of the theatre; the theatre not to be opened before Christmas; to be mine in virtue of a clear lesseeship; not for the committee to have the power of letting it during my vacation, etc. . . . .

March 24. Wrote out the heads of my stipulations in my agreement with Drury Lane proprietors. Lord Glengall *[Richard Butler, Earl of Glengall]* and Dunn called; I read my stipulations, which were considered admissible. Lord Glengall was earnest to carry the proposed agreement into effect. . . .

March 26. Mrs Warner called —*talked very much.* She is quick-tongued, I never felt it before; I listened, watching my opportunity, and spoke on the business of Drury Lane theatre; the old sore subject came up, Miss Faucit. I brought it to this point—either make your bargain with me *en métier*, and leave me to reduce it as I can, or come to me in the confidence of a friend as you have done before. She left me to write an answer, which I suppose I shall receive. . . .

April 6. [At Drury Lane] The General Committee was sitting; we met them. I explained my views; they deliberated. We met them again, and they gave me the theatre, in which undertaking may God prosper me.

Macready's Haymarket engagement had ended on 13 March. At the end of March he had a brief engagement in Newcastle; and from mid-April to the end of the month he appeared in turn at Birmingham, Bristol, Exeter, and Plymouth

Birmingham, April 13. Acted Macbeth with great spirit, *i.e.* began it so, and felt that my acting begins to want spirit, which I must attend to. Was marred and utterly deprived of my effects by the 'support' of a Mr — and others in the last act. Was in a violent passion, and in that behaved very ill. . . .

April 14. . . . I tried to act Richelieu well, and did my best with a company and a Mr C— that would paralyse a Hercules. . . .

April 16. . . . Acted Werner with much care, and in most respects very well, but was inconvenienced by Ulric, who was raw though willing, and cut up root and branch by Mr C—.

Exeter, April 23. Acted Cardinal Richelieu as well as the wretched murdering of the other characters would let me. . . .

Plymouth, April 26. Acted Macbeth in my very best manner,

positively improving several passages, but sustaining, the character in a most satisfactory manner. . . . Colonel Hamilton Smith[1] and Wightwick came into my room. Wightwick came here to tea with me and sat late. . . . I have improved, Macbeth. The general tone of the character was lofty, manly, or indeed as it should be, heroic, that of one living to command. The whole view of the character was constantly in sight; the grief, the care, the doubt, was not that of a weak person but of a strong mind and of a strong man. The manner of executing the command to the witches, and the effect upon myself of their vanishing was justly hit off. I marked the cause. The energy was more slackened—the great secret. A novel effect I thought good, of restlessness and an uneasy effort to appear unembarrassed before Banquo, previous to the murder. The banquet was improved in its forced hilarity of tone; the scene with the physician very much so. It was one of the most successful performances of Macbeth I ever gave.

He returned to the Haymarket.

London May 3. Acted Evelyn fairly. . . . A gentleman sent me a snuff-box, a very pretty one, from the boxes as a token of his admiration.

May 5. Obtained Mademoiselle Rachel's[2] address and called on her after rehearsal. Saw first some male *attachés*, and afterwards herself and mother. She is a very engaging, graceful little person, anything but plain in person, delicate and most intelligent features, a frank, a French manner, synonymous to pleasing. I talked with her some little time; invited her to dine on Sunday, which she accepted; asked her if she would visit the theatre, which she wished to do.

May 8. Read in the newspaper the death of Barnes, editor of *The Times*.[3] It was a sort of surprise to me, but an event that I heard of with indifference. Perhaps of the men who were never acquainted with me none ever did me so much injury, or willed to do me so much as this man, but all strife is now at rest. . . .

May 9. . . . Coming in, dressed and read in *Courier*, Balzac, and Sevigné—laughing at whiles—to accustom myself to thoughts in French. Madame and Mademoiselle Rachel, Colonel and Mrs Gurwood, Mrs Norton, Eastlake, Young, T. Campbell, Kenney, Dr Elliotson, and Quin came to dinner. A very pleasant and cheerful day we had. . . . I

[1] Colonel Hamilton Smith, of Plymouth, was an authority on theatrical costume. He designed the Shylock costume the Devonport-born Samuel Phelps wore at his Haymarket opening as Shylock in 1837.
[2] Rachel (Elisabeth-Rachel Félix, 1821–1858), actress.
[3] Thomas Barnes (1785–1841), eighth editor of *The Times*, 1817 until his death.

was—indeed, all were—delighted with Rachel; her extreme simplicity, her ingenuousness, earnestness, and the intellectual variation of her sweet and classic features. There was but one feeling of admiration and delight through the whole party at and after dinner. . . . Dear Rachel seemed very happy and very loth to go away. Bless her! I wish her *all* success.

[Among those in this entry are Colonel John Gurwood (1790–1845), who edited 'The Wellington Dispatches'; Mrs Caroline Norton (1808–1887), poet and novelist, grand-daughter of R. B. Sheridan, who married the Hon. George Norton in 1827 and was separated from him in 1836; Sir Charles Lock Eastlake (1793–1865), artist; Charles Mayne Young (1777–1856), actor; Thomas Campbell (1777–1844), poet; and Charles Lamb Kenney (1821–1881), son of James Kenney (the dramatist), a godson of Lamb, and a critic and author.]

May 15. Miss Faucit came in. I told her not on any account to give up her engagement with Mr Webster. She said she would not, if she could help it! She asked me whether I would not 'give' her 'the same terms' she has at the Haymarket, which she was 'obliged to ask'. I was obliged to say *yes*.

May 15 was the last night of the Haymarket engagement, Macready paid brief visits to Dublin, Liverpool, and Birmingham.

Dublin, May 20. Our houses are indifferent. After an absence of four years—during which crowded houses have attended the performances of Mr C. Kean—it is rather hard to hear persons place my performance of Othello above Kean's—(which I do *not*)—and act it to £60. . . .

London, July 5. After dinner went to the Opera House *[in Haymarket.]* Read in Corneille's *Cinna* the scenes of Emilie. Watched with intense eagerness the performance of the part by Rachel. I must confess I was disappointed; she has undoubtedly genius; grace in a high degree, and perfect self-possession. But she disappointed me; she has no tenderness, nor has she grandeur. She did not dilate with passion; the appeal to the gods was not that grand swell of passion that lifts her up above the things (too little for its communion) of earth to the only powers capable of sympathising with her. She did not seem to commune with the *Manes* of her father. Her apostrophe to the liberty of Rome was not 'up to the height of the great argument'. She was stinging, scornful, passionate, but *little* in her familiar descents, and wanting in the terrible struggle, the

173

life and death conflict, between her love and revenge. The 'sharp convulsive pangs of agonising pride' and fondness were not felt. She is not equal to Mars *[Mlle Mars (1779–1847), French actress]* or Miss O'Neill, but she is the first actress of her day.

Macready was now back at the Haymarket, where he acted for Webster from 3 July to 7 December.

July 16. We went to the Opera House, to see Rachel in *Horace*. My opinion of her was very greatly raised. If I might apply a term of distinction to the French acting, I should say it is sculpturesque in its effect; it resembles figures in relief, no background, and almost all in single figures, scarcely any grouping, no grand composition: this sort of individual effect may be good for the artist, but not for the illusion of a play. With the drawback consequent on this national peculiarity, Rachel in Camille was generally admirable. . . . In the last scene she was all that a representation of the part could be. It was a splendid picture of frenzied despair.

He now had arrangements for Drury Lane very much on his mind. He met the committee on 26 July and discussed the state of the theatre; and he was busily reading plays

August 6. Finished the play of *Plighted Troth*—a play written in a quaint style, but possessing the rare qualities of intense passion and happy imagination. . . . Wrote to Rev. C. F. Darley [the] author. . . .

[The Rev. Charles F. Darley was the brother of the poet George Darley, and the author of 'Plighted Troth; or, A Woman Her Own Rival,' a tragedy.]

August 8. Considered for more than an hour the subject of Sir Robert Walpole as one for Bulwer's pen. . . . Resumed my search in *History of England* for matter for Bulwer. . . .

August 13. Letter from Darley, and from the lady who calls herself Mrs St Aubyn, wishing to see me this evening. I might gratify my curiosity if without trouble, but *voilà tout!* I answered her—in the hope that I may shake her off.

August 14. . . . Met a very beautiful woman in Portman Square, who had written to me as Mrs St Aubyn. I found it was an assumed name, and that she was the mistress of a Lord —. I had thought she had been connected with the St Aubyns. *Addio, mia bella!*

August 18. . . . Went to keep my appointment with Mrs St Aubyn, to tell her that I could not see her again. She begged *very hard* that I would, told me part of her story—of course a sad one—that she had been promised marriage and seduced by a Mr —, a barrister; that she was not the particular mistress of Lord —; in fact, that her mysterious carriage with me was to keep her partiality from the knowledge of Mr C. Kean who was 'very kind' to her. I was amused. She wished to make me promise to see her again— I avoided it.

August 23. Mrs St Aubyn, with a gentleman, occupied the stage private-box. She is very beautiful. I inquired who she was, and it seems she had been noticed as constant in her attendance on C. Kean's performances.

September 7. Read in bed several scenes of *Two Gentlemen of Verona* which I think I have now clearly arranged in my own mind.

September 13. . . . Poole called, and in the course of conversation alluded to some persons talking of myself and Mr C. Kean as actors!!! Now really, it is almost an excuse for expatriation, for anything in the shape of *escape* short of suicide, to think that one has lived and *had a mind* and *used* it for so many years to be *mentioned* at last in the same breath with Mr C. Kean! Particularly offensive.

September 22. Received a letter from Dickens mentioning to me his purpose of going to the United States, and asking my opinion as to the best course to be pursued with regard to his children—whether to take them or leave them. I answered him on the instant, recommending him not to take them with him.

September 23. As I was going to bed Dickens called in, having sent a note first, and sat with me some time canvassing his contemplated voyage to the United States. He spoke of Mrs Dickens's reluctance and regret, and wished me to write to her and state my views, putting them strongly before her. When he was gone, I wrote to her, enclosing the note to him.

September 27. A very fervent and grateful letter from Mrs Dickens, in reply to mine, acquiescing in all I urged upon her. Letter with a *triste* report of herself from Helen Faucit. . . .

October 4. On this day I enter upon the lease and management of Drury Lane theatre. I humbly implore the blessing of Almighty God upon my efforts.

Engaged at the Haymarket, where he acted in Zouch Troughton's dull cardboard-drama 'Nina Sforza' (staged for Helen Faucit's benefit), and ended his engagement with two performances of Claude Melnotte, Macready would not open Drury Lane until 27 December. One of his tasks now was

*the instruction of a Miss Fortescue whom he had seen in July acting
Barnaby Rudge at the English Opera House with 'great vivacity and grace
and power'. On 14 November he described her as 'a very sweet little girl.
Mrs Fortescue is a counterpart of Mrs Nickleby'. Julia Fortescue (d. 1899)
married in 1848 the third Lord Gardner.*

December 4. Bulwer looked in, but would not wait. Went to Dickens's.
where I saw Landor, Elliotson, Quin, Stanfield, Maclise. The Talfourds
extremely disagreeable.

December 7. . . . Miss Fortescue came and continued her lessons. I
am greatly interested in her success. . . . Went to the Haymarket theatre.
Acted Claude Melnotte with vigour, gaiety, and energy, inspired and
animated by the good house and the feeling they displayed towards
me—perhaps I never acted it better; it was the *last time*. Was called for
and very enthusiastically received. I bowed my adieux. . . .

December 10. Reconsidered the question of acting the unimportant
parts of Harmony [in Mrs Inchbald's *Every One has his Fault*] and
Valentine [in *The Two Gentlemen of Verona*], and came to the decision
that everything should be done to raise and sustain the character of the
theatre; that my reputation could scarcely be affected in any way by the
assumption of these parts, or, at least, not injuriously; and that it would
be a sad calculation to think of propping my reputation by the ruins of
the theatre. I saw that it was right to do them. Read Valentine. Read
Harmony.

*There were immediate troubles: the equipment of the theatre which he had
had to put into complete order, though the proprietors would allow him only
an inadequate reduction in rent; the officials' want of energy; the utter
incompetence of the superintendent of the ladies' wardrobe; deficiencies in
Miss Fortescue's rehearsing in* The Two Gentlemen. *However,* The
Merchant of Venice, *as opening play, was coming up well, and on 27
December the venture began.*

December 27. . . . Went round the various places. Gave direction on
direction. My mind was over every part of the house. My room very
uncomfortable. Lay down, but got little rest. Was much disturbed by
being called for as the play began; resisted for a long while, but was at
last obliged to go forward. My reception was most enthusiastic. I acted
Shylock very nervously—not to please myself. I saw the pantomime
afterwards.

[That night, and for the first time at a Shakespeare revival, small playbills were distributed among the audience, giving the order of the scenes and the names of their painters. Others in the cast with Macready included Phelps as Antonio, Anderson as Bassanio, George Bennett as the Duke, Henry Compton as Launcelot Gobbo, Mrs Keeley as Nerissa, and Mrs Warner as Portia.]

[The pantomime was 'Harlequin and Duke Humphry's Dinner; or, Jack Cade, the Lord of London Stone.']

December 28. . . . Read over Harmony. Acted it tolerably well. Was not known by the audience at first. . . . The play seemed to have made an agreeable impression, about which I was very anxious, as being a comedy. Mrs Carlyle was in Catherine's box, and very glad to see me.

December 29. Rehearsed the play of *The Two Gentlemen of Verona*, which occupied us a very long while; it was not finished until five o'clock. Acted Valentine imperfectly, and not well. . . . Miss Fortescue did not equal, in the impression she seemed to make, my expectations. I felt very much on her account. Let us hope. Took counsel with my officers on what should be done with her. All and Catherine were of opinion that *Romeo and Juliet* should not be hazarded.

December 30. Looked at the newspapers, which were very cordial in their notice of *The Two Gentlemen of Verona*, and kind in their opinion of Miss Fortescue. Sent for and spoke to Miss Fortescue about last night; she acknowledged that she had not done justice either to herself or me. She promised to be more attentive.

December 31. . . . Acted Valentine indifferently. . . . Spoke with Miss Fortescue after the play. . . . She was very languid in her acting.

[Poor Miss Fortescue, it was decided, could not play Juliet and it was decided to do Gerald Griffin's tragedy of Gisippus *instead. Even so, James Anderson would remember, in his autobiography, that in 'The Two Gentlemen of Verona' 'Miss Fortescue played the part of Julia most delightfully. She made a great sensation, and was much and deservedly applauded for she was all that could be desired in the character.' We have to suppose that she had been deemed too successful for a novice in the highly competitive world of Drury Lane.]*

1842

January 1. Dear Dickens called to shake hands with me. My heart was quite full; it is much to me to lose the presence of a friend who really loves me. He said there was no one whom he felt such pain in saying good-bye to. *[The Dickenses left their four children in the Macready's care.]*

January 2. In conversation with Messrs Serle and Brydone, it came out on the part of Mr Brydone, when speaking of the accounts, that no bills, no material had been paid for!! It was a thunderbolt to me! I did not know what position I was in—I might be ruined! I was very angry...

January 4. . . . Gave directions to C[harles] Jones *[Treasurer of Drury Lane]* from whom I learned that my liabilities would amount to at least £2500!!! This is very cruel. Gave him directions to write out a circular, refusing to pay any bills unaccompanied by my written order, previously given. . . .

January 17. . . . A letter in verse from Mrs St Aubyn. I am vain enough, God knows, but might be much more so!

January 19. . . . Ordered that, after this evening, the money of women of the town should be refused altogether at the doors.

February 1. . . . A noble article, the third leader, in *The Times*, on the attack of *John Bull*.

['John Bull' had said that a staircase was provided at Drury Lane for women of the town, that a refreshment room had been set apart for their use and for such of the public as might choose to resort to it, and that they were admitted to the house 'along with the respectable portion of the public from the second circle upward'. Macready replied wrathfully that he could not think of anything less inviting than the dismantled, unpapered, unpainted, and seatless lobby of the third circle, patrolled constantly by a policeman. He ordered that the money of 'all persons of supposed improper character' should be refused at the door; and 'The Times', edited now by John Thaddeus Delane, congratulated him in a third leader on 1 February, calling him 'the man who has done more than any other individual to make Shakespeare popular'.]

February 5. Gave my whole attention during the day to various matters connected with the opera *[Acis and Galatea, adapted and arranged for representation from the serenata of Handel]*. Directed the rehearsal. The curtain was let down, and the stage swept five minutes before the half-hour past six. Stanfield and the assistants painting to the last minute. Saw the performance of the opera, which was beautiful; have never seen anything of the kind in my life so perfectly beautiful. . . . 'Gratulations were passing everywhere. . . .

February 6. Rejoiced in my absence from Mr Ducrow's funeral, which was attended by a fearful set—Messrs Bunn, etc. When will my funeral come? Let it be as simple as the return of dust to dust should be. . . .

February 18. Note from Helen Faucit *[who had joined the company]* absurdly complaining of being cast [as] Catherine *[in the afterpiece of Catherine and Petruchio]* for Monday night. She last complained of Mr Webster for not putting her in it. Answered her.

February 21. Wrote to Mr J. Dickens. Sent him £20, desiring him not to mention it to his son. Forster had advised £10—but he is Dickens's father, though——*[John Dickens (?1785–1851), Charles Dickens's Micawberish father, 'as kind-hearted and generous a man', said his son, 'as ever lived in the world'.]*

February 23. Acted Gisippus, I must admit, not well, not finished; not like a great actor. The actor was lost in the manager. The effect of the play was a success; but I am not satisfied. I hope I shall be able, if I escape severe handling in this instance, to be more careful in future. . . .

[Gisippus; or, The Forgotten Friend was a contrived, mediocre piece in facile blank verse by an Irish writer Gerald Griffin (1803-1840). Anderson played Fulvius, a Roman tribune, rival of Gisippus, a Greek (Macready), for the love of Sophronia (Helen Faucit).]

February 27. . . . Wrote a note to Betty, giving him the freedom of Drury Lane theatre. . . .

March 4. Note from Browning; looked at the paper. Went to Drury Lane, reading *Athelwold [by William Smith]*, a printed play sent to me yesterday—another instance of the extraordinary growth of dramatic power in our time. . . .

March 16. Mrs Nisbett and her mother called, and entered on the matter of her visit. Her terms were £35 per week. She waived the question of a Benefit, leaving it to circumstances and my consideration. . . . She signed her engagement for next season at £35 per week, the two next, if she remained on the stage, at £40. . . . *[Louisa Nisbett (1812–1858) was a popular comedienne, who married Sir William Boothby.]*

Macready was still recruiting.

March 26. Received an intimation that Mr and Mrs C. Mathews *would* come to Drury Lane if they could receive remuneration for their services. Took Serle, Willmott, and Anderson into consultation upon it. We sifted the matter as we best could, and the conclusion was that we could not make them worth their cost. . . .

[After three years Mathews and his wife (Madame Vestris) had failed at Covent Garden. Charles Kemble and his co-proprietors had impounded scenery, wardrobe, and properties against arrears of rent alleged to be £14,000 (though Planché put the figure at £600), and Vestris and Mathews found themselves with nothing but their debts and a piece of plate presented by their company. During their very brief stay, barely more than a month, at Drury Lane, they had few opportunities. Vestris appeared only as the Duchesse de Chartres in Planché's 'Follies of a Night' (sixteen performances), given with 'Marino Faliero'; Mathews appeared as Palliot in the same play, and as Fag ('The Rivals'), Goldfinch in 'The Road to Ruin', and Roderigo ('Othello'), also in a pair of farces.]

March 29. . . . Offered them £40 per week for next season.

March 30. . . . Beazley called and informed me of Mr C. Mathews's refusal of £40 per week for himself and his wife. We talked for some time; he said from them that they would find their own clothes, and submit to costume, and be in all respects good subjects, but that they did not like half-past-nine-o'clock rehearsals. I offered them £50. . . .

April 4. Wrote note to Mrs Carlyle, thanking her for the gift of a brooch which was once Flora Macdonald's. Acted Macbeth. . . . The Queen and Prince Albert were present.

April 5. To Maclise, and was very much pleased to see his grand picture of Hamlet, which was splendid in colour and general effect. With some of the details I did not quite agree, particularly the two personages, Hamlet and Ophelia. Drove to Edwin Landseer's and saw some of his charming works. Went on to Etty, and was delighted with his gorgeous colours and ravishing forms. . . . *[Sir Edwin Henry Landseer (1802–1873), and William Etty (1787–1849), were fashionable painters of the time.]*

April 8. Note from Beazley about the Mathewses. Answered it, expressing my belief they were coquetting. Acted Gisippus for the last time. . . . Now here is a complete defeat of my calculations. I thought it a material object in opening a theatre to have such a play. It has produced nothing, and been well spoken of. There is some weakness in it, which I have not yet exactly pointed out.

April 9. I agreed to give Mr and Mrs C. Mathews the terms for which they stood out, viz. £60 per week. It is a very great salary, but it is paid in consideration of enfeebling an opposition as well as adding to my own strength. . . . Called at Beazley's and found there Mr C. Mathews and Madame Vestris. I met them very frankly and good-humouredly; heard much that was irrelevant, and some things that amused me; at last concluded an engagement with them for two years. . . . Parted with them, they starting off in their carriage, I in my shattered old hack cab!

April 19. Rehearsed the play of *Plighted Troth*, which occupied me the whole day. Mr Darley was present. . . .

April 20. Went to the theatre, trying to keep my thoughts on the acting of my part. Rehearsed the play of *Plighted Troth*. Became confident in hope about it. Looked at the chance of a brilliant success. Serle spoke to me. Rested. Acted nervously; but *the play was unsuccessful.* Long consultation afterwards on what should be done. Anderson, C. Jones, Serle, Willmott, and Forster. I wished to do justice to the author, and we agreed at last to give it another trial. Chance, I fear, there is none. *Eloi!* A most unhappy failure; I have felt it deeply, deeply.

Plighted Troth: a Dramatic Tale, by C. F. Darley, *a very long, Elizabethan-style drama on a religious controversy (Catholic versus Protestant), was Macready's unluckiest misjudgment. Believing the gloomy, turgid affair to be a work of 'fine thoughts expressed in massive language', he had approached it with confidence. But it lasted only a single night. Darley had called his chief character Gabriel Grimwood: Eliza Grimwood happened to be the name of a girl brutally murdered in Waterloo Bridge Road, and the gallery fastened on this. 'Look here, old bloke,' somebody shouted, 'who cut Eliza's throat?' The louder the gallery laughed, the colder Macready's acting became. During the first scene George Bennett[1] sprained his ankle, and whenever he limped on, the pit told him to 'hook it, to the hospital!' At the end of the play, after Elton had stabbed Macready with a table-knife and the dead man had fallen beneath the table, Bennett—emerging from a bed and limping down to look at the body—trod heavily on Macready's hand. 'Beast!' cried the tragedian. 'Beast of hell!' He lay down angrily, and died all over again, and at length the curtain fell to hysterical laughter.*

April 21. Came down, wretchedly low at heart, worn, done, and depressed by the issue of last night and the want of sleep. I did not sleep at all through the night. I cannot imagine how I could have been so mistaken. Surely I could not believe that to be poetry, thought, energy,

---

[1] George Bennett (1800–1879), actor; with Macready at Covent Garden and Drury Lane; later, 1844–1862, with Phelps at Sadler's Wells.

imagination, and melody of rhythm which was totally devoid of all these? . . . Mr Darley called. We talked over the matter of last night. He was much depressed, and I agonised for him. He deserved to succeed. The result of our conference was that he could not make the alterations suggested to his play by the day's rehearsal, and, therefore, that he would wish the play to be withdrawn.

April 22. Received a note from Dr Ashburner, informing me that Darley would call on me, and wishing me to speak encouragingly to him. God knows I need no prompter to act in kindness and sympathy towards him. A note—a most kind note—from Bulwer in relation to Mr Darley's play. I enclosed it to Mr Darley, with a cordial expression of sympathy and a cheque for £34.

April 23. At dinner received a most affecting note from Darley that almost reconciles one to the misery that has been my lot this week.

May 7. . . . Saw a Mr Ryder rehearse two scenes of Pierre [Venice Preserv'd] and thought he showed more promise of becoming a useful actor than any novice I had seen for a long time. Engaged him. . . .

[John Ryder (1814–1885), actor, was the son of a river pilot from the Isle of Thanet and noted for his deep baritone voice (said to vary between organ and hunting horn). He would accompany Macready twice to America.]

May 8. . . . Went to Bulwer's—walked round the grounds [at Fulham]. A dinner-party of journalists and critics (!) assembled— Leigh Hunt, Bell of the *Atlas*,[1] Ainsworth, Forster, Jerdan, Blanchard; there were also Quin and Villiers, M.P. for Wolverhampton. One of the dullest, most uncomfortable days I have spent for some years. I asked Quin once the time; he said, 'A quarter-past nine; you thought it was eleven.' I was not very well pleased with Bulwer inviting me to in-different company and a very bad dinner when I could so much more pleasantly and profitably have employed my time at home or elsewhere.

May 12. After the play went to the Queen's theatre [in Tottenham Street] to see a man of the name of Fuller do the Clown. It was a dread-ful endurance. What places these minor theatres are! Surely it is the duty of a Government to have some care of the *decency*, if not the *moral influence* of places of public amusement, both of which were set at naught by the exhibitions before and behind the curtain at this disgusting place of obscene and ribald absurdities.

May 20. Weary! weary! . . . Rehearsed with much care (what occupied a long morning) the play of *Marino Faliero [by Byron; Macready's*

---

[1] Robert Bell (1800–1867), editor of *The Atlas*.

Benefit night]. Rested and thought over my character. I could not sleep. Acted Marino Faliero in parts very well; the interest of the play grew upon the audience, and the curtain fell upon the death of Faliero with their strong sympathy. . . . *[In the cast were Macready as Marino Faliero, Hudson as Bertuccio Faliero, Anderson as Lioni, Phelps as Israel, Bennett as Benintende, Elton as Bertram, Helen Faucit as Angiolina.]*

May 23. *[Last night of season]* Through the day gave every interval of thought to the speech I had to deliver at night. Rehearsed the play of *Othello.* Heard of some paragraphs in the papers about summonses being served upon me for *rates*—the first I had heard of it. I was very angry. . . . Acted Iago very unfinishedly, very poorly. *[Anderson's benefit: he played Othello.]* Spoke my speech falteringly and ill. I have had too much upon my head. Fox and Forster came into my room. I was so nervous, for all recollection of the words left me entirely. I had too much to do.

Between 27 May and 24 June he was acting in Dublin and at Birmingham. Helen Faucit appeared with him in each city. He left by rail for Liverpool on 26 May, having one of the mail carriages to himself all the way except between Coventry and Birmingham, and reading various plays including Farquhar's The Recruiting Officer *'which does not suit the theatrical genius of our time'. That night he crossed to Kingstown, 'a sofa for my berth'.*

Dublin, May 31. Called on Miss H. Faucit, and gave her some general notions respecting Lady Macbeth, of which she rehearsed a part with me. . . .

June 1. Spoke to Miss Faucit about her habit of acting with her arms in to her side, and thus bringing herself so close to another person as to destroy all outline; also about her *smothering up* the last scene. She behaved very weakly upon these kind and good-natured remarks, and I thought would have had an hysteric in my room. I was distressed and annoyed.

June 2. Spoke a few words with Calcraft, asking him if he thought Miss H. Faucit might accompany me to Glendalough, if her maid went with her. He thought there could then be no observation. Acted Claude Melnotte very well to a dull audience commanded by the Lord Lieutenant.

June 6. . . . Was very much struck with Miss Faucit's rehearsal of Lady Macbeth, which surprised and gratified me very much. Acted Macbeth as well as my harassed mind and worn-down body would let me. Called for and well received. Would have taken on Miss Faucit, but she, against my directions, had undressed, so left her to Calcraft. Spoke with Calcraft and her afterwards about her Benefit—and with her about her acting, which was *remarkably* good.

June 11. . . . Bought a waistcoat for Forster—gay one!—poplins for my women. Acted Gisippus as well as a disgusting ill-bred party in the stage private box would let me by their noise.

Birmingham, June 21. . . . Rehearsed *Gisippus*, and pointed out to Mr Anderson the actual son of Crummles among the actors—not to be mistaken. Called on Helen Faucit and spent a very pleasant hour with her. Wrote to Letitia and to Catherine.

June 22. Note from [Helen Faucit]. The means adopted to place her heart in a state of repose—to *satisfy* her affection, as she said and, I am sure, believed, appears now to me only to add fuel to the ardour of her passion. I now again lapse into doubt and fear, and in *youth*, I begin to imagine, there is no love without an intermingling of sexual love. It is therefore *dangerous*, and to be avoided.

[During this Birmingham visit, as Sir Theodore Martin recorded in the biography of his wife, 'Helen Faucit' (1900), Macready and his leading lady went over to Stratford-upon-Avon to visit Holy Trinity Church and the Birthplace. 'Their names, inscribed on a beam in the principal room, though faint, are still discernible, and are eagerly sought for by countless visitors. Close by them Robert Browning has, in later days, placed his bold autograph—well pleased, no doubt, that it should be near to those of the two artists to whom he had owed much.']

June 23. Wrote a few lines—wishing to direct her views to the danger of losing sight of her *understood relationship* with me—to ——. Acted William Tell with a company that would have strangled the efforts of Roscius himself. . . .

June 24. *Wedding Day*. Passed a sleepless night! For all the enjoyment, the comfort, the delight, the happiness this day—eighteen years ago— has brought me, I thank God, and next I bless the dear, dear earthly cause and participator in my worldly bliss—my blessed Catherine. . . .

London, June 29. . . . I was lying on the sofa when a person entered abruptly, whom I glanced at as Forster?—no. Jonathan Bucknill *[Macready's cousin]?*—no. Who was it but dear Dickens himself *[just back from America]* holding me in his arms in a transport of joy. God bless him!

July 2. Helen Faucit called, in very good spirits. The sight of her cheerfulness imparted its influence to me.

July 4. . . . Went in cab, reading Alfred Tennyson's[1] beautiful poem, to see —. I was truly, truly rejoiced to leave her in so comfortable a state of mind. She said she felt so happy, now that she was secure in her understanding with me, that she could speak to me without restraint. . . .

Eastbourne, July 8. [Holiday]. Read several poems of Tennyson. Some I liked; some I thought puerile; some evincing a mean affectation of simplicity. . . .

July 10. Letter from —, in an altered tone from that which she has lately used to me. I am uncertain of the cause, but shall be too glad to know—although my feelings towards her have undergone no change— that she has subdued all that was too painfully strong in her attachment to me.

London, July 12. . . . Went to Dickens; found Landor, Maclise, and Forster there. Dickens had been mesmerising his wife and Miss Hogarth, who had been in violent hysterics. He proposed to make a trial on me; I did not quite like it, but assented; was very nervous, and found the fixedness of the position—eyes, limbs, and entire frame— very unpleasant, and the nervousness at first painful. Reasoned myself out of it, and then felt it could not affect me.

Eastbourne, July 19.—A letter from —, that gave me the deepest concern; from a state of comparative health it struck me down into illness at once. My nerves were unstrung, my head in pain, and my spirits painfully depressed the whole day. She is fretting her heart with self-upbraidings for her affection to me; when the understanding has been established between us that this affection shall never violate any time, law, or propriety, but be an attachment purely of heart and mind, and that such understanding seemed to make her so *very happy*. I am quite at a loss to divine the cause of this change.

London, July 27. Tried to understand the Income Tax paper, which perplexed and annoyed me. . . .

July 29. Went out in good time; called on Dickens, who gave me his introductory chapter to his book on America. *I do not like it.* . . .

Eastbourne, July 31. Examined as strictly as I could the probable expenditure for Drury Lane theatre before the opening, and the means to meet it. It is very heavy to encounter, but I have no retreat. . . .

London, August 11. Read part of Dickens's *America*, the style and matter of which *I did not like.*

August 26. Looked over my Drury Lane expenditure, and calculating how much it has cost me, find that I am minus what I should have possessed—£8000. This is a sad contemplation—the earnings of a life

[1] Alfred Lord Tennyson (1809–1892), later Poet Laureate.

of labour! I certainly never intended, never dreamed, never agreed to be made liable to such an amount. . . . *[The thought did not prevent him from sending, early in September, £50 to Anderson whose eldest child had just died.]*

London, August 29. On my way to London *[from Eastbourne]* I read Marston's[1] tragedy of *The Patrician's Daughter*, which is a most interesting and touching play. I will act it, if I am prosperous.

During the first fortnight of September Macready acted in Liverpool, Manchester, and Bristol. Drury Lane re-opened on 1 October, with As You Like It, *Mrs Nisbett as Rosalind, Macready as Jacques, Anderson as Orlando, Ryder as the Banished Duke, Mrs Stirling as Celia, Miss Phillips as Phebe, Keeley as Touchstone, Mrs Keeley as Audrey. In this endearing revival (though Louisa Nisbett's brunette Rosalind could not have been reasonably cast), Mrs Stirling (1813–1895) gave as Celia what Forster called, in 'The Examiner', 'the prettiest, quietest, most sensible, most graceful, and, if we may say so, most open-hearted piece of acting we have seen of the kind for many a day'.*

October 1. Went to Drury Lane theatre, calling at Delcroix's to purchase rouge. Attended to the business of the theatre, which was most harassing. Rehearsed the play of *As You Like It*, which kept me very late. Business, business all the day and all the evening. Was called for by the audience before the play began; very enthusiastically received. . . . I acted Jacques as well as I could. Was called for after the play and led on Mrs Nisbett. Stanfield and my own people came into my room. . . .

October 8. Went to Drury Lane theatre, but first looked through Mr M. Lemon's farce, which I found to be really objectionable as to the part assigned to Mr C. Mathews. I was run away with by the broad humour of the piece. Spoke with Helen Faucit about her acting last night [Julia in *The Rivals*]. Mr C. Mathews held a very long and *very silly* conversation with me, which I tried to receive as patiently as possible. I see he is not to be managed to any advantage. He was obliged *repeatedly* to admit in the presence of Serle that nothing could be more kind or courteous than my conduct had been to him. . . .

The next production was a very elaborate King John. *Macready, as a subtle and sinister John could chill the stage, especially in the Macbeth-charged dialogue with Hubert. Anderson was the Bastard; Helen Faucit,*

[1] John Westland Marston (1819–1890), dramatist, critic, and later a stage historian (*Our Recent Actors*).

Theatre Royal, Drury Lane.

The Public is respectfully informed, that this Theatre will be RE-OPENED
his Evening, SATURDAY, October 1st, 1842
When **Her Majesty's Servants** will perform the Play of

AS YOU LIKE IT

FROM
THE TEXT OF SHAKSPEARE.

first Movement of BEETHOVEN'S PASTORAL SYMPHONY will be given as an OVERTURE t
the Play, and the Entre-Acts will be selected from the same Work.

Duke,	*living in exile,*	Mr. RYDER,
	(His first appearance.)	

First Lord,		Mr. ELTON,
Second Lord,	*Lords attending upon the Duke*	Mr. H. PHILLIPS,
Amiens,	*in his banishment.*	Mr. ALLEN,
Jaques,		Mr. MACREADY,

e Frederick, *Brother to the rightful Duke, & usurper of his dominions,* Mr. G. BENNETT
Le Beau, *a Courtier attending upon Frederick,* Mr. HUDSON.
Charles, *his wrestler,* Mr. HOWELL,

Oliver,		Mr. GRAHAM,
Jaques,	*Sons of Sir Rowland de Bois,*	Mr. LYNNE,
Orlando,		Mr. ANDERSON,

lam, and Dennis, *Servants to Oliver,* Mr. PHELPS, and Mr. ELLIS,
Touchstone, *a Clown,* Mr. KEELEY.
Sir Oliver Mar-Text, *a Vicar,* Mr. MELLON,
n, and Sylvius, *Shepherds,* Mr. W. BENNETT, and Mr. STANTON
William, *a country fellow, in love with Audrey.* Mr. COMPTON
s, *attending upon the banished Duke,* Miss P. HORTON, and Miss GOULD
s attending Duke Frederick, Mr. ROBERTS, Mr. WALDRON, Mr. BENDER
C. J. SMITH. Mr. CARLE, Mr. HARCOURT, Mr. SEVIER, Mr. STILT, &c.
s attending the banished Duke, Mr. REDFEARN, Mr. YARNOLD, Mr S. JONES,
rs. Walsh, May; J. Beale, Walker, Collet, Leigh, Gilbeigh, Simmons, George, Price; T. Price, Macarthy,
Barclay, Cowbrick, Miller, &c.
Foresters, Mr. STRETTON, Mr. J. REEVES,
Messrs. Clifford, Hance, Hill, Pigeon, Wemis, Johnson, Tyrrell, Foster, Richards, Ryan, &c.
rds, Messrs. Paulo, Brady, Roffey, Burdett, Sharpe, Priorson, Gouriet, King, Gilbert, J. Roffey, Lake, Upsdell, &c
salind, *Daughter to the banished Duke.* Mrs. NISBETT,
(Her first appearance here these Six Years)
Celia, *Daughter to Duke Frederick,* Mrs. STIRLING,
Phebe, *a Shepherdess,* Miss E. PHILLIPS,
(In consequence of the illness of Miss Fortescue)
Audrey, *a Country Wench,* Mrs. KEELEY.
of the Court, Mesdames Byers, C. Byers, Goward, Perry, Boden, Smith, Foster, Newcombe, King, Mapleson
Williams, Jackson, &c.
Shepherdesses, Miss WEBSTER,
mes Maile, Reede, Greene, Sutton, Berringer, Carson, Lee, Hunt, Schmidt, T. Marsano, Travis, A. Travis, &c. &c
PREVIOUS TO THE PLAY.

GOD SAVE THE QUEEN,

WILL BE SUNG BY

OMER, Mr. H. PHILLIPS, Miss P. HORTON, Mr. ALLEN, Miss GOULD, Mr. STRETTON, Mrs. SERLE
REEVES, Miss TURPIN, Mr. REDFURN, Mr. S. JONES, Messrs. J. Beale, Clifford, Cofler. Gilbeigh, Lee, May
ns, Walker, Walsh, &c. Mesdames H. Boden, Byers, C. Byers. Forster. Goward, Perry. Smith. King, Newcombe, &c.

Constance; Phelps, Hubert; Ryder, Pandulph. Critics described the glitter-
ing panoply of France and England before the gates of Angiers.

'*We have had nothing so great as the revival of* King John. *We have had*
no celebration of English History and English Poetry so worthy of a National
Theatre,' *wrote the faithful Forster in '*The Examiner*' on 29 October. The*
*production is recreated in the facsimile prompt-book, '*William Charles*
Macready's King John', *edited by Charles H. Shattuck (University of*
Illinois, 1962). Sir Theodore Martin recorded that, when Helen Faucit's
*Constance left the stage after the grief-torn first scene of the third act, '*she*
was generally carried fainting to her room'.*

October 24. Acted King John fairly. . . . Helen Faucit much depressed
and very unhappy at not having realised the expectations she had raised.

October 25. Little refreshed by last night's rest, which was attended
with very little sleep, my mind being full of the evening's scenes and
events. Looked at the newspapers, and read a very eulogistic description
of what I had attempted to do, by Fox; a very malignant attack on me in
the *Morning Post* by a Mr Johnson, and a very ignorant, vulgar article in
the *Morning Herald;* an ill-written notice in praise in *The Times.* With
such *critical* appreciation of my labours, I begin to fear they will
produce little harvest of good. The time is, I fancy, *past.* Helen Faucit
came, in very low spirits, to speak to me of last night. *Wretched house!*

November 5. About to begin rehearsal, having seen Stanfield, when
Mr C. Mathews wished to speak to me. Madame Vestris followed him
into my room and began a *scene* which lasted two or three hours—on
the lady's part much 'Billingsgate' and false assertion, on his much
weakness and equivocation. I sent for Anderson and Willmott, and
Serle came in afterwards. Serle directly contradicted his assertions; his
engagement was produced and was in direct contradiction of his statements. It was very offensive. I felt my own strength and was very cool. I
would not relinquish their engagement, but offered to *refer* the pecuniary
point. *She* threw down her part in *King Arthur [Dryden and Purcell]*
and left the room, stating that she would not act after next week if the
full salary were not paid. We sent for Cooke to take measures about
King Arthur. Consulted on a public refutation of her falsehoods, and
after dinner drew up a notice which was placed in both green-rooms.

King Arthur, garishly mounted, was staged—with fair success—on 16
November. A young singer called Sims Reeves was taken from the crowd to
sing the Warrior.

November 21. . . . Read the abuse of myself from the *Sunday Times*

—a quantity of low, ribald falsehood, which did not anger me at all. I believe it was written to provoke a prosecution.

November 22. After dinner went to Covent Garden and saw the first scene of *The Tempest*. A ship was introduced and all the poetry cut out—worse acting or more inapplicable means to an end I never saw. *[During Charles Kemble's last brief and fated management. Vandenhoff was Prospero and Miss Rainforth the Ariel.]*

November 25. . . . Heard very disgusting news, that the infamous wretch Bunn had been brought in as lessee of Covent Garden theatre by Messrs Moore and Surman; that the players were succumbing to him and only anxious to make their engagements with him. The proprietors of Covent Garden had shown themselves, as usual, most *dishonourable men*.

['The Globe' reported on 26 November: 'Mr Bunn is to be the new manager of Covent Garden from Christmas next. The performers are making arrangements to keep the theatre open on their own account till that time. The change, which was only decided on the 24th inst., was on the part of the proprietors consenting to take £20 a night instead of £35 until the new management.']

Macready decided to risk young Westland Marston's The Patrician's Daughter, *a verse tragedy of the spiritual conflicts of modern life. Dickens composed a prologue. Lady Mabel, an Earl's daughter, tricked by a scheming aunt, rejected her lover, Mordaunt, a young Radical statesman. Five years later the man, now a baronet, had his revenge by disowning her on the verge of their wedding, much as Claudio flung aside the 'rotten orange' in the church scene of 'Much Ado About Nothing'. Reconciliation came too late; but Mabel could just say 'I am happy—very happy' before she died in her lover's arms. It was an improbable piece; but Helen Faucit would later have some provincial success with it.*

December 1. . . . Spoke to Anderson about speaking Dickens's prologue, which he declines doing. He *ought* not to have done so [*i.e. declined*]. I fear his self-opinion will prevent him ever rising to the point I wished. Tried to learn it myself. Talked long with Serle. Heard that the Covent Garden proprietors had engaged Mr Bunn as the person most inimical to me. . . .

December 10. First night of *The Patrician's Daughter*. Spoke the prologue (by Dickens) tolerably well. Acted uncertainly the part of Mordaunt, but the play was much applauded. I was told that I was called for, and was annoyed and disconcerted to hear calls, which I

thought were for Miss Faucit [Lady Mabel], and which I believe them to be, but which they tell me were for the author. I gave out the play and left the matter to settle itself. Dickens and Forster came in (I spoke a few words to Helen Faucit)—they thought it a great success.
[Dickens's prologue ran, in part:

> *Awake the Present! Shall no scene display*
> *The tragic passion of the passing day?*
> *Is it with man, as with some meaner things,*
> *That out of death his single purpose springs? . . .*
> *Awake the Present! Though the steel-clad age*
> *Finds life alone within its storied page,*
> *Iron is worn at heart by many still. . . .*
> *Learn from the lessons of the present day.*
> *Not light its import and not poor its mien;*
> *Yourselves the actors, and your homes the scene.*

Besides Macready as Mordaunt and Helen Faucit as Lady Mabel, the cast included Phelps, Hudson, Elton, Ryder, George Bennett, and Mrs Warner. The play, received tentatively, had eleven performances during the season.]

December 12. . . . Saw the *Morning Chronicle*, which was very fervent in its praise of the new tragedy. Went to Drury Lane theatre. Saw the other newspapers. The *Morning Post* contained a most scurrilous and abusive article, with many false statements. . . .

December 26. My beloved Catherine was safely delivered of a daughter *[Lydia Jane (1842–1858)].*

December 31. A sad, sad close to a year of labour and unrest, that has strewn snow upon my head and wrung my heart. . . .

A NEW TRAGEDY,

CALLED THE

PATRICIAN'S DAUGHTER,

WRITTEN BY

J. WESTLAND MARSTON, Esq.

Will be produced on THURSDAY.

The PROLOGUE written by

Mr. CHARLES DICKENS,

Will be Spoken by Mr. Macready.

The Earl of Lynterne, (a Statesman) Mr. PHELPS, Lord Chatterly, Mr. SELBY,

Sir Archer Taunton, Mr. M. BARNETT, Captain Pierpoint, Nephew of Lord Lynterne, Mr. HUDSON

Mordaunt, afterwards Sir Edgar Mordaunt, Mr. MACREADY,

Heartwell, } Politicians. { Mr. ELTON,
Lister, { Mr. G. BENNETT,

Deancourt, } Friends of Mordaunt: { Mr. W. H. BLAND,
Colville, { Mr. ROBERTS,

Physician, Mr. RYDER, Guests of Lord Lynterne, Mr. STANTON, Mr. HARCOURT, &c,

Mordaunt's Servant, Mr. C. J. SMITH, Notary, Mr. YARNOLD,

Lord Lynterne's Servants, Messrs. BENDER, BRADY, PAULO, &c.

Lady Mabel Lynterne, Daughter of the Earl, Miss HELEN FAUCIT,

Lady Lydia Lynterne, his Sister, Mrs. WARNER, Lady Chatterly, Miss ELLIS

Lady Taunton, Mrs. SELBY, Attendant on Lady Mabel, Mrs. WATSON.

VIVAT REGINA.

W. S. Johnson, Printed Soho.

1843

January 1. The year begins to me with labour and difficulty, with care and deep anxiety. My enterprise thus far has only tended to reduce my means, and I have now adventured them as far as I think it prudent to go. I will not advance one farthing more than I see absolute occasion for. . . .

January 4. Mrs Warner came to mention some distressing involvements of her husband, and to ask me if I could advance her £100. I spoke with great kindness to her and urged her to try and have the business settled without calling on me, but that to save her furniture I would accommodate her, if needful. . . .

January 20. Acted Mordaunt very fairly. Helen Faucit spoke with me, somewhat weakly and pettishly, about her dress. I was not pleased with her behaviour. . . .

January 25. Considered well and read scenes of *Athelwold* [by W. Smith] to Catherine, who did not seem impressed with the part of Athelwold, but very much with that of Dunstan. I was shaken in my purpose as to its immediate production, and turned to Browning's *Blot in the 'Scutcheon.*

January 28. Went to Drury Lane theatre, finishing by the way *A Blot on*, etc. . . . Willmott, to whom, on Anderson's declining, I had entrusted the reading of *Blot on*, etc., came and reported to me that they laughed at it, and that Anderson passed his jokes on it—not very decorous for an official! I fear—I fear this young man's head is gone.

[Macready calls it 'A Blot on the 'Scutcheon' throughout the journal; but, except in this entry, we use the recognised form. Hastily written, the tragedy was an eighteenth-century tale of love, seduction, and family honour, with a fourteen-year-old heroine in whose chamber window a signal light glowed behind a purple pane.

Impatient with the play, Macready showed his distaste by allowing John Willmott to read it to the cast after Anderson's refusal. Though by no means a 'ludicrous incapable person', as Browning described him (to William Archer) many years afterwards, Willmott was one-legged and elderly; his matter-of-fact rendering of the passionate scenes caused laughter in the company.]

January 29. Browning called, told him of the reading on Saturday and the conduct of the actors. Advised him to the alteration of second act.. . .

January 31. Went to Drury Lane theatre. Found Browning waiting for me in a state of great excitement. He abused the doorkeeper and was in a very great passion. I calmly apologised for having detained him, observing that I had made a great effort to meet him at all. He had not given his *name* to the doorkeeper, who had told him he might walk into the green-room; but his dignity was mortally wounded. I fear he is a very conceited man. Went over his play with him, then looked over part of it. Read it in the room with great difficulty, being *very unwell*.

February 1. Received notes—one enclosing 5s. with a desire that I would advertise the day of my birthday in *The Times*. Read Browning's play. Rose, and read and cut it again. Serle called, and I told him of my inability to meet my work—that I *could not* play this part of Browning's unless the whole work of the theatre stopped, that I thought it best to reduce it to its proper form—three acts, and let Phelps do it on all accounts. He concurred with me. I wrote a note to Browning.

February 4. Rehearsed Browning's play, *A Blot in the 'Scutcheon*.

February 6. Mr Phelps was too ill to play tonight. I decided on under-studying his part in Browning's play.

February 7. Rehearsed Browning's play, with the idea of acting the part of Lord Tresham, if Mr Phelps should continue ill. Browning came and in better humour than I have lately seen him.

[Macready, bearing an impossible load, was acting Melnotte, King John, and Othello on successive nights; he was rehearsing Benedick and had begun to read 'Comus'.]

February 10. Began the consideration and study of the part of Tresham, which was to occupy my single thoughts till accomplished. About a quarter past one a note came from Willmott, informing me that Mr Phelps would do the part, if he 'died for it', so that my time had been lost. Arrived, I applied to business; offered to give to Browning and Mr Phelps the benefit of my consideration and study in the cuts, etc. I had made one I thought particularly valuable, not letting Tresham die, but consigning him to a convent. Browning, however, in the worst taste, manner, and spirit, declined any further alterations, expressing himself perfectly satisfied with the manner in which Mr Phelps executed Lord Tresham. I had no more to say. I could only think Mr Browning a very disagreeable and offensively mannered person. *Voilà tout!*

[The cast included Phelps as Tresham, Anderson as Mertoun, Helen Faucit as the fourteen-year-old Mildred, and Mrs Stirling as Guendolen.

Although it was received hopefully, it would have only three performances.
With meaning Browning wrote in Helen Faucit's album on 4 March:

> *Helen Faucit, you have twice*
> *Proved my Bird of Paradise!*
> *He who would my wits inveigle*
> *Into boasting him my eagle,*
> *Turns out very like a Raven;*
> *Fly off, Blacky, to your haven!*
> *But you, softest dove, must never*
> *Leave me, as he does, for ever.*

February 11. Directed the rehearsal of *A Blot in the 'Scutcheon* and many valuable improvements. Browning seemed desirous to explain or qualify the strange carriage and temper of yesterday, and laid much blame on Forster for irritating him. Saw the play of *Blot in the 'Scutcheon* which was badly acted in Phelps's and Mrs Stirling's parts—pretty well in Anderson's, very well in Helen Faucit's. I was *angry* after the play about the call being directed without me. . . .

February 22. Heard that the Covent Garden actors had accepted *half-salaries* from Mr Bunn—the wretches! They deserve the fate they have mainly contributed to bring on themselves.

February 24. Rehearsed *Much Ado About Nothing* and *Comus*. Acted Benedict [Benedick] very well. The audience went with the play and with *Comus*. They called for me after both pieces. *[According to Anderson this Benedick was as melancholy as a mourning coach in a snowstorm. But Lady Pollock ('Macready As I Knew Him') would testify that he was 'all mirth', and his smile 'the pleasantest thing in the world'.*

March 3. I entered this morning upon my *fiftieth* birthday. How very little of self-approval attends the review of my past life—how much of self reproach! . . .

March 18. Went out; met Browning, who was startled into accosting me, but seeming to remember that he did not intend to do so, started off in great haste. What but contempt, which one ought not to feel, can we galled spirits feel for these wretched insects about one. . . .

March 19. In conversation with my dearest Catherine, she gave her opinion that it would be necessary for me in the event of an unsuccessful termination to our season, to go alone to the United States. This looks cheerily, inasmuch as there is opportunity for exertion and prospect of reward, perhaps the means of recovering all I have lost, and adding to my gains. . . .

March 23. Helen Faucit called; I was not pleased with an evidence of pettishness in her. Acted Iago better, I think, than I ever have before done. Sent on Mr Anderson, but did not go on myself. . . .

March 27. Fox called in the middle of the day. He told me that he stopped the insertion of a paragraph *[in 'The Morning Chronicle']* in Mr Bunn's handwriting, speaking of himself as 'Like Cincinnatus called from the plough, Mr Bunn had been summoned to resume the reins of management' at Covent Garden. . . .

April 5. Walked home; enjoyed very much the air and exercise—the first time that I have walked home from the theatre, I believe, this season! Received note and MS from Bulwer. Read two acts of his play.

April 7. . . . I signed the bills, which are very heavy. Our season is not only irredeemable, but more loss must be incurred. . . .

April 9. Wrote a note to Bulwer, declining his play. *[Charles H. Shattuck identifies this with the incomplete 'Darnley', dealing with the theme of egotism and published posthumously in 1882. Bulwer wrote only four acts. Charles F. Coghlan, the actor and dramatist, supplied a fifth when, as 'The House of Darnley', the play—with Ellen Terry in the cast— failed in London during 1877.]*

April 10. . . . Heard of —'s letter with an account of Major —'s making love to her. Was in an ill-humour with the world and almost with her, as part of it, for her very fickleness and venal lightness. But what this world is! I hope she may be married to Major—, but what a world! What a world!

April 12. Helen Faucit called in at four o'clock, and I went over part of Lady Macbeth with her, and endeavoured to raise and dilate her mind to the conception of the full grandeur of the character, which she only sees from a distance at present, but which she shrinks into littleness before, as she comes near it. I took great pains with her. . . .

April 14. Talked with dearest Catherine over our prospects, and the only course (which involved our temporary separation) that lay before us. We now regard it more cheerfully than we used to do. . . .

April 17. . . . Acted Macbeth unequally; I was depressed at times by the extreme nervousness of Helen Faucit, who lost all management of herself. I recovered when alone.

April 18. Note from Helen Faucit—suffering from illness, but in a very unkind and impatient spirit. Talked—and despaired!

April 26. The darling children acted *Comus* in the drawing-room after dinner, interesting and amusing me very much; they recited the poetry very well indeed, and only gave me a fear lest they should imbibe a liking for the wretched art which I have been wasting my life upon. God forbid! . . .

April 29. Received the news that Covent Garden theatre was closed. Without indulging in any feeling of vindictiveness or exultation, I cannot but regard with satisfaction the termination of this wretched attempt to degrade our miserable art still further and oppress its poor dependents by the obtrusion of such a wretch and such a villain as that Bunn. If I desired vengeance, it is given to me. I only feel satisfied for the effect in a professional point of view.

May 5. . . . Spoke to Miss Fortescue, who declined to act Maria [The School for Scandal]. I do not understand this. . . . I acted Comus. Spoke to Miss Romer; to Helen Faucit, who seemed disposed to expect me to do an injustice. She little knows me, if it be so. . . . [Emma Romer, Mrs Almond, 1814–1868, singer, played Sabrina in 'Comus'.]

May 6. Went to Drury Lane theatre; attended to business; Lord Spencer called, respecting the hire of the theatre for an agricultural dinner in July 1844. He seems to me a used-up man, not very well-mannered, a farmer, and a twaddle. He disappointed me very much. These are the men to govern states—oh God! Rehearsed The School for Scandal. Met the committee and had a long conference with them. They will not be able to come to terms with me. Acted Joseph Surface very fairly.

May 8. Helen Faucit was in ill-humour about not playing Lady Macbeth, upon which I spoke to her very roundly, telling her I would not do an injustice for any one. Catherine called for me, and we went to Greenwich to dine with Stanfield. Our party consisted of the Dickenses, Quin, Jerdan, Liston, Maclise, E. Landseer, Grant, Allan and niece, Forster, who was stentorian, Ainsworth, etc. Cheerful day.

May 18. Rose at five o'clock, weary, sick, and uncomfortable; applied briskly to this unpleasant task of learning the words of Athelwold [in W. Smith's tragedy] which I soon mastered. Looked at the paper. Went to Drury Lane theatre. Rehearsed the play. Rested, being very, very tired. Acted, or rather scrambled through, Athelwold; was called for. After the play spoke with W. Smith, the author, who came in. I have acted against my own judgment in taking this part, but I did it for the author's interest, and to serve Helen Faucit. It has been a heavy task.

['Athelwold' was a Saxon tragedy. It was acted twice only with a cast headed by Macready, Helen Faucit, and Phelps. This was the second complete failure with a new play in a very short time. Sheridan Knowles's 'The Secretary', 24 April, had had three performances.]

May 19. I felt all the painful languor of overwork. Looked at the paper and saw, what I had before felt, that I had really made a sacrifice to the author and the play of *Athelwold* in taking the part upon myself.

May 28. Called on Sir William Curtis *[of the Drury Lane Committee]*; spoke to him on the subject of my continuance, told him I would not pay any more money, that I did not seek to leave the theatre, but was quite ready to go—demonstrating to the public that I did not *desert* the duty I had undertaken. He was very cordial, very courteous, very kind, engaged to call a committee, and left it to me to arrange with the actors the reduction of their salaries. . . .

May 29. Spoke to Mrs Nisbett on the subject of next season. She subscribed to the risk of one-third of her salary. Spoke to Keeley upon the reduction of one-third of salary next season; he agreed to it most heartily; to Hudson *[James Hudson (1811–1868)]*—the same; to Mrs Stirling—the same. Acted King Henry IV. The house was very good, for which I am most thankful.

May 30. Spoke to Mrs Warner on the subject of her salary reduced one-third next season. She demurred—the only one who has not cheerfully accepted it. . . . Acted Leontes tamely. Spoke to Anderson and Phelps about the reduction of salaries—both agreed; Anderson, *if* not going to the United States.

On 2 June Macready knew that he and the Drury Lane Committee would never agree. He was not an amenable bargainer. Within a few days a playbill informed the public that Mr Macready would relinquish the direction of Drury Lane on Monday 12 June, 'his last appearance in a London theatre for a very considerable period'. The Queen annoyed him by commanding for 12 June, instead of Much Ado About Nothing *as he had wished, a bill of* As You Like It *and the farce of* The Thumping Legacy *by John Maddison Morton (Keeley as Jerry Ominous. 'The selection does me no good.') Ultimately his farewell night at the Lane was transferred to 14 June.*

June 12. *[Command performance]*. . . . Acted Jaques very well. Was called for and the Queen sent to order me to go on, but I was undressed. Lord G.— *[the Earl of Glengall, of the Drury Lane Committee]* was as officious as if he had been stage manager at £2 per week. . . . When the Queen came from her box, she stopped Lord Delawarr and asked for me. She said she was much pleased, and thanked me. Prince Albert asked me if this was not the original play. I told him: 'Yes, that we had restored the original text.' After lighting them out, I went into the scene-room, which was filled with people, all delighted with their evening.

June 14. *[Farewell]* . . . Very low in spirits, could scarcely repress the tears that rose to my eyes when Miss Horton spoke to me. Rehearsed the two or three short scenes of *Macbeth*. Gave directions to Sloman, etc., to put the scenes and properties in good order to be rendered up to the proprietors. . . . Rested and thought over my character and my address. Was in the lowest state of depression—was actually ill from my state of mind. Spoke to Mr Willmott upon what was needful to be done. On appearing in Macbeth, the whole house rose with such continued shouting and waving of hats and handkerchiefs that I was quite over-come. I was never so affected by the expression of sympathy by an audience. When wearied with shouting, they changed the applause to a stamping of feet, which sounded like thunder; it was grand and awful! I never saw such a scene! I was resolved to act my best, and I think I never played Macbeth so well. I dressed as quickly as I could, and went forward to receive another reception from that densely crowded house, that seemed to emulate the first. It was unlike anything that ever occured before. I spoke my speech, and retired with the same mad acclaim. Dickens, H. Smith, Forster and Stanfield, Serle, came into my room. They did not seem struck with the speech.

June 16. . . . I passed round the scene-rooms and saw all put away in the best order. I could have wept to think of all those efforts and expendi-ture come to nothing! I desired Jones to give up the theatre to Dunn. I could not bear to look at it again. Came home dejected to the last degree. *[That season he had appeared at Drury Lane 133 times.]*

On 19 June at Willis's Rooms, the Duke of Cambridge[1] presented a testi-monial from Macready's admirers, a massive and complicated design in which, at the base of a pedestal upon which Shakespeare stood, Macready sat in silver, 'habited in the costume of the early stage', and with a volume in his hand that symbolised his restoration of the early text of Shakespeare. About him were the Muses. The inscription which oddly omitted Drury Lane offered the testimonial to William Charles Macready 'in commemoration of his management of the Theatre Royal, Covent Garden, in the seasons of 1837–1838 and 1838–1839. . .' The Duke 'spoke better than I have ever heard him'. Macready, in reply, said he had 'aimed at elevating everything represented on the stage'. His journal entry ended:

The Duke took his leave, and I, after a few words with Bulwer, whom I saw, left the room, sought my carriage, disgusted with myself and sick

[1] Adolphus Frederick, first Duke of Cambridge (1774–1850), seventh son of George III.

of all—except the love which I felt many of the assembled multitude to bear me, and yet to what good? . . .

July 1. Read the number of Chuzzlewit's landing in America, *which I do not like*. It will not do Dickens good, and I grieve over it.

July 17. Still very unwell, and kept in bed late from the state of my head. Mr Phelps called, and I saw him; he came to speak about the debt due from him; in the course of conversation I asked if he would like to go to America—as it occurred to me. He said 'of all things'. We talked on and I promised to consult the agent (Maywood) on the matter. I stated that I could guarantee nothing, but if the chance of £30 per week and his expenses to and fro offered as likely, would he be satisfied? He said he would. . . .

July 23. . . . Messrs Phelps and Maywood came to dinner, and we talked over the subject of his accompanying us to the United States. I would not urge him, nor press him for an answer; he would take some days to consider of it.

Phelps had already decided not to accept. As they left the house, Maywood said to him, 'Don't you see that his absence will be your opportunity? If you remain at home, you'll step into his shoes,' Phelps, impressed, wrote to Macready: 'Some years ago, when I thought of returning to the country, you said to me: "He who remains in the field may change defeat into victory at any moment." ' Dramatic; but Macready had merely wanted Phelps to travel because he liked him. Soon another actor accepted.

August 3. Mr Ryder called, and I proposed to him to accompany me to the States. Heard that Mr Bunn was the lessee of Drury Lane. This is, on the part of the committee, shameful—to the art, actors, and the public. . . .

August 5. Mr Ryder called to say that he would be happy to accompany me to the United States.

August 22. A Mr Tenniel[1] called to see me. Dined with Mrs Norton; met Lady Conyngham, Lord Melbourne, Sidney Herbert, Köhl, and the Sheridans. Rogers came in in the evening.

['The dinner-party is noteworthy as including three persons who were proto-types of prominent characters in George Meredith's novel 'Diana of the Crossways', namely Mrs Norton, Lord Melbourne, the former Prime Minister, 1779–1848, and Sidney Herbert, statesman, later Lord Herbert of Lea, 1810–1861.' (Note by William Toynbee, 1912).]

[1] Sir John Tenniel (1820–1914), artist. Later illustrated *Alice in Wonderland* and was for more than fifty years on the staff of *Punch*.

August 26. Went to Richmond, to the *Star and Garter*, where I was received by the party expecting me, Dickens, Maclise, Braham, E. Landseer, Fox, Dillon, F. Stone,[1] Stanfield, Forster, George Raymond, Quin, H. Smith, Carew, an amateur singer. A very elegant dinner, and enjoyed by a company in the most perfect harmony of feeling and spirits. Dickens proposed the only toast of the evening, my health, etc., in a very feeling and eloquent speech. I had not had time before to ponder the circumstances of my departure, and I quite broke down under it. I could not speak for tears, or very insufficiently. Afterwards a most joyous evening, and the warmest emotions of regard and regret pervaded the party.

September 1. Forster told me at dinner that he had written a very strong letter to Dickens, endeavouring to dissuade him from accompanying me on board the steamship. I thought for Dickens' sake he was quite right, but did not feel the full amount of mischief to myself.

September 2. Received a present from Forster of shirt-studs, very handsome, which I had rather he had not given. . . . Read the number of *Chuzzlewit*, the most powerful of the book which Dickens is now employed upon, but as bitter as it is powerful, and against whom is this directed? 'Against the Americans' is the answer. Against how many of them? How many answer to his description? I am grieved to read the book. Received a letter from him telling me that he had received a strong expostulary letter from Captain Marryat[2] on the subject of his accompanying me, and that, on my account, he would therefore deny himself the indulgence of shaking hands with me on board ship. His letter was generous, affectionate, and most friendly. But why did he say *Marryat* had written, when it was *Forster?*

---

[1] Frank Stone (1800–1859), painter.
[2] Captain Frederick Marryat (1792–1848), novelist; during 1837–8 he travelled in Canada and the United States.

IV
Home and Abroad
(1843–1851)

Farewell, Macready, since to-night we part;
   Full-handed thunders often have confessed
   Thy power, well used to move the public breast.
We thank thee with our voice, and from the heart.
Farewell, Macready, since this night we part;
   Go, take thine honours home; rank with the best,
   Garrick and statelier Kemble, and the rest
Who made a nation purer through their Art.

Thine is it that our drama did not die,
   Nor flicker down to brainless pantomime,
   And those gilt gauds men-children swarm to see.
Farewell, Macready; moral, grave, sublime;
Our Shakespeare's bland and universal eye
   Dwells pleased, through twice a hundred years, on thee.

Sonnet by Alfred Tennyson, the Poet Laureate, read by John Forster at the farewell dinner to William Charles Macready in London on 1 March 1851.

1843

To Liverpool, September 4. Rose at a very early hour; prepared for my departure; kissed my beloved children. Very nearly losing our train through the negligence of the cabman, arrived, and started at the moment from the railway station. A sleepy, dull journey. Reached Birmingham; amused with the passengers there. Landed and set off in the Liverpool train. Very much wearied and distressed with fatigue. Forster and Thompson[1] were at the railway waiting for us. Went to Adelphi, from thence to the river, where we took boat to near the *Caledonia*, a very comfortable ship, in which I saw my luggage land. . . . Forster dined with us, and we passed a cheerful evening.

September 5. Took leave, after some fond and sad talk, cheerfully and well, of my dearest wife and sister. Went with Forster to the quay. We reached the ship and came on board. What a scene! Bade dear Forster farewell; he was greatly affected. I looked at my fellow-passengers— eighty. Thought of my wife; watched the gorgeous sunset and the soft moon. Took tea; watched Liverpool, or where it was, till the lights could no more be seen.

After a reasonably calm voyage Macready landed at Boston on 20 September, and on the following day was in New York and ready to begin work.

New York, September 21. . . . Saw Mr Ryder and D. Colden, to whom I submitted my letters of introduction. Went to rehearsal, with which I took much pains and, of course, found a material very different from what I had lately been accustomed to; found that I had done right in bringing Mr Ryder. Forrest came up to me as I was standing over a New York paper in the reading-room of the hotel. I was very glad to see him, and he came up to my room and sat with me some time, civil.

[It was more than six years since Edwin Forrest's visit to England. There on 23 June, 1837, he had married Catherine Sinclair at St Paul's, Covent Garden. Since returning to America he had consolidated his fame: his parts, Shakespeare aside, had included two of Macready's, Richelieu and Melnotte.]

---

[1] Thomas James Thompson (1812–1881), traveller and collector; friend of Dickens. Alice Meynell was his daughter by his second marriage.

September 22. . . . Forrest came up to my room and sat with me some time, inviting me to dine on Thursday week. . . . Mr Longfellow called. *[Henry Wadsworth Longfellow (1807–1882), poet. In his journal for 6 October 1842 Macready had noted that, on an 'As You Like It' night at Drury Lane, 'Dickens, Maclise, Forster, and Mr Longfellow, a professor at one of the U.S. universities, came into my room.']*

September 24. Met Mr Penn, or Pell, and Mr Griffiths. A cheerful day. It was Mr Penn who observed of Dickens that he must have been ungrateful and therefore a bad man. I defended and explained as I best could his morbid feeling about the States. . . . Went to Mr Sedgwick's. Saw Mrs *Butler*, whom I dared not ask after her husband. An agreeable evening.

September 25. Went to the [Park] theatre, and acted Macbeth. What shall I say? With every disposition to throw myself into the character as I had never so completely done before, I was, as it were, beaten back by the heat, and I should certainly have sunk under it, if I had not goaded myself repeatedly to work out my thoughts and vindicate my reputation. The audience did not applaud very much; but really it would have been too much to expect successive rounds of applause under such an atmosphere. My reception was most enthusiastic and very loudly cheered and with repeated cheers. The audience seemed held by the performance, though Lady Macbeth was a *ridiculous* drag-chain upon my proceedings. I am glad I have brought Mr Ryder. . . .

[For a long time, under Stephen Price, who had managed it for more than thirty years, the Park was America's major theatre. When Price died in 1840 its fortunes were declining, and Edmund Shaw Simpson (1784–1848), its manager when Macready came, was finding the struggle hard.]

September 26. Called on Pierce Butler and sat some time with Mrs Pierce B—. Pierce Butler came in as I was going away. Rehearsed Hamlet. Could not collect an exact opinion on the effect of last night's performance; did not choose to look at the newspaper.

September 29. Acted Cardinal Richelieu but indifferently. I was not in the vein, and though I tried and tried I was not up to the high mark.

September 30. . . . Forrest called and took me out to see the reservoir of the aqueduct; afterwards to see Mrs Forrest. Dined with Pierce Butler, Bryant,[1] Mr and Mrs Longfellow. Mrs Butler's conversation was such that, had I been her husband—I should observe that Mrs Butler spoke admirably well, but quite like a man. She is a woman of a most extraordinary mind; what she said on most subjects was true—the

[1] William Cullen Bryant (1794–1878), poet and editor.

stern truth, but what in the true spirit of charity should not have been said in the presence of one who was obliged to listen to it. Alas!

October 3. Dined with Forrest; met a very large party, too large for comfort, but it was most kindly intended. . . . I like all I see of Forrest very much. He appears a clear-headed, honest, kind man; what can be better?

October 5. Forrest called on me, and agreeably to his wish, I underwent of the operation of being *daguerreotyped*. Eheu! for the operation and heu! heu! for the product (I thought to myself and could I be so ugly!) I was very much amused.

October 18. Acted the part of Othello with every possible drawback; the actors were all *slow-coaches* (*incompetent*) around me. I fought against it and succeeded in interesting the audience, but my effort here not to lose ground must be great indeed.

October 19. Spoke to Mr Ryder about his tameness and inaccuracy; he is well-meaning but weak, and not made of the stuff to run far ahead of his fellows. Acted Werner unsatisfactorily to myself; I *cannot afford* to expend my spirits and alacrity by recreation or exercise on the days of performance. . . .

Philadelphia, October 21. Went to the National theatre, where I saw Forrest act King Lear. I had a very high opinion of his powers of mind when I saw him exactly seventeen years ago; I said then, if he would cultivate those powers and really study, where, as in England, his taste could be formed, he would make one of the very first actors of this or any day. But I thought he would not do so, as his countrymen were, by their extravagant applause, possessing him with the idea and with the fact, as far as remuneration was concerned, that it was unnecessary. I reluctantly, as far as my feelings towards him are interested, record my opinion that my prophetic soul foresaw the consequence. He has great physical power. But I could discern no imagination, no original thought, no poetry at all in his acting. Occasionally in rage he is very strong and powerful, but grandeur in his passion there was *none*; pathos, *none*. The quiet portion—and much, too much, was quiet—was heavy and frequently inaudible; irascibility of *temperament* did not appear; there was no *character* laid out. The audience were very liberal, very vehement in their applause—but it was such an audience!—applauding all the disgusting trash of Tate as if it had been Shakespeare, with might and main. But an actor to speak the words of Tate—with Shakespeare's before him—I think criticises his own performance; and of Forrest's representation I should like to say that it was like the part—false taste. In fact, I did not think it the performance of an artist. In the storm. . . . he walked on in perfect quietude; there was throughout nothing on his mind, fastened *on* and tearing and convulsing it with agony, and certainly his frenzy 'was not like madness'. His recognition of Cordelia the same. *He did not fully comprehend his poet. . . . [Later]* There was much to praise in Forrest's execution frequently; he seems to have his person in perfect command, but he has not enriched, refined, elevated and enlarged his *mind;* it is very much where it was, in the matter of poetry and art, when I last saw him. . . . He had all the qualifications, all the material out of which to build up a great artist, an actor for all the world. He is now only an actor for the less intelligent of the Americans. But he is something better—an upright and well-intentioned man.

Macready was now acting at the Chestnut Street Theatre in Philadelphia, built on the model of the Theatre Royal, Bath, and holding 2,000 people.

October 23. Acted Macbeth equal, if not superior, as a whole, to any performance I have ever given of the character. I should say it was a noble piece of art. . . . The Miss Charlotte Cushman who acted Lady Macbeth interested me very much. She has to learn her art, but she showed mind and sympathy with me; a novelty so refreshing to me on the stage. . . .

[Charlotte Saunders Cushman (1816–1876) was a celebrated actress. Trained as a singer, she worked her way into leading dramatic parts and had made a conspicuous success of Meg Merrilies in one of the versions of 'Guy Mannering'. Association with Macready improved her work a great deal, but she also borrowed his mannerisms. She had, too, a strange facial resemblance, a similar 'depression of nose', protruding chin, broad, prominent brow. When she came to London Gilbert à Beckett would put her into verse:

> *What figure is this which appears on the scene?*
> *'Tis Madame Macready—Miss Cushman, I mean,*
> *What a wondrous resemblance! The walk on the toes,*
> *The eloquent, short, intellectual nose;*
> *The bend of the knees, the slight sneer of the lip.*
> *The frown on the forehead, the hand on the hip.*
> *In the chin, in the voice, 'tis the same to a tittle,*
> *Miss Cushman is Mister Macready in little. . . .*
> *No fault with the striking resemblance we find,*
> *'Tis not in the person alone, but the mind.]*

October 28. Saw some papers; one, signed Barlow, affecting to make a comparative criticism on Mr Forrest and myself in Macbeth; it was too

Macready as Iago, engraved from a painting by H. Tracey.

Macready as Lear, with Helen Faucit as Cordelia.

Macready as Macbeth, engraved from a painting by H. Tracey.

Macready as Werner, engraved from a painting by H. Tracey.

Thomas Noon Talfourd.

Charles Dickens, aged 27, from a painting by Daniel Maclise, R.A.

James Sheridan Knowles, from an engraving of a drawing by T. Wageman.

Sir Edward Bulwer-Lytton, Bart.

bad, as the ignorant creature showed in what he was obliged to state that Mr Forrest did not understand the character; nor does Mr Forrest understand Shakespeare. *He is not an artist.* Let him be an American actor—and a great American actor—but keep on this side of the Atlantic and no one will gainsay his comparative excellence. . . .

Forrest had begun to assert his rivalry by acting the same parts—Macbeth and Richelieu, for example—in direct opposition to Macready.

October 31. . . . I quite abandon all idea of settling in this country. The press is made up, with a few exceptions, of such unredeemed scoundrels, and the law is so inoperative that 'the spurns which patient merit from the unworthy takes' in England are preferable to the state of semi-civilisation here. . . .

November 6. Called on and met Pierce Butler, who went with me upstairs and left me with Mrs Butler and Miss Sedgwick. We talked a little while very pleasantly, but upon my observing that she [Mrs Butler] did not do justice to the talents committed to her—that she might do much beside writing powerful plays, that she might in a country like this influence society, etc.—she burst into tears, our conversation became more restrained, and I took leave of her, she appearing anxious to see me again, as, I believe, really regarding me . . .

November 9. . . . [Mr Ryder told me that] one [verbal] critic in the earnestness of his advocacy of Mr Forrest said to another, who was extolling me for my intellectual qualifications: 'Oh! damn intellect!' Mr Forrest's engagement at New York has failed; as it was got up in *opposition* to me and so *carried through*, I cannot affect regret at it.

From 10 to 29 November Macready was in Boston, appreciating the social life, loathing the other actors, and seeing something of Charlotte Cushman whom he had hoped would appear with him, but whom the manager refused to engage.

Boston, November 10. Ryder called in the morning and gave me an account of Mr Pelby [the manager] which seems to promise anything but an agreeable—indeed a profitable engagement. He is a vulgar man of very indifferent character. He has advertised his daughter for Lady Macbeth—she is reported to be drunken, and Mr Wallack says does not understand one word of what she says! I must *do my best*, but this is a dreadful drawback. . . .

November 12. . . . Note from Miss Cushman, announcing her arrival and wishing to see me. I am in a strange country, and I think it is only a duty to myself to be strictly circumspect. I have not the slightest purpose, dream, or intent of wrong or folly, and therefore I keep it at arms' length. Wrote to her, promising to see her tomorrow, which I will do in the common room.

November 13. Looked over Macbeth, being most anxious about my performance. Went to the theatre and rehearsed it; had sad misgivings as to the effect of Lady Macbeth, who does not understand the words she has to speak, and speaks words that no one can understand. . . .

November 14. . . . Dined with Longfellow; everything very elegant. Mrs L— is a very agreeable woman. . . .

November 15. Was nearly four hours and a half rehearsing Hamlet, so distressed and crippled am I by the conceit and inefficiency of the players of this company. . . .

November 16. Waldo Emerson called, and sat with me a short time. . . . I liked him very, very much—the simplicity and kindness of his manner charmed me. . . . *[Ralph Waldo Emerson (1803–1881), poet and essayist.]*

November 18. Called on Miss Cushman and chatted with her some time. She told me of a conversation she had heard between two watch-makers—one of whom had seen Mr Forrest and myself, the other had not seen me—to convey his idea of the two men, the one observed, 'Why, you see Forrest is a watch upon a common lever and Macready's a chronometer'. . . .

November 22. Acted Hamlet with resolution against weariness and weakness, and for the most part very effectively. The Daggers about me are *dire!* One said to the Ghost, '*If thou art privy to thy country's peace, which happily foreknowing may avoid, speak!*' *['Daggers' refers to barn-storming actors. From Colman the younger's 'Sylvester Daggerwood' (1796), in which the title part is an actor from 'the Dunstable company' seeking to arrange for his London début.]*

November 27. . . . Supped on broiled oysters, with some of the ingenious and beautifully composed—I should say *constructed*—drinks that are conspicuous in this country. . . .

Macready returned to New York on 30 November. On 4 December he had a glum rehearsal of The Bridal, *Miss Cushman—who had had her part a month before—knowing nothing of what she had to do.*

December 5. Talked with Miss Cushman about her want of energy and purpose in studying her art. She made the *usual* excuses. She told me that Mrs Butler was literally wretched, that Butler's feeling to her was absolute aversion; I do not know her authority for saying so much—that Mrs Butler had written to her that the only consoling reflection on her birthday was, that another year of wretchedness being gone, she was so much nearer its termination. Miss Cushman said that but for her children she [Mrs Butler] would go on the stage again. *That would not do.*

December 6. Acted Melantius unequally—some parts good, in others felt a want of strength, in others was cut up by the people (particularly by the person acting Archas, the jailer; this man was conspicuously absurd and deficient) with me—Miss Cushman particularly.

December 8. Went to the rehearsal of Benedict [Benedick]; was much dissatisfied with several. Saw enough of the unsteadiness of Miss Cushman to perceive that the *first* qualification of an artist is not there. . . .

December 9. Looked at some American Saturday papers, which state that Miss Cushman more than shared the applause of the audience with me in *The Bridal.* If it was so, I never heard one hand of it. She is an *intriguante,* I fear, a very double person. . . . An American dinner: ter[r]apin soup, bass-fish, bear, wild turkey, canvas-back duck, roasted oysters, etc. Delicious wines. . . .

For a few nights before Christmas he acted in Boston, and from Christmas Day to the end of the year in Baltimore.

Baltimore, December 27. . . . Letter from Miss Cushman—oh! I do not like thee, Dr Fell!

December 28. Acted Hamlet. Cut up from the beginning to the end—striving, struggling vainly against the *wretches* that were sent on with me. I never remember anything worse. Polonius in a bag-wig of King Charles—not speaking three lines of the text consecutively—Horatio speaking *my* speeches! and acting, as if on purpose, to annoy me; Rosencrantz and Guildenstern cutting out and making nonsense of the dialogue. Altogether disgraceful.

[While Macready was in America the Theatre Regulation Act of 1843 changed the face of the London stage. Drury Lane and Covent Garden, under their cherished letters patent, had in theory an all-the-year-round monopoly of 'legitimate' drama. Though 'minor' theatres towards the end were going forward boldly, without complex evasions, they were always in peril of the common informer and the Lord Chamberlain. Now all this was over; the classical drama could be acted anywhere. Macready, before going to America, had presented a petition to the House of Commons, declaring

that the patentees were unworthy of their exclusive rights. By then the Government had made up its mind. Planché noted the new freedom in a Haymarket entertainment, 'The Drama at Home' (1844). The Drama, about to emigrate, was stopped by Portia in her 'Doctor of Laws' gown:

> *I say you're free to act where'er you please,*
> *No longer pinioned by the patentees.*
> *Need our immortal Shakespeare mute remain*
> *Fixed on the portico of Drury Lane;*
> *Or the nine Muses mourn the Drama's fall*
> *Without relief on Covent Garden's wall?*
> *Sheridan now at Islington may shine,*
> *Marylebone echo Marlowe's mighty line;*
> *Otway may raise the waters Lambeth yields,*
> *And Farquhar sparkle in St George's Fields;*
> *Wycherley flutter a Whitechapel pit,*
> *And Congreve wake all 'Westminster to wit.'*

1844

Between 1 and 19 January Macready was at Charleston; later, after a few days in Savannah, he and Ryder travelled by coach, rail, and river-boat to New Orleans which they reached on 3 February.

Charleston, January 3. . . . Was delighted with the warm sunshiny day, the fresh air, the foliage of the wild orange, the palmetto, the roses in bloom, the violets, the geraniums, etc., but was pained to see the coloured people go out of the way and show a deference to us as to superior beings. . . .

January 8. Acted Hamlet, I scarcely know how. I strove and fought up against what I thought the immobility of the audience; I would not be beaten cravenly, but such a performance is never satisfactory—at least to the actor. . . . I died game.

January 13. Ogilby called, and confidentially related circumstances of great atrocity occurring in this State. An overseer, against his master's orders, flogging a runaway negro, tying him up all night, getting up in the night to repeat the torture, and repeating it till the wretched creature died under the lash. The felon was acquitted. A person supposed by another to trench upon ground which he claimed, was, in the midst of his own labourers, shot dead by the villain in open day; the felon was acquitted. . . .

January 14. Ryder informed me that Mr N. P. Willis, in his Washington letter, stated that 'Mr Macready was continuing southward, his attraction diminishing as he proceeded'. What a miserable reptile must this be ! . . . *[Nathaniel Parker Willis (1806–1867), an American journalist.]*

January 19. . . . Could not please myself in the performance of Hamlet, with all the pains I could take. Ryder, as the Ghost, got upon the trap and could just get out the words 'pale his ineffectual fire'. When he had finished, the trap ran down and he disappeared, to his own consternation as much as mine. . . .

On the first stage of the journey to New Orleans, through Georgia, the train held to a rate of about four miles an hour; at one stop all got out and pushed the car and engine. During the afternoon (27 January) it became so cold that

Macready and Ryder walked for about three miles. In order to keep the engine fire alight the railmen had to chop wood by the roadside. That night, at Griffin, Macready slept in a frigid room with single-boarded walls, an open-beamed roof, broken jug, somebody's trunk, and a door without lock. Next there was a three-day journey, in a two horse wagon (that tossed them about like bags of cotton) to Checaw in the state of Alabama. In heavy rain between Caseta and Checaw (30 January) the wagon overturned: no one was hurt. 'When thrown over, all were in confusion and alarm, struggling to get out. I called to them to be still and quietly take their turns.'

Rising long before daylight to entrain from Checaw to Montgomery, Macready and Ryder observed their landlord's wife, a girl of fourteen who had run away with him. The rail track lay along, and through, a high bluff that overlooked the Tallapoosa River, and they had for companions 'a seven-foot colonel' in a blanket coat, a major in a ragged one, and a judge in one of frieze. Again the train stopped for enforced forestry. 'Come, Judge,' *said someone,* 'take a spell of chopping!', *and he responded with goodwill. From Montgomery (31 January) Macready and Ryder sailed down river in the* Charlotte *('Bulwer's novel of* 'The Last of the Barons' *divided, and only divided, my attention with this wild and grand and beautiful scenery of the Alabama'). At Mobile (2 February) they changed boats and reached New Orleans in the early morning.*

New Orleans, February 3. Rose from my hard and ache-giving berth about half-past four o'clock; dressed and sauntered up and down the wooden pier thinking of home and the great distance I was from it, and all it contains. Passed into the sort of village, half French, half English, in its shops' inscriptions and was interested and struck by the resemblance it conveyed, in the architecture of its small houses and gateway or arch, to an old French village or small town. . . . Went to rehearsal at eleven; did not like either theatre or actors. Rehearsed *Hamlet*.

Macready was acting in New Orleans until 1 March; in Mobile from 4 to 15 March; and in New Orleans again until the end of the month.

New Orleans, February 11. A Mr Cronin called—a professor, I believe of elocution—to tell me that in my scenes of passion he could not hear a single word, and that he had a very fine organ, requesting me to attend more to the improvement of *the vocality;* I do not know his object in coming; it was either silly, for some knavish purpose, or impertinent; matters little which.

February 18. . . . After dinner rode along the Levee, saw the shipping and warehouses of this wonderful place; the waterworks, with their muddy contents; the steamboats coming in; the Mississippi winding round, and the buildings, wealth, and bustle of the place. The people seem so happy! . . .

February 29. . . . Rehearsed Iago. Saw Forrest, who came on the stage. Acted Iago well.

March 1. . . . The night has been rainy, and the morning is wet, but it is warm moisture, thick and steamy. My system is quite relaxed and oppressed; a sensation of general debility is most distressingly upon me. My clothes feel damp upon me and clinging as I change each posture. I am quite unequal to my work. Looked at the papers—the daily trash that is offered up. Pah! Rehearsed *King Lear*, with a perfect conscious-ness of my utter inability to do justice to my own conception of the character. I am weary of this atmosphere and this place. Dined early. Rested, and thought over my great part of King Lear, feeling that I could not satisfy myself in it, but wishing to do my utmost. A note from some *curiosa*—wishing to see me, but whom I could not answer—signing herself *Augusta*. Went to the theatre, very weak. The house not what it ought to have been, certainly not. I rallied against my lassitude, and made a very fair fight for poor Lear; parts of it I acted very fairly, and I think made a strong impression on the audience. Some parts I did really well. Was called for; an apology was made by Smith for my change of dress, which the audience were not very patient under, and in a very short time I appeared before them and addressed them. *[Sol Smith, comedian, and one of the managers of the St Charles Theatre.]*

Mobile, March 4. Acted Hamlet. I thought I never acted the first scene with the Ghost so well; the audience this night was very numerous. Persons going away in some of the steamboats had prevailed on the masters to delay their start till midnight in order to visit the theatre. Many *rowdy* people were there, women of the town—in short, it was an audience attracted by sheer curiosity. Perhaps I was not up to my mark, though I strove very resolutely.

March 12. Dickens's misjudgment is as clear to me as is the noonday sun, and much is to be said in explanation and excuse, but Dickens is a man who fills such a place in the world's opinion, the people cannot think that he ought to need an excuse—alas! the greatest man is but a man!

March 16. Started with a fresh breeze against us for New Orleans; liked everything in Mobile except the hotel and theatre; glad to go forward as beginning my return to dear, dear home. . . .

*March 27. *[He was entertained to a dinner, with the Mayor presiding]*. In shaking hands with about fifty people, agitated too with the uncertainty of my own self-possession when called upon to speak, I could not retain the many names that were given to me. Mr Mure I knew,— Mr Bullitt I talked with; and a very great bore of a Senator—one whose Senatorial importance was as great an enjoyment to himself, and as great an affliction upon others, as Otway's old Antonio *[Venice Preserv'd]*. Garcia, President of the Senate, was an interesting looking person, but Soulè, the leading French advocate, is one of the handsomest, most picturesque, most intellectual heads I have ever seen. . . . The dinner was as handsome as it well could be: turtle &c, &c. When the business of appetite was ended—during which my thoughts were endeavouring to keep unbroken in my mind the chain of thoughts connecting my speech—I drank wine with a great many. The American custom is peculiar. Each has his bottle, or bottles, of wine which he sends to whomever he wishes should pledge him, and out of his bottle the friend he compliments acknowledges his courtesy. This continues, not only during dinner, but to the very end of the evening: an ill-considered custom, subjecting a guest to such a dangerous and infinite variety of wines. [Several toasts were drunk; Macready replied to that of his health; and, after great cheering, he observed to himself: 'Many seemed surprised that I should have been able to speak at all'.] My health was given *at least* twenty times. . . . The bore of a Senator forgot himself and addressed his convives as *'Gentlemen of the Jury'*, which of course made a great roar, in which the Negroes joined most heartily. It was compliment on compliment . . . Mr Mure, British Consul, spoke vulgarly and ignorantly . . . I grew weary, rose to say good-night . . . and shaking hands with all in my reach, as I passed, I went up to my room. Burnley and Paton came in and kept me up an hour discussing *stump* politics.—I dropped asleep, my pen in my hand and cravat off, alas!

Macready sailed up the Mississippi to St Louis. After acting there and at Cincinnati, he reached New York on 7 May.

St Louis, April 15. Acted Iago, taking much pains with the part. The audience did not *notice* me on my appearance; to Mr Ryder,

* Entries prefaced by an asterisk, between 27 March and 16 August, have not been published before, and are transcribed from the original diary leaves in the Raymond Mander and Joe Mitchenson Theatre Collection, London, by permission of Messrs Mander and Mitchenson.

Messrs Field and Farren they gave long and loud plaudits in receiving them! Throughout the play, too, they really bestowed as much, if not *more*, applause upon the unmeaning rant and gabble of these people than they gave to me; and really I *tried* to act Iago in my old earnest, 'honest' way, but the difference is not of importance to them. In my last scene, which I was acting in a very true manner, as I was taking my departure from the room, the *continued* vulgar speeches, ejaculations, and laughs of some ruffians in the second tier quite overcame my patience. I threw up the attempt and walked right off.

Cincinnati, April 29. Acted Iago as well as I could, being so ill; very much *disgusted* with the house, which was very bad, I am sick of American audiences; they are not fit to have the language in which Shakespeare wrote.

April 30. I was very unwell, have suffered much. Acted Virginius very feebly to a very poor house; suffering from debility. . . . My southern and western tour is ended; thank God for all it has given me. I feel, however, overwrought.

*New York, May 8. Saw Mr Pelby [the Boston manager] in the course of the morning, who spoke to me of Boston as if we had parted on the most satisfactory terms. . . . Saw the impressions sent me by Holloway of Postlethwaite's engraving from Thorburn's miniature,[1] which I think is very clever. Could not avoid noticing the brilliancy of the scene which the Park presents at night—the lights of the Theatre, museum, shops, restaurants, etc., make quite an illumination below, and the glory of the heavens above is grand in its expanse and radiance far beyond our more northern skies. I remember well the strong effect of a similar impression made on me at Venice in the Piazza di San Marco—but there was music and association to add to the crowd of thoughts and feelings that excited me, and there was youth and its animal spirits, which were almost in themselves intoxicating.

His New York engagement continued until early June. After this there was much strenuous work (with a good deal of travelling) until the middle of October when he sailed for home from Boston. He camped in the Adirondacks with David Colden; he heard the violinist Ole Bull at Rochester; he acted for a few nights at Buffalo (on his wedding anniversary, 24 June, he 'drank a bottle of champagne to my dear wife' and played Hamlet 'to a bad house—oh, Buffalo!') he visited Niagara; he crossed into Canada for a season at Montreal; toured in New England; played at Philadelphia in the

[1] Robert Thorburn (1818-1885), fashionable miniaturist.

first part of September, at New York during the second half, and finally at Boston until he sailed.

May 27. We are the chief attraction, I may say the only one, in New York at present. Reproved the Birnam Wood messenger very sharply; he deserved it. Spoke to Miss —, who, it seems, laughed in the banquet scene; my object in speaking to her, desiring her to call here, was to prevent the recurrence of such inconveniences as I had encountered; but she promised *to behave* for the future.

May 30. Acted Hamlet; the latter part, i.e. after the first act, in a really splendid style. I felt myself the man. . . . Hamlet has brought me more money than any play in America.

*June 12 *[in the Adirondacks].* . . . The business of erecting our camp occupied us until the night began to close in. On two fir stems laid on two uprights we placed six poles of young fir trees over which, for a thatch, we laid four layers of spruce bark which was dexterously peeled off by our adroit pack-man Johnson, and the sides were diligently closed up with boughs and leaves of birch and dwarf maple. Our fire against the rock was in front of the camp, and our bed within was made with branches of spruce and overlaid with the balsam pine which was soft. . . . and very sweet to the smell. We drank our tea, with bacon and trout, took our cigars, and wrapped in our large blankets, lay with our feet against the glorious fire, listening to the hunting stories of John Cheney and his hair-breadth 'scapes in encountering panthers, bears, and wolves and chasing deer, until twelve, when an uneasy listening among two or three, with 'Hush! did you hear that?—there!—there!—Something behind the camp' etc., made me prick up my ears. I could hear nothing, but all the rest were confident of the sound of a heavy, stealthy step among the bushes behind us. Cheney got the pistol and timber axe, and got up. Colden and myself lay still. I had the bowie-knife, which I felt was a defence. They were on the watch and heard the tramp down towards the stream. I rose for a few minutes, but neither heard nor saw anything except the palpitations of a comrade near me. I went back to my blanket after a time. Cheney increased the fire and lay down again, returning to his stories until we all dropped asleep. Colden most kindly insisted on my leaving a place which exposed me to a draught of air from the corner of the rock, and I fear took cold from his care of me. The stars were bright when I looked out above, for the thickness of the wood gave me no horizon. I . . . thought of my home, and dropped asleep.

* June 21 *[at Rochester]* . . . I sought and after many inquiries found the miserable, dirty, minor Theatre up three pairs of stairs, where the

216

be-puffed Ole Bull the violinist was giving his only concert to the people of Rochester. It was not a flattering specimen of an American concert room. There was no care or regard for appearance—unshorn beards, fustian, linen, coats, blouses, or anything. . . . It was not what the smallest country town in the old country would display in its Theatre or in an exhibition room. . . . I inquired for some time vainly for Mr Gregg—at length I found him in the pit—there was only pit and gallery in this dirty hole of a place—lit by, I think, four lamps and two candles. His reception of me was courteous and I found him a most gentlemanly and agreeable man in my short conversation with him. I heard Ole Bull. Is this a high art? What is its effect? On what does your mind run while listening to him? Do you think of the air? of the composition? of the melody? Not once. . . . You think of nothing but the individual—his 'tours d'artifice'—his tricks—his legerdemain—which are startling. . . . He has been ignorantly praised and is pandering to a false, a vicious, and vulgar appetite. The musical taste of this country will not be improved by the memory of Ole Bull's performance. . . .

Montreal, July 5. . . . At dinner read much of *Ion*, which thrilled and affected me again quite with the old feeling. I was very much moved. I could not help thinking how in this world we let petty feelings disturb those more charitable ones, which should cherish regard for what is amiable in man and indulgence for what is weak or worse. It is to be lamented that I have ever known Talfourd out of his literary calling; he is unequal but—I wrote a kind letter to him.

July 6. Looked at the papers for English news. . . . I perceive that some persons have presented a piece of plate to—Mr Bunn for his 'uniform urbanity in the season of 1843–1844' *[at Drury Lane]*. This wretch, who not only robbed almost every player he had dealings with, but constantly insulted those whom he dared with language of the most offensive and blackguard kind.

*August 16 *[at a hotel near Boston]*. We stepped into the shop of a droll sort of artist, a Mons. Edouard who cuts out likenesses in black paper. Felton[1] sate at my request, but the hour of dinner was so near that the cutter-out observed he could not help thinking he had a knife in his hand, and we agreed to visit him after. Some of his likenesses were very fair. We returned to the hotel, and in due time took our places at the dinner-table. To my concern and regret Mr Blood *[a singer Macready had known in London]* (whose advertisement as *Mr McMichael, giving specimens of Irish Minstrelsy* I had noticed) sate down nearly opposite to

---

[1] Cornelius Felton, of Harvard, whom Dickens called 'heartiest of Greek Professors', and who was also Longfellow's friend.

us. I would not look the way he sate, but perceived that he talked gaily and with an air of indifference during dinner. [Later] Mr Blood came and sate down by me, observing 'You do not seem to recollect me'. I answered, 'I recollect you, Mr Blood, but you are, I understand, under another name here, by which I should naturally suppose you would not wish to be recognised by your former acquaintances, nor should I imagine you would desire to recognise them.' He murmured that 'if he had an opportunity of speaking with me alone, he could explain things to me', and as I did not resume the conversation, he left me. I really did not do this out of harshness. I do not pretend to judge him, or any man, but I could not approve his conduct.

New York, September 6. Called on Simpson, who gave me some account of the London theatricals. Mr Bunn had ejected *the drama* from Drury Lane theatre. This is well. Mrs Nisbett was losing herself rapidly, poor woman! Miss Helen Faucit has engaged for Paris next winter; also that Mr Forrest was resolved to go there and act. I could not be concerned about it in any way.

Philadelphia, September 7. Went to Walnut Street theatre; saw Forrest act Damon *[in John Banim's* Damon and Pythias*]*—a very dull, heavy-mannered, unpleasant performance. He is not a good actor—*not at all an artist*. He acts Hamlet on Monday in opposition to me, and, I hear, made this engagement to oppose me! This is not the English generosity of rivalry. *[Forrest, who had trailed Macready through the South, was now acting at the Walnut Street in Philadelphia while Macready was at the Chestnut Street Theatre. But on this occasion—in spite of a challenge with Hamlet—the rivalry was not alarming.]*

September 9. Mr Forrest in Hamlet at the Walnut Street theatre had not more (if he had that sum) than $200 to his Hamlet. If it be so, he is justly punished for his ungentlemanly conduct.

September 14. Rehearsed carefully and laboriously four acts of *Werner;* saw the impossibility of Mr Conner delivering the words of the part or even scrambling through Ulric; he could not even *read* the text of his part. It was too serious to be angry about. . . . I proposed that an apology should be made for this Mr Conner, and that he should *read* the part; it would quiet his mind, and get the play through. Miss Cushman said he would play a trick—he would have a fit; it seems he was drunk last night. Well, it was settled. We finished the play, and I went home dreadfully tired. Evening came. I went to the theatre; acted the first act of Werner excellently; went on to Josephine and Ulric in the second; had not spoken six lines before Ulric—Mr Conner—gave a reel (*not a good one*—I have no faith in it) and fell!!!—a fit! What was to be done? Nothing appeared to me but to substitute *The Stranger*. An apology was made, our dresses changed, and *The Stranger* acted. *['Conner' was Edmund Connor.]*

Later that night Macready, in a farewell speech, said: 'I feel more sensibly the cordiality of my reception here from some unworthy attempts that have been made to excite a prejudice against me and my countrymen engaged in this profession, on the plea of being foreigners [Copying the speech into his journal, he added the word 'Excitement'] But such influences, I know, could not reach you. . . .'

September 15. Saw Forrest, talked with him, and went to sit with Mrs Forrest, whom I like as pretty and amiable. Talked with them for some time. He told me of Mr Conner's *fits*.

New York, September 25. The anniversary of my opening the Park theatre, New York, since when I find myself, with all my expenses paid, about £5,500 bettered in pecuniary circumstances, for which I gratefully, devoutly and earnestly thank God.

His New York farewell was on 27 September (King Lear) *and his final performance of the tour* (Macbeth) *at Boston on October 14.*

Boston, October 14. . . . Acted Macbeth well, where I was not *cut up* by the men on the stage. Was *savagely angry* with Mr Ryder and *quite forgot myself*. Oh, passion! passion! what a wretched, senseless, ruinous guide thou art! Was called for. Spoke. The audience attentive but not enthusiastic.

Back in London early in November, Macready arranged to act in Paris during the following month for a season arranged by John Mitchell, who founded a famous ticket agency in Bond Street, and who from 1842 to 1854 was lessee of the St James's Theatre which housed so many French companies, and became recognised indeed as 'the French theatre' in London.

December 4. Set out, Catherine and self, for the Dover station. Dined at Folkestone, where we were detained till four o'clock by the non-arrival of the packet. Went on board a nasty, miserable little boat, called the *Water Witch*, stowed full of passengers; good deal of wind and very heavy sea made our passage, of four hours' duration, perfectly miserable.

Paris, December 11. Alexandre Dumas[1] called and left a box for the

[1] Alexandre Dumas *père* (1803–1870), novelist and dramatist.

Odéon. We went and saw his play of *Christine*—poor old Mlle Georges,[1]
quite an old woman, acted Christine. So dull a play I scarcely ever saw.

December 13. . . . Dickens dined with us, and left us at half-past five,
taking with him the last pleasant day that I expect to pass in Paris.

*[Dickens had been in Paris on his way back from London to Genoa. In
London Macready had heard him read 'The Chimes' at Forster's rooms in
Lincoln's Inn Fields.]*

December 16. Acted Othello *[in the Salle Ventadour; Helen Faucit as
Desdemona]* with great care, often with much reality, but I could not
feel the sympathy of the audience; they were fashionable, and from the
construction of the theatre, not within the range of my *electric contact*, to
coin an expression; the shocking delay between the acts was another
cause for a certain heaviness I felt to pervade the evening.

*[The Salle Ventadour was used as a rule for Italian opera. Edouard Thierry
blamed Macready's over-accentuated declamation. Jules Janin, indignant
at the way in which Othello 'masked' Helen Faucit when, kneeling and
hidden by his robe, she addressed the Venetian Senate, wrote of 'le grand
paravent de Macready.']*

December 21. Went to theatre, rehearsed Virginius, a very trouble-
some rehearsal. It seems that Miss H. Faucit is not more smitten with
Paris than I am—the audience are too fashionable, or too far off from
the actor. We shall not act more than our twelve nights; the theatre is
too large.

December 30. News of Miss H. Faucit's illness, and inability to play.
. . . The business was at last arranged for Mrs Serle to do her best with
Ophelia. Acted Hamlet as well as I could. The audience were interested.
but not so tumultuous in their applause as on the previous evening.
Mrs Serle made a very fair effort. . . . *[Mrs Serle, wife of T. J. Serle
(who was stage-managing in Paris), was the actress Cecilia Novello.]*

[1] Mlle Georges (1787–1867), French tragic actress.

1845

Paris, January 1. Received an Edinburgh paper, in which I was very much vilified and calumniated to raise the name of Miss Helen Faucit—things were said that must have come from her directly or indirectly.

[The Paris season caused a break between Helen Faucit and Macready. When she agreed with Mitchell to go to Paris, she had arranged to take Lady Macbeth, Ophelia, and Virginia on the understanding that she would also have other parts—Juliet for one—more identified with her. On Macready's return from America he put aside the Faucit choices and substituted his own: thus she had only a single night ('Romeo and Juliet') in a favourite part. But Paris, to Macready's annoyance, received her with enthusiasm. At the end of the season she wrote: 'Either Mr Macready has grown more selfish and exacting, or I am less capable of bearing with such ungenerous conduct. In either case I am far better away from him.']

January 8. Acted Macbeth with effort, not so well as Monday, but in spite of the *distressing* blunders and mismanagements, I think with power and discrimination. It is, however, certain, if that be any proof of skill or power, that the audience applauded Miss Faucit's sleeping scene much more than anything else in the whole play. . . . I was called for, and Mr Serle, as I thought *very impertinently*, said: 'You had better take on Miss Faucit, for it was noticed.' I was really *stung* by the unauthorised intrusion of his advice, and said: 'When I want your advice I will ask for it!'

January 14. Saw Mitchell on business, and understood from him his meaning in alluding last night to the endeavours of an envious clique to annoy me; he meant the friends of Miss H. Faucit; but *is it possible* that she could wish they should act so unworthily? I will not believe it. . . .

January 15. . . . Bowes told me distinctly that *Miss H. Faucit's friends were my enemies*, and left me no room to doubt on the subject.

On 16 January he acted Hamlet before the King [Louis Philippe, 1773–1850] and Queen in the private theatre of the Tuileries.

January 16. . . . In my mind I never gave such a representation of the part, and without a hand of applause; but indeed there was an attempt in the first scene by some one who, I suppose, became sensible of his offence against decorum, 'and back recoiled, he knew not why, even at the sound himself had made'. In the fourth act, where I have nothing to do, I did cast a glance at the royal box; saw the white fuzz of the Queen's head and the old King on the other side of the centre; the *salle* had altogether a very brilliant appearance, the pit was filled with military. . . . After the play one of the King's *suite* in Court uniform waited on me, and, with expressions of his Majesty's pleasure, etc., presented me with a long packet or parcel. I hastily dressed. Miss H. Faucit, as I passed her, said: 'Such a pretty bracelet.' I hurried home to Catherine, told her all the news, and looked at the poniard sent by the King.

January 19. . . . Went with De Fresne to call on Victor Hugo, in the Place Royale; the storm obliged our driver to drive the carriage under the colonnade. The house, old and cold, was quite a poet's mansion. The *salon*, hung round and ceilinged with tapestry, had large pictures; it had a gloomy air, though not dark, and looked like a poet's room. Victor Hugo received me very cordially, and was most earnest in his expressions of admiration and respect to me. I talked with several there, and had a circle of the young men around me. I saw his daughter, who was pretty. He accompanied me to the door when we left, and was most cordial in his adieux to me. *[Victor Marie Hugo (1802–1885), poet, novelist, and dramatist, lived on the first floor of 37 rue de la Tour d'Auvergne, a big house that backed upon the Palais-Royal.]*

Macready was back in London during the last week in January. Edwin Forrest, who seemed to be haunting him, would be opening during February at the Princess's in Oxford Street, with Charlotte Cushman as his leading lady. Macready had only some provincial engagements ahead.

London, January 29. A Mr —, a barrister, called on the subject of some dramas of about 3,600 lines each, which he had made, and put into Longman's hands, upon the reigns of the Plantagenets, joining with it a history of the Church; I backed out as courteously as I could. . . . Called on Forster. Found him and Leigh Hunt at dinner; sat with them about an hour. Hunt is a *bore*.

February 3. Sat and talked with Forster; he very strongly argued for the restoration of Hamlet's speech when the King is praying. It is worth thinking of.

February 12. Catherine brought me the Louis Philippe poniard from Smith's, and with it the information that the French King's present— 'Oh Majesty, how high thy glory towers, when the rich blood of kings' *[King John, II.i.]*—is silver-gilt!!!

Macready as Henry IV, from a painting by John Jackson, R.A.

Macready, a portrait attributed to Daniel Maclise, R.A.

Macready, 1850. A portrait bust by William Behnes.

Macready in retirement, an engraving from a photograph.

Newcastle, February 23. Read a confirmation of the account of Forrest's disastrous and total failure in Macbeth. I had only seen him in Lear and Damon, which were very dull performances, but not otherwise offensive, but in Macbeth he seems to have provoked the patience of the audience. I am truly sorry for him (without wishing him *great* success) and deeply sorry for his wife.

London, March 2. Called on Mr and Mrs Forrest, with whom were several people; to me he observed that he was going to Paris, where he would be 'better appreciated than he is here'. I fancy not.

[Macready had now another grudge against Forrest. He would have preferred Charlotte Cushman to Helen Faucit as his leading lady in Paris, but she decided on the Forrest season. The plays, received indifferently, included 'Othello', 'Macbeth', 'King Lear' (possibly the best, though Forster called Forrest a 'roaring pantaloon'), and 'Metamora' by John Augustus Stone. From early April (but without Charlotte Cushman) Forrest went to the provinces.]

March 3. On this day I enter on my fifty-third year.

Sheffield, March 5. Acted Hamlet pretty well, taking the company, etc., into account. Called for. What a farce has this absurd usage now become.

March 9. Read over some poems of Wordsworth; certainly where he is good, he is very good; but he is often obscure, often wordy to extreme weariness and often weak almost to silliness; his egoism is, moreover, not very amiable; but he gives great lessons and kindles aspiring feelings.

London, March 22. . . . Mr B. Smith . . . told me, evidently with reluctance, that the jewels in the poniard given me by that *shabby dog*—Louis Philippe—are sham!

Macready acted in Manchester, Glasgow, Whitehaven, Belfast, Dumfries, and Carlisle. He was back in London in mid-May. In Manchester (27 March) he read with exasperation of the Irish Academy's testimonial to Helen Faucit for her Dublin performance of Antigone ('ridiculous to call such trash as the language of Antigone (in a version by W. Bartholomew) the Greek poetry, and as absurd to talk about Helen Faucit's education —she being utterly uneducated. Unluckily the stage is the profession of all others for empiricism'). At Whitehaven, where he acted Hamlet Shylock and Richelieu late in April, 'the set around me were enough to paralyse inspiration'.

London, May 16. *[At the Lyceum Theatre for one of the burlesques presented by Robert and Mary Keeley.]*—Who would not blush for the character of his country's taste and refinement who saw an audience crowded to listen to such stuff so wretchedly acted; it is disgraceful to taste, and in the exposure made of the legs of a great number of women, it is indecent and immoral. Oh—England's drama!

Macready, making many visits to the provinces, did not appear in London until the autumn. During July talk of a Haymarket engagement came up; but he and Webster could not agree. Ultimately, J. M. Maddox, of the Princess's, accepted the proposal, though neither Charlotte Cushman, who seemed disinclined to appear with Macready, nor Helen Faucit, who would not act on terms inferior to his, joined the cast; and when the season began on 13 October, Mrs Stirling would be the leading lady.

Birmingham, May 29. I went to the theatre. . . .Saw Mr Ryder, but neither actors nor manager were there, nor were they coming—'it was only Hamlet', and they knew it quite well!!! I wish they did!

London, July 22. Catherine received an anonymous letter accusing Miss H. Faucit of depreciating me and reflecting upon her. Anonymous letters are not worthy of belief, and this I have no doubt exaggerates the truth—though I fear Miss Helen Faucit forgets what she owes to me.

St Helier, Jersey, August 13. . . . Received a letter from Forster with reports of his negotiation. Two curious pieces of information he gives me; one, that Miss Cushman will not engage at all with Mr Maddox, *if* it is to act with me. This is perfectly intelligible in the contemplation of the woman's perfect inconsistency; the other, that Miss H. Faucit's friends say that she must have whatever terms are given to me. What my terms have to do with Miss H. Faucit it is not easy to perceive. But I let them go their own way. . . . Acted Othello quite as a study, but I was grievously discomposed by the miserable ass that was put on for Iago. The man was *'acting'* so outrageously all through the play, grimacing, mysticising, and ranting, that it was with the utmost difficulty I could bring back my mind to my character. . . .

London, September 1. Mr Maddox . . . told me that Mr Forrest acted at his theatre for *nothing*. . . . Went to Sadler's Wells theatre and saw *Macbeth [with Samuel Phelps, now manager of Sadler's Wells, and Mrs Warner]*—most creditably put upon the stage and very well done indeed *for such a locality*. As a piece of art considered positively, it has been greatly overpraised. Read in the *Connoisseur* that some paper has been accusing me of being 'jealous of Miss Faucit's success in Paris'.

*[Dickens, always an actor at heart, had collected his friends for a perfor-
mance of Ben Jonson's comedy at Miss Kelly's theatre (later the Royalty)
in Dean Street, Soho. John Leech (1817—1864), the comic artist;
Augustus Dickens (1827–1866), Charles's youngest brother; Douglas
William Jerrold (1803–1857), dramatist, author of 'Black Ey'd Susan'.
Mark Lemon (1809–1870), the Brainworm, was editor of 'Punch' from
1841-1870.]*

London, September 20. . . . Went to Miss Kelly's theatre; saw the
play of *Every Man in his Humour*. Several of the actors were very fine as
amateurs: Forster in Kitely; Dickens, Bobadil; Leech, Master Mathew;
Lee, Cob; young Dickens, Cash, were very fair; Jerrold very bad in
Master Stephen. Old Knowell was also very fair. But it was a dull
business. Fitzgerald criticised Forster unintentionally in saying: 'At one
time he spoke in so strange a tone that he was very near making us laugh.'
The fact was he played Kitely as a tragic character—the grand mistake;
otherwise it was very commendable. The farce between Dickens and
M. Lemon was very broad and laughable. Saw Lady Blessington, etc.,
Mrs Carlyle, Quin, Mr King, etc. With the greatest difficulty got our
party out and off, and in Oxford Street, out of Serles' carriage into a
cab, torrents of rain falling, and drove to 9, Powis Place, Great Ormond
Street. Here I waited with Jerdan, Maclise, Stanfield, etc.—I think an
hour—my cold torturing me. At length Dickens, Jerrold, Forster, etc.,
and Count D'Orsay (!) arrived; Talfourd also, who accosted me very
cordially. I took some oysters, and consented to go up to supper, but got
near the door, and before it was half over took an opportunity to escape.
I was very unwell.

September 28. Mr Maddox *[J. M. Maddox (Medex), of the Princess's,
a Jewish speculator.]* called, again to speak to me about Miss Cushman;
this woman is full of the idea of her own importance, and will not listen
to any other notion. We must try to work through the engagement—
without *her* would be easy enough, but without *any* actress!

October 6. Reflected much on the tendency to selfish and envious
feelings in my nature. *I have no right* to be dissatisfied with any performer, male or female, whether I have helped them to obtain distinction
or no, for choosing the course that seems most eligible to them, even
though that course be in direct hostility to my interests. Should I hesi-
tate in accepting an engagement from which I expected benefit, upon
the surmise or belief that it would operate disadvantageously to any other
persons on the stage? It is clear *I should not*. What right then have I to
impugn others' actions, which are quite independent, or to murmur in

my secret heart at their arrangements? Let me try to think with resolute judgment and to *feel* liberally on such points. Wrote to Bulwer on his supposition that I was offended with him.

On 13 October, as Hamlet at the Princess's, he began his first London engagement for well over two years. It lasted until 21 November. Mrs Stirling was his leading lady.

October 13. Acted Hamlet fairly, but my strength failed me, though not, I think, to be perceived, in the closet scene. The reception which the audience gave me was something quite of itself; the only instance to which it can be at all likened, though in a smaller theatre, was my last night at Drury Lane, which was *awful*. But this, both at the entrance and upon the call, was quite a thing by itself. Maddox came and thanked me. Forster came round and discoursed very coolly on the evening's effects. . . .

October 14. . . . Read the papers, which, particularly *The Times*, were most gratifying—most comforting to me. . . . Kind note from John Delane [*John Delane (1817–1879), editor of 'The Times' 1841–1877.*].

October 15. Acted King Lear—unequally. Some things I did well, sometimes I was deficient, I thought, in power. . . .

October 19. Forster came to tea and informed us that Bradbury and Evans, with Paxton,[1] Duke of Devonshire's agent, and another capitalist, a Birmingham man, had agreed on starting a daily paper [*The Daily News*] on a very large scale, and that Dickens was to be at the head of it. Forster was to have some share in it, and it was instantly to be got into train for starting. I heard the news with a sort of dismay, not feeling myself, nor seeing in others, the want of such a thing. I fear the means and chances have not been well enough considered.

October 21. . . . Read an account of the reception of Miss Helen Faucit and Mr Anderson at the Haymarket [*in 'The Lady of Lyons'*], which seemed cordial and kind, but not verging towards enthusiasm. . . .

October 25. Looked at papers. It is not without satisfaction that I see the claims of Miss Helen Faucit (which have been urged in so hostile a spirit to me, and so unjustly as to facts) now distinctly and certainly most honestly adjudged by the public voice, which gives her the praise with which I have always readily heralded her name, but limiting it to

[1] Sir Joseph Paxton (1801–1865); designed the 'Crystal Palace' building for the Great Exhibition of 1851.

its point of desert. She is a very pleasing, clever, and good actress, but she is not a great one. She is not Mrs Siddons, not Miss O'Neill, not Mlle. Rachel.

October 26. Forster came to dinner; he urged upon me giving permission to my family to see me act. I do not know; I have a feeling about their seeing me as a player. Perhaps I am wrong.

November 2. Forster called and read me Dickens's Prospectus of the new morning paper—or rather I read it over twice attentively. It increased my apprehensions. I objected to several parts of it, but my objection is one and all. I feel that he is rushing headlong into an enterprise that demands the utmost foresight, skilful and secret preparation and qualities of a conductor which Dickens has not. Forster agreed to many if not all of my objections, but he did not seem to entertain much hope of moving Dickens.

November 3. *[After 'Othello']* . . . Spoke to Maddox about his wretched rascal of a property man, who behaved most shamefully. He promised to discharge him. He *ought* to be discharged. . . .

November 4. Wrote a note to Mr Maddox requesting him to forgive the property man (though indeed he does not deserve forgiveness) which he answered promising he would. . . .

November 14. Had some little conversation with Maddox, who told me that Vestris and Mathews's engagement at Dublin was a complete failure owing to the potato disease—a black look-out!

November 15. . . . Dressed, dined early and went to the amateur play *[again 'Every Man in his Humour']* at the St James's theatre. As an amateur performance it is exceedingly good, but the commendation is held of no account with the actors, and they desire to be judged on positive grounds. Judged therefore by the poet and by the art, by what the one affords the opportunity of being done, and what the other enables the actor to do, the performance would not be endured from ordinary, or rather regular actors by a paying audience. They seem to me to be under a perfect delusion as to their degrees of skill and power in this art, of which they do not know what may be called the very rudiments. . . .

November 16. Forster called, not in very high spirits about last night's performance, though it was very creditable. . . .

November 18. Went with White *[The Rev. James White, 1803–1862, retired clergyman, dramatist and contributor to 'Household Words']* to the Haymarket theatre; saw two last acts of *Lady of Lyons*; an indifferent house. Anderson is deteriorated; Helen Faucit in some respects improved, in some fallen off.

November 21. Acted Hamlet as well, or better, than I ever did . . . and thus ends this brilliant engagement.

From 23 November to 15 December Macready was in Dublin; thence after three nights in Belfast and a final night in Dublin, he returned to London.

Dublin, November 24. . . . Acted Hamlet before one of the most—there is no qualification of the term to leave its fair description—the most blackguard audiences I ever encountered. They were grossly insulting in their continued noise and absurd words, breaking in upon the language of the play. They called 'Order' at every burst of applause, and frequently completely stilled it. I was greatly provoked, but went through it without noticing the brutality of the ruffians, who had congregated together to prevent others from listening to Shakespeare. . . . I dislike and despise them.

Nightly he was 'distressed to a degree that irritates and agitates my nerves to a point of intense suffering. . . . The most loathsome and offensive engagement I ever underwent.'

December 8. Letter from Bulwer Lytton, proposing the translation and adaptation of Sophocles' *Œdipus Tyrannus*, and, as I understand it, offering it to me for purchase for £600, but would leave £300 contingent upon the run. If I understand him rightly, this is rather mingling the trader with the friend. Answered Bulwer, not accepting his offer.

London, December 23. Took a cab in Oxford Street to call on Forster, with whom I had some conversation about Bulwer. I took the opportunity of telling Forster that Bulwer's expression, in his letter to me at Dublin, of 'desiring to *serve me* by writing a new play' was not very generous nor correct; that, understanding, as I believed I did, his position, it was certainly to '*serve himself*'. Forster said undoubtedly, and that Bulwer would not use such a term in speaking or writing to him on such a subject.

December 24. At dinner we burned the Yule log, and had the dear children round us; to the little ones I told a story, and afterwards to the four elder read parts of the first and second acts of *Macbeth*. . . .

December 27. . . . Forster now *draws in* about the paper, and seems to feel it is a wrong step and that Dickens is not qualified for the situation of director. *His tone is quite altered now.* He told me that Dickens was so intensely fixed on his own opinions and in his admiration of his own works (who could have believed it?) that he, Forster, was useless to him as a counsel, or for an opinion on anything touching upon them, and that, as he refused to see criticisms on himself, this partial passion would grow upon him till it became an incurable evil. I grieved to hear it.

1846

January 2. Went out with Edward to call on Forster; found Dickens and his tailor at his chambers, he encased in his doublet and hose; it is quite ludicrous the fuss which the actors make about this play! *[Fletcher's 'The Elder Brother']*—but I was sorry to hear of intemperate language between them, which should neither have been given or received, as it was. . . .

January 3. Note from Forster, *pestering* me about his cloak—to 'wear it, or not'—absurd. Went to see the amateurs act *The Elder Brother [at Miss Kelly's theatre]*; the best-filled part in the play was Miramount by Lemon, but the play was not well acted. Miss Fortescue was pleasant, but rather wanting in *délicatesse*. Forster was quite beyond his depth—indeed, rather entirely out of his element in the part of Charles. The whole play was dull and dragging. . . . *[Dickens took the part of Eustace.]*.

During much of January Macready acted in the West of England, at Exeter and Plymouth.

Plymouth, January 12. Went to rehearsal *[at the Theatre Royal]* where I was much annoyed by the manifest indifference of these persons, who call themselves actors, in the scenes which I had several times rehearsed with them on Saturday. They made the *very same* mistakes, proving that they had never looked at their books, had made no memorandum, nor in fact, ever thought upon the business for which they received the price of their daily bread. . . .

[J. R. Newcombe was lessee of the Theatre Royal ('rising in column'd pride and Attic grace') from 1845 to 1887.]

January 13. Letter from Mrs —, full of talent and most entertaining, but giving me considerable pain, in the information it gave of Helen Faucit speaking in unkind terms of me. Acted Cardinal Richelieu, not at all to please myself; was cut up, root and branch, by these horrid players—but the audience chose to be satisfied. Wightwick came into my room, walked with me to hotel, and supped. Gave me some very salutary objective criticism.

January 15. Read and noted Mr White's play of *The King of the Commons*, which I like. Acted Othello pretty well, considering the disadvantage under which I stood with an inaccurate Iago, shocking Desdemona, bad Emilia, and wretched Cassio. Oh, such a company for Shakespeare!

January 16. Wightwick took tea and talked with me critically of my performances; mentioned some good objections to *the* soliloquy in Hamlet. I will attend to them.

January 20. Went into the old church *[of St Andrew]*; read the inscription over Mathews's grave—a falsehood; he was a *player*, and no more; a mere selfish player, without one feeling of the gentleman—a fit 'friend' for Theodore Hook. *[Charles Mathews (1776–1835) died in Plymouth where he landed after a voyage from America, and was buried in St Andrew's, the city's mother church. He was the father of Charles James Mathews.]*

January 22. Slept much of my journey to Exeter; a young gentleman in the coach knew and addressed me; a lunatic, in charge of his keeper, was on the top . . . *The Daily News* has nothing very striking or startling in it—nothing, I think, to stimulate curiosity or excite expectation. Dickens's letter from the road to Italy I did not fancy; it is too familiar, I think, for a letter in a newspaper detailing actual occurrences with a real signature. Sent off a few words by way of a starting cheer to Dickens on the sight of the first *Daily News*.

Macready had a season at the Princess's from 26 January to 27 February.

London, January 30. Read the papers; pleased with the leading articles of *The Daily News*, but when *The Times* came its superiority was so manifest that I am *in despair* for the result of the *Daily News*.

February 3. Looked at paper, *Daily News*; nothing in it; this cannot do; *three columns* of citations from country papers about the Special Express; yesterday two and a half columns! How can this interest its readers? The persons employed do not understand their business.

February 5. . . . Thackeray, Dickens, and Fox came, Maddox and his brothers. I read to them *The King of the Commons;* White *[the author]* reading the scenes of Laird Small. I thought all parties seemed very much pleased, and was buoyed up in my own mind with the hope of success. White, Fox, Dickens, Thackeray, and Forster came to dinner. When gone, Fox gave me his opinion as adverse to the expectation of great success for the play. I was sorry and disappointed to hear it. I cannot judge of it in my present state myself. Forster spoke to me at dinner in so rude a manner, so grossly impertinent, telling me my opinions were 'unworthy of me', etc., that Dickens expected I should reply very angrily to him, and White was surprised at his tone and language. He forgets himself.

February 6. . . . Called on Dickens and talked with him on *The King of the Commons*. He did not think it strong; he was *disappointed* in it. . . . Note from Thackeray, sticking up for White's play.

February 9. Acted Cardinal Richelieu tolerably. . . . Forster came into my room. He seemed in very low spirits about *the Paper*, and said he 'had always felt as I did about it—it was precipitate; that no one could be a worse editor than Dickens', etc! Alas!

February 12. Forster called; he told me that Dickens had abdicated the editorship of *The Daily News*, and that he was editor. He seemed elated with his position and looked forward to improving the paper. I doubt his ability to do so sufficiently for success. . . . Forster read a letter from Tennyson, and a copy of verses.

February 13. Wrote to Bulwer, *confidentially*, recommending him to contradict, if he could, the assertions of his having written *The New Timon [in which he attacked Tennyson]*.

[The second part of 'The New Timon: A Romance of London'—a poem that appeared anonymously—included such couplets as

> The jingled medley of purloined conceits,
> Outbabying Wordsworth and outglittering Keats

and

> Let school-miss Alfred vent her chaste delight
> On 'darling little rooms so warm and bright'. . . .

Bulwer replied to Macready from Rome 3 March: 'I should feel much obliged if you would use "my distinct and most positive authorization to contradict the report".' *Yet he was clearly the author.]*

Tennyson's reply included the lines ('The New Timon, and the Poets'; signed by 'Alcibiades'):

> What profits now to understand
> The merits of a spotless shirt—
> A dapper boot—a little hand—
> If half the little soul is dirt?'

In later years Tennyson said that Forster had sent these lines to 'Punch' without his knowledge; he regretted them. His further poem, 'An After-thought', which appeared, unsigned in 'Punch' soon after 'The New Timon,

*and the Poets', began with the words, 'Ah, God! the petty fools of rhyme/
That shriek and sweat in pigmy wars . . .,' and ended 'The noblest answer
unto such/Is perfect stillness when they brawl'.*

February 26. Looked at papers. In *Punch* read the lines of Tennyson
on Bulwer Lytton, as the author of *The New Timon*. It is not easy to
conceive any verses more bitter, more graphic, more full of scorn, and
powerful in their high and master tone. Their bitterness the author felt
after having written them, and, in his charitable spirit, in his sense of the
littleness of revenge, of the nobleness of forgiveness, he desired Forster,
to whom he sent them, to destroy them. Forster, the friend and confi-
dant of Bulwer Lytton, writes back to Tennyson, saying that though
Lytton was his friend, yet justice was more dear than friendship to him;
that Lytton denied the authorship of *The New Timon*, but that he, Forster, did not believe his denial, and, such was his sense of justice and of
Tennyson's wrong, that if he wished it, on re-consideration, he, Forster,
would publish them! Tennyson was stung by Forster's letter to descend
to retaliation, to fling away his magnanimity, and in the *Punch* of today,
auspice Forstero, the lines are printed.

*On 28 February Macready left for an engagement in Edinburgh which
would last until mid-March. Almost at once there occurred the incident
which would shadow much of the rest of his professional life.*

Edinburgh, March 2. Acted Hamlet really with particular care,
energy, and discrimination: the audience gave less applause to the first
soliloquy than I am in the habit of receiving, but I was bent on acting
the part, and I felt, if I can feel at all, that I had strongly excited them,
and that their sympathies were cordially, indeed, enthusiastically, with
me. On reviewing the performance I can conscientiously pronounce it
one of the very best I have given of Hamlet. At the waving of the handkerchief before the play, and 'I must be idle' *[Macready here would flirt
his handkerchief above his head with an air of extravagant jauntiness]*, a
man on the right side of the stage—upper boxes or gallery, but said to be
upper boxes—hissed! The audience took it up, and I waved the more,
and bowed derisively and contemptuously to the individual. The
audience carried it, though he was very staunch to his purpose. It
discomposed me, and alas! might have ruined many; but I bore it down.
I thought of speaking to the audience, if called on, and spoke to Murray
about it, but he very discreetly dissuaded me. Was called for, and very
warmly greeted. Ryder came and spoke to me, and told me that the

hisser was observed and said to be a Mr W—, who was in company with Mr Forrest! The man writes in the *Journal*, a paper, depreciating me and eulogising Mr F—, sent to me from this place.

March 3. Fifty-three years have I lived, today. Both Mr Murray and Mr Ryder are possessd with the belief that Mr Forrest was the man who hissed last night. I begin to think he was the man. . . . *[Forrest, who had been acting in Aberdeen, had a week's break before going to Carlisle, and had come to Edinburgh to watch his rival.]*

March 4. Mr Ryder told me that a Mr Smibert, a Mr Aitken, and some other, had informed him that they were in the box with Mr Forrest on Monday night, and *saw him* hiss on the occasion alluded to. He also told me that a person, Mr Mills, an amateur, had told Mr Murray positively that he also saw him, and that it was *Mr Forrest!* In the course of the rehearsal the police officer came to Mr Murray and told him that it was Mr Forrest who had hissed on Monday night, and that it was set down in the report of the night (a practice here) to the police office by the officer on duty, regularly entered among the occurrences of the evening. It is alluded to in *The Scotsman* of today with a direct reference to Mr Forrest. Indeed, it seems placed beyond all doubt. . . . I do not think that such an action has its parallel in all theatrical history. The low-minded ruffian! The man would commit a murder, *if he dare*.

March 5. Went to rehearsal. Here I heard from Ryder that Mr Forrest was again in the boxes last night, as he says, conspicuous by laughing and talking in my principal scenes. Poor creatures! . . .

March 6. Rehearsed. Heard from Mr Ryder that Mr Wyndham, one of the actors, had been told by a bystander that Mr Forrest justified his act of *hissing* on the plea that he gave applause to actors, and he had an equal right to hiss them! *Mr Forrest!*

March 7. Ryder came and told me that in the *Chronicle* of today was *an admission and an attempt at justification of Mr Forrest's outrage!* I am glad that all uncertainty on the question is at an end. But what a wretch is this Mr Forrest! Read *The Times* and the Edinburgh *Courant*, which has a sort of civil notice by a very hypercritical connoisseur. These people can see genius in all the harlequin quackeries, devoid of a glimpse of idea, of Mr C. Kean, and inspiration in the rant of Miss Helen Faucit, to which the houses are crowded. But I am not one of the Edinburgh wonders.

March 9. . . . Acted Hamlet. Read over Hamlet. Felt rather nervous and uneasy from the uncertainty of whether this American ruffian may not have left some colleague or hireling here instructed to renew the insulting outrage on me. Reasoned against it, but it is scarcely possible to acquire *full confidence*—indispensable to acting—under such an apprehension of doubt. Acted Hamlet with care, but had upon me the restraining feeling of doubt and want of confidence in my audience, against which I battled as well as I could. . . .

After the Edinburgh engagement Macready travelled back to London by way of the Lakes (where he called on Wordsworth, 'ill in bed and had had his leeches this morning', and Miss Martineau); York, and Derby. In York an actress, Mrs —, to whom Macready had once given some advice, and who clearly had interested him, took the trouble to tell him 'much of Helen Faucit's abuse of me, and representation that I had ill-treated and injured her.' Macready commented in his journal, 'I am grown seared to it; it does not now affect me.' On the next night Mrs — gave him 'a somewhat fuller account of Miss H. Faucit's conduct, which seems to be in the worst style and taste of caballing actresses.'

London, April 1. Mr Ryder called, and informed me of an article in the *Sunday Times*, which denied that Mr Forrest had been guilty of the offence imputed, and that the statement was made by the *Times* and *Examiner* to benefit me at his expense! Unluckily it was the *Scotsman's* statement which Mr Forrest himself has confirmed, observing he 'would do the same again'. I listened with the utmost complacency to Mr Ryder, and told him I could not degrade myself to notice anything of the sort. . . .

April 4. Called on Forster. He spoke about Tennyson, Bulwer, and *Punch*—not quite satisfactorily. I told him I had written to Bulwer on the subject of *The New Timon*. He has not done well in that business. He showed me *The Times* in which is a letter of Mr Edwin Forrest, admitting that he hissed me on my introduction of a 'fancy dance' into *Hamlet*; that he had a right to do so; that he was not solitary in the act; and that he often led the applause which he regretted others did not follow. There are other falsehoods in the letter. . . .

[Forrest, after playing in Manchester and in Ireland, made his last appearance, on 11 May, at Cork. After holidays in Ireland and in Spain, he returned with his wife to London on 8 August, and they sailed from Liverpool to New York a week later.]

April 7. Called at Edwin Landseer's; saw a noble picture of a Stag at Bay. . . .

Macready prepared for another engagement, 13 April to 19 June, at the Princess's, and he accepted an offer of £1000 for five weeks across the water at Stirling's Surrey Theatre.

May 2. . . . At Dickens's suggestion (with no relish on my part), Edwin Landseer, Stanfield, Dickens, Talfourd and myself went to the Lyceum to see General Tom Thumb [*Charles Stratton, a dwarf; fourteen years of age, he was twenty-five inches high and weighed fifteen pounds*].

May 5. . . . Met Mr B. Disraeli and Mr K. Macaulay [*Kenneth Macaulay, barrister, and cousin of the historian*], from both of whom I had the honour of a cut. This is rather amusing, considering that both of these men have felt my notice of some value to them!

May 9. Gave the morning to *King of the Commons*, which I cannot like—it is hasty and trashy. Rested. Acted King Lear very languidly and not at all *possessed* with the character.

May 14. Note from Forster excusing himself from dining with us today. It is not that I am disposed to take offence at one or two rudenesses or slights committed by a friend, but the frequency of them wearies one's patience, and, where very questionable behaviour has been added, excites at least indifference. Began to read in *King of the Commons*, but was stopped by a ludicrous cause of alarm in the non-arrival of Messrs Gunter's cooks and dinner. Sent down to them—at last to our relief they arrived. It was a ridiculous perplexity. . . .

May 15. . . . Note from Forster, complaining of my note of this morning—a little *touch of conscience*, I fancy. I answered his note.

May 20. Acted King James, in Mr White's play of *The King of the Commons* very fairly, considering all things. Was called and very warmly received. Forster came into my room to speak of some *misses* in the play.

[*This was a romantic drama on the life of King James V of Scotland. Mrs Stirling was the heroine. Ryder, Leigh Murray, Cooper, and Compton were in the cast. Its reception was tepid.*]

May 23. Saw that disgusting wretch Mr Bunn in Covent Garden!—a reflection on the world and on mankind! Bought a farewell present for my little godchild, Katie Dickens. A note from Forster with the MS. of *Œdipus* by Bulwer. What I have read I do not like—it lacks simplicity of style and picturesqueness and *reality*.

May 25. A very long note from Forster, addressed to *me* alone, making admissions and confessions of his feelings and wishing to establish a better understanding. He desires no answer, but that cannot be. I must explain to him the causes of my coolness for *his own sake*. . . .

May 26. . . . My whole morning was engrossed by writing a letter to Forster, in which I frankly, but with very considerable *reservation*, in tenderness to him, stated objectionable points in his conduct which led to estrangement between us.

May 28. Received a long letter from Forster, which, I fear, puts *reconciliation* out of the question. . . .

May 30. Exceedingly annoyed by the necessity of answering this letter of Forster's, which was a cloud of words to hide facts—busied with it. Wrote my answer to Forster, whose position with me is so much altered that it must depend upon himself whether our earlier understanding is ever restored. . . .

May 31. A note from Forster with an admission that he had been wrong, and asking me to give him back the two notes he had written to me —requesting our understanding might be restored, and asking me to go down and see Landor who was to dine with him. I answered him very kindly and cordially, enclosing him the two letters. After dinner went down to Forster's and sat with him and Landor for some time. Much talk on Milton, Shakespeare, Virgil, Horace, Homer, etc. Reconciled to Forster.

June 4 *[at Mrs Procter's ball]*.—Not very crowded or distingué. Saw . . . Browning—who did not speak to me—the *puppy!*—a dull party.

June 7. Bulwer Lytton called. I was sorry to see him so peculiar in his dress—most particularly extravagant in his attention to the costume of his face, which he makes unpicturesque and coxcomical. . . .

June 19. Acted King James better than usual, wishing my last night at the Princess's to leave a pleasing impression—as I think it did. . . . Heard news of the other houses, Drury Lane with the vaunted attraction of the ballet, acting on Monday to £31! Haymarket to £10, etc. We therefore are still high in the scale. . . .

June 25. Looked at paper. Read the detailed account of Haydon's suicide; it is most sad—most dreadful for the surviving relations, but it is a termination of a life that does not surprise me. . . .

[Benjamin Robert Haydon (1786–1846), artist: arrested for debt in 1823, he continued to be financially embarrassed throughout his life; his achievement never matched his ambition and his 'Autobiography' reveals a paranoiac tendency.]

July 13. Went to St James's theatre. Saw Rachel in the *Horaces*. Her acting in Camille was very good, but there was a deficiency of physical force, and, in consequence, her vehemence was too scolding, too cat-like in the spitting out of her reproaches. . . .

He played in the Channel Islands between 21 June and 5 August. His daughter, Cecilia Benvenuta, was born in London on 20 August. Between

23 August and 4 September he was in Manchester, and on 7 September he began two engagements at the Surrey Theatre that lasted, with a short break, until 7 November.

Manchester, August 23. Arrived at Manchester; I had my usual nervousness upon me, which is most extraordinary, most ridiculous; but so it is, the entering into a town where I am going to act, the sight of my name in the playbills on the walls affects me most unpleasantly. How strange!

August 25. . . . A Mrs — called, and wished me to hear her read Lady Macbeth. I heard her recite part of the first scene, which was indeed ridiculous; her husband, who has nothing and is living as he can, is the son of Sir —, the police magistrate, and has taken his degree of M.A. I told her it was hopeless, and as she said her husband had not had a dinner for three days, I gave her 10s.

London, October 18. White, Maclise, King, and Forster came to dinner. Forster was in one of those humours in which he displays a rude and low-bred indifference to his friends, with a general churlishness of manner that is literally offensive. It was remarked, immediately that he left the room, by White, and directly we came upstairs, by Catherine. Maclise says it is not possible to associate with him!

Forster had reason to be troubled. He had quarrelled with the proprietors of the Daily News *on a point of ethics, and Macready described his ultimate resignation (22 October) as 'most honourable'. On 8 November Macready went to Manchester (where on the 10th he read 'Macbeth' at the Mechanics' Institute), and from 23 November to 4 December he acted at the Theatre Royal in Plymouth.*

Manchester, November 8. Left home for Manchester. At the station asked for a coupé, and was told it was engaged. Whilst arranging my seat in the carriage, a person of the station came to tell me that there was one seat in the coupé unoccupied, but that 'Mathews and Vestris' had the others, and perhaps I might not like it. I laughed and said 'Certainly not', and that I was much obliged.

Plymouth, November 23. Went to rehearsal, found the company most wretched; some not arrived, and Mr Newcombe *[the manager]* utterly ignorant of his business. The rehearsal was one of the most hopeless exhibitions I have almost *ever* seen. Rested and thought on Hamlet, resolving not to let the inaccuracy and incompetency of these wretches— they are no better!—disturb me. But we began with waiting twenty minutes for Marcellus, who, when on the stage, stunk of tobacco and a public-house to *sicken* the stomach—oh!—and all this I might have avoided had I been prudent in taking care of the money I have earned. Bitter, bitter reflection! . . .

November 26. Acted King Lear—trying—but with such a company would 'sink a navy'!

November 28. Wightwick called with Mrs W— for me, and took me in a carriage to Flete, the seat of Lady Elizabeth Bulteel. I was introduced to her, admired her; really, a most engaging woman. . . . Lady Morley was with her, and Mr Courtenay also. We lunched. I went over the house, which is a monument of the feeling, taste, and talent of the deceased proprietor and builder.

December 1. Acted King Lear with much care, for I saw the old colonel [Hamilton Smith] in the boxes, who had come on purpose to see it, and I wished to give him all the pleasure I could. The house was really *awful!* Not six people beside his party in the boxes!—the rest of the house proportionate. It is hard to know what to do against the advice of persons on the spot; but I ought to have ended last night. . . .

Macready ended the year with two nights ('Hamlet' and 'Werner') at Canterbury. 'The Horatio and Marcellus were infinitely worse than the disgraceful promise of their rehearsal. . . . The weather is dreadfully cold.'

1847

With a fortnight's break during the second half of March, Macready was in the provinces between 3 January and 1 May.

Bristol, January 10. A letter from Lane to Catherine, informing her of Mrs Butler's intent to return to the stage. I am not, perhaps, qualified to judge. I hope she is right, but fear she is wrong. She is a woman of unquestionable genius, and many good qualities, but in judgment, I think, she is deficient. If she succeeds, it will be so far well for her; if she has not great success, her enemies will speak harshly of her.

Bath, January 14. Read paper; saw correspondence between *Fanny Butler* and Mr Bunn, she asking £100 per night, he declining in a letter written, of course, in *bad English*, and offering £50!

Bath, January 19. . . . . Acted Macbeth very fairly. Unluckily, cut poor Cooper's head, but not badly. . . . Before the play spoke to one of the players, Mr Swift, and apologised to him for coarse and impatient language I had used last night.

Dublin, February 1. Looked at paper, in which was an extract from a Belfast journal, that 'Miss H. Faucit, the greatest actress of the day, had left and was to be succeeded by Mr Macready, the greatest actor.' Now, certainly, if comparisons are odious, so are such classifications. . . .

Edinburgh, February 16. Read No. 5 of *Dombey and Son*, a most afflicting piece of story, but the growing ill is more deeply touching than the death of the child itself; in which the *hurry* introduced, and the too much vagueness militate against the full effect. But it is full of genius and beauty.

Greenock, February 23. . . . Two women, mother and daughter, called on me about a piece—dramatic—written in *vairse*—and made quite a scene! With difficulty I got them to go away.

Glasgow, March 7. A Mr Jeffrey, who had sent last night to ask my autograph for himself, sent his little daughter, a child, with the album of some young lady, asking its insertion there also, with a line from any dramatic poet. The leaf marked for me contained Miss H. Faucit's name, with the signature of *Helena* Faucit. A feather shows the direction of the wind. The conceit and affectation attributed to her is put beyond doubt in my mind by this little instance. I am greatly mistaken in my reasoning (which very likely I am) if real talent of any very high grade can co-exist with such want of truth and genuineness.

London, March 13. Caught a glimpse of Mrs Carlyle. Thought, talked, and consulted upon what we are to do. *America* appears our only *certain* dependence! I do not *like* it, but must make the best of it, if we cannot live here.

He began to consider 'getting our friends in committee to arrange courses of subscription nights for two seasons, the last being my farewell of the British stage, then taking two seasons in America, and settling down in Cambridge, Massachusetts'.

Birmingham, April 22. Rehearsed; very much pleased with the acting of a little dumpy dumpling-figured girl of the name of Sanders, who acts Albert. There was a truth and freshness about her that I have not seen for many a day. Acted William Tell very feebly, being much fatigued, and greatly put out by a miserably vulgar little ugly woman—like a dressed-up charwoman—whom they had put into Emma! Very much pleased with Albert.

London, May 3. . . . Letter from King, of the Dublin theatre, informing me that the theatre is smashed and Calcraft in the Marshalsea prison for debt. I should feel deep concern for him if I had not concern for myself in the loss of £150 he has unwarrantably detained—belonging to me! My old luck!

May 9. Called on Mrs Butler. . . . She gave vent a little to her over-burdened spirit, lamenting the state of the drama to which necessity had compelled her to resort. Told me that Maddox had asked her, if she could renew, to act with me . . . that she could not give him an answer before Tuesday, and that he had stated his inability to wait so long, therefore it was given up. She hoped a chance might come yet for her acceptance of his offer. She wept—what I thought, alas! were bitter tears—I fear of wounded pride and disappointment; I am truly sorry for her. . . .

May 13. White came and dined with us, and we went together to the amateur play at the St James's theatre. Saw there Landor, Mrs M. Gibson, Lord Ellesmere, Lady Essex[1] and Miss Johnstone, and Sheridan Knowles. The play, *Hernani*, translated by Lord Ellesmere, was in truth an *amateur* performance. . . . Forster was by far the best, and with a little practice would make a very respectable actor. In Mrs

[1] Catherine Stephens (1794–1882), actress and singer ('Enchanting Kitty Stephens'); in 1838 she married the 81-year-old fifth Earl of Essex who died just a year later.

Butler I saw the *proof* that I had been *most honest* and *most discriminating* in my original judgment. *She is ignorant of the very first rudiments of her art.* She is affected, monotonous, without one real impulse—never in the feeling of her character, never true in look, attitude, or tone. She can never be an actress, and this I never ventured to think before. . . .

May 14. Jenny Lind called. She is simplicity itself, and puts to shame all our actresses, or all actresses. *[Jenny Lind (1820–1887), singer, was known as 'The Swedish Nightingale'.]*

From 24 May to 18 June Macready was at the Princess's. Mrs Warner, Mrs Stirling, Ryder, and William Creswick were in the company.

May 24. . . . Acted Hamlet at Princess's theatre, very fairly; but I am growing old; my youthful vigour and elasticity—alas! where are they? . .

June 18. Acted King Lear with much care and power. . . . Jenny Lind was in one of the stage boxes, and, after the play, there was a great excitement to see her. I was called on; the audience tried to make me come on after the first act, but of course I would not think of such a thing. The enthusiasm of the audience on my taking leave was very great.

July 19. Went with Edward *[Major Edward Macready (1798–1848), Macready's brother]* to see Rachel in *Phèdre.* It was a very striking performance, all intensity; all in a spirit of vehemence and fury that made me feel a want of keeping; I could have fancied a more self-contained performance, more passionate fondness—not fury—in her love, and more pathos. I could imagine a performance exciting more pity for the character than she inspired, and equal effect in the scenes of rage and despair.

July 24. Went with Forster to Putney Heath to dine with Jerrold. He was *very glad* to see me. His family and young Blanchard, a Mr Hills, Leigh Hunt, Maclise, and the Dickenses were the party. Leigh Hunt I thought *particularly disagreeable.* Disputative and tedious—affecting great benevolence and arguing most malevolently. He is a good-tempered coxcomb—but coxcomb heart and soul—not meaning harm to any but a coxcomb.

September 9. Went to dine with Forster. Met Stanfield. Forster became very quarrelsome over his wine; so much so as to call forth the expostulatory candour of Stanfield. When I *would not* let him quarrel with me, he tried to turn on Stanfield: it is a *disease of temper in him.*

Another Princess's Theatre season lasted from 4 October to 7 December. Charlotte Cushman was now in the company. She played Lady Macbeth, Queen Katharine, and Emilia.

October 4. Acted Macbeth as well as I could after so long a respite. . . . Led on Miss Cushman, who thanked me for the civility.

October 6. Acted Othello, under the great disadvantage of Mr Cooper—an incarnation of stupidity for Iago.

October 17. Went out with Catherine to Mortlake to call on Mr and Mrs Henry Taylor; proposed to him to have *Philip van Artevelde* acted. He seemed pleased with the idea, and would consider it. He appointed to come to me with Mrs Taylor on Tuesday at seven to hear the play read.

[Macready had admired 'Philip van Artevelde' for a long time. He read Henry Taylor's dramatic poem towards the end of July 1834 and called it in his journal 'the work of a master spirit, whose politics, I fear, are strictly Tory.' Sir Henry Taylor (1800–1886) was an official of the Colonial Office; knighted in 1872. Macready 'arranged' the stage version of 'Philip van Artevelde' (the last new play in his record) with the greatest care, and it was finely mounted by Clarkson Stanfield.]

October 19. Mr and Mrs Taylor, Elliot, Mr and Mrs Spring Rice, Dickens, Stanfield, White and Forster came to the reading, Nina and Katie were present. The effect was very great. Taylor said he had no idea of such theatrical power being in the work. He assented readily to its performance.

October 21. Began the day with the business, which I expected to last for two or three hours, of preparing a copy of *Philip van Artevelde* for the theatre. I was busily, very busily, employed in it the whole day, and it is not nearly finished. H. Taylor called in the morning, and gave me some altered lines. He also read me his idea in which the second Stadt House scene should be played. Never let it be said that a poet knows best how his scenes should be acted; he knows nothing about it—at least he has no power of conveying a shadow of an idea of a meaning. I heard and—.

October 29. Acted Othello, I think, very well. Led on Miss Cushman who, according to Mr Maddox, said, *in the presence of Mr Forster*, 'He and his whole theatre might go to hell', etc. He persisted that she repeated this! Our art!

November 4. Forster dined; was sorry to hear him speak as if the long and intimate friendship between himself and Dickens was likely to terminate or very much relax. They have both faults with their good qualities, but they have been *too* familiar. I hope Dickens is not capricious—not spoiled; he has, however, great excuse.

November 5. It is very wrong—very wrong—to suffer my temper to be thus affected, but even now I am suffering from the excitement of disgust and indignation into which this wretched Jew [Maddox] has thrown me. But I will meet him with the most studious silence and cut short any future attempt at conversation. This fellow, among other things, admitted—'*You* wished to do things well, *I* wish to get money.'

November 17. Acted Cardinal Wolsey, as I thought very well, to a very insensible audience. Am I deteriorating as I grow older? . . .

November 19. Acted Cardinal Richelieu. . . . Maddox—pah!—and Forster came into my room. The person who should have played Marion de Lorme fell down—*as they said*—in a state of intoxication after her first speech. A Mrs Selby dressed, and read the scene after long delay.

November 20. Rehearsed *Philip van Artevelde*, but was afraid to exert myself on account of my throat. I do not know what to think. There are people of absolute danger; Father John; the Pape; Van Æswyn, if not very careful; and Adriana is very bad, unmeaning, and dull. There is no disguising this, and where is there help? But I must now do my best, and hope, and trust. God speed me well.

November 22. Production of *Van Artevelde*. . . . Failed; I cannot think it my fault. Called for, of course. Forster, Dickens, Stanfield, Maclise, Spring Rice and his brother came into my room. I am very unhappy; I wish I were dead! My toil and life are thrown away. My disappointment was very severe, and I saw so much that might have grown out of its success for ever gone from me. I certainly laboured more than my due in regard to the whole play, and much of my own part of van Artevelde I acted well; but the play was so under-acted by the people engaged in it that it broke down under their weight.

[The play, which presented eloquently the revolt of Ghent against the Lords of Flanders, was poorly acted by most of the principals except Macready himself and John Ryder (van den Bosch). Among the other names were John Cooper, James Vining, Susan Cushman (sister of Charlotte) as Clara, and Emmeline Montagu as an Adriana of whom Macready, in later life, said to Lady Pollock: 'In her timid confession of love, [she] bellowed it out so that the boards shook with it. Was it not difficult to cherish her for this?' ('Macready As I Knew Him'). Susan Cushman had her moment of fame on the English stage when , in 1845–1846, she acted Juliet to her sister's Romeo at the Haymarket and elsewhere.]

November 23. Rose very late, having passed a sleepless and uncomfortable night. Saw the papers, which—I should instance *The Times* and *Chronicle* as especially disgusting—did not raise my spirits; but I soon looked matters directly in the face. A very sweet letter from dear Dickens, which was much to compensate me for the injustice of the papers ['I never saw you more gallant and free than in the gallant and free scenes last night; it was perfectly captivating to behold you']. . . . A very cordial letter of thanks from Henry Taylor.

November 24. Very affectionate note from Forster. Answered it briefly. . . . Acted Philip van Artevelde ten times better than the last night. . . .

November 30. Henry Taylor came and talked about the play. I was obliged to tell him of my fears. I paid him £100—of which Mr Maddox had paid me £50. . . . Read the December No. of *Dombey and Son*, which I did not like. I thought it obscure and heavy. Maddox called, and expressed with great fairness his necessity of closing *Philip van Artevelde's* career on Friday. Alas! Alas! Forster called, too ill to dine. Knowles dined. . . .

December 5. Dickens and Charley came in, and sat long. I fear dear Dickens called to ascertain our feeling about the last number of *Dombey*. I could not speak as I wished, and therefore did not allude to it.

On 7 December he played Henry IV's death scene at a Covent Garden performance for the purchase of Shakespeare's Birthplace. It must have meant something to be back for a few hours at the Garden (now an opera house) to talk with Willmott, and to meet such players from his past as Mrs Warner, Priscilla Horton (Mrs German Reed), Webster, Keeley, Phelps (now at Sadler's Wells), Charles Mathews and Madame Vestris, Mrs Glover, Mrs Nisbett (now Lady Boothby), Helen Faucit, Mrs Stirling. One player, whose name Macready omitted, was Fanny Kemble Butler; after Queen Katharine's death scene she was too emotionally upset to take her call. His scene came first, with Leigh Murray, from the Princess's, as Hal.

December 7. Went to Covent Garden theatre. . . . I told [Willmott] I had decided on quitting the stage. He thought I was quite right in such a judgment. . . . Acted King Henry IV not well—chilled by the audience and the vast expanse which separated me from the people. Called. Sent to inquire if Miss H. Faucit was dressed. She was not. Lady Boothby [Mrs Nisbett] wished to see me. She came into my room, and we had a little talk. She is a warm-hearted creature, whom I like very much. . . .

December 12. Looked through *The Cenci* [Shelley] as a matter of form The *idea* of acting such a monstrous crime, beautiful as the work is! . . .

December 18. . . . Mr Robinson, a pert young man, called to ask me what he ought to do in going on the stage. I told him to go off it!

December 23. A Mr Beaumont called, an acquaintance of the late

Dr Sleath, to impose a play upon me to read! I gave him very broad hints that it was a heavy draft upon my time, but he was insensible to any thought but his own convenience and wish, and left his play. *[Later]* Looked over Mr Beaumont's *Maccabee;* found it *trash;* folded it up and addressed it with a note to him.

December 25. Interchanged with all my dear family the wishes belonging, of usage, to this dear day. Fox and Forster came to dinner and we passed a very pleasant evening. The children repeated Milton's Ode to the Nativity. We had a game at whist. My heart is thankful.

1848

Until the middle of February Macready was in the provinces. A Princess's Theatre engagement lasted from 21 February to 14 April, now with Fanny Kemble Butler as leading lady: the post had been declined by the American actress, Anna Cora Mowatt (1819–1870, also author of the social comedy, 'Fashion', 1845.)

Bath, January 4. Looked at *The Times*. Read a most encomiastic notice of Mr Brooke's performance of Othello *[at the Olympic, London]*. I have seen this actor, and can most *purely* and truly say his acting warrants no such praise; he has no pretensions to genius, judgment, taste, or any artistic quality. He has physical advantages, but a most common mind, and no real passion. . . . *[Gustavus Vaughan Brooke (1818–1866); drowned in the wreck of the steamship 'London' in the Bay of Biscay when bound for Australia. Helen Faucit said of him: 'He was a very fair actor; some thought a very good one; but never could be distinguished in his art because of his want of true dramatic instinct and imagination.']*

Sheffield, January 18. Sat down to ruminate thoroughly on the plays to be done at the Princess's. . . . Turned to Shakespeare, considered *Timon*, suggested by Forster, which could not be made interesting on the stage, in my opinion. Thought of *King Richard II*, went over the part, thought it promised the best of all. My age is an objection that I must encounter, and may overcome, by truth and passion. Read the play, and became confirmed in my opinion and settled in resolution, if Mr Maddox will do anything for it.

Manchester, January 22. A Miss——, the person who rehearsed Regan, called here in a cab about ten o'clock, and detained me until I quite lost my patience and had the greatest difficulty not to show it. She came about a statement made, as she said, by Mr Beverly the manager that she was put out of Mrs Oakly *[in The Jealous Wife]* because I thought her so detestable in Regan! I directly and emphatically contradicted her assertion about ten times. The fact was, I was contented with her in Regan, and understood she was to rehearse Mrs Oakly to see if she could do it. Afterwards Mr Beverly said she had relinquished it, and Mrs Weston was to do it. The woman appeared to me *excited*, and went on with such unconnected rigmarole that I really could not bear it. I certainly do not think her 'better than she should be', as they say.

January 26. Read the paper. In it I perceived the advertisement of the Olympic theatre in which the lessee, Mr Davidson, announces Mr G. V. Brooke as 'the greatest living tragedian'. This is another evidence of the puppet-show condition to which the London theatres have descended!

London, February 19. Rehearsed Macbeth, Mrs Butler the Lady Macbeth. I have never seen any one so bad, so unnatural, so affected, so conceited. She alters the stage arrangements without the slightest ceremony, and, in fact, proceeds not only *en grande artiste*, but *en grande reine*. She is *disagreeable*, but her pride will have a yet deeper fall, I feel confident. . . .

[One could hardly have expected Macready and Fanny Kemble Butler to work in harmony. She wrote dolefully to Harriet St Leger during the season: 'He growls and prowls and roams and foams around the stage, in every direction, like a tiger in his cage, so that I never know which side of me he means to be, and keeps up a perpetual snarling and grumbling so that I never feel sure that he "has done" and that it is my turn to speak.' As for Macready's blank-verse method: 'What is called the "natural" style in speaking blank verse is simply chopping it up into prose. . . . It demands the same care and method that music does.']

February 21. Acted Macbeth, I *think*, with peculiar strength, care, and effect; was occasionally disconcerted by this monstrous pretender to theatrical art, who to me is most unnatural and bad. . . .

February 22. Went to rehearsal of *King Henry VIII*. Mrs Butler was weeping at the scene of Wolsey. She is living in an atmosphere of self-delusion. There is nothing genuine in her, poor woman! . . .

February 23. Acted Cardinal Wolsey with great care. Mrs Butler was the Queen, and C. Kemble in the stalls knocked so loud and often with his stick—often almost *alone*—that the people called '*Turn him out!*'

February 24. Mrs Butler's rehearsal of Desdemona struck me as a very correct and forcible conception of that beautiful character, and if she would give herself up to the study of execution, she might yet become a very fine actress. Her *intention*, which is admirable, is seen in her acting the part; but her affected voice, her leaning her head, her walk, etc., so many affectations prevent her from *being Desdemona*.

February 25. Acted Othello with all the strength I had, and, I think, *well*. Called and led on Mrs Butler. News of the abdication of *Fagin*—Louis Philippe. . . .

March 3. Birthday, *æt.* fifty-five. Acted King Lear in my best manner which was appreciated by the audience. . . .

March 17. Acted King Lear very fairly. Spoke to Mrs Butler, *who is a very indifferent actress to be placed in a prominent position.*

From 24 April to 8 May he acted at the Marylebone Theatre (in Church Street, Marylebone), managed by Mrs Warner. On the night of the 24th, after his Hamlet, she came into his room and gave him from the managers a cheque for £300.

April 26. Letter from Mrs P. Butler, acquainting me with her inability to act on the Siddons Monument night, in consequence of a summons to appear on the 5th of June to answer a suit of divorce brought against her by Pierce Butler on the ground of 'desertion'. I was truly sorry to read it. Faults on both sides would have made mutual forgiveness 'wisest, discreetest, best.' Walked to theatre. Rehearsed Macbeth. Mr Ryder called, and expressed his unqualified readiness and willingness to accompany me to the United States on the understanding that it was a 'speculation' on his part, etc.

He had some provincial engagements, including Chester (18 May) 'where at sixteen I took charge of a company nearly all three weeks in arrear.'

London, May 21. . . . Called on poor Dow. Saw his wife, her brother, and three of Dow's children—tenanting a second floor in Norfolk Street. He keeps his bed. He was very glad to see me—was much changed, his face swollen, his eyes and mouth swollen—alas! a stranded vessel! He wished to die in peace and to have a perfect understanding with all men, particularly his old friends. I assured him that no feeling had ever existed in my mind at variance with him—explained to him how *he had* estranged himself from us, etc. . . . Going out, I spoke to Mrs Dow, who told me [Dr] Elliotson had said she must not encourage any hope! I inquired of her about their pecuniary circumstances, and her tears answered me. . . . It rained as I came out, and I took a cab home. Wrote a note to Mrs Dow, expressive of my concern for her, and enclosing her a cheque for £20, begging her to accept it, as most agreeably to her—as a loan, or a gift to the children. Sent it by Lester. . . . Note of warm acknowledgment from Mrs Dow.

June 3. . . . Went with Catherine and Willie to the opera, Mr Lumley having obligingly sent us a box. Jenny Lind sang and acted Lucia with wonderful power and sweetness, but the *thing*—the opera, as an amusement, is such a revolting absurdity that I cannot reconcile myself to it.

June 9. Note from Forster, who I fear is not in the best temper with me; if at all in an ill one it is *most unreasonably* that he is so. Went to Sir John Soane's house[1] or museum, a quaint piece of coxcombry and gimcrackery, absurd I think to be left as it is, alone, for it is scarcely worth the trouble of *going* to see. The sarcophagus of Belzoni ought to be in the British Museum; the Hogarths, Canalettos, the Sir Joshua, and Lawrence's portrait of Soane should be in the National Gallery.

June 29. Dined with Dickens—meeting Mrs Crowe *[Catherine Crowe, 1800–1876, writer]*, Mr and Mrs Muspratt (late Miss S. Cushman),[2] Hillard *[George S. Hillard, American man of letters]*, Mr and Mrs Stanfield, and Forster, whose insolent coldness and supercilious bearing were too much for my patience. I returned his behaviour by not noticing him through the whole evening. I had put one letter into his hand, as I placed another in Dickens's. I would not take a paper from a servant as he took mine from me! He spoke to me at the end of the evening, because he saw that he had carried his impertinence too far. I answered very coldly. I had a note from Dickens in the course of the day with one from Miss [Charlotte] Cushman, very cavalierly *consenting* to act Queen Katharine, if her expenses were paid. I answered that I would willingly dispense with such aid.

[Macready was moved to protest at the rowdily discourteous reception of a French company at Drury Lane. The play, Dumas's 'Monte Cristo', 'a grand drama in ten acts and eleven tableaux', was designed to occupy two evenings as performed by the Théâtre Historique, from Paris, under M. Hostein. Several members of the British stage—including Charles Kean, Webster, Buckstone, Charles Mathews, Farren, Harley, and others— objected strongly; and on the first night an anti-French faction in the audience made so sustained a din for three hours that barely a word was audible. Macready, in a letter to the French company, regretted the 'disreputable proceedings', whereupon Webster, Charles Kean, Mathews, and the rest immediately protested to him through a solicitor. Macready returned an unwavering and dignified reply, and that was that. The play, having been shouted down through two nights at Drury Lane, did get a hearing, but with no kind of success, when Mitchell put on the company at the St James's. In spite of this storm in a teacup, several leaders of the stage rallied to Macready's benefit, a Royal Command performance at the Lane on 10 July.]

[1] Sir John Soane (1753–1837), architect, presented his house in Lincoln's Inn Fields, and his art treasures, to the nation.
[2] Susan Cushman's first husband, an American, having deserted her, she married Muspratt, an Englishman, in 1848.

July 10 *[the performance commanded by the Queen, and for Macready's benefit, before his departure for America: the first three acts of 'Henry VIII' followed by 'The Jealous Wife'].* Called for Dickens, with whom I went down in the carriage to Drury Lane theatre. . . . Dickens was very active all day, answered letters for me, and took on himself various arrangements. He was the acting manager; the play was very respectably set upon the stage. I lent Mr Phelps my dress for King Henry VIII. Rehearsed two pieces: saw Braham *[who had come from retirement to sing the National Anthem]*, Knowles, Forster—who asked me 'in what he had offended me'; I told him that the stage was no place for such a subject. He was very active through the day. Rested. Requested Forster to apply for seven or eight policemen in plain clothes to be placed in the pit, which he fortunately did. On going on the stage, indeed, as it appeared from the beginning of the anthem, an organised disturbance, similar to that got up for the expulsion of the French actors, was violently persisted in by a few persons in the pit and galleries. My reception was very great, and the house, with Her Majesty and the Prince in state, was most brilliant. Noise continued through the scene, and in the next, wishing to ascertain the nature of the disturbance, I sent to ask leave to address the audience. The Queen granted it, and I told the galleries that, under-standing they were incommoded for want of room, I had to assure them that, happy as I had been in receiving favours from them for many years, they would now add to their obligations by receiving their money and leaving the theatre. Applause, but not tranquillity, ensued, and it was only in the banquet scene that the play *[Henry VIII]* began to be heard. I took great pains, both in Cardinal Wolsey and in Mr Oakly. The Queen left at the end of *The Jealous Wife*, and I was called on and most warmly greeted.

[Phelps was Henry VIII; Charlotte Cushman, Katharine; Mrs Warner, Mrs Oakly. On the playbill were Mrs Nisbett, Priscilla Horton, Mrs Stirling, Miss Rainforth, Hudson, Ryder, Willmott, and several more from past years.]

July 11. . . . Received a printed letter addressed to the members of the theatrical profession inciting them against me—another evidence of the unprincipled character of this rascally class!

July 15. Note from Ransom *[Macready's banker]*, informing me that £489 3s 6d had been paid to my account by my committee. No account of the house yet sent me!

July 22. Letter from Thackeray, sending me the copy of *Vanity Fair* he had promised me, with the inscription on the leaf—presented 'to Mrs Macready.' I am not satisfied of his sincerity towards me.

July 23. Displeased with Thackeray's behaviour, which may have no purpose in it, though I think it has. Dickens called; he told me the receipts at Drury Lane, before the people took back their money, was above £1200—above £90 was returned.

July 24 [*Trafalgar Hotel, Greenwich*]. Stanfield, Maclise, Mr and Mrs Horace Twiss arrived; then Mr and Mrs Dickens, Miss Hogarth and Catherine, and Troughton, and we sat down to one of those peculiar English banquets, a whitebait dinner. [*Also in the party were White; John Kenyon (1784–1856), the 'littérateur' and friend of the Brownings; Hillard, and another American named Silliman ('a very agreeable man,' said Macready, 'whom I had met at dinner in New York').*] We were all very cheerful—very gay; all unbent, and without ever forgetting the respect due to each other; all was mirth unrestrained, and delighted gaiety. Songs were sung in rapid succession, and jests flung about from each part of the table. Choruses broke out, and the reins were flung over the necks of the merry set. After 'Auld Lang Syne', sung by all, Catherine giving the solos, we returned home in our hired carriage and an omnibus, hired for the nonce, Kenyon and I on the box of the carriage. A very happy day.

Between 30 July and 14 August Macready had engagements at Swansea, Bristol, Birmingham, and Hull.

Hull, August 13. Read on my journey ninety pages of *The Princess* [*Tennyson's new poem*]. I cannot say that I hold a very high opinion of it—it seems in its language such *determined* poetry that peculiarity of phrase seems sought for or excogitated.

London, August 26. Wrote to Forster, offering to shake hands with him before I go. . . .

August 27. Note from Forster saying he would come up, but that he was 'unconscious of the cause' of my displeasure. I wish he would be more ingenuous for his own sake; because if there was no cause, I had done him an *unpardonable wrong;* but however—Forster called—we were friends—and we sat. . . .

September 1. . . . Went with Catherine and four eldest children to Elstree; enjoyed the ride with them, the beauty of the country, the recollection of every house and tree, the wandering over and through our old house, Elm Place, where so many of our children were born; walked through the neglected grounds and marked the shrubs and trees, now grown very high, that I had planted. . . . Every step was a memory.

To Liverpool, September 6. Our dinner was a very silent, very mournful one; no one seemed disposed or able to talk, and tears stole down the cheeks of several of us. . . . Went to station with Catherine, Willie, and Edward. Deceived by the railway guide, were *an hour* before the time. Dickens and Forster came and remained with us. . . . Reached Liverpool late.

Liverpool, September 7. Acted Cardinal Wolsey and Mr Oakly tolerably well to a very good house, which was surprising to me when I heard that Jenny Lind was singing in St George's Hall! . . . Took leave of Mrs Warner, saw Mr Simpson. . . .

September 9. Set sail for America.

Macready, in the Arcadia, *with John Ryder, reached Boston on 24 September. He had soon the pleasure of greeting old acquaintances—the Longfellows among them—and of making new ones: Charles Eliot Norton (1827–1909, biographer and critic); Oliver Wendell Holmes (1809–1894, essayist, novelist, and poet; at this time he was Professor of Anatomy and Physiology at Harvard and had written little). But he was aware also of opposition, of the malice with which a newspaper spoke of the 'independence' of Forrest in hissing him at Edinburgh. Though he had come with a belief in the American mode of life, affection for his friends, and a wish to make a home for himself and his children, doubts clouded him: the projected house at Cambridge began to fade. He opened in New York on 4 October with* Macbeth.

New York, October 12. Acted Hamlet *[at the Astor Place Opera House]* not without some uncertainty as to whether some friends of Forrest might not be in the theatre on purpose to give colour by their disapprobation to the 'justice' of his outrageous conduct in hissing me for my illustration of the 'idle' assumption of Hamlet on the King's approach; but there was spontaneous applause, and after a short interval, as if it were remembered that this must have been the point of Mr Forrest's exception, another confirmatory round. I was very much cut up in the play, but made the best fight I could. Called at the end.

October 16. Acted Brutus with great care and energy, but I fancy the '*gentle*' Brutus was utterly misunderstood or fell flat upon the audience, who were ravished with the bawling and rant of Mr G. Vandenhoff, whom they called on at the end of the *third* Act!!! They allowed the play to finish, and I really would not let disgust have any influence upon me, but played my best to the end, and took no notice whatever of myself. . . .
[George Vandenhoff, 1813–1885, actor, John Vandenhoff's son, had last

acted with Macready in Philadelphia in 1843. In 'An Actor's Note-book; or, The Green-room and Stage' (1860) he saw Macready as a harsh egotist, a man who excelled in executive power and certainty of effect, not in imagination or poetic feeling.]

He was acting in Boston from 30 October and Philadelphia (Arch Street Theatre) from 20 November.

November 2. . . . Acted Othello as well as I could with my indisposition on me, and a Desdemona of 50, patched up to 45.

November 4. On this day, henceforward marked as one of my most sad anniversaries, my beloved brother, the playfellow of my boyhood, the cherished *protégé* and pupil of my youth, the friend of my life, Edward Nevill Macready, died.

November 8. . . . *I will not live in America*—rather, if I *live to leave it, I will not return to die here—I will not.* . . . Acted King Lear, with a Goneril—perhaps sober, but acting the distressful!—with a Cordelia talking nonsense, haggard and old as Tisiphone, and affecting the timid; a Fool singing *horribly out of tune*, but by far the best of the bunch; that great lout, Mr Ryder, as bad as the worst of them. I acted *against* it all, striving to keep my self-possession, and I acted well. The curtain fell, and the audience, who would have cheered on a thick-headed, thick-legged *brute* like Mr Forrest, took no notice of this, my best performance. This is the civilisation—the growing *taste* of the United States!

Philadelphia, November 18. Met Mr Forrest walking with some person. He bowed to Gould, who saluted him; I did not look towards him. I had been telling Gould before that I should not speak to him if I saw him, and that I should decline any offer to meet him, as that would be to acquit him of the unworthy and ungentlemanlike conduct he has displayed to me.

November 20. Acted Macbeth. Before the play Mr Ryder came to inform me there would be a disturbance. I would take no stimulant; had fortunately eaten a light dinner, conscious of having done nothing even questionable. I was prepared. I heard great shouting at Mr Ryder, who was evidently mistaken by the deputed rioters for myself. Went on, and applause, with the hissing, coarse noises, etc., of the ruffians there, attended my entry. I received it unmoved, and went on braving it. It continued, growing more and more faint through the scenes, the rioters, sometimes well informed, trying to interrupt the more effective parts of the performance, but becoming gradually subdued until applause roused them again. They were sufficiently quiet before the end of the first act. They heard the dagger soliloquy, manifestly enrapt, and the applause was a genuine burst, but of course again a signal for the ruffian blackguards assembled. The murder went triumphantly, and the second act ended as having stilled them. I went through cheeringly and defyingly, pointing at the scoundrels such passages as 'I dare do all,' etc. The third act had also evidently a strong hold upon them; in the early part a copper cent was thrown at me, missing me, which particularly excited the indignation of the audience, and when I went on a bouquet was thrown to me. I mention all I can recollect. The fourth act passed smoothly after my entrance. In the fifth act, as if the scoundrels were aware that it was a strong point for me, they began with more than their primary violence of noise and outrage. A rotten egg was thrown on the stage. I went in active and cheerful defiance through it, though injured in the more touching and delicate effects, and in the last scene threw all my heart into the contest, and wound up with great effect. The majority—the large majority—of the audience were enthusiastic in their demonstrations of sympathy with me, and of indignation against these ruffians. I was called, and I went on—of course, the tumult of applause and the attempts of those wretches was very great—I stood to be heard, and that for a long time, touched and moved at first by the genial and generous warmth of the bulk of the audience. . . .

When he could speak, he said simply that he had been warned of possible organised opposition, that he had confidence in American good feeling, and that he was sure they would not sanction gross injustice. Somebody shouted 'Nine cheers for Macready'! Three or four feebler ones were raised for Edwin Forrest. Macready went on to deny that he had shown hostility to an American actor in England. But that actor had hissed him in a public theatre, something he felt no American would condone. He retired among fervent cheering; the Recorder of Philadelphia came round to say that he would walk home with him as a bodyguard; and they parted late, at Macready's hotel.

Forrest had opened at the Walnut Street Theatre in the same play on the same evening and continued these tactics. 'A week of theatrical rivalry' said the 'Public Ledger'; 'Macready has to contend with age, Forrest is in the prime of a vigorous and robust manhood.'

Thunder accompanied the rest of the engagement, which closed on 2 December. On 22 November Edwin Forrest published in the 'Philadelphia Public Ledger' a so-called 'Card' in which he agreed that he had hissed Macready, and that he had openly avowed it. He averred that Macready, moved by jealous fear, had suborned the English Press against him—notably Forster, 'a "toady" of the eminent tragedian'—and that in consequence he had been hissed upon the London stage before his own action in Edinburgh. He denied having helped to raise 'an organised opposition' in America. His advice was to do nothing—merely to 'let the superannuated driveller alone'.

November 22. . . . Went on the stage to the most hearty reception—cheers on cheers; *one* miserable Forrester '*tried it on*' in the middle of the pit with some call about Forrest, but he was *submerged*, actually drowned, and never came up again. I acted Othello under great disadvantages—uneasy—off my balance—abroad; but I tried to do my best, and got through tolerably. Was called, and most enthusiastically greeted.

December 1. Papers, with a most offensive notice in the *Ledger*, mixing up that ruffian and myself, and suggesting 'the street, the field, the town-court or the newspapers' as the best arenas for our squabblings or fights. . . .

December 2. Acted Hamlet with care and energy; took especial pains to make the meaning of '*I must be idle*' clear, which was followed by cheers on cheers after the first applause, when it was understood by the house that this was Mr Forrest's '*fancy dance*'. Oh, fie! fie! The play went off triumphantly. I said, 'Ladies and Gentlemen. . . . The remembrance of my visit here will always be companied with the ready testimony of my gratitude for the truly noble and generous earnestness with which you have defended me, a stranger, from the grossest outrage, the grossest injustice'. . . .

Yet Macready had less sympathy than he had hoped. Forrest was a valued national figure, a brother-democrat, while Macready was one of what an attacker would call 'the codfish aristocracy'. On 3 December he left Philadelphia for New York where he spent a week and gave two Shakespeare readings. On 9 December he went to Baltimore. There he stayed only a week instead of the expected fortnight because Forrest had gone down as well and—using the technique employed in Philadelphia—put on at the Holiday Street Theatre the plays that Macready was presenting at the Front Street.

Baltimore, December 12. Looked at the Baltimore papers, speaking of the performances last night *[Macbeth]* in terms of equal general praise, or perhaps implying the superiority of Mr Forrest. People here—my friends—talk of the victory I have obtained, the triumph I have won! Victory! over what or whom? A large portion of the American public, the more intelligent and gentleman-like, have been shocked and ashamed at Mr Forrest's 'card', written in the worst taste, and convicting himself of falsehood in one or two particulars—and they believe that I am true, or for the most part so. A large portion—the democrat party—crowd to see him at the theatre, cheer him in the most tumultuous and pointed manner, calling forth his thanks for their 'support', etc., and the papers speak of him in the same admiration and respect that they would of a real artist, and a real gentleman! And I am to live in this country! Rested. Acted Cardinal Richelieu with pains and effect. A rascal in the pit set up a yell at the end of the loud applause in the first act, and there was some disturbance with him in the third—they said he was removed. Was called, and some person proposed three cheers, which they gave. I am grown insensible.

Richmond, December 20. Acted Hamlet—taking much pains, and, as I thought, acting well; but the audience testified neither sensibility nor enthusiasm, and I suppose it is either not good, or 'caviare to the general'. They gave me the skull, for Yorick's, of a negro who was hung two years ago for cutting down his overseer.

On 31 December he wrote: 'A year of awful, stirring, fearful and afflicting events is this day brought to a close.'

1849

Macready's principal engagements during the first four months of 1849 included the last three weeks of January in Charleston (he delayed his departure to New Orleans because of a cholera epidemic there); then four weeks in New Orleans, to the middle of March, and—after a river voyage— 2 to 14 April at Cincinnati, and 16 to 21 April at Louisville. On 28 April he was in New York.

Richmond, January 4. . . . For the first time I saw in the glass today that I really am an old man. My mind does not feel old. . . .

Charleston, January 15. Looked at paper, in which it is observed that 'some people think the Hamlet of Vandenhoff senior superior to Macready's.' What ignorant and what conceited dunces in literature and art these people are! It is the fact! Rehearsed. Oh, the company!

Griffin, February 2. Resumed the reading of that delightful book, Thackeray's *Vanity Fair*. It has surprised and *conquered me*.

Montgomery, February 3. Finished, with great reluctance, *Vanity Fair*. The story hangs a little after the death of Osborne; and the tour on the Continent, I think, might have been spared with advantage. Dobbin's return to Ostend is very good, as is his going away; but Becky is, to say the least, quite enough on the scene, and Jos is rather a bore; the Pumpernickel set are stupid. But the book is an extraordinarily clever one, and, differing in its kind, is second to none of the present day, which is an admission I make almost grudgingly for Dickens's sake; but the truth is the truth.

New Orleans, February 19. Acted Virginius; miserably cut up by almost all parties, but an old, ugly, and very affected Virginia is in itself such utter damnation of the play that I need not enumerate the attendant imps on this monstrous piece of diabolism.

March 3. Kept my birthday (*æt.* fifty-six) in sympathy with the dear ones at home, and drank their healths in a small glass of hock, full to 'the highest top-sparkle'. God bless them. Acted Henry IV, Joseph Surface, very fairly.

March 7. Acted Cardinal Richelieu! not to my satisfaction, being greatly disconcerted by—what?—Ha! upon how small a thing the success of an actor's perfect identification depends—upon my beard being loose, and torturing me for four acts with the fear of its dropping off!

March 10 *[Last night at New Orleans]*. Acted Hamlet (with an out-wearied body, but a mind and heart determined to *win or die*) in a most superior manner, in one of my *happiest* moods, though sorely tried by physical debility, but the *spirit* was *indomitable*. Called. Went forward and addressed the crowded audience, who had purchased their seats by *their own suggestion at auction*.

March 11. . . . Now if I die, I leave my family £20,000, besides my furniture, plate, prints, etc. Thank God! thank God! thank God!

Macready left by river-steamer on 22 March.

March 24. Mr Clay, or Henry Clay as he is called, came on board last night at Natchez, but was not at the breakfast-table. I went to my old study under the wheel, and saw the shores, the boats, the flat-boats, and all the life of this great watery world as I raised my eyes occasionally from the interesting life of that master of stupidity and crime, King James II *[in Macaulay's history]*. . . . Mr Clay came to the upper deck, and sat with me some time. He is much, much older than five years ago. Came to Vicksburg, a town pushing itself into life and note. Some of the inhabitants, rustic-looking men, came on board to pay their respects to Mr Clay, and some guns were fired on shore in compliment to him.

March 26. Rose in good time to see the city—all towns are cities here —of Memphis; like all the rest of these spick-and-span new places, industry and energy observable everywhere. . . . Walked on upper deck, pleased with the pink blossom of the red-bud, profusely growing in some of the woods.

Louisville, March 29 *[Having spent a night at Louisville, he changed boats]*. . . . Went on board the steam-boat *Benjamin Franklin*, a very large, handsome boat, the interior decorated in Gothic arches the whole length and very elegantly arranged, but more cramped than the *Peytona*, and much more unpleasant motion. . . . Went early to bed, but something in the machinery had given way, and after blundering and botching and creeping along and stopping, we at last made a *wait* of about three hours at Madison. I was awoke by the jerking of the engine as we resumed our course, and getting up, half-dressed, lay down again, but to a very uncomfortable night.

Cincinnati, April 2 *[having arrived on 30 March]*. Went to rehearsal. Found a most disgracefully imperfect Horatio, who had rehearsed on Saturday and now knew nothing of words or business, one of those wretches who take to the stage as an escape from labour, and for whom the treadmill would be a fitting punishment. Rested. Acted Hamlet to a rather rickety audience, but I tried my utmost, and engaged the attention of at least the greater part of the auditory. In the scene after the play, with Rosencrantz and Guildenstern, an occurrence took place that, for disgusting brutality, indecent outrage, and malevolent barbarism, must be without parallel in the theatre of any civilised community. Whilst speaking to them about 'the pipe', a ruffian from the left side gallery threw into the middle of the stage the half of the raw carcase of a sheep! Of course, there is no commenting on such sheer brutality. The audience were, of course, indignant, and when I came on in the closet scene, quite stopped the play with their prolonged and vehement applause. I felt for them; and I feel for humanity in the degrading circumstance. Was called and went on, and, bowing, came off.

April 11. Especially disgusted by a reference in a New York paper which discusses the *possibility* of certain friends of mine and this black-guard Forrest making the occasion of my appearance a signal for conflict! Are not the vulgar wretches, the stupid, unprincipled dolts of this country, enough to drive a wise man mad! . . . Walked in the streets with Mr Ryder. We went into three or four book-shops, and I was struck with the coarse, rude manner in which, in all of them, the people there answered our civil questions. . . .

April 13. Telegraph from Gould, informing me of Mr Forrest being engaged at the Broadway, opening on 23rd. So that it is now apparent all this villainous proceeding on his part has been to get up an excitement in the hope it will draw money to him! *My God!*

New York, April 28. Dined with the Coldens. Went with them after-wards to Mrs Butler's Reading of *King Henry VIII*, which was *too bad—I could not stay*. . . .

April 30. Read paper in which Mr Forrest's 'repudiation' of his wife without cause assigned, and with the admission of her unimpeached character, and having borne him four children, is stated merely in its native fact, and in terms much more complimentary to him than other-wise. The tenderness of the American Press towards that scoundrel is an uncontradictable evidence of its rascality and baseness.

May 2. Looked at paper—*New York Herald*. One is as good as another! An article headed with that disgusting beginning, *Forrest and Macready*. It is really too bad. . . .

[Macready's New York season was to be at the Astor Place Opera House. The Astor Place, which had a life of not much more than six years, was opened in 1847 and named after John Jacob Astor who developed the neighbourhood. It held 1,800 people. For Macready's season it was leased

by Colonel William Niblo (the proprietor of New York's popular Niblo's Garden) and James Henry Hackett (1800–1871), the American character actor, celebrated Falstaff, and father of the romantic and Shakespearean actor, James K. Hackett (1869–1926). In the cast of 'Macbeth', besides Macready, were Mrs Coleman Pope as Lady Macbeth, Mr Wemyss as Duncan, and William Chippendale (manager) and John Sefton (stage director) as two of the Witches. Macduff, usually acted by Ryder, was the American C. W. Clarke, brought in by Macready for one night in an effort to temper the anti-British feeling. On that night of 7 May there were three Macbeths in New York, for Thomas Sowerby Hamblin (1800–1853) had also decided to play the part at the Bowery Theatre; Ryder went down to appear as Hamblin's Macduff.]

Forrest, who had begun a season at the Broadway Theatre on 23 April, announced Macbeth *for the night of 7 May when his rival was due to open at the Astor Place Opera House in the same part. Macready went resolutely forward.*

May 7. Rehearsed with much care. . . . Rested. Went to [Astor Place] theatre, dressed. My hairdresser told me there would be a good house, for there was—an unusual sight—a great crowd outside. My call came; I heard immense applause and three cheers for Mr [C. W.] Clarke in Macduff*[In the acting version used by Macready, Macduff spoke Ross's lines in Act I, scene ii.]*. I smiled and said to myself, 'They mistake him for me.' I went on—the greatest applause, as it seemed, from the whole house. I bowed respectfully, repeatedly. It still kept on. I bowed as it were emphatically (to coin an expression for a bow), rather significantly that I was touched by such a demonstration; it continued. I thought, 'This is becoming too much'. It did not cease, and I began to distinguish howlings from the right corner of the parquette. Still, I thought, it is only like the Western shriek—a climax of their applause. At length I became sensible there was opposition, and that the prolongation of the applause was the struggle against it; I then waited for its subsidence, but no cessation; I at last walked forward to address them, intending to say—'I felt pain and shame, which the intelligent and respectable must feel for their country's reputation, and that I would instantly resign my engagement rather than encounter such disgraceful conduct.' They would not let me speak. They hung out placards—'You have been proved a liar', etc.; flung a rotten egg close to me. I pointed it to the audience and smiled with contempt, persisting in my endeavour to be heard. I could not have been less than a quarter of an hour on the stage altogether, with perfect sangfroid and good-humour reposing in the consciousness of my own truth. At last there was nothing for it, and I said 'Go on', and the play, *Macbeth*, proceeded in dumb show. I hurrying the players on. Copper cents were thrown, some struck me, four or five eggs, a great many apples, nearly—if not quite—a peck of potatoes, lemons, pieces of wood, a bottle of asafoetida which splashed my own dress, smelling, of course, most horribly. The first act, at least in my scenes, with these accompaniments, passed in dumb show; I looking directly at these men as they committed these outrages, and no way moved by them. Behind the scenes some attempted to exhibit sympathy which I received very loftily, observing, 'My concern was for the disgrace such people inflicted on the character of the country'. The second act closed in exactly the same way. I dressed for the third and went on; the tumult was the same, the missiles growing thicker. At last a chair was thrown from the gallery on the stage, something heavy was thrown into the orchestra (a chair) which made the remaining musicians move out. Another chair was hurled by the same man, whom I saw deliberately throw it, then wrench up another, and throw it too—I bowed to the audience, and going up to Mr Chippendale, observed that I thought 'I had quite fulfilled my obligation to Messrs Niblo and Hackett, and that I should now remain no longer'. I accordingly went down and undressed; Colden was there, and seemed to apprehend danger out of doors; I did not. However, I took my dirk, but thinking it unworthy to carry it, threw it down again. Colden (who made too much of it), Tallmadge *[Recorder of New York]*, and Emmett *[This was Robert Emmett, nephew of the Irish patriot of the same name.]* walked home with me; there was no sign of any attempt in the back street, but there was a crowd at the front door, which Colden had not been able to penetrate, and which the Chief of the Police *[G. W. Matsell]* informed me afterwards, made the strongest efforts to break into the house. . . . I was in the best spirits, and we talked over what was to be done. Several things proposed, rejected, and certain things decided on, but so hastily that when they were gone I perceived the course was yet to be fixed on. A Mr Bennett—stranger—came, as he said, from young Astor and other names of the first, he said to say that this should be resisted, and to convey to me the expression of their regret, etc. I was not quite sure of my man. . . . My landlord, and one of the heads of the police, called to show me a deposition taken from one of the rioters who had been captured, and who, because he cried very much, was set at liberty. I asked leave to copy the deposition and I am about to do it, and I suppose I shall have a long night's writing. And this is my treatment! Being left

alone, I begin to feel more seriously the indignities put on me, and entertain ideas of not going on the stage again. Pray God I may do what is
right. . . .

May 8. Rose in good time with headache. Look at papers. *New York
Herald* which gave a semi-facetious, insidious, and, as regards myself,
incorrect account of the brutality of last night. Saw other papers . . .
good notices.

*Macready decided not to act that night and was disinclined to appear again.
But a petition signed by forty-seven leading New Yorkers (including David
Colden, Washington Irving, and Herman Melville) urged him to stay;
eventually he agreed to repeat* Macbeth *on 10 May. That morning hand-
bills throughout New York asked simply: 'Working men! Shall Americans
or English rule in this city?' and went on: 'The crew of the English steamer
has threatened all Americans who shall dare to express their opinion this
night at the English Aristocratic Opera House! We advocate no violence,
but a free expression of opinion to all public men!' This was signed 'American
Committee', here used as a cover not only for supporters of Forrest but also
for various fanatical societies advocating 'America for the Americans'.*

May 10. The Recorder called, Mr Tallmadge, and assured me that
every measure should be taken to insure the tranquillity of the house
tonight, etc. . . . At rehearsal I saw the performers, all in good spirits;
ran through the scenes of *Macbeth* for fear the excitement of Monday
night might have put the *business* from their memories. Spoke with
Messrs Sefton and Chippendale, expressing my own opinion that there
would not be the slightest demonstration of opposition. They thought
there might be a hiss or perhaps two at the beginning, but that it could
be instantly silenced. . . . Was inconvenienced by the smell of the
asafoetida in the green cloth at the side of the stage, and gave directions
that it should not be used tonight. Returned to hotel. *[William Henry
Chippendale, 1801–1888, who acted in America between 1836 and 1853.
On his return to London he spent nearly two decades at the Haymarket.]*

[Later] I went gaily, I may say, to the theatre, and on my way,
looking down Astor Place, saw one of the Harlem cars on the railroad
stop and discharge a full load of policemen; there seemed to be others at
the door of the theatre. I observed to myself, 'This is a good precaution'.
I went to my dressing-room, and proceeded with the evening's business.
The hairdresser was very late and my equanimity was disturbed. I was
ruffled and nervous from fear of being late, but soon composed myself.
The managers were delaying the beginning, and I was unwilling to be

behind the exact hour. The play began; there was some applause for Mr Clarke (I write of what I could hear in my room below). I was called, and at my cue went on with full assurance, confidence, and cheerfulness.

My reception was very enthusiastic, but I soon discovered that there was opposition, though less numerously named than on Monday. I went right on when I found that it would not instantly be quelled, looking at the wretched creatures in the parquette, who shook their fists violently at me, and called out to me in savage fury. I laughed at them, pointing them out with my truncheon to the police, who, I feared, were about to repeat the inertia of the previous evening. A blackboard with white letters was leaned against the side of the proscenium: '*The friends of order will remain silent*'. This had some effect in making the rioters more conspicuous. My first, second, third scenes passed over rapidly and unheard; at the end of the fourth one of the officers gave a signal, the police rushed in at the two sides of the parquette, closed in upon the scoundrels occupying the central seats and furiously vociferating and gesticulating, and seemed to lift them or bundle them in a body out of the centre of the house, amid the cheers of the audience. I was in the act of making my exit with Lady Macbeth, and stopped to witness this clever manoeuvre, which, like a *coup de main*, swept the place clear at once. As well as I can remember, the bombardment outside now began. Stones were hurled against the windows in Eighth Street, smashing many; the work of destruction became then more systematic; the volleys of stones flew without intermission, battering and smashing all before them; the Gallery and Upper Gallery still kept up the din within, aided by the crashing of glass and boarding without.

The second act passed, the noise and violence without increasing, the contest within becoming feebler. Mr Povey, as I was going to my raised seat in the banquet scene, came up to me and, in an undertone and much frightened, urged me to cut out some part of the play and bring it to a close. I turned round upon him very sharply and said that 'I had consented to do this thing—to place myself here, and whatever the consequences I must go through with it—it must be done; that I could not cut out. The audience had paid for so much, and the law compelled me to give it; they would have cause for riot if it were not all properly done.' I was angry, and spoke very sharply to the above effect. The banquet scene was partially heard and applauded. I went down to change my dress, the battering at the building, doors, and windows growing, like the fiends at the Old Woman of Berkeley's burial, louder and louder. Water was running down fast from the ceiling to the floor of my room and making a pool there. I inquired; the stones hurled in had broken some of the pipes. The fourth act passed; louder and more fierce waxed the furious noises against the building and from without; for whenever a missile did effectual mischief in its discharge it was hailed with shouts outside; stones came in through the windows and one struck the chandelier; the audience removed for protection behind the walls; the house was considerably thinned, gaps of unoccupied seats appearing in the audience part.

The fifth act was heard, and in the very spirit of resistance I flung my whole soul into every word I uttered, acting my very best and exciting the audience to a sympathy even with the glowing words of fiction, whilst these dreadful deeds of real crime and outrage were roaring at intervals in our ears and rising to madness all round us. The death of Macbeth was loudly cheered, and on being lifted up and told that I was called, I went on, and with action earnestly and most emphatically expressive of my sympathy with them and my feelings of gratefulness to them, I quitted the New York stage among the acclamations of those before me. Going to my room I began without loss of time to undress, but with no feeling of fear or apprehension. When washed and half dressed, people came into my room—consternation on the faces of some; fear, anxiety, and distress on those of others. 'The mob were getting stronger; why were not the military sent for?' 'They were here.' 'Where'? 'Why did they not act?' 'They were not here; they were drawn up in the Bowery.' 'Of what use were they there?' Other arrivals. 'The military had come upon the ground.' *[Soldiers of the Seventh Regiment, cavalry and infantry, more than two hundred in all.]* 'Why did they not disperse the mob there?' These questions and answers, with many others, were passed to and fro among the persons round me whilst I was finishing my hasty toilet, I occasionally putting in a question or remark. Suddenly we heard a volley of musketry: 'Hark, what's that?' I asked. 'The soldiers have fired.' 'My God!' I exclaimed. Another volley and another! The question among those surrounding me (there were, that I remember, Ruggles, Judge Kent, D. Colden, R. Emmett, a friend of his in some official station, Fry, Sefton, Chippendale, and I think the performer who played Malcolm, etc.) was which way was I to go out? News came that several were killed; I was really insensible to the degree of danger in which I stood, and saw at once—there being no avoidance—there was nothing for it but to meet the worst with dignity, and so I stood prepared.

[Outside, though the Sheriff of New York had given a solemn warning, the mob, mostly youths, pressed in upon the police; the cavalrymen, their horses

restive and almost unmanageable, had to retire, and the remaining soldiers
were penned in a crowd of twenty thousand people on a night of thickening
darkness, the street lamps out. Ultimately, firing was imperative; General
Hall ordered his men—seventy were left, in front of the theatre—to fire
above the heads of the crowd and against a blank wall. The noise carried off
his order; soldiers, mishearing, fired straight into the crowd. In spite of
casualties, the crowd—believing that blanks were used—still surged forward.
This time the soldiers fired low and several men fell. When the rioters
attacked again, now in two sections, the troops fired obliquely, one half to the
right, one to the left, volleys that caused much of the carnage. At length a
space about the theatre was freed; two brass cannon, charged with grape,
were brought on, to command Broadway and the Bowery; and slowly the
mob began to disperse.]

They sent some one to reconnoitre, and urged the necessity of a change in my appearance. I was confident that people did not know my person, and repeated this belief. They overbore all objections, and took the drab surtout of the performer of Malcolm, he taking my black one; they insisted, too, that I must not wear my hat; I said, 'Very well; lend me a cap.' Mr Sefton gave me his, which was all cut up the back to go upon my head. Thus equipped I went out, following Robert Emmett to the stage door; here we were stopped, not being allowed to pass. The 'friend' was to follow us as a sort of *aide*, but we soon lost him. We crossed the stage, descended into the orchestra, got over into the parquette, and passing into the central passage went along with the thin stream of the audience moving out. We went right on, down the flight of stairs and out of the door into Eighth Street. All was clear in front—kept so by two cordons or lines of police at either end of the building, stretched right across. We passed the line near Broadway, and went on threading the excited crowd, twice or three times muttering in Emmett's ear, 'You are walking too fast.' We crossed Broadway, still through a scattered crowd, and walked on along Clinton Place till we passed the street leading down to the New York Hotel. I then said, 'Are you going to your own house?' 'Yes'. We reached it, and having opened the door with a latch-key, closing it after us, he said, 'You are safe here; no one will know anything about you; you shall have a bed in ten minutes or quarter of an hour, and you may depend upon us all in this house.' I sat down in the drawing-room, talking of the facts about us, and wondering at myself and my condition, secretly preparing myself for the worst result, viz., falling into the hands of these sanguinary ruffians. A son of Emmett's was there, Robert; in about a quarter of an hour Colden came in.

Several men had been killed, how many not certainly known yet. 'You must leave the city at once; you must not stay here!'

It was then a consultation between these excellent friends, I putting in an occasional opinion objecting or suggesting upon the safest course to pursue. At length it was decided, and Robert was sent out to find Richard, another son, probably at the Racket Club, to put the plan in execution. He was met by Robert in the street, and both returned with additional reports; the crowd was still there, the excitement still active. Richard was sent to the livery stable to order a carriage and good pair of horses to be at Emmett's door at four o'clock in the morning 'to take a doctor to some gentleman's house near New Rochelle'. This was done and well done by him; Colden and Emmett went out to reconnoitre, and they had, as I learned from Emmett, gone to the New York Hotel, at the door of which was still a knot of watchers, and to Emmett's inquiries told him, if any threats were made, to allow a committee of the crowd to enter and search the house for me. Emmett returned with my own hat, one from the hotel, and I had got Colden's coat. An omnibus drove furiously down the street, followed by a shouting crowd. We asked Richard, when he came in, what it was; he said, 'Merely an omnibus,' but next morning he told me that he asked the men pursuing 'What was the matter?' and one answered, 'Macready's in that omnibus; they've killed twenty of us, and by G— we'll kill him!' Well, all was settled; it was believed that twenty had perished.

Robert went to bed to his wife. Emmett went upstairs to lie down, which I declined to do, and with Richard went down into the comfortable office below before a good fire, and, by the help of a cigar, to count the slow hours until four o'clock. We talked, and he dozed, and I listened to the sounds of the night and thought of home, and what would be the anguish of hearts there if I fell in this brutal outbreak; but I resolved to do what was right and becoming. The clock struck four; we were on the move; Emmett came down; sent Richard to look after the carriage. All was still in the dawn of morning; but we waited some ten minutes—an age of suspense—the carriage arrived. I shook the hand of my preserver and friend—my heart responded to my parting prayer of 'God bless him!'—and stepping into the carriage, a covered phaeton, we turned up Fifth Avenue and were on our way to safety. Thank God. During some of the time of waiting I felt depressed and rather low, but I believe I showed no fear, and felt determined to do my duty, whatever it might be, acting or suffering. We met only market carts, butchers' or gardeners', and labourers going to their early work; the morning was clear and fresh, and the air was cooling to my forehead, hot and aching with want of sleep. The scenery through which we passed, crossing the Manhattan, giving views of the various inlets of the sound, diversified with gentlemen's seats, at any other time would have excited an interest in me; now one's thoughts, or series of thoughts, with wanderings to home and my beloved ones, gave me no time for passing objects. I thought, as we passed Harlem Station, it would never have done to have ventured there. Some of the places on the road were familiar in my recollection, having been known under happier circumstances.

Boston, May 11. Reaching New Rochelle a little before seven o'clock, we got breakfast, and Richard decided on leaving me here; but in the bar-room the landlord asked me, 'Did you come from New York this morning?' I was taken aback. 'Yes'. 'Did you hear of a riot there last night?' 'Yes I did.' 'Was it a very bad one?' 'Yes, I believe so,' and I walked out. Seeing Richard, I suggested the advisability of his accompanying me to New Haven in case of similar occurrences in the cars, when I might be at fault, and he could take the office of spokesman, to which he readily assented. He told me (we wondering how the news could have got here, nineteen miles) that the subject had been discussed in a conjectural sort of style at the breakfast table, after I had left it, but that all spoke favourably of me; on the platform of the station among the arriving passengers were two, one of whom, I saw, knew me. Richard E. thought not; I became convinced of it, and my belief was verified by the annoying consequences. He told some acquaintances, as the cars arrived, of the fact; they communicated to others, and my identity was enjoyed by successive crowds of starers, to whom and from whom the news was handed down along the whole course of the railroad, even to Boston city. We got the different papers, and there read the horrible details, fifteen killed—it turned out to be seventeen—and several wounded! The conductor was particularly civil and attentive to me. Richard E. left me as I entered the Springfield cars at New Haven. Here a group of four began a conversation at me, I sitting near them, but on the same side, 'wondering if I should play tonight again,' etc. I sat silent; another person came and sat behind me, and, leaning over, asked me, 'Are you going to act at Boston?' 'No.' 'Shall you read there?' 'No.' 'Um—a terrible business last night?' 'Yes, very shocking,' etc. Reaching Boston I got into a cab, no one near me, and drove at once to my dear friend, George Curtis [1824–1892, essayist, editor, orator], whose invitation yesterday received, appeared almost providential. He soon after came in, and was heart-glad to see me; the telegraph had given the main facts. . . .

May 12. Woke early; unable to dress myself from want of clothes or shaving and dressing implements. Thought much and long on letters and things to be done. Curtis told me, whilst I was dressing or trying to dress, that my servant had come. Colden, who had written to me by him, had sent him away with every portion of my luggage. This was not quite what I wished, but perhaps there was no alternative. He brought some brief accounts of the state of things in New York. All quiet, but groups collected, and crowd round the theatre.

On 13 May Macready received a violent threatening letter, and the Mayor called to assure him that Boston knew the rules of hospitality and justice. The inquest verdict on the thirty-one casualties of the riot reached him on the 15th: 'That the deceased persons came to their deaths by gun-shot wounds, the guns being fired by the military, by order of the civil authorities of New York, and that the authorities were justified, under the existing circumstances, in ordering the military to fire upon the mob; and we further believe that if a larger number of policemen had been ordered out, the necessity of a resort to the use of the military might have been avoided.'

By 16 May excitement had abated; on the evening of 20 May Macready read Milton and Dryden to Curtis, Longfellow, Dana, Judge and Mrs Warren, David Colden, and several others; and on the clear, bright morning of 23 May, his affairs settled, he went by carriage with George Curtis across the ferry to East Boston and got on board the Hibernia. Two friends, one of them Charles Sumner (who looked very much like Macready) had come to say good-bye. Soon the vessel began to move; Macready waited there, on deck alone, until he saw the monument on Bunker's Hill grow dim in the distance.

On 7 June he arrived in London. Soon there was a steady round of provincial engagements until on 8 October he began a season at the Haymarket that—varied by some performances in the country—lasted until mid-December.

London, June 22. Proceeded to [Buckingham] Palace. Colonel Phipps came to the room to which I was shown, apologising that the Prince was then in his own. Told me that he was instructed to inform me that the Queen wished to have theatrical performances at Windsor this Christmas as before, and wished me to act Brutus and Hotspur. I stated my readiness to show my duty to Her Majesty, and that her wishes were commands to me; that I was in the habit of acting Brutus, but that I had long discontinued the performance of Hotspur, not intending to resume it; that I should have to restudy the character—unfitted by years to personate it, etc., intimating that, if I played two nights, it must be in some other character. All most courteously. I urged the necessity of knowing the time as soon as possible, on account of my engagements, etc. He was to write to me, and we parted with the best understanding.

June 23. Wrote an answer to Colonel Phipps, fixing Thursday, December 27, as the night for my performance at the Castle—eheu!

Birmingham, June 26. Delighted—constantly did the thought, the sense of *delight* recur to me—to find myself in *England*, to find myself under the security of law and order, and free from the brutal and beastly savages who sought my life in the United States. . . . The audience gave me a reception such as I have never witnessed out of London, and *very, very rarely even there*. They stood up all through the house, waving hats and handkerchiefs till I was anxious to proceed.

June 28. Acted Hamlet under very distressing, incapacitating circumstances: a dress not fitting me; my hair, I do not know how; a sword every minute sticking in my shoes and breaking in my hand when trying to use it—altogether miserable, but I did my best under these disadvantages. Called.

Sherborne, Dorset, August 6 *[He had gone there, thinking of his retirement, to look for a house, and had found one that pleased him]*. . . . It is old-fashioned in its adaptation to the needs of a family: there is no attempt at commodiousness or contrivance, but I think, at a very cheap rate it might suit us (provided we can contract our expenditure to my proposed annual expenditure, £700) better than most other people of moderate means, and a person of fortune would be a fool to live there. There is a great deal to recommend it to us. . . . The rent of house and garden without the field was £50. Called on Lord Digby's steward, and, after waiting some time, saw him and talked over the house— Sherborne House—its rent, etc. I gave him my name which, I said, he perhaps had heard, as it was in some sort a public one. He asked if I were any connection of *the* Macready. I informed him that, if he chose so to designate me, I was *the* Macready. His manner became more interested. I explained to him frankly my views and motives.

Brighton, September 11. Looked at the *Examiner*. A long article on Browning's poetry, which, except his *Paracelsus*, I cannot think anyone would read twice who had choice of any other poet.

September 12. This morning in the rain two elderly, coarse and lusty women passed by me, coming out of a shop. They had quite gone by when I remembered—through the *fat* and *red* and *age*—one with whom I had once been in love, Miss Stephens, now Dowager Lady Essex, and her niece Miss Johnstone. '*So fades, so languishes.*' . . .

London, October 8. Acted Macbeth *[at the Haymarket, the company included Mrs Warner, Priscilla Horton, Howe, Keeley, and James William*

Wallack ('Gentlemen Jem': 1791–1864).]. Mr Webster staggered me about the house just before I went on, implying that it was not full; there was, however, no appearance of room anywhere. The cheering on my entrance was very great from the whole house, but it did not seem to me that wild abandonment to a delighted feeling that the audience at the Princess's showed five years ago. It may be, and I think *is*, the difference of a Haymarket audience—the *stock* part is false in its habits. I never acted better, in many parts never so well, so feelingly, and so true. I said to Mrs Warner once, 'I never played that scene so well, and yet they do not seem to feel it.' She observed, 'They are not educated to it', meaning, they have been accustomed to things so different they cannot quite appreciate it. The play ended most enthusiastically. . . .

October 10. Acted Hamlet . . . I am not announced as *the* attraction of the theatre, and the public do not respond to the invitation to see me as *one of the company*. The audience was as *flat* as the people accustomed to attend Mr C. Kean's performances can be expected to be.

October 16. Rehearsed *King Lear* with several characters absent and several not cast! Planché calls the Haymarket 'The Patent Self-Acting Theatre'.

November 1. Went to the rehearsal of *Othello*. Oh! the waste of time by these *stage-managers* as they are called. A life frittered away in self-important displays of vacuity of mind.

Canterbury, November 11. . . . A very rude and coarse person, a Jew, addressed me in the refreshment-room at Ashford to ask whether I 'was well patronised last night'. I was quite at a loss to answer the man's impertinence, but, like others, he supposes players may be spoken to by any one!

London, November 22. Returning from rehearsal today I saw a poor-looking man with four children of different ages, one in his arms, straggling after him. 'Need and oppression stared within their eyes', they were on the other side of the way and I *did not like*, i.e. was ashamed to cross over to them. I said to myself, if I had met them and no one saw me, I would give them something. I went on with active combatings in my mind and was going *right on*, or rather wrongly on, with the conclusion that they had passed, and that perhaps they might not be legitimate objects of charity, when the principle of *right before all* came to my aid, and forced me back. I followed them and gave the poor man something.

November 23. Acted Macbeth but moderately the two first acts, but hearing that Peel[1] was in the theatre, I played my very best in the three

[1] Sir Robert Peel (1788–1850), politician and sometime Conservative Prime Minister.

last. I am not sure that the audience fully appreciated me; it is the most difficult criticism to criticise acting well.

November 28. Acted King Lear very fairly. Sent to speak to Mr —; he was loth to come—at last came. I told him that I had only desired to see him to say that I had no intention of saying anything offensive or disagreeable to him on Monday night; that he came on me in a moment of business and great excitement, and that had he been the King of England I should have repelled him in like manner; had he spoken to me afterwards quietly on the subject, I should have explained to him *then* how it occurred. He is an ass, and, being a player, of course a low-bred person. Mr Wallack, whom I addressed very civilly, was really *impertinent*, not in a way that I find I can notice now, but I shall not allow it to pass.

November 30. Acted Macbeth. Mr Wallack came, without invitation, to try over the fight, and, though he had *again* been *rude* this evening, sought occasion to clear it up. I took him upon his own words, and, having listened to him with the most profound patience, and upon that rebuked him for *interrupting me*, showed him that he had no right to take offence with me for what was not my fault. He made many protestations and—humbug! . . . Read in bed the number of *Copperfield*, which does not interest or move me much.

December 4. The Dickenses, Stanfields, Dr Elliotson, Jerrold, Oxenford,[1] and Forster dined with us; a cheerful day. Jerrold is delightful. Gave dear Stanfield his stick.

Shrewsbury, December 13. Read my letters from Catherine, from Webster, from Colonel Phipps, and from Bulwer, one of the most delightful letters I have ever received—full of *bonhomie*, humour, and wit, and what, of course, gives a zest to all, an offer of a house of his close to his park either to live in or to use as a place of occasional resort. Now whether this is only the generous and friendly impulse of the moment, or whether it is a pondered thing, it is most amiable, and I cannot but feel most affectionately and gratefully to the heart that could entertain such a thought. Its practicability is another question—I mean the practicability of the acceptance of the offer. Wrote to Colonel Phipps, asserting my earnest desire to do the possible to meet her Majesty's wishes. *[The Command performance at Windsor was now to be on 1 February.]*

Chester, December 18. Acted Macbeth under slaughterous obstruction. Never was worse dealt with. The Lady, oh!—Banquo—Lennox. In fact, it was wholesale murder. B—, who was complaining to me of

[1] John Oxenford (1812–1877), drama critic of *The Times*, and dramatic author.

being 'a pauper' yesterday, was drunk in the Witch tonight. The cause of his being rejected at theatres is too easily accounted for. . . .

Charles Kean had been chosen during the winter of 1848 to direct the annual Windsor Castle performances: a choice Macready could not complain about since he had been in America when the appointment was made. The next play would be 'Julius Caesar', and through Webster, Macready suggested the name of an actor, Webster's own nephew, for the part of Lucius, Brutus's young servant.

December 27. . . . Received a note from Webster, in which he mentioned that Mr C. Kean had stated any person to be 'impertinent' who suggested the cast of any character in *Julius Caesar*, and desired him to tell me so. My usual indignation rose to my throat, but almost *immediately* subsided. I felt the miserable creature's folly disclosing his envy; decided on *temper, temper*. Went to Maclise and gave him a long sitting. Thought of the terms of the note I should return to Webster. Came home and wrote to him, retaining copy of same. Note from Webster, endeavouring to extenuate the character of the expression used by Mr C. Kean. *[Kean had also written a very reasonable letter to Macready saying that he 'would very willingly have endeavoured to make any arrangement that could have added to your personal convenience and comfort, had you applied to me in time'.]*

December 28. Went by Great Western Railway to Windsor. The day bitterly cold, with drifting snow and sharp frost. Proceeded to the castle; after some time, cooling my heels in the basement lobbies, saw Mr Roberts, to whom I carried a letter from Colonel Phipps. He showed me the Rubens Gallery, the theatre of the castle, explaining to me the position of the stage, etc., the dressing-rooms, and all that was needful. He then took me round the state-rooms, displaying the furniture to me, about which I was indifferent, but was charmed with the pictures of the Old Masters I saw there; West and Lawrence made me turn very sick. Colonel Phipps was out shooting with the Prince. . . . Returned home by Slough. Note from Mr C. Kean *[the explanatory letter]*, apparently wishing to supersede the message sent by Mr Webster, but in very bad taste—half-civil, half-supercilious tone. Wrote to Mr C. Kean, declining a direct correspondence with him, as he had before addressed me through his solicitor, and acknowledging his note *and his message*.

December 29. Went in carriage to Maclise, sat to him; from him to Mr Wallack, with whom I arranged all my business of Brutus and rehearsed with him. He told me that there had been words between

273

Messrs Webster and C. Kean, and that Mr Webster had very sharply put down this conceited and silly fellow. Returned to Maclise and sat or stood in the dress of Werner for him. . . . Letter from Mr C. Kean—of most inane and senseless *bluster*—an intimation of readiness to attack or defend himself!

What Kean said was: 'In reply to your note I beg to acquaint you that I addressed you solely in my ministerial capacity, as Director of the representations commanded by her Majesty at Windsor, and in discharge of the duties deputed to me by her Majesty. I will therefore venture to suggest that we should not mix up any private difference with this transaction. When these duties are at an end I shall always be ready to account to you for any slight which you may suppose, however erroneously, that I have passed upon you, and equally ready to guard against disrespect to myself.

Exeter, December 31. . . . Found a company—even *worse than my fears!*—in all respects *disgusting*—the manager superlatively and preeminently so. Rehearsed!—to impress myself with the conviction of its inutility, and to try to prepare myself for the night. Acted Macbeth—oh! such a night—I striving for patience —the Lady Macbeth the *very worst* I ever saw in all my life; Macduff very little better; Witches execrable; no music; dresses and properties shabbiness itself. The Macduff, I firmly believe, desired to cut me in the fight. I thought he had drugged himself, Malay-like, with brandy or something to do it! My sword broke, which I had *apprehended*, and was very angry with Mitchell. He was very rude and increased my wrath. Oh, this temper, this wretched temper, the cause of so much misery to me. I fear I shall die with little improvement in my endeavour to subject it to reason and wisdom. . . .

1850

Throughout January Macready was on his round of farewells, playing in Exeter, Bath, Bristol, Bradford, Leeds, and Liverpool. Next, the Windsor Castle performance on 1 February. He was intensely worried about the illness of his eldest child, Christina Letitia (Nina), a girl of nineteen.

Bristol, January 18. Acted King Henry IV very well; and Lord Townly [*The Provok'd Husband*] better, I think, than I have ever before done it. . . . After his farewell speech I was quite overcome, and unable to check the tears that rolled down my cheeks. . . .

Leeds, January 26. Letter from dear Catherine with accounts of Nina, blessed child, that rather increase my apprehensions, and depress and fret me with the uncertainty of her true condition. I feel I can but pray and hope, but my fear is growing on me. . . .

Liverpool, January 30. Rehearsed, and with a set of actual *curs*, ignorant and rude as men can well be. Each day brings us nearer to the end of it. Acted Shylock. I do not know how; I only know I tried to act it well. Came away before the fifth act began. Note from a Mrs or Miss Chatterton wanting an *interview!* They all want interviews!

Liverpool, January 31. Busy with affairs for this Palace performance. I now find the trouble, the labour, and the expense so great, that I am almost angry with my own quixotism in giving way to the proposition. . . . Inquired of Mrs Warner about the mode of returning; learned that *the* train—the players' train—will not be likely to start before one, or half-past one o'clock, and on the previous occasion *she* reached home at *three*. I must therefore either take a special engine, or sleep at Windsor. If the special be too expensive, I must encounter the less expense and greater derangement. . . . Acted Iago, taking much pains. The Othello, Mr Barry Sullivan [*tragedian, 1821–1891*], was really indifferent, and vociferously applauded. The Roderigo, Mr Brown, was *drunk!*

[Many had a special admiration for Macready's Iago. Lady Pollock said: 'He looked like the camp soldier, his bearing was frank and free, his speech suited with it; he was rough and straightforward in his ways; it was natural to think him honest. . . . The face that was so frank was also intellectual, and no one could be surprised that Othello listened to him.' Again: 'Iago's motive was found in his own nature; he contrived mischief with satanic

275

*ecstasy, he exulted in his sense of power when he planned an injury.'
'Macready as I Knew Him'.]*

London, February 1. Found my beloved Nina beyond all evasion of even hope, ill; seriously, alarmingly ill. . . . Almost bewildered with perplexity in regard to what I had to do! Note from Colonel Phipps. Attended, as well as I could, to affairs. Dressed; went to Windsor by railway, taking at the Paddington Station a special engine to return at night, for which I paid seven guineas. Dined at Castle Inn. Went in cab to the Castle; passed with my ticket into my room, a very handsome one, partitioned off from a passage; pictures of Moretto, Tintoretto, Parmigiano, exquisite, etc. Dressed; was kept in a state of irritable expectation. Mr Wallack came to speak to me. Acted Brutus in a style of reality and earnest naturalness that I think did, and I felt ought to, produce an effect on my auditors. I cannot describe the scene; my Nina agitates my heart and shakes my nerves; I cannot write. Colonel Phipps came to see me from the Queen and Prince Albert to express how much they had been pleased. I requested him to offer my duty, and that I was most happy in the opportunity of offering any testimony of my respectful homage. Came away by special train. Carriage was waiting for me. Reached home [Clarence Terrace] about half-past twelve o'clock.

February 3. Carried my dear sick child downstairs. Sat with her. Dickens called and sat. He went up to see dear Nina, suggested his servant Anne going down to Hastings for lodgings, and said he 'did not think she looked worse than when he last saw her'. . . . Dr Bright and Elliotson came. After seeing my beloved child, they came to see me in my study where I was waiting for them. They spoke to me, and from their language I collected that the case was desperate. I felt that hope was gone. . . . Went to the station as desolate, as agonised at heart as any wretch could be. My journey through the night *[to Liverpool]* was one long thought of my dear, dear child.

Liverpool, February 5. A telegraph arrived with the blessed words, to Elliotson's observation that 'she *may* rally', she cannot rally. *[Later]* Reached Holyhead an hour behind our time—I fancy from the impediment of the gale that was blowing. It was so bad that two or three parties, one of foreigners seemingly wealthy, decided on *not crossing*. . . . The night was awful. The gale was in our teeth, and the sea literally raging. To make things worse, we had a most inattentive and cowardly steward —could gain neither attendance nor information through the night. . . . The seas broke over us to that degree that it was fearful to hear the lashing of the waters rolling on the deck above us. I feared the fires being extinguished, or the hold filling. The captain, it seemed, was in apprehension of the funnels not holding! Had they gone, we were gone. He came down to look at the glass, to draw some comfort from what he saw or thought he saw—the rising of the glass—that the gale was breaking. He said in all his life he had never encountered '*such a terrific night*'. He did not know where we were—could see nothing. Thus we were beating about; once catching a light, which he thought Balbriggan light—but not daring and not knowing how to take any decisive course till daylight. He then got view of points—Howth, etc., and made south for Kingstown, which we reached at half-past ten o'clock! I believed once or twice in the course of the night that my time was come.

Dublin, February 6. . . . Heard that nothing like the gale of the night had been known *[at Kingstown]* since 6 January, 1839. . . . We had been fifteen hours instead of four on our passage.

Macready made his farewells in Dublin and Belfast, and crossed to Liverpool. Nina had gone to Hastings; Letitia, who was with her, wrote to Belfast to say that the pulse was not so quick, and stronger. It was false fire. Six days later, after Macready had said good-bye to Liverpool, in the parts of Wolsey and Lord Townly, a telegram summoned him to Hastings.

Liverpool, February 19. Something past one o'clock—my servant gone to seek a special engine to convey me to Hastings to catch one last living look of my dear blessed Nina. I know not what is my state of mind; I am certain my head is strange and heavy, but I have packed up my clothes, made my arrangements as were needed—clearly; and I sit here awaiting, with anxiety to depart, the carriage that is to take me away. I cannot, to myself, disentangle this state of mind. This day brought me accounts teeming with promises of comfort and joy. . . . I rose to receive a handful of letters, all full of good news—Catherine's and Letitia's —with an account of my Nina more promising than any I have yet received! A sweet, consolatory one from Forster. Acted, with great care and peculiar effect, Cardinal Wolsey and Lord Townly. Went forward, the whole house stood up to hear me, and such a house as is rarely to be seen. Everything to gratify the pride and vanity of a person in my position, and the telegraphic dispatch was waiting me at my hotel. Here is indeed a lesson of what life is; who can say he is happy or prosperous in this world? who dares to boast or feel confidence in what he enjoys? I have thought my Nina the strongest and healthiest of all my dear ones, and as I write—perhaps—I feel dull and half-stupid—I do not know what to do.

*Mitchell, Macready's servant, went to Lime Street, Edgehill, and Everton
in search of the superintendent and a special engine. It could not be procured. Macready left Liverpool at 6 a.m., hurried to Hastings from London,
found Nina 'pale, emaciated, weakened', and heard from the doctor that
there was no ground for hope. There were three days of desperate suspense.
Then, on 24 February, Nina died.*

Hastings, February 24. . . . Mrs Allen came to call me about six
o'clock; I found my blessed child breathing with extreme difficulty,
quick and short. She gave me her hand, said she was very ill. I uttered
what words I could of comfort. She wished Dr Mackness to be sent for.
I saw it was utterly vain, and dearest Letitia, who stood by her holding
her other hand, seemed not to desire him to be sent to, but I could not
resist a wish of hers, as I had not hitherto done, nor could I deceive her
at such a moment. I sent Mrs Allen for him; she lay dying before us, but
fell again into sleep, breathing quick and very short. Mrs Allen,
returning, rang at the bell; I went down to let her in. As I came up, I
heard Letitia's voice loud in lament. She, my beloved child, had just
ceased to breathe. . . .

*Catherine, who was expecting a child, could not leave London. Macready
was as overcome as he had been at Joan's death; again, in anguish, he
considered his vanity, selfishness, envy, in page after over-wrought page
forced from him by his grief. The funeral over, at Kensal Green on 28
February, he had to return to the farewell tour: Newcastle, Edinburgh
(where in 'Hamlet', his house applauded the waving of the handkerchief to
show it had not forgotten Forrest), and later, Birmingham.*

Edinburgh, March 23. . . . I do not know what to think of the proposed Exhibition of 1851. It seems to me too vast to be an amusement
for sightseers, and too extensive and too various to permit of its being a
study. Then, it must make many idle persons: to be seen it must be open
some months. I am not disposed to cavil, but I fear it will derange the
course of business very much in this country. There may be, however,
beneficial results, which even the projectors do not themselves foresee.
Let us hope it. Acted Richelieu.

March 24. On this day my beloved wife was delivered of a son, and
whilst my heart was grieving for the absence of one blessed object of love,
another was presented to me, and my fears for my dearest Catherine
tranquillized. Thank God! *[Jonathan Forster Macready, 1850–1908.]*

March 27. Read a very angry article in *The Times* on Talfourd respecting his charge in a case of murder. I can say with perfect kindly feeling for *him* personally that I did not, and do not think, he has *moral courage* for the office of judge.

London, April 7. . . . Forster came to dinner. Brought me a sort of regretful message from Browning, and brought me his book, *Christmas Eve*.

Glasgow, April 13. Tried to read Browning's poem. I cannot relish it; I cannot approve it.

April 16. . . . Tried once more to read Browning's poem—I *cannot* like it.

On 22 May he went to Sherborne to sign the lease of his house, and on 4 June he took Daniel Maclise to see it.

Sherborne, June 4. Called for Maclise and went with him to the South-Western Station. Left London under a very smiling sky, and talked away, pleasantly enough. He told me of a coolness between Thackeray and Dickens—that Thackeray in '49 had been invited to the R.A. dinner and Dickens not, that this year Dickens was asked and wrote a very stiff note, *declining!* How weak are the wisest of us! If the invitation were a right, what pleasure would be received, what paid in it! At Southampton we took a very moderate luncheon. Maclise pointed out the Duchess of —, a plain and very common-looking woman, with her children resembling her. It is enough to make the blood of truth boil to hear the sycophantic falsehoods of toadies talking about the personal beauty of our aristocracy as distinguished from our common people. . . . Came on from Dorchester to Sherborne. I was much gratified to see Maclise so pleased with the scenery as we passed along. He was quite excited by the view of the Vale, though the haze very much obscured the landscape. He liked all.

London, June 19. In the evening Curtis called, and still later we were surprised by the entrance of Carlyle and Mrs C—. I was delighted to see them. Carlyle inveighed against railroads, Sunday restrictions, almost everything, Ireland—he was quite in one of his exceptious moods. I love, however, to hear his voice. Mrs C— left one of his *Latter Day Pamphlets*, with a corrected sheet, from which he had expunged an eulogistic mention of me, thinking 'I might not like it'. He little knows what value I set on a word of praise from him. . . .

June 20. The Dickenses, Talfourd, and Forster dined with me and seemed to pass a very happy day. I scarcely remember seeing friends more perfectly happy and enjoying in a more unrestrained spirit the pleasure of conscious interchange of regard than on this occasion. . . .

Lyme Regis, July 18 *[while on holiday]*. Looked at paper, read in it of Mrs Glover's death. It seems she was quite unequal to the effort of appearing last Friday night, and her son was apprehensive she could not last long. She was an actress of high talent; in private life she had no principle of honesty, was possessed of great spirits, and a very sarcastic biting style of conversation. She was not likely to make or retain friends. Poor woman! Her father worked in my grandfather's employ as an upholsterer, his name was Butterton which on coming to the stage he changed to Betterton. Byron speaks of an interview with him. Of such are theatres made up.

August 3. *[a visit to Bulwer Lytton at Knebworth]*. . . . Reached Knebworth, a very beautiful park, not quite so happily undulating as Sherborne Park, but the house and ground immediately around it a most finished specimen of a baronial seat. The order, the latest Gothic; the architecture, internally, in perfect harmony, though sometimes of different periods, with the outer ornaments of the building. Bulwer Lytton gave me a very cordial reception, and after some delay with our luggage, brought on by a fly, we went to the drawing-room, or rather to the upper drawing-room, where a very elegant dinner was served. The day was very cheerful. D'Eyncourt, junior, and Forster, with some of the neighbourhood, were added to our party. We were late in going to bed, Bulwer taking his long cherry-stick pipe and Forster his cigar.

August 4. Bulwer sent a message to me, as I was dressing, to inquire if I would like a walk with him, which I was very happy to do. We went through the park and along the road that skirts, discoursing on religion, the immortality of the soul, youth, marriage, and much interesting matter. When we came back, we changed to persons, D'Orsay, Lord Hertford, of whom he related anecdotes, showing him to be possessed of more talent than I had supposed. *[Later]* . . . I like him more and more. I wish his health gave him more enjoyment. His place is beautiful. Went in the carriage to Welwyn, in fly to Hertford; thence very slowly and uncomfortably by rail to London.

In mid-August Macready had an engagement at Cork. On 4 September he spent his first night in Sherborne House whither the family had moved, and it was there that he 'read a flaming puff, apparently written by himself, on whom?—Mr Bunn—the scholar—artist—I know not what! It made me almost sick.' On 10 September he had his last visit to Clarence Terrace, and next day left for Edinburgh.

To Edinburgh, September 11. Read the *Daily News*, which I did not dislike; *Punch*, and some papers in *Household Words*. Handed *Daily News* to the gentleman next me, evidently a foreigner, and was surprised and pleased at his introducing himself to me as Mazzini! *[Giuseppe Mazzini, 1805–1872, Italian nationalist.]* We had some talk of mutual friends, Italy, etc.

Dundee, September 13. Sent to Glover, who came and sat whilst I took tea. Among the news he told me that it was believed Miss H. Faucit was married to Mr Martin. . . . *[(Sir) Theodore Martin, 1816–1909, poet, biographer, and translator. Practised as a solicitor in Edinburgh; became head of a London firm of Parliamentary agents. Wrote, with Queen Victoria's approval, the 'Life of the Prince Consort.' His 'Helena Faucit (Lady Martin)' appeared in 1900, two years after his wife's death.]*

Perth, September 17. Walked to theatre, along the river bank, on the Inch, thinking of the days when, thirty years since, I admired these scenes and fell in love with my dear Catherine. *[In the summer of 1820, when playing at Aberdeen, Montrose, Dundee, and Perth, he had become warmly attached to the girl, Catherine Frances Atkins, then not quite fifteen (he was twenty-seven), who acted Virginia to his Virginius and the Prince of Wales to his Richard III. On his last night in Scotland, presenting her with the handsomest shawl he could buy in Perth, he told her that if, at any time, he could help, she would know where to ask. They were married in London on 24 June 1824.]* Rested. Drunken property-man came to ask for me! Went to theatre; heard that 'the company' had been drinking, but luckily only noticed it as observable in one person. Acted Cardinal Richelieu not very well, against the grain, with bad actors, and to a house not crowded as one might have expected. . . .

Dundee, September 18. . . . Read the account of the arrival of Jenny Lind among that degraded population of New York. . . .

Aberdeen, Greenock, Glasgow, Paisley ('Acted Cardinal Richelieu; the house quite disappointed me, and depressed me. This is my last country performance'); thence, on 3 October, to London.

London, October 3. Read *Punch*. Amused, of course. . . . Purchased two last numbers of *Copperfield* and read parts of each; was very much affected and very much pleased with them. His genius is very great.

Sherborne, October 8. Letters, two, from Gould, with an account of Jenny Lind in New York, whose first six concerts appear to have amounted to the enormous sum of £30,000.

On 28 October he began his series of farewell performances at the Haymarket Theatre, which would last until 3 February 1851.

October 28. Acted Macbeth. How? I was disappointed by the sight of the house, which was not full. I was not satisfied with the feeling of the applause; it seemed to me the effort of a minority; still, I resolved to do my very best and I 'went in to win'—if I could. I thought the audience cold; yet on I strove, undeterred by the apathy with which they accompanied my still sustained endeavours. Mrs Warner told me she thought I was playing in my best manner, but the audience did not satisfy me on the point until the banquet scene, when they burst into unanimous and long-continued applause. The play ended triumphantly, but it was at the cost of very great labour to me. . . . The house was a mystery and a gloom to us. There is *not a bite!* Is it not strange that the only actor remaining of a school of art should pass away in neglect and with the indifference of the public?

He played Hamlet: he 'felt' his Lear on 2 November; on the 4th Bulwer-Lytton was delighted with Richelieu. Werner next; Othello—and not a critic present ('not even my friend Forster'). He read Hamlet to his old school at Rugby on 12 November preserving the excitement, and as pleased with his listeners as they with him. But 'I suffer from the least thing—it is terrible!' *he wrote on 18 November when the Vice-Chancellor (Dr Plumptre) dilly-dallied about a Hamlet reading at Oxford, fearing maybe that a player might harm University morals. Cambridge assented at once. In the event both Universities heard the reading during February.*

November 23. . . . .My mind is much depressed and impressible. Acted Cassius, tried to carry through the burning spirit of the impatient republican, but moved with heavy weights hanging to me in the actors of the play. Called. As I passed the stage-box, the gentlemen near it uttered loud in my ear, 'God bless you!' That was worth the audience. The Brutus was very bad. Forster thought that he neutralized my performance—especially in the quarrel—*to a critic*, that should not have been. *[Brutus was played on this occasion by Edward Loomis Davenport, 1815–1877, an American actor who came to London in 1848 with Anna Cora Mowatt, and remained for some years. In 1849 he married Fanny Vining, of the theatrical family.]*

November 27. Acted Hamlet in my very, very best manner; it is the last time but one I shall ever appear in this wonderful character. I felt it, and that to many, to most, it would be the last time they would ever see me in it. I acted with that feeling; I never acted better. I felt my allegiance to Shakespeare, the glorious, the divine. Was called and welcomed with enthusiasm. The house—private boxes (aristocracy) excepted—was *great*.

December 1. Thought over King Richard II. In considering its capabilities, the degree of interest it possesses, or rather that it does not possess, the absence of effect—equal to the principal *second* rank of *first characters* as Wolsey, King John, Brutus, Cassius, Shylock, Virginius, etc.—the production of it in the *judging [?grudging]* Haymarket style, in which not even a grand historical *picture* is displayed; in considering *all this*, I am struck with the want of judgment and pertinacity of opinion which Forster has shown in urging it, and of course making Webster (*grasping at anything*) eager to do it. I fear it will *damage* the engagement —'I do fear it.' It *cannot* do it good; that is my opinion, which I note down before the event. . . .

December 2. . . . Went in tolerably equable spirits to act, but was put out and flurried by the neglect and mistakes of that dolt, that imbecile, Mr —. Struggled against it. Acted—unequally—in what *I* call a '*first night*' fashion—not as I should have done had the things been smooth and the people in their places. 'My prophetic soul' was but too painfully certified of its reasonings for—what I had not been led to expect—the house tonight was not only bad, but certainly the worst we had played to! Called. Forster came into my room and admitted he was wrong—(alas!)—and that I had been right. Changed the play for next Monday. Tried to rearrange the list of plays, quite deranged by this signal failure of tonight. . . . *[Richard II, which caused very little interest, was repeated only once. Davenport, playing 'seconds' this season instead of Wallack, was Bolingbroke, and Miss Reynolds the Queen.]*

December 3. Called on Forster, who suggested my going to dine with Dickens. I read some conversations of Goethe till ready to go. Dined with the Dickenses—he not well. After tea we had two rubbers at whist! Dickens gave me the bound volume of *Copperfield*. Walked home part of the way with Forster.

December 5. Am now sunk into the habit of late rising, half-past eight, which leaves me no time for anything before a ten o'clock rehearsal. The excitement of my system I have not time to lull, and thus day after day alternates between languor and feverish endeavour. What a mode of blindly, and, as it were, furiously, fretting and struggling through life! For so it is. Wilkins called. I wished to give him this one parting order to please him, poor fellow. He spoke to me of having seen all my first nights of characters, except two; talked of George

Barker, of his great wealth, which made me reflect. I was in the enjoyment of a very excellent income for a bachelor I think £1000 a year, when he could scarcely have had more than £150, if so much. He said to be now worth £10,000 per annum, and I not much more than £1,200. I am not at all dissatisfied, discontented, or repining at this disposition of things. I only pray that my income may be maintained. I am grateful for it. As I reflect, look back on my past life, the thought of being rich, the ambition to be so, never once entered into my mind. I was most anxious to be independent; and, after having purchased my brother's company, thought of retiring (1829) on what I then, without children, regarded as independence, £400 per annum. God sent us children, and all my plans were altered. Still, I could not think of wealth for them, as they came fast and dear, but diminished my own means to secure them by insurances the means of education and subsistence in case of my death. Thus I am what the world would call a poor man. I trust, in reality, a contented and grateful one. *[Macready left £20,000.]*

December 8. Dined with Dickens; sent note to Kenyon. Met Bulwer, Jerrold, Hawkins, and Forster. Bulwer was not very lively; rather dull. His deafness is rendered more distressing to himself in society, because he will not admit it, and invite a more distinct mode of address to him. He seems ashamed of what all would condole with him on, and sympathise with him for.

December 9. Acted King John. Part of the audience came to the play, not to see it, but to *act themselves* in a foolish demonstration of hostility to Papistry. The consequence was, they interrupted the course of interest in the play, and, together with Mr —'s blundering stupidity, marred my best scene. Was called. Bulwer and Forster came into my room.

December 11. . . . . Proposed Joseph Surface for the last Saturday. Wrote to Forster, thinking, on reflection, Joseph Surface might be *beneath* my position. *[He had always disdained the part. In 1835 one of the clauses in his Drury Lane contract with Bunn stipulated 'That W. C. Macready shall not be required or asked to act the characters of 'Sir Giles Overreach', 'Joseph Surface', or 'Rob Roy'. . . .']*

December 12. Called on Forster, and spoke again about *School for Scandal*, on which he was to consult Dickens. . . . Acted Virginius. The company all abroad in what they had to do. Forster came into my room and gave his changed opinion, *on good grounds*, against acting the *School for Scandal*.

December 15. Forster came in to call for me—went together to dine at Dickens's. The Foxes and Paxton were there. Fox is always the same, intelligent and philosophic. Paxton was new to me, a self-educated man —from a mere gardener. I was delighted with him; his account of the nurture of the Victoria lily, a water-plant (river), was one of the most interesting narratives I ever listened to. . . .

Forster spent Christmas with the Macreadys at Sherborne.

Sherborne, December 25. Gave up the day to 'far niente' pleasures and mere enjoyment. Forster made me show him all over the house, with which he was greatly pleased. Walked out with him, Willie and Edward, into the park; were checked in our way by showers of rain, which turned us home again after looking at the best part of the park. . . .

1851

London, January 3. Acted Virginius, one of the most brilliant and powerful performances of the character I have ever given. . . .

January 6. Acted Macbeth in a first-rate manner—always speaking of my own efforts as in *comparison with myself*—no one else.

January 8. . . . Read through Bulwer's play, written for the amateur actors. It is very good, but it requires actors to perform it, and actors to produce it—to know how to *work up* the scenes, where to omit, heighten. I fear their power of doing justice to it. Wrote cursory remarks, which I enclosed for Bulwer in a note to Forster.

[This was 'Not So Bad As We Seem; or, Many Sides to a Character', written specially by Bulwer for the Guild of Literature and Art (successful authors banded to help the unsuccessful). It would be acted by Dickens's amateurs before the Queen at Devonshire House on 16 May. 'Most lively and agreeable' wrote Macready at the end of his 'cursory remarks' on 8 January; 'I have been "greatly pleased" with it.' Time has been unkind to the piece, a drama of the reign of George I, and when it was acted (for another special occasion) at Devonshire House in the autumn of 1921, a critic called it 'excruciatingly inflated' and chose for mockery such lines as 'Scheme now, plotting brain! Dare now, Stubborn will!' and 'The plot thickens around me.']

January 9. Forster came into my room. Spoke about Bulwer's play. Told me that he had mentioned to me that Bulwer would call on me on Sunday about it. *Most certainly* I never *heard* him say anything of the sort. But *I* may have been unobservant or inattentive, or *he* may have been forgetful. There is a misapprehension between us. I do not know where it lies. *He* is evidently urgent that Bulwer should preside at the dinner suggested to be given to me, I am strongly opposed to it. I think if Monsieur le Prince (Heaven help the mark!) declines, as I am sure he will, to preside on such an occasion. It ought to be a commoner, a real commoner—no baronet or titled person, and that man *not a personal friend* of mine. If it were right to have a personal friend, Dickens is the person most fit. I shall rest well contented, I think, to escape the fret and *wretched* anxiety of it. Wrote to Bulwer.

January 10. Mrs Warner came into my room to tell me confirmatory tidings of what I had mentioned to her, viz. Miss Faucit's abuse of me.

She had heard direct from the *Foleys*—sculptors—who said, 'Miss F.'s offer to act for me showed an amiable nature, as forgiving or forgetting injuries'. This elicited question, and the charges were stated, that I had stopped the run of *Nina Sforza*—that I had used her ill, from jealousy, at Paris!!! It is too pitiful to be angry with. [*R. Zouch Troughton's tragedy 'Nina Sforza', was staged at the Haymarket on 1 November, 1841. In his biography of Helen Faucit, Sir Theodore Martin says simply: 'The play ran for eighteen nights, and would have run longer but for the close of Mr Macready's engagement.'*]

January 12. Forster called. Bulwer came, and we went over his play, I giving all the views and advice I could. But the amateurs *will never be able to do justice to it*, and the play will, I fear, be lost. Bulwer wanted me to set to work and write down my views, etc., but this I was compelled to say distinctly *I could not do until after my own business was over*. I fancied he did not seem quite so pleased as he had been. But I cannot help it. *I cannot do* it till my mere business is done.

January 14. . . . Read Mrs Forrest's declaration in the action of divorce. She states that Mr Forrest gave money at Boston and New Orleans to get up the excitement against me.

January 16. . . . Acted Virginius, for the last time, as I have scarcely ever—no, never—acted it before; with discrimination, energy, and pathos, exceeding any former effort. The audience were greatly excited. Called. Wrote to Forster, enclosing him 'the part' of Virginius and the parchment I have always used in the second act, in the performance of the character. I was deeply impressed by the reflection that in this character—which has seemed one of those exclusively my own, which has been unvaryingly powerful in its effects upon my audience since the first night, in 1820, when I carried them by storm, when Richard Jones came round from the front of the theatre, Covent Garden, into our dressing-room and, laying his hand on my shoulder, exclaimed, 'Well, my dear boy, you have done it now'—that I should never appear in this again, and now I have done it, and done with it! I was much affected during the evening, very much, something with a partial feeling of sorrow at parting with an old friend, for such this character has been to me, and, alas, no trace of it remains. The thought, the practice, the deep emotion conjured up, the pictures grouped so repeatedly throughout the work, live now only in memory. Alas, for the player who really has made his calling an art, as I can stand up before all men and say I have done!

January 18. Dined with Justice Coleridge to meet the Wordsworth Memorial Sub-Committee. Before dinner, whilst looking at some

Christmas books, I asked, 'Have you seen Ruskin's Christmas book? It is charming.' *[The Black Brothers]* 'Indeed'. 'Oh!' I went on, 'it is a most delightful book.' Mr J. Coleridge observed, 'Do you not know him? This is Mr Ruskin.' And I was introduced. I like the family very much, and passed a pleasant, cheerful day. . . .

January 19. Read a very good article by Forster, not quite strong enough, on the invidious and secretly malignant article on Southey by Lockhart in the *Quarterly Review*. Is there a man living who has fewer persons to love him than that man Lockhart? In Edinburgh, where he passed his youth and so many years of his life, and had the shelter and countenance of Scott, I was told he had not one friend and scarcely an acquaintance—a good test of a man's disposition. Called on Forster. Met Bulwer Lytton at his chambers, who asked me to read his play again, which I promised to do, and also to *arrange* it for him, with which he was greatly pleased.

January 22. Acted Iago with a vigour and discrimination that I have never surpassed, if ever equalled. There were persons in the theatre who appreciated the performance, but it was disgustingly manifest that there were a parcel of Yankee claqueurs in the gallery, who gave applause to the most vapid and senseless inertness of the miserable Othello *[the American Davenport]* 'without remorse or dread', and the audience, with a sort of American stolidity, endured it! I was really sickened; still I did not abate my exertions nor relinquish one jot my firm hold of the mind and purpose of the character. I do not think I ever acted it so powerfully. That last performance of Iago was, in my mind, a commentary on the text, an elucidation and opening out of the profound conception of that great creative mind, that almost divine intelligence, Shakespeare, which had not been given before in the inward feeling of the part: the selfishness, sensuality, and delight in the exercise of his own intellectual power I have never seen in Cooke or Young, nor read of in Henderson, as being so developed. . . .

January 23. Acted Benedict [Benedick]—as well as I could with a most unfit representative of Beatrice [Miss Reynolds] and two stupid dolts in the Prince and Claudio, that almost baffled every attempt I made to be understood. It was only when I was *alone* in the garden scene that I could *assert myself* before my audience, and that they could *satisfactorily respond* to me. The '*art declining!*' What *art*? Are these *low-bred*, uneducated *fellows* from *counters* or warehouses with the ignorance of Messrs C. Kean and Anderson—one who has been at a school, Eton, and *learned nothing*, and the other *not*, but got an appearance of knowing something—are *these* fellows to comment on, and illustrate Shakespeare? Forster had come into my room. The performance made a strong impression on the audience despite of my drawbacks. . . .

January 24. Looked at paper, in which was a slight notice of Benedict [Benedick], that in ordinary course would have been well enough, but as a thing never to be seen again, and the last performance but eight of the first English actor, was neither worthy of the great journal *[The Times]* nor of the artist. Acted Brutus as I never—no, never—acted it before. . . . I think the audience felt it. Of course there must be dunces among them, and Yankees.

January 27. Acted Othello. It was very curious how nervous I was of acting before my children *[who had not previously been allowed to see him on the stage]*. . . . I was most anxious to act my very best. I tried to do so, but am not sure that I succeeded. The audience were cold, and, as Mr Howe observed, 'slow'. But this could scarcely be otherwise with such an atrocious stick in Iago as Mr Davenport; it was really and utterly devoid *of all meaning*. I fought up, and I think I acted well, but I cannot think the play gave satisfaction.

January 28. Letitia and darling Katie called. She told me, through her tears, in reference to last night, that she 'should be glad when I had left the stage. She had rather I was away from it, and entirely with them—all theirs; that if my art was sustained and made a noble pursuit, it might be different; but, as it was, she did not like to see me associated with such minds as those about me.' It is well that with minds so trained these dear children should have seen me. I trust it may be for good. . . .

January 29. Acted Hamlet; certainly in a manner equal to any former performance of the part I have ever given. . . . The character has been a sort of love with me. . . . Beautiful Hamlet, farewell, farewell! There was no alloy to our last parting. . . .

January 30. No word in *The Times* on *that performance* of Hamlet last night; nor has there been any notice of it this season. Surely this is too bad. Played Cardinal Richelieu with all my energy. The audience very much excited. . . . Gave Mr Howe my Philip van Artevelde's sword.

January 31. Acted Macbeth, trying to produce a powerful effect on my dear children, and the house crowded to overflow. Certainly succeeded in the display of great power. . . .

February 3. Last performance at the Haymarket. . . . Most anxious to make my last performance *one to be remembered*. Nervous, anxious, and uneasy. Went to the theatre and collected myself, preparing for a great effort. Acted King Lear, certainly in a superior style to what I ever did before. Power, passion, discrimination, tenderness constantly kept in mind. Called at the fall of curtain and went forward, lingering to see if the audience expected me to speak; it seemed as if they did not, and I left the stage. They called again, and after some time I had to appear again. After waiting some time the noise subsided, and I said: 'Ladies and Gentlemen,—The period of my theatrical engagements is reached this evening, but, as my advertisements have signified, there is yet one occasion more on which I have to appear before you, and to that, the last performance in which I shall ever hope to strive for your approbation, I reserve the expression of the few words of acknowledgment and regret that I may desire and endeavour to offer you, my true, patient, and long-approved friends.' This was kindly received. White, Talfourd, Dickens, Forster, Willmott, Manby, Webster, came up to my room. I do not know how many letters were waiting me, and almost all on the subject of places for my Benefit. My theatrical engagement is concluded. My professional life may be said to be ended. I have only to act one night more for my own benefit, in regard to which I am bound to no man; I have acquitted myself of my dues—I am free! Nearly fifty-eight years of my life are numbered: that life was begun in a very mediocre position—mere respectability; my father maintained a good character as an honest and a liberal man; my mother was a woman of good family, of superior intellect, excellent heart, and of high character, but at ten years of age I lost her counsel and example. . . . I have attained the loftiest position in the art to which my destiny directed me, have gained the respect of the honoured and respected, and the friendship of the highly gifted, amiable, and distinguished. . . . My home is one of comfort and of love, and I look towards it with cheerfulness and delighted security, and most gratefully and earnestly do I bless the name and thank the bounty of Almighty God, who has vouchsafed such an indulgence to me, undeserving as I have been, and sinner as I am. . . .

February 4. Read a long review of my professional character in *The Times*, kind and complimentary, whilst taking the analytic process to prove its own truth. Went out with Willie and called on Forster; found Bulwer Lytton and Dickens there. They went into the business of the *[testimonial]* dinner, which made me very low. . . .

February 11. Webster came and offered £5 for every dress; there were twenty-five, but I withdrew the armour. The deduction of this would of course, reduce the sum total, and therefore I said if you give me the round sum of £100 I shall be satisfied. To that he instantly agreed, and, I think, has a very excellent bargain, but he met me in a very gentlemanlike tone. I am glad to be rid of the clothes, etc., and glad to have the £100 in my pocket. Dined with Mrs Dickens. Walked home;

note from Kenyon. Tried to think on the subject of my dinner speech. It seems that the tickets are in active request already, and that the room will not contain the applicants.

February 12. A very becoming and grateful note from Phelps, acknowledging my Richelieu's order.

[Phelps's original letter is in the Raymond Mander and Joe Mitchenson Theatre Collection, London. He is thanking Macready for the gift of the Order which the creator of Lytton's Richelieu had worn on the stage for so many years:

8 Canonbury Square,
Islington. February 12.
My dear Sir.—You have given a high value to a memorial which, had it been granted at my own request, would have possessed comparatively little. My gratification at receiving it is greatly increased too, as it gives me an opportunity of saying how much I am indebted to my four years' professional connection with you—of assuring you that the important service rendered at an eventful period of my life has never been forgotten, and that all the members of my family are likely to recollect you not only as a great actor but as a good man.

That for many years you may be enabled to say—'Beatus ille qui procul negotiis'—is the sincere wish of
My dear Sir
Yours very faithfully
Saml. Phelps

Phelps was quoting from the 'Epodes' of Horace, a passage that, in full, has been rendered (by Wickham) as 'Happy the man who far from schemes of business, like the early generations of mankind, ploughs and ploughs again his ancestral land with oxen of his own breeding, with no yoke of usury on his neck!'

February 13. Note from Forster, enclosing one from home, with the wish of Charles Kemble to come on the stage at my leave-taking and shake hands with me before the audience!!! What ideas of taste some persons have! . . . Forster is now in one of his usual scrapes; he has undertaken much more than he can at all do justice to. Dickens gives orders and goes to Paris. The result is, he [Forster] gets angry, and is likely to quarrel!

February 18. Heard that the box-office door at Drury Lane theatre was besieged at eight o'clock in the morning by crowds, and that it was filled with a rush at ten! This is all very touching to me. The dinner, by advertisement, removed from London Tavern to Hall of Commerce in consequence of the great demand for tickets.

Macready must have a last brush with someone. He chose his old colleague James Anderson, then director of Drury Lane and bowed by the task. Meaning to help, Anderson had inserted names on the playbill of 'Macbeth' —his own name, and those of Vandenhoff and Cooper, of the Drury Lane company, among the Singing Witches. What he meant to be a friendly gesture Macready called 'a piece of vulgar insolence without parallel' and ordered the names to be deleted. Later, after rehearsing at the theatre, he shook hands very coldly with Anderson, who—said the ever-observant Mrs Warner—'coloured' and moved away. Macready was consistent to the last hour. On 25 February he read over Macbeth for the last time as a player, and next morning woke to the final duties of his professional life.

Pit and gallery crowds swarmed outside Drury Lane on the afternoon of 26 February. Every seat in the boxes (three pounds), stalls, and 'slips' had been sold days before. A crowd gathered to see the crowds; three thousand people were outside the theatre at half-past six; carriages, wheel to wheel, filled the roads. Within, the companies of the Haymarket and Sadler's Wells supported Macready: Mrs Warner as Lady Macbeth, Samuel Phelps as Macduff. As Macbeth entered, uttering the spurious line, 'Command they make a halt upon the Heath', Drury Lane rose at him, and from the front of the stalls, the edge of the boxes, to the back of the gallery where (said Dickens) shirt-sleeved men were striking out their arms like swimmers, everyone in the great house was up, waving handkerchiefs and hats, stamping like thunder, and crying with a voice heard by the crowd in the drizzling night outside, 'Macready! Macready!' And again: 'Macready! Bravo!'

The diary:

February 26. *Farewell to the Stage.* . . . Dressed in the room which I had fitted up for myself when manager and lessee of the theatre, and as I heard the shouts and cries of the assembled crowds at the doors, thought with thankfulness to God, on the time when I listened to those sounds with a nervous and fretful feeling, my fortune and my children's weal depending on the result of my undertaking. Acted Macbeth as I never, never before acted it; with a reality, a vigour, a truth, a dignity that I never before threw into my delineation of this favourite character. I felt everything, everything I did, and of course the audience felt with me. I rose with the play, and the last scene was a real climax. I did not see who assisted me to my room, I believe it was Mr Simpson of Birmingham. I dressed as rapidly as I could *[in plain black, wearing (as friends would realise) black studs in memory of Nina's death just a year before, and carrying a hat with a band of crape]*, and, thinking of what I had to do, gave notice of 'being ready', that dear old Willmott might, according to his wish, clear the entrance for me. I thought over what I had to say, and went forward. To attempt any description of the state of the house, of the wild enthusiasm of applause, every little portion of the vast assembly in motion, the prolongation, the deafening cheers, would be useless. After waiting for a time that I have never in my experience seen approached, I advanced. On my first entrance, before I began Macbeth, while standing to receive the enthusiastic greetings of my friends, the audience, the thought occurred to me of the presence of my children, and that for a moment overcame me, but I soon recovered myself into self-possession and assumed Macbeth returning from his triumph. On the occasion of my address I was deeply touched by the fervent, the unbounded expression of attachment from all before me, but preserved my self possession. I addressed them in these words: 'Ladies and Gentlemen,—My last theatrical part is played, and, in accordance with long-established usage, I appear once more before you. Even if I were without precedent for the discharge of this act of duty, it is one which my own feelings would irresistibly urge upon me; for, as I look back on my long professional career, I see in it but one continuous record of indulgence and support extended to me, cheering me in my onward progress, and upholding me in mortifying emergencies. . . .'

It was a brief, grave speech. He regretted that his 'ambition to establish a theatre, in regard of decorum and taste, worthy of our country, and to have in it the plays of our divine Shakespeare fitly illustrated, was frustrated by those whose duty it was, in virtue of the trust committed to them, themselves to have undertaken the task.' *He was glad that the corrupt text had been banished. He had little to add except that he was resolved to retire with his powers still unfailing rather than to linger, weakening, on the stage. With tears irrepressible in his voice and eyes, and many listeners in tears also, he ended:* 'With sentiments of the deepest gratitude I take my leave, bidding you, ladies and gentlemen, in my past professional capacity, with regret, a last farewell.'

Drury Lane rose at him once more. A voice from the upper gallery cried: 'The last of the Mohicans!' For a few minutes he bowed repeatedly to the waving, clapping, cheering throng, while outside, people who could not enter but who had waited patiently for the end, added their own cheers. Macready bowed for the last time, turned, and walked firmly through the cleft of the

*applauding actors; and as he came to his dressing-room, a final wave of
'Macready! Macready!' shattered against the footlights.*

The diary:

. . . The address was frequently interrupted by expressions of
satisfaction and sympathy, and occasionally with the warmest applause;
the picture of the theatre as I bowed repeatedly in returning my thanks
was, in my experience, unprecedented. No actor has ever received such
testimony of respect and regard in this country. My dear countryman
Willmott, good old fellow, came into my room; Dickens, Jerdan,
Mr Hogarth, applying for the address; Bulwer Lytton, White, Forster,
Jerrold, Mark Lemon, Oxenford, for the address; Lever and Norton
from Manchester, whom I was delighted to see, and whom I welcomed
most cordially when I recognised them. Manby, etc., came in, all
delighted with the evening, and pleased, as they expressed themselves,
with the address. I gave one copy of it to Oxenford, and another to
Hogarth, on the condition he sent slips to the other papers. Mrs Reed
[Priscilla Horton], Mrs Lacy, Mrs Warner, Mrs Gill, and Mr Cooper
came in; the persons present were amused at my kissing each of the
ladies. I sent for Mr W. West, at his request promised him my autograph
and gave him my Order of the Bath, worn in Lord Townly. When they
had gone, except Forster, I sent for Katie, Willie, my sisters, and Hetta,
who came in to see me, of course excited and penetrated by what they
had witnessed. I gave Hetta my riband of the Bath for Marianne.[1] There
was a crowd waiting to see me get into my cab, and they cheered me,
kind hearts, as I drove off. There was a crowd at the pit door at half-
past one.

Thank God!

*One thing remained: the testimonial dinner at the Hall of Commerce in
Threadneedle Street, organised by Dickens who arrived in a blue dress-coat,
brass-buttoned and silk-faced, a satin vest with a white satin collar, and an
elaborately embroidered shirt. Sir Edward Bulwer Lytton presided, and the
list of stewards—most of whom were there—seemed to cover Macready's
career: Dickens, Talfourd (but the author of 'Ion', Mr Justice Talfourd
now, was absent on circuit), John Delane, W. J. Fox, John Forster,
Douglas Jerrold, old Charles Kemble, John Kenyon, Mark Lemon, Daniel
Maclise, Bryan Waller Procter, Samuel Phelps, Samuel Rogers, Clarkson
Stanfield, Alfred Tennyson, W. M. Thackeray, James White, Benjamin*

---

[1] Marianne Skerrett (Pollock's note: 1875) had held for many years a confidential position in attendance on the Queen; she and her sister Hetta were connec-
tions of Macready.

Webster, Charles Mayne Young, and several more. The great crowd of guests included such people as Serjeant Adams, Albany Fonblanque, (1793–1872, journalist, editor of the Radical 'Examiner', 1830–1847), James Wallack, John Leech, Tom Taylor (1817–1880, dramatist, editor of 'Punch'), John Willmott, Augustus Egg (1816–1863, painter), John Oxenford, Zouch Troughton, author of 'Nina Sforza'.

It was an evening of many speeches. Lytton, giving Macready's health, praised an actor who was original because he never tried to be original, but who sought to be as truthful, as conscientious, in his art as in his actions; he had identified himself with the living drama of his period and half created it. Macready, replying, did not say much, but he said it with dignity and an actor's art, displaying (said 'The Times') 'considerable emotion during some portions of his address.' Dickens spoke wittily, Fox too long, and Thackeray too uncertainly; Charles Kemble tried to speak, but fumbled into silence; Phelps—whom Macready named, in effect, as heir to the dramatic throne—slipped off before he was called; and John Forster, proposing 'Dramatic Literature', read the sonnet that Tennyson, Poet Laureate, had written for Macready, with its lines:

> *Thine is it that our drama did not die,*
> *Nor flicker down to brainless pantomime,*
> *And those gilt gauds men-children swarm to see. . . .*

It was midnight before the dinner ended. Macready's journal entry was very brief:

March 1. Was quite overcome by weariness of nerve and spirit, my strength seemed beginning to give way under this unrespited excitement. Thought quite composedly over what I should say, resolved to confine myself to my thanks, etc. Dared not, with all the pains I had taken, venture on the matter I had prepared. Felt very nervous and uncomfortable. Dressed, and with dear Willie went to the London Tavern; waited with Mark Lemon, whom we found there, till Dickens came. Lemon and Willie then went to the Hall of Commerce, and Dickens and myself after a time followed them. Saw Bulwer there, Quin, Lord Clanricarde, Lord Warde, who asked to be introduced to me. I sat between Bulwer and [Chevalier] Bunsen *[the Prussian Minister]*. The hall was splendid in its numbers and admirable in its arrangement. The occurrence will be noticed in the prints. I was delighted to learn in Van de Weyer's speech that George Sand[1] had published her book (the *Château des Désertes*) inscribed to me.

[1] George Sand (1804–1876), pseudonym of French novelist.

Next day he was back in Sherborne, but within less than a fortnight he came to London again.

London, March 12. Went to Dickens's to dinner. Met Bulwer Lytton, Mark Lemon, D. Jerrold, Egg, Forster, etc. The day was given up to the business of the performance [*of 'Not So Bad As We Seem'. Dickens, Forster, and Mark Lemon had the leading parts.*] and amusing it was to notice their many grounds of debate, and assurances of success. Mr Egg thought that Willmott as prompter might put them too much into conventional habits.

March 18. Called on dear old Mr Rogers. Heu! *quantum mutatus.* I shall never see him again. He talked much and I sat long. He talked much of poetry, quoting passages, and I citing from his own. He spoke of sonnets to which he had a great dislike, and thought them the Procrustean bed for thought. He sent his love to Catherine, and seemed, as I parted from him, to have the persuasion that it was for the last time. I turned as I left the room, and his two hands were lifted up to his head in the action of benediction on me.

March 19. As I review the circumstances of this last visit of mine to London, the notice is forced on me of the respect and regard universally manifested towards me. I have felt no embarrassment in the presence of men the most distinguished, and have been addressed and treated by them as on a footing of most perfect equality. Though experiencing usually much courtesy, I have never felt this independence of position before. I can look my fellow-men, whatever their station, in the face and assert my equality.

Winchester, March 21. My income this year I reckon at £1,285, my expenses at £882, leaving my balance for Willie's college terms, etc., £403.

London, May 3. Went to the Exhibition [*in Hyde Park*]. Was struck with the splendour of the view on reaching the centre, looking round at the transepts, and up and down the cross. The most beautiful single objects were the park trees growing within the building, the *coup d'œil* was very striking, very imposing, the detail very surprising, very beautiful. With all its extraordinary magnificence, my feeling was, that if I had not seen it, I should not have regretted it very much. . . . Went to the Royal Academy Exhibition. Delighted with much that I saw; Maclise's Caxton is the picture of the year. E. Landseer has a most brilliant fancy of Titania and Bottom, and some excellent things besides. . . . An unknown name, Faed, very good. . . . Went home to dress, having seen Stanfield, Hart, Herbert, Maclise, Bulwer, Dickens, etc. [That night] Returned to Academy. . . . The usual routine was passed. The Prince spoke very well; Lord John but so-so; Macaulay indifferently for such men. The Duke as usual. To our astonishment and I may say horror, Eastlake, in associating literature with the arts, mentioned the names of Dickens, myself, and Bulwer. I could have sunk into the earth. Dickens was for the first time on such an occasion completely taken aback; he rose, as did I, thinking to cover myself under his speech. Bulwer would not. Dickens made a very fair reply, and we sat down. I was called on to rise. Oh God! I was compelled; and said a few words, I know not what, about being urged by Dickens and others, and about my debt to the pictorial art, etc. I cannot remember anything, except that I was terribly distressed. The evening passed off, however, very pleasantly, and Talfourd and myself agreed to go and take tea at the Athenaeum. I was putting on my coat, as the Duke of Newcastle came up and shook hands with me very cordially, joining in conversation with us. We went to the club. Then Edwin Landseer came in and sat with us very pleasantly. Saw Thackeray for a moment as I was passing out.

May 4. Forster called, went with him to Rogers. Found the old man very cheerful, thinner than when I last saw him, but in very good spirits. He told all his stories 'over again'. . . . Spoke of Scott, Byron, and Moore, and of his own poetry, quoting us a particularly fine line, 'Their very shadows consecrate the ground.' Took leave of dear old Rogers once more. I think indeed for the last time. I cannot make out his character. He is surely good-natured, with philanthropic and religious feelings, but his fondness for saying a sharp thing shakes one's certainty in him; his apparent desire, too, to produce effect, I think, sometimes awakens doubts of his sincerity in some minds. Dined with Dickens. Maclise and Forster were there. Dickens related a *mot* of Jerrold's: P. Cunningham's *[a friend of Dickens; son of the Scottish writer, Allan Cunningham]* stating that he had been eating a strange dinner, calves' tails. Jerrold observed, 'Extremes meet.'

During the rest of the year Macready settled into his country retirement in the Sherborne house which his friend, George Wightwick, the Plymouth architect, had adapted for him. The stage was behind him for ever. A day would come when Dickens, fired by his own success, urged Macready to give Shakespearean readings in London. The reply came, very simply, in the words of Byron's Werner 'I have done! I have done! I have done with life!' Long before this, he had made his decision.

Sherborne, December 31. It is very late as I begin to enter my parting words to the eventful year on this its record of my thoughts, feelings, and sufferings. Continued my work, too late begun, upon my account books. Heard Walter part of his lesson. Read in English History with Willie, and afterwards, in French, Thierry's *Conquête d'Angleterre*, with Willie and Katie. Took a warm bath. Received gardener's character. Sat with Catherine, who, thank God, seems better. Not quite well after dinner. Rested in her room. Read French and geography with my adult class. Heard Walter his lessons. Looked at the paper. Continued my books and partially arranged my accounts. It is very late. Adieu to 1851, one of the most eventful years of my eventful life. For all, thank God, thank God, thank God. Amen.

Epilogue
(1852–1873)

'Only a name is ours, a forlorn fame.
Repeat its royal name:
Troy, once in thunder born. . . .'

Macready, after his retirement, lived for twenty-two years. They were often sorrowful. Very soon, in September 1852, Catherine—who was tubercular, as several of her children were—died at Plymouth where he had accompanied her on a visit. She had been very ill; Macready, though he had long feared the end, was overcome. 'The elasticity of my mind seems gone', he wrote to Bulwer-Lytton. While reading *Romeo and Juliet* aloud to a group (that included Lady Pollock) in the summer after Catherine's death, he broke down uncontrollably at Romeo's 'O my love, my wife!' Early in 1853 Macready lost his thirteen-year-old son Walter. He tried to absorb himself in his new occupations. He revived the failing Literary and Scientific Institution; he taught labourers' children at a night-school of his own establishment; and in 1855 he began to write the chapters of autobiography, reflective and detached, that were so unlike the constant storm of the journal.

The chapters were never finished. Henry, subject to epileptic fits since his illness of 1840, died at the age of eighteen in August 1857; ten months later the fifteen-year-old Lydia (Lillie) died of scarlatina; and on 5 November, 1858, Letitia Macready died,[1] the severance of a life's association. In his loneliness, Macready had to marry again, and he did so at St John's Church, Clifton, during the spring of 1860. He was sixty-seven. His second wife, the much younger Cécile Louise Spencer[2], an intimate friend of his daughter Katie, knew nothing of the stage, but she recognised her husband's genius and cared for him affectionately to the end of his life. They moved at once from Sherborne to Cheltenham and a much smaller house at 6 Wellington Square. There, on 7 March 1862, Macready's last child was born: Cecil Frederick Nevil.

During these ten years he had been to London occasionally. Thus in October 1855 he attended a dinner to Thackeray at the London Tavern and met many of his friends ('Dickens, Jerrold, Pollock, Stanfield, Murphy, Fladgate, Charles Knight, Longman. . . .'), an assemblage 'most cordially disposed to be happy'. In the following year he saw the ruins of the Theatre Royal, Covent Garden, destroyed by fire at the close of a *bal masqué* in March 1856:

April 4. Passing by Covent Garden Theatre, I stopped the driver and directed him to the entrance. The *custos* made much objection to my

[1] Letitia (1794–1858) was sixty-five.
[2] 1827–1908. She was thirty-three at her marriage.

entrance, but on giving my card, and insisting that Mr Gye *[Frederick Gye, the director]* would desire that I should have admittance, he yielded, and called a fireman to show me the interior. It was, as ruin ever is, a melancholy sight; but it did not affect me. It was not my theatre, the scene of my anxieties, my struggles, my trials and my sufferings, and my triumphs: that had long since been erased.

Just after this he visited Paris, where Dickens was staying, and went to a rehearsal of George Sand's *Comme il vous plaira*, a curious version (Jaques married Celia) of *As You Like It*, most trivially directed. In 1857 he saw Dickens's amateur company in what he described with tact as an 'uncommonly good' performance of Wilkie Collins's disastrous Arctic melodrama, *The Frozen Deep*, at Dickens's own home, Tavistock House.

II

So the years went by. He wrote his grave, kindly letters. He would talk about the theatre to chosen listeners, such as the Pollocks; and now and then his journal might have a touch of the old asperity: an Etonian testimonial to 'Mr C. Kean' he looked upon as 'one of the fruits of the most systematic cultivation of imposture and humbug that I have ever known.' Frequently his friends visited him: such familiars as Dickens,[1] and, at length, Forster who was forgiven, thanks to Dickens, after what appears to have been a typical *gaffe* about Macready's second marriage. Life at Cheltenham in the eighteen-sixties was steadily tranquil. Then, of a sudden, Macready's griefs were renewed. Once more Plymouth was a place of tragedy. He had gone down with his wife in March 1869 to meet Katie, the thirty-four-year-old consumptive daughter who was very near to him, and who had been wintering in Madeira. When the ship arrived in Plymouth Sound, he learned that Katie had died on the homeward voyage and had been buried at sea. And still there was a loss to come: the death of William, his eldest son, in Ceylon during November 1871.

By now Macready's hands were paralysed. He could neither hold a book nor read; but when he was alone he could recall many of his parts, every word and pause ('and the very pauses have eloquence'). His speech

---

[1] In 1869 Dickens gave one of his readings at Cheltenham. The ailing Macready, suffering from aphasia and very frail, was brought round to see him after 'Sikes and Nancy', the *Oliver Twist* murder, and managed to exclaim: 'It comes to two Macbeths!'

had waned to a blurred whisper. This was the Macready Helen Faucit, Lady Martin, found when she and her husband visited him in London whither he had gone for treatment during the spring of 1871. Helen Faucit had not met him for twenty years. On the first afternoon: 'He is changed, and yet not changed—like a great ship, past its work, but grand in its ruin.' Next day she went again. When he looked at her as he woke from his sleep, and smiled in sudden enchanted recognition, she remembered the face of his Lear, long ago, as he opened his eyes to find Cordelia beside him. 'His snowy hair and fine form, the eager eyes, and the tender tones of the broken voice made a deep impression upon me.'

He had only a short time left. The years had taken many of his friends and foes: Talfourd, as far back as 1854 (when a Judge, he collapsed while charging the Grand Jury at Stafford); Charles Mayne Young, Maclise and Stanfield and Sheridan Knowles, Bunn and Charles Kean and Edwin Forrest. Dickens died in 1870—a profound grief—and, in January 1873, Lord Lytton. In April of that year Macready had a slight bronchial attack from which he never rallied. Conscious to the last, he died in the morning of 27 April: he was eighty years old. A week later, on 4 May, he was brought from Cheltenham to the vault at Kensal Green where his wife, his sister, and five of his eleven children had been buried, and the names of two others, Katie and William, were also upon the marble tablet.[1]

It was twenty-two years since John Forster, who followed the coffin of his friend, had read Tennyson's ode among the glitter of the farewell banquet. On this last morning it may have returned to his mind:

Farewell, Macready, since this night we part;
Go, take thine honours home.

[1] The surviving children were Edward (b. 1836), the disappointment of the Macready sons, and the date of whose death is unknown; Cecilia Benvenuta (1847–1934), Jonathan Forster Christian (1850–1908), and Cecil Frederick Nevil (1862–1946).

Some Books

I have noted the two basic editions of the Diaries. Other books (all published in London, unless otherwise stated) are Lady Pollock's *Macready As I Knew Him*, 1884; William Archer's *William Charles Macready*, 1890; J. C. Trewin's *Mr Macready: A Nineteenth Century Tragedian and His Theatre*, 1955; Charles H. Shattuck's excellent edition of the Bulwer-Macready correspondence, *Bulwer and Macready: A Chronicle of the Early Victorian Theatre* (University of Illinois Press, 1958); Alan S. Downer's *The Eminent Tragedian: William Charles Macready* (Harvard, 1966; Oxford, 1967). General the Rt. Hon. Sir Nevil Macready, Bart., recalls his father in the first chapter of *Annals of an Active Life*, 1924.

A few of the many books on various figures in Macready's career are: James R. Anderson's *An Actor's Life*, 1902; Alfred Bunn's *The Stage: Both Before and Behind the Curtain*, 3 vols., 1840; Sir Theodore Martin's *Helena Faucit, Lady Martin*, 1900; John Forster's *Charles Dickens* (1874), Una Pope-Hennessy's *Charles Dickens: 1812–1870* (1945), and *The Letters of Charles Dickens: Vol. One, 1820–1839*, edited by Madeline House and Graham Storey (1965); Richard Moody's *Edwin Forrest: First Star of the American Stage* (New York, 1960); Richard Renton's *John Forster and His Friendships*, 1912; W. May Phelps and John Forbes-Robertson's *The Life and Life-Work of Samuel Phelps*, 1886.

For drama criticism there are the works of Leigh Hunt, Hazlitt, G. H. Lewes, and John Forster, as well as J. Westland Marston's *Our Recent Actors* (1888) and Arthur Colby Sprague's *Shakespeare and the Actors* (1945). Charles H. Shattuck has edited *William Charles Macready's 'King John'*, a facsimile prompt-book (University of Illinois, 1962).

Richard Moody has described *The Astor Place Riot* (Indiana University, 1958). Some other books are mentioned in the Notes.

J.C.T.

Index

The Journal of William Charles Macready, 1832–1851

Abridged and Edited by J. C. Trewin

Besides being a great actor and the friend and associate of Dickens, Bulwer Lytton, Browning, and most of the principal figures in the drama and literature of his time, William Charles Macready (1793–1873) was a compulsive diarist. His journal of twenty-one years, during most of which he was at the head of the English stage, is a candid and absorbing self-revelation.

"No one could undertake the re-editing and compression of the diaries with more authority and understanding than Mr. Trewin. . . . Mr. Trewin's concise interpolations provide an authentic background to the diarist's entries and so enable us to take them in our stride as an absorbing narrative."
—*Times Literary Supplement*

"Judged by this admirable abridgement Macready's journal ranks high, both as an early Victorian peep show and as the strangely moving portrait of an unamiable but far from unlovable man."
—*The Observer*

Cover design by **Gary Gore**

SOUTHERN ILLINOIS UNIVERSITY PRESS

CARBONDALE, ILLINOIS 62901

SBN 8093-0423-6